TRANSPORTATION AND

GLOBAL CLIMATE CHANGE

Other ACEEE Books on Energy Policy and Energy Efficiency

Regulatory Incentives for Demand-Side Management
Energy Efficiency and the Environment: Forging the Link
Efficient Electricity Use: A Development Strategy for Brazil
State of the Art of Energy Efficiency:
Future Directions
Energy-Efficient Motor Systems:
A Handbook on Technology, Program,
and Policy Opportunities
Residential Indoor Air Quality and Energy Efficiency
Electric Utility Planning and Regulation
Energy Efficiency: Perspectives on Individual Behavior
Energy Efficiency in Buildings: Progress and Promise

ACEEE also publishes numerous reports on a variety of topics
addressing energy policy and energy efficiency, including
transportation. For a catalog of publications,
write: ACEEE, 2140 Shattuck Avenue, Suite 202,
Berkeley, California 94704.

TRANSPORTATION AND
GLOBAL CLIMATE CHANGE

Edited by
DAVID L. GREENE
DANILO J. SANTINI

American Council for an Energy-Efficient Economy
Washington, D.C. and Berkeley, California
1993

Transportation and Global Climate Change

Published by the American Council for an Energy-Efficient Economy, 1001 Connecticut Avenue, N.W., Suite 801, Washington, D.C. 20036 and 2140 Shattuck Avenue, Suite 202, Berkeley, California 94704

Cover art copyright © 1952 M. C. Escher Heirs/Cordon Art—Baarn—Holland

Cover design by Chuck Myers, American Labor Education Center, Washington, D.C.
Book typeset by Wilsted & Taylor, Oakland, California
Printed in the United States of America by Edwards Brothers, Inc.

Library of Congress Cataloging-in-Publication Data

Transportation and global climate change/edited by David L. Greene, Danilo J. Santini.
    p. 383   23 cm.
    Includes bibliographical references and index.
    ISBN 0-918249-17-1: $28.00
    1. Greenhouse gases—Environmental aspects—Congresses. 2. Transportation, Automotive—United States—Energy conservation—Congresses.
3. Transportation, Automotive—United States—Energy consumption—Congresses. 4. Synthetic fuels—United States—Congresses. 5. Climate changes—Congresses. I. Greene, David Lloyd, 1949– . II. Santini, Danilo J., 1945– .
TD885.5.G73T72   1993
363.73'87—dc20   93-15469
                                           CIP

NOTICE

 Printed on recycled paper.

To Albert Chesnes and Eugene Ecklund, for their leadership in transportation energy technology and alternative fuels

Acknowledgments

The 1991 Asilomar Conference on Transportation and Global Climate Change was organized by the Transportation Research Board of the National Research Council, Section F—Environmental and Energy Concerns, with the leadership of the Committees on Energy Conservation and Transportation Demand and Alternative Fuels. Sponsors and cosponsors included the U.S. Environmental Protection Agency, the U.S. Department of Energy, the U.S. Department of Transportation, the Transportation Research Board, the American Council for an Energy-Efficient Economy, and the Department of Energy, Mines and Resources of Canada. Organizational assistance was provided by the Department of Civil Engineering of the University of California at Davis. The sponsorship and support of each of these organizations is gratefully acknowledged. We also thank ACEEE's director of publications, Glee Murray, for managing the book's publication. The estimates and opinions expressed by authors within this book are those of the authors and not necessarily those of the institutions sponsoring the conference or those sponsoring the authors' participation at the conference.

Preface

In 1991 the National Research Council of the National Academy of Sciences published the report *Policy Implications of Greenhouse Warming*, a review of contemporary knowledge about global warming and potential responses to this threat. The report recommended, in part, strengthening "research on social and economic aspects of global change and greenhouse warming" and reducing "the emission of greenhouse gases during energy use and consumption." In the same year, committees on energy and alternative fuels of the Transportation Research Board, an arm of the National Research Council, began to carry out these recommendations by organizing the first U.S. conference focusing on the potential of the transportation sector to reduce the emissions of gases that might cause global warming.

In the summer of 1991, a diverse group of experts in various aspects of transportation systems gathered at the Asilomar Conference Center in Pacific Grove, California, to address this issue. For some, the idea that global warming would be a serious transportation problem was new. That the transportation sector is a major and growing source of greenhouse gas emissions is certain. What impacts those emissions will have on the global environment, how urgently we must act to curb them, and how effectively and efficiently we can do so are all highly uncertain and often controversial questions. The 1991 Asilomar Conference on Transportation and Global Climate Change recognized that the problem, if determined to be large in magnitude and serious in consequences, would have no "quick fix" but would require a comprehensive long-run strategy. Such a transportation strategy must address growing global demand, energy efficiency, and alternative, noncarbon energy sources. The 1991 Asilomar conference marked the beginning of focusing the expertise of the transportation research community on this enormously complex issue.

This book, a result of that conference, documents the efforts of a group of transportation experts to examine the U.S. transportation sector's ability to reduce or offset greenhouse gas emissions either by conservation of conventional transportation fuels or by substitution of alternative energy sources having fewer net greenhouse gas emissions. The various chapters examine choices to be made over the next several decades and consider supply options, conversion systems, end use, and external effects. In addition to options for "focused research and development . . . on a variety of alternative energy supply sources" that "could change the priorities for energy supply within the fifty-year time span" addressed in the NAS study, the authors also explore policy mechanisms that may be needed to bring about necessary changes. Costs of technologies and scheduling problems of technology switches (phasing) are discussed by some authors, thereby providing information supporting the NAS's admonitions to "avoid shocks caused by rapid price changes" and to avoid options that require great expenses at this time.

The conference organizers invited international experts from academia, government agencies, government-funded research institutions, industry, "think tanks," and other consulting agencies. The intent to cover a range of transportation-related issues is reflected in this book, which first puts the U.S. transportation system into a world context and then examines the components of the U.S. system with the purpose of estimating the feasibility and means of reducing greenhouse gas emissions from each transport mode. The chapters reflect considerable uncertainty about what can be achieved. Scientific uncertainty is reflected in significant differences between contributing authors in reduction estimates, not only across modes, but also within modes, even with similar technology. Thus, the problem of scientific uncertainty about global climate change is not limited to projecting the consequences of a CO_2 build-up.

This book represents an initial effort to reduce scientific uncertainty and improve knowledge for future decisions within one of the many areas—transportation—where such research activities are necessary. In this initial effort, communication between transportation experts has begun, and the best professional judgments of these experts have been documented. Although some of these estimates and judgments differ in important respects, there is also much common ground, which only becomes apparent when the whole is assembled, as has been done here. Having documented initial estimates, the participating experts and others can, in future conferences, work toward refining estimates of engineering realities and of the ability of the social and economic systems to substitute technologies that can reduce greenhouse gas emissions.

Foreword

The Nature of the Problem

Though scientists are confident that concentrations of greenhouse gases, such as carbon dioxide (CO_2), are increasing in the atmosphere, and that their increase will eventually lead to a rise in average temperatures around the globe, the magnitude and regional effects of global warming are highly uncertain. Models cannot yet predict temperature and climate changes at a scale on which environmental impacts can be reliably estimated. This fundamental uncertainty about the danger to be avoided has thus far stymied efforts to formulate effective global climate change policy for transportation. Unfortunately, at present we have no obvious, off-the-shelf, technical fix that would allow significant reduction of CO_2 emissions in the transportation sectors of all countries. We do have, however, a host of promising technologies with the *potential* to allow significant reductions in CO_2 emissions from the transportation sector in industrially advanced countries, such as the United States. The best of these, however, cannot be regarded as "on the shelf," ready for use. With continued research, we may be able to develop many of these technologies, along with policies capable of mitigating the greenhouse gas problem at a reasonable cost.

A theme of the 1991 Asilomar Conference on Transportation and Global Climate Change was the search for a "no regrets" greenhouse gas policy for U.S. transportation. The "no regrets" concept was defined to require that CO_2-reducing policies make sense for reasons other than just their CO_2 reduction effects. Such policies should be worth carrying out even if their CO_2 reduction benefits are valued at zero. The magnitude, effects, and certainty of the anticipated global warming problem are too vague to justify assigning a dollar value to CO_2 reductions. The "no regrets" concept is clearly minimalist in that regrets can arise from doing too little as well as from doing too much.

The term *greenhouse effect* comes from an analogy between the atmosphere and a greenhouse. Like the glass in a greenhouse, the atmosphere allows solar radiation, which is mostly in the short-wavelength visible spectrum, to pass through it and be absorbed by the earth's surface and transformed into heat. This heat is radiated back to the atmosphere in the long-wavelength infrared spectrum. Generically, a greenhouse gas is any gas that tends to absorb and later release more of this infrared radiative energy than do the gases in the atmosphere as a whole. The net addition of such gases to the atmosphere tends therefore to increase the retention of heat energy in the atmosphere, thereby increasing average atmospheric and surface temperatures. A complicating factor is the decay and conversion of gases from one chemical species to another. The current emissions of a gas that decays rapidly may not have a warming effect a few decades from now, whereas current emissions of one that decays very slowly may have a warming effect centuries from now.

Gases can tend to create a warming effect even if emitted in small quantities if their effects are potent enough. Chlorofluorocarbons (CFCs) are greenhouse gases of this type. Other gases are far less potent but are emitted in large quantities and tend to be nonreactive, remaining in the atmosphere for a very long time. Most prominent of these are carbon dioxide and methane (CH_4). According to the Intergovernmental Panel on Climate Change (IPCC), a pound of methane has several times the warming effect of a pound of carbon dioxide, and methane emissions are increasing more rapidly than carbon dioxide. However, because of the sheer volume of emissions, carbon dioxide is the most important greenhouse gas. The list of greenhouse gases and the degree to which each of them contributes to global warming is a changing one, with inclusions and deletions subject to scientific developments and perhaps to other nonscientific considerations as well. The top members of the list at this time are CFCs and carbon dioxide.

CFCs are largely a U.S. innovation, to which motor vehicle air conditioners contribute. International agreements, such as the Montreal Protocol, have already reduced worldwide use of CFCs. Carbon dioxide is emitted into the atmosphere when hydrocarbon-based fuels are burned (oxidized). Such fuels include oil, natural gas, and coal. International carbon dioxide reduction or control agreements have not yet been established, though many nations have adopted control goals.

Since the Industrial Revolution, the earth's forests have been cleared and burned for settlement, and the hydrocarbons under the earth's crust have been extracted and burned at accelerating rates. Burning converts the carbon in the burned material to carbon dioxide, whose concentration in the atmosphere has been increasing. Plants on the earth's surface and in the ocean can reclaim carbon through photosynthesis, but the expansion of human populations has reduced the amount of plant matter available for photosynthesis. The injection of additional carbon from fossil fuels into the biosphere has further exceeded the capacity of plants to recycle the carbon. Consequently, carbon dioxide has been building up in the atmosphere. The rate of atmospheric carbon dioxide increase over the last two decades has been directly measured at a monitoring station on the Mauna Loa volcano in Hawaii. Concentrations prior to this time, including prehistoric times, have been estimated by sampling ice cores in Antarctica. These records clearly indicate that since the Industrial Revolution we have significantly increased the level of carbon dioxide in the earth's atmosphere. The recent *rate* of carbon dioxide build-up is unprecedented in the world's history, although the *level* of carbon dioxide has often been exceeded in the geologic past. Consequently, scientists are concerned that the *rapidity* of the warming effects could exceed the ability of biological systems to adapt, even with the presumed assistance and management of the process by humans.

Some question the inevitability of global warming in response to the build-up of greenhouse gases, or question its seriousness. Others question whether we should address global warming by attempting to reduce the emissions of gases contributing to warming (greenhouse gases) or by attempting to cope with the climate change as it develops. Such climate adaptations might include migration, the building of new cities and infrastructure, and changes in the nature and distribution of crops. The contributors to this book have focused primarily on the emissions reduction approach, because it poses the greatest challenges for transportation.

It is hard to comprehend how difficult it would be to actually stop the build-up of greenhouse gases and to stabilize the amount of carbon dioxide and methane in the atmosphere. The problem is so enormous that few have even attempted to address it comprehensively. (The final chapter of this book presents a scenario of what would be necessary for the United States to control its transportation-sector greenhouse gas emissions.) Stephen Schneider of the National Center for Atmospheric Research, an atmospheric scientist and one of the leading advocates of the emissions control approach, concedes that his primary hope at this time is to reduce the rate of growth of atmospheric concentrations of carbon dioxide and methane while scientists attempt to develop accurate models to predict the rate of climate change at both a world and regional scale. He argues that even if the predictive science is uncertain, the evidence of warming is strong enough to recommend immediate action. But what kind of action, and how much should we be willing to spend?

The ill-fated 1992 Rio Environmental Summit proposal for nations to agree to stabilize carbon dioxide emissions, even if implemented and collectively adhered to, would *not* eliminate growth in the atmospheric concentration of carbon dioxide. Such an agreement would simply *slow* the rate of growth and the rate of warming. However, it would certainly represent a major feat, from both a technical and a sociopolitical point of view, and would place the world in a far better position to cope with the problem of actually stabilizing or reducing atmospheric concentrations of carbon dioxide in the event of a scientific consensus that such action would be necessary.

Today, fossil energy is fundamental to the world's economy. Its use to provide power for heating, cooling, lighting, communications, cooking, industrial production, and transportation is ubiquitous and highly dispersed. Methane from agricultural activities and carbon dioxide from deforestation are also major sources of greenhouse gases. When each contributing sector in each individual nation considers the degree to which it contributes to the problem, it is easy to conclude that each individual source is unimportant and therefore cannot make a significant contribution to solving the problem. The U.S. transportation sector contributes only a small part (perhaps 5%) of estimated world greenhouse gas emissions. However, every contributor in every nation can make the same argument. Thus, fairness and equity are likely to be as crucial as economic efficiency to formulating successful international global warming control strategies.

The Problem in a World Context

The initial three chapters in this volume attempt to put the problem of the U.S. transportation system into perspective among worldwide transportation systems. Chapter 1, "Highway Vehicle Activity Trends and Their Implications for Global Warming: The United States in an International Context," by Michael P. Walsh, takes the broadest historical and international view, though it focuses exclusively on motor vehicles. Walsh includes estimates of past worldwide motor vehicle ownership, starting in 1930, and projects trends through 2010. He provides broad functional breakdowns of motor vehicle use for various world economic blocs and shows the remarkable differences between North American motor vehicle use and that in the rest of the world. One of the significant problems in international negotiations is the fact that less developed nations do not consider it fair that the United States should be allowed to retain its high rate of automobile use while they may be asked to postpone or even forego the ambition to ever achieve such a rate of use. Walsh also places motor vehicle greenhouse gas emissions in the context of the growing international problem of urban air pollution, to which the world's growing vehicle fleets are major contributors.

Chapter 2, "Trends in Transportation Energy Use, 1970–1988: An

International Perspective," by Lee Schipper, Ruth Steiner, and Stephen Meyers, also compares international patterns and trends. This chapter provides relatively detailed estimates of transportation energy use in most sectors for the United States, other industrially advanced nations, and some less developed nations over the last two decades. If U.S. citizens are to be expected to accept significant changes in the nature of their transportation system, models from other nations can suggest what may be possible. Since other postindustrial nations use far less transportation energy per capita and per dollar of income than the United States, this chapter's examples of how they do it are potentially very valuable. It is equally important that we understand the factors that make the U.S. transportation system different from those of Europe and Japan. And although Schipper, Steiner, and Meyers show how other nations use less transportation energy than the United States does, they also show that these nations are increasing their use of transportation energy. Consequently, the sobering characteristic of the trends presented in this chapter is that they suggest the rest of the world is becoming more motorized, more like the United States, rather than the reverse.

Chapter 3, "The Effects of Transportation Sector Growth on Energy Use, the Environment, and Traffic Congestion in Four Asian Cities," by Mia.Layne Birk and Peter Reilly-Roe, examines energy consumption at the city level rather than the national or multinational level. By selecting four fundamentally different Asian cities, Birk and Reilly-Roe illustrate how variable the rate of motor vehicle use is across the world, making tangible the fact that the motor vehicle consumes not only fuel but also urban space. Reading their narrative, one can clearly see that urbanized areas that developed before the advent of the automobile are fundamentally incompatible with it. Unless the structure and traffic control systems of urban areas are consistent with the design of the vehicles that fit into them, the result is likely to be a far more congested, inefficient, and highly polluted city.

Birk and Reilly-Roe describe what happens when the rate of automobile use rises in an evolving city whose core was built before the automobile became available. In doing so, they show that the aspiration of developing nations for as many automobiles per capita as in industrialized nations is effectively an aspiration to replace the urban structure of the past. As a general proposition, it appears that the amount of investment in, and planning of, transportation system infrastructure tends to lag the rate of spending on vehicles in developing cities. Thus the future growth of motorization in the developing world will depend critically on public infrastructure investment decisions. Birk and Reilly-Roe note the lack of trained technicians and political structures as well as the lack of capital to accomplish transportation planning in developing nations and cities.

The Light-Duty Vehicle

United States voters recently chose an administration committed to emphasizing investment in public infrastructure. Investment in transportation infrastructure has the potential to reduce congestion, permitting vehicles to operate more efficiently. Further, the prior administration signed into law the Intermodal Surface Transportation Efficiency Act of 1991 (ISTEA), which allows funding to be more readily shifted to public transportation. This may provide U.S. metropolitan planners an opportunity to move toward a mix of modes more typical of the other industrialized nations examined by Schipper, Steiner, and Meyers.

Chapter 4, "Designing Incentive-Based Approaches to Limit Carbon Dioxide Emissions from the Light-Duty Vehicle Fleet," by Robin Miles-McLean, Susan M. Haltmaier, and Michael G. Shelby, evaluates three key policy options for stabilizing the CO_2 emissions of light-duty vehicles: an oil import fee, a gasoline tax, and a gas guzzler tax with a gas sipper rebate. The latter two are "revenue neutral," with collected fees being returned to the private sector rather than funding government expenditures. The gasoline tax approach differs from the guzzler/sipper tax by returning tax revenue to employers (businesses) through "cuts in the employer-paid portion of payroll taxes," whereas the guzzler/sipper approach returns tax revenue to buyers of fuel-efficient vehicles. The results suggest that new-car fuel economy in miles per gallon need only rise to the low thirties by the year 2000 and the high thirties by 2010 to stabilize CO_2 emissions from light-duty vehicles. Unfortunately, as later chapters discuss, light-duty vehicles are not the part of the transportation sector with the most rapid growth of CO_2 emissions. Thus, an answer for light-duty vehicles is only part of an answer for transportation as a whole.

Miles-McLean, Haltmaier, and Shelby assume continued reliance on gasoline-powered vehicles. Fuel switching is not discussed. A representative mpg number for the years 2000–2010 from their study—35 mpg—would require a 27% improvement in the mpg of conventional gasoline vehicles (a 21% reduction in fuel consumption per mile). Chapter 5, "IC Engines and Fuels for Cars and Light Trucks: 2015," by John L. Mason, examines the additional level of efficiency that is theoretically possible through improved engine efficiency. Mason argues that about a third of the theoretical limit of a 21% efficiency improvement in the spark-ignited (gasoline) engine is possible in the next twenty years. The resulting 7% estimate falls well short of the 21% improvement that is needed in that time frame. Though some would dispute Mason's estimate, nonetheless it is clear that all the required improvement cannot come from the engine alone. Better transmissions, tires, and more aerodynamic bodies would be necessary, as would some weight reduction. A point that Mason's chapter makes clear is that there are theoretical limits to the capability of a given technology.

Chapter 6, "Vehicle Efficiency and the Electric Option," by Paul B. MacCready, proposes a more ambitious goal: a substantial *decrease* in greenhouse gases and local pollutants by the year 2005. Recognizing the difficulty of this goal, MacCready focuses on the need to replace conventional spark-ignited (SI) internal-combustion-engine (ICE)-powered vehicles with electric-drive vehicles. Such vehicles—both all-electric and electric-hybrid vehicles—are argued to have particular advantages in congested stop-and-go driving. If the projections of significantly worsening congestion are correct, the theoretical advantages of these vehicles would become even more desirable in the future. MacCready also emphasizes that these vehicles can use fuels other than gasoline, creating desirable long-term options. In the near term, MacCready points out that these vehicles might also be individually effective in reducing imported oil use.

Chapter 7, "The USDOE Vehicle Propulsion Research and Development Program," by John J. Brogan and Sek R. Venkateswaran, provides some drawing board specifics on the types of vehicles proposed by MacCready. Brogan and Venkateswaran illustrate that the best of these vehicles can theoretically be far more efficient than a gasoline vehicle and can also use several other fuels. Compressed natural gas, methanol, and hydrogen are discussed, but other fuels are also possible. The fuel cell vehicle discussed by Brogan and Venkateswaran has the advantage that its ultimate theoretical efficiency is far greater than that of the ICE engine, which is limited by the ideal cycles for this engine type, as pointed out by Mason.

Chapter 8, "Solar Hydrogen Transportation Fuels," by Joan M. Ogden and Mark A. DeLuchi, extends the analysis of the advanced light-duty vehicle to include an analysis of the production of the fuel that goes into the vehicle. The most efficient of the vehicles projected by Brogan and Venkateswaran is the hydrogen-fueled proton exchange membrane (PEM) fuel cell hybrid vehicle. Ogden and DeLuchi show how such a vehicle could be powered by solar-derived hydrogen fuel. They also include a methanol-fueled hybrid vehicle using methanol from biomass in the "solar hydrogen" family of vehicles, so they discuss the methanol-fueled PEM fuel cell hybrid as well as a solar-electrolytic hydrogen system. Of all the technologies on the horizon, the hydrogen fuel cell vehicle appears to have the greatest potential as an ultimate solution to greenhouse gas emissions by transport vehicles.

Freight and Other Transportation

Chapter 9, "Why Is Energy Use Rising in the Freight Sector?" by Marianne M. Mintz and Anant D. Vyas, examines the expanding role of freight and commercial travel in the context of trends in fuel consumption and travel in all transportation sectors in the United States. Mintz and Vyas show that automobiles and light trucks consume the most energy in the transportation sector, confirming the focus of several chapters of this book on the light-duty vehicle. However, they also show that projected energy use by heavy trucks is next-greatest to that of light-duty vehicles and that a continuation of current trends could lead to a situation in which "commercial" highway vehicle energy use (including commercial light trucks and cars) could exceed the energy consumption for personal use. Demand for aircraft fuel is third-largest after that of cars and trucks. Breaking down fuel consumption into gasoline, diesel, and jet fuel, Mintz & Vyas project that the demand for middle distillates (diesel and jet fuel) will continue to expand, whereas gasoline demand is likely to flatten out.

Mintz and Vyas discuss the role of the structure of the economy, pointing out that the shift to services leads to many more business trips in light trucks. They point out that the adoption of efficiency devices on trucks has not led to the energy savings expected by truck operators who have been surveyed. Congestion is offered as a possible factor behind increased truck energy intensity. On the whole, Mintz and Vyas are pessimistic about the ability to improve the operating efficiency of heavy trucks. This is consistent with Mason's finding of a slightly smaller achievable fuel economy improvement for diesel engines than for spark-ignited engines.

Chapter 10, "Characteristics of Future Aviation Fuels," by Oren J. Hadaller and Albert M. Momenthy, addresses the remaining and fastest-growing large consumer of energy in transportation—air travel. The point made by Hadaller and Momenthy is that reductions in CO_2 emissions from aircraft will have to be accomplished by improvements in efficiency, not by fuel switching. Hadaller and Momenthy illustrate why petroleum-based jet fuels are ideal aircraft fuels. They also focus on the cost of fuel as a deterrent to the adoption of alternative fuels in aircraft. Past reductions in fuel consumption per passenger have been accomplished in part by enlarging aircraft, a process that would have to continue if significantly greater levels of efficiency were to be achieved.

Restructuring the Transportation System

Finally, Chapter 11, "Transportation on a Greenhouse Planet: A Least-Cost Transition Scenario for the United States," by John M. DeCicco et al., addresses a "least cost" transition scenario for the United States designed to accomplish sharp reductions in CO_2 emissions. It is the only comprehensive proposal presented in the book, covering all of transportation and a number of problems. The term *least cost* has been borrowed from the utility industry, where advocates of energy conservation have been attempting to get the regulatory process to consider all ways of meeting the final goal of providing the services that utility customers desire, not only the expansion of supply. The term calls for a broadening of perspective and an inclusion of more alternatives.

In that sense, the "least cost" analysis of DeCicco et al. looks beyond the narrow consideration of only one transportation mode or one method of reducing CO_2 emissions. On the other hand, the term *least cost* must be considered indicative only, since the authors do not actually attempt to assess the costs to the economy of the policies, as Miles-McLean, Haltmaier, and Shelby do. The DeCicco strategy proposes new-car fuel economy levels well in excess of those proposed by Miles-McLean, Haltmaier, and Shelby. New-car fuel consumption per mile drops by more than half, though the technical analysis by Brogan and Venkateswaran suggests that—for a given size of vehicle with current characteristics—such a reduction may not be possible, even in advanced vehicles. On the other hand, it is possible to achieve such improvements if consumers will trade off other vehicle attributes for higher mpg.

The DeCicco et al. analysis shows that very ambitious CO_2 reduction goals will require both major efficiency improvements and fuel switching. Even though the efficiency assumptions/projections are aggressive, DeCicco et al. find it necessary to assume switches to bio-fuels and electricity to reach the ambitious goals they have set. Whereas Mason estimates an achievable efficiency gain of about 7% (of a maximum 21%) in spark-ignited engines, DeCicco et al. estimate an achievable gain of efficiency of 29.8% by adding contributions from roller cam followers (1.5%), overhead camshafts (6.0%), advanced friction reduction (6.0%), intake valve control (6.0%), four valves per cylinder (6.8%), and multipoint fuel injection (3.5%).

In one sense, the DeCicco et al. analysis is conservative. While calling for enormous efficiency improvements for the gasoline-powered vehicle, the authors are not requiring advanced vehicles such as those discussed by MacCready and by Brogan and Venkateswaran. The list of options discussed in this book is more extensive than that included by DeCicco et al. Perhaps those new, theoretically promising technologies can be successfully substituted to achieve similar results. Whether the costs of those technologies would create net societal benefits, as DeCicco et al. assume, is an important and open question. The concept of least-cost planning asserts that consumers are interested in the level of service they receive per dollar of cost, not the technological method by which the service is produced. An incomplete or incorrect consideration of consumer preferences can lead to failure of a proposed alternative when it is built and put into the marketplace. Future evaluations of advanced technologies must consider the full range of consumer preferences in assessing the costs of technical solutions, a subject we merely touch upon here.

Widespread adoption of new transportation technologies is very costly to society during the time that the most rapid changes are accomplished—even when the decision to adopt is correct. On the one hand stands the danger of entrenched interests investing too long in the refinement and defense of the old technology. On the other hand is the danger of advocates of change being willing to invest in new technology before its worth or viability has been proven. Entrenched interests systematically overestimate the potential of their own technology and the drawbacks of their competition, whereas advocates of change respond in kind but in the opposite direction.

Final Comments

The contrasts in assessments of what is technically and practically achievable in this book show the importance of the dialogue established at the Asilomar conference. The desire of the conference organizers was to offer a range of experts an opportunity to provide the scientific, academic, and business communities their best estimates of what is technically achievable and—if possible—their assessment of the cost. The wide divergence in the size of some of the estimates found in this book shows that the organizing committee succeeded in including a range of points of view.

Since atmospheric scientists and consumers have not yet decided what level of CO_2 emissions the world should achieve, several of the authors in this book have explored "what if" scenarios concerning the goals that society might choose to adopt, and then have assessed which technological approach might best achieve that end. The exercise clearly shows that dramatic shifts of CO_2 emission rates will require major technological changes in the transportation system. The diversity of estimates presented suggests that the transportation policymakers, planners, and researchers still have a considerable amount of work to do to formulate effective policy as atmospheric scientists and society at large try to narrow the range of uncertainty about the importance of reducing greenhouse gas emissions.

Earlier we stated that the "no regrets" policy discussed at the conference is a minimalist policy. The conference participants, who included scientists concerned about the health of the globe and economists concerned about the health of the economy, developed and discussed a number of proposed "no regrets" recommendations. It was agreed that none of the proposed recommendations would be reported unless a consensus was reached. As a result, there are no "sense of the conference" recommendations that can be reported here. On the one hand, this is a discouraging outcome, given the minimalist nature of the fundamental policy being considered. On the other hand, as political scientists might have told us, the requirement that a consensus be achieved was undoubtedly a maximalist goal fated to prevent any recommended "no regrets" policy.

It would be a mistake to assume that the "veto power" was exercised only by economists concerned about effects on economic growth. Another dynamic is that among scientists over whether to commit to minimalist policies when, for some, the perceived risks of global warming require the rejection of inadequately strong policies in favor of a continued battle for stronger policies. Further, even when using the concept of "no regrets," the valuation of costs and benefits of reduced fuel use differs greatly among scientists and economists who study the issue. Finally, to the extent that economists might have exercised veto power, it should be noted that the winter of 1990–1991 was a period of recession, and it was not clear whether recovery was assured. Given their nature, the economists present might have been concerned with being associated with a reputed consensus that recommended imposing more regulatory or taxation costs on the economy while in the midst of a recession.

The one "no regrets" policy that did achieve consensus was that the search for knowledge should continue, and that the conference should be repeated periodically.

Contents

Highway Vehicle Activity Trends and Their Implications for Global Warming: The United States in an International Context

Michael P. Walsh

O ver the past century, huge amounts of air pollutants and gases have been released into the atmosphere that now pose risks to human health, natural ecosystems, and the earth's climate (WRI 1990, ch. 2). Many kinds of industrial and agricultural activities have contributed to these releases. Fossil fuel combustion, massive deforestation, the release of industrial chemicals, and agricultural development have amplified the natural greenhouse effect, increasing the risk of global warming. The release of industrial chemicals containing chlorine and bromine has contributed to the depletion of the ozone layer (Gribbin 1988), and fuel burning and industrial development are responsible for most of the planet's air pollution, including acid rain and urban smog.

Motor vehicles are a major contributor to both the build-up of greenhouse gases—potentially the most serious of these problems—and the creation of smog and acid rain. Carbon dioxide and other pollutants emitted in large quantities from motor vehicles are major contributors to global warming. Vehicles produced or registered outside of the United States and highway vehicle modes other than passenger cars

This chapter is based on work previously carried out for the World Resources Institute and an ongoing collegial relationship with Argonne National Laboratories.

are assuming increasing significance in the problem of vehicle emissions. This chapter summarizes the nature of these problems and the role played by motor vehicles in causing them.

The Global Warming Problem

Greenhouse warming occurs when certain gases allow sunlight to penetrate to the earth but partially trap the planet's radiated infrared heat in the atmosphere. Some such warming is natural and necessary (IPCC 1990b). If there were no water vapor, carbon dioxide, methane, and other infrared-absorbing (greenhouse) gases in the atmosphere trapping the earth's radiant heat, our planet would be about 60° F (33° C) colder, and life as we know it would not be possible.

Over the past century, however, human activities have increased atmospheric concentrations of naturally occurring greenhouse gases and added new and very powerful infrared-absorbing gases to the mixture. Even more disturbing, in recent decades the atmosphere has begun to change through human activities at dramatically accelerated rates. According to a growing scientific consensus, if current emissions trends continue, the atmospheric build-up of greenhouse gases released by fossil fuel burning and industrial, agricultural, and forestry activities is likely to turn our benign atmospheric "greenhouse" into a progressively warmer "heat trap," as Norway's prime minister, Gro Harlem Brundtland, has termed this overheating.

How much do various human endeavors contribute to climate change? Recent estimates (WRI 1990, ch. 2) indicate that by far the largest contributor (about 50%) is energy consumption, mostly from the burning of fossil fuels. Chlorofluorocarbons (CFCs), the second-largest contributor to global warming, account for about 20% of the total. Mostly known for depleting the stratospheric ozone layer, these stable, long-lived chemicals are also extremely potent greenhouse gases. Deforestation and agricultural activities (such as rice production, cattle raising, and the use of nitrogen fertilizers) each contribute about 13% to 14% to global warming.

Carbon dioxide (CO_2) accounts for about half of the annual increase in global warming. The atmospheric concentration of carbon dioxide, now growing at about 0.5% per year, has already increased by about 25% since preindustrial times. Half of this increase has occurred over just the past three decades.

Globally, about two-thirds of anthropogenic carbon dioxide emissions arise from fossil fuel burning, the rest primarily from deforestation. In the United States, electric power plants account for about one-third of the carbon dioxide emissions, followed by motor vehicles, planes, and ships (31%); industrial plants (24%); and commercial and residential buildings (11%).

The third-largest contributor to global warming (after the CFCs) is methane (CH_4), accounting for about 13% (Hansen et al. 1988, 79) to 18% of the total warming (USEPA 1989, 13). Sources of this culprit gas include anaerobic decay in bogs, swamps, and other wetlands; rice growing; livestock production; termites; biomass burning; fossil fuel production and use; and landfills (USDOE 1990, 1.4). Methane may also be arising from the warming of the frozen Arctic tundra. The atmospheric concentration of methane is growing by about 1% annually.

Ozone (O_3) in the lower atmosphere (the troposphere) is the principal ingredient of smog. This gas is created in sunlight-driven reactions involving nitrogen oxides—NO_x (as distinct from nitrous oxide, N_2O), given off when either fossil fuels or biomass are burned—and volatile organic compounds from a wide spectrum of anthropogenic and natural sources. In Western Europe, road transportation accounts for an estimated 50% to 70% of NO_x emissions and almost half of anthropogenic emissions of organic compounds (Lubkert & de Tilly 1987). In the United States, highway vehicles are the source of about 31% of NO_x emissions and about 44% of volatile organic compounds. Tropospheric ozone contributes about 8% to global warming.

Nitrous oxide (N_2O) accounts for about 6% of current enhanced warming (USEPA 1989, 15) and also contributes to depletion of the stratospheric ozone layer. Exactly where nitrous oxide comes from is still uncertain, but prime suspects include the use of agricultural fertilizers and, perhaps, the burning of biomass and coal. Available evidence indicates that emissions tend to increase with the use of three-way catalytic converters. From a review of available literature as well as some new testing on nine vehicles, GM Research has concluded that vehicular emissions of N_2O are about 125Gg in the United States and about 200Gg worldwide. "Based on this value and the rate of N_2O increase in the stratosphere, vehicles in the United States emit about two percent of anthropogenic N_2O emissions" (Dasch 1992).

As greenhouse gases accumulate in the atmosphere, they amplify the earth's natural greenhouse effect, profoundly and perhaps irreversibly threatening all humankind and the natural environment. Although most scientists agree on the overall features of such warming, considerable uncertainties still surround its timing, magnitude, and regional impacts (IPCC 1990b).[1] Major unanswered questions include whether

---

[1] For discussions of the various possible impacts, see the pertinent chapters of WRI (1990).

the additional clouds that are likely to form will have a net cooling or warming effect, how the sources and sinks of greenhouse gases will change, and whether the polar and Greenland ice sheets will grow or retreat. At any rate, the complexity of the global climate system is daunting, and the interactions between the atmosphere and the oceans are still imperfectly understood.

Unless measures are soon taken to reduce the release of greenhouse gases, by as early as 2030 they could reach levels equivalent to twice the carbon dioxide concentrations of preindustrial times (USEPA 1990c). According to the most informed scientific opinion, continued "business as usual" growth in greenhouse gas emissions will lead to

- an increase in the global average temperature of 2° C (3.6° F), with a range of 1.4° to 2.8° C (2.5° to 5° F), over preindustrial levels by the year 2030 (IPCC 1990a)

- sea level rises great enough to threaten wetlands, accelerate coastal erosion, exacerbate coastal flooding, and increase the salinity of estuaries and aquifers[2]

- changes in rainfall patterns

- more intense tropical storms

- more severe droughts, especially in midcontinental regions, resulting in dislocations and reduced agricultural output

- the loss of many unmanaged ecosystems

Some of these changes could be gradual. The United Nations–sponsored Intergovernmental Panel on Climate Change (IPCC) has estimated that sea levels may rise an average of 6 to 20 inches above current levels by 2050 if present trends continue (IPCC 1990b). However, the totally unanticipated opening of the Antarctic ozone hole heightens scientists' anxiety about how quickly such significant and poorly understood phenomena can develop. Many experts fear that climate changes, once initiated, could occur faster than expected.

How Motor Vehicles Contribute to Global Warming and Air Pollution

Worldwide, cars, trucks, buses, and other motor vehicles are playing an ever-increasing role in global climate change and air pollution. As

---

[2] The remaining impacts are discussed in Abrahamson (1989).

large oil consumers, motor vehicles are major sources of carbon dioxide; volatile organic compounds (VOCs) and nitrogen oxides, the precursors to both tropospheric ozone and acid rain; carbon monoxide (CO); and chlorofluorocarbons (CFCs) (DeLuchi et al. 1988). All of these gases contribute to greenhouse warming either directly or indirectly; CFCs also contribute to depletion of the stratospheric ozone layer.

Carbon Dioxide

Virtually the entire global motor vehicle fleet runs on fossil fuels, primarily oil. For every gallon of oil consumed by a motor vehicle, about 19 pounds of carbon dioxide (containing about 5.3 pounds of carbon) go directly into the atmosphere.[3] In other words, for every 15-gallon fill-up at the service station, about 300 pounds of carbon dioxide are eventually released into the atmosphere. Globally, motor vehicles account for about a third of world oil consumption and about 14% of the world's carbon dioxide emissions from fossil fuel burning. For the United States, motor vehicles are responsible for about 50% of oil demand and about 25% of carbon dioxide emissions.

Tropospheric Ozone

Although ozone in the lower atmosphere does not come directly from motor vehicles, they are the major source of ozone precursors throughout the industrialized world. Over the past one hundred years, "background" ozone levels have approximately doubled (Volz & Kley 1988) and monitoring data suggest that ozone concentrations are increasing by about 1% per year in the Northern Hemisphere (Ciborowski 1989, 217).

Historically, the strategy of the U.S. Environmental Protection Agency (EPA) for reducing the concentrations of ozone (the principal ingredient of smog) has been to tightly restrict volatile organic compound emissions. But, recent research indicates, further controls of nitrogen oxides releases may also be needed (Sillman, Logan & Wofsy 1990). Without them, the continued emission of nitrogen oxides will increase ozone problems in downwind rural areas and some urban areas.[4]

---

[3] Direct tail-pipe emissions only. Transportation, refining, and distribution account for perhaps 15% to 20% of total emissions.

[4] There is an emerging consensus that NO_x control is more necessary than previously believed. This was reflected in the National Academy of Sciences (NAS) report "Rethinking the Ozone Problem in Urban and Regional Air Pollution." This report concludes that "State of the art air quality models and improved knowledge of the ambient concentrations of VOC's and NO_x indicate that NO_x control is necessary for effective reduction of ozone in

Controls of nitrogen oxides are also needed to reduce the deposition of nitric acid, an important component of acid rain.

Besides contributing to the greenhouse problem, ozone pollution also adversely affects human health, crops, other vegetation, and materials. Eye irritation, coughing and chest discomfort, headaches, upper respiratory illness, increased asthma attacks, and reduced pulmonary function can all plague people exposed to ozone (ALA 1989). This gas has also been shown to reduce crop productivity, with U.S. annual losses of several billion dollars, and to kill ponderosa and Jeffrey pines in California and eastern white pines in the eastern United States (MacKenzie & El-Ashry 1989).

Widespread and pervasive, smog looks to be a long-term problem in many areas of the world unless more stringent controls are adopted. About 112 million Americans reside in areas where the current air quality standard is violated (USEPA 1990b, 15).

Carbon Monoxide

Carbon monoxide—an odorless, invisible gas created when fuels containing carbon are burned incompletely—poses a serious threat to human health. Participating in various chemical reactions in the atmosphere, carbon monoxide also contributes to smog formation and the build-up of methane.

Exposure to carbon monoxide results primarily from motor vehicle emissions, though in some locales wood burning is also an important source. People with coronary artery disease who are exposed to carbon monoxide during exercise experience chest pain (angina); exposure also alters their electrocardiograms (ALA 1989, 10). Although ambient carbon monoxide levels have been reduced across Europe, Japan, and the United States, the problem is far from under control. In forty-four major U.S. metropolitan areas with a combined population of some 30 million people, the national carbon monoxide air quality standard is currently not being met (USEPA 1990b, 6, 15).

Global carbon monoxide concentrations in the lower atmosphere are increasing by between 0.8% and 1.4% per year (Khalil & Rasmussen 1988). For the five countries for which data on carbon monoxide

---

many areas of the United States. . . . Ozone is predicted to decrease in response to NO_x reductions in most urban locations. Models show that ozone concentrations rise in some urban cores, such as New York City and Los Angeles, in response to NO_x reductions but decrease in downwind areas, where maximum amounts of ozone are found. Choosing not to reduce NO_x in those urban centers, while ameliorating a local problem, could exacerbate the ozone problem in downwind regions. . . . If the anthropogenic VOC inventory is as badly underestimated as recent studies indicate, areas that were previously believed to be adversely affected by NO_x controls might actually benefit from them."

Table 1-1. Motor Vehicle Share of OECD Pollutant Emissions, 1980		
Pollutant	Total Emissions (1,000 tons)	Motor Vehicle Share (1,000 tons)
NO_x	36,019	17,012 (47%)
HC	33,869	13,239 (39%)
CO	119,148	78,227 (66%)
Source: OECD (1987).		

emissions are available, transportation accounted for 59% to 84% of releases (WRI 1988, 168). In the United States, 67% of the carbon monoxide emissions in 1988 came from transportation (USEPA 1990b, 56).

Carbon monoxide can elevate concentrations of tropospheric ozone and methane in several ways. First, carbon monoxide helps convert nitric oxide (NO) to nitrogen dioxide (NO_2)—a crucial step in ozone formation (USEPA 1986, 3–15ff.). Second, the hydroxyl radical (OH) that eventually removes carbon monoxide from the atmosphere is also the principal chemical that destroys ozone and methane. If carbon monoxide levels increase, OH concentrations will fall and regional concentrations of ozone and methane will rise.

Comprehensive data are not available on global air pollution emissions from transportation and other activities. For the twenty-four Organization for Economic Cooperation and Development (OECD) countries, however, motor vehicles are the dominant source of emissions of carbon monoxide (CO), oxides of nitrogen (NO_x), and volatile organic compounds (hydrocarbons, HC) (see Table 1-1).

Chlorofluorocarbons (CFCs)

Highly potent greenhouse gases, CFCs also reduce the protective stratospheric ozone layer (Gribbin 1988). During the Antarctic spring, the ozone hole spans an area the size of North America. At certain altitudes over the Antarctic, the ozone is destroyed almost completely.

If CFCs continue to deplete the world's stratospheric ozone layer, ultraviolet radiation will increase and so will ground-level ozone formation. Even a moderate loss in the total ozone column would significantly boost peak ozone levels at the earth's surface. By allowing more ultraviolet radiation through the ozone shield, such a loss is also expected to increase the number of skin cancers and impair the human immune system. Increased ultraviolet radiation might also harm the

Table 1-2. Estimated U.S. Consumption of CFC-12 for Mobile A/C, 1985

Use	CFC Consumption (1,000 tons)	% of Total
Initial charge of units		
United States	14.7	27.2
Imported	2.8	5.2
Aftermarket	1.0	1.8
Recharge of units		
After leakage	13.5	25.0
After service venting	18.2	33.6
After accident	3.9	7.2
TOTAL	54.1	100.0

Source: USEPA (1987).

life-supporting plankton that dwell in the ocean's upper levels, thus jeopardizing marine food chains that depend on the tiny plankton.

A major source of CFCs in the atmosphere is motor vehicle air-conditioning, and in 1987 approximately 48% of all new cars, trucks, and buses manufactured worldwide were equipped with air conditioners (UNEP 1989). (CFCs also are used as a blowing agent in the production of seating and other foam products, but this is a considerably smaller vehicular use.) Annually, about 120,000 metric tons of CFCs are used in new vehicles and in servicing air conditioners in older vehicles. In all, these uses account for about 28% of global demand for CFC-12. According to the EPA, in the United States, vehicular air conditioners are the single largest users of CFCs, accounting for about 54,000 metric tons of CFC-12 demand in 1985 (USEPA 1988, 10) and roughly 16% of total U.S. CFC use in 1989 (USEPA 1990a) (see Table 1-2). As agreed under the Montreal Protocol, CFCs are to be completely phased out of new vehicles by the turn of the century.

Historic Patterns of Vehicle Production and Use

In 1950, there were about 53 million cars on the world's roads, 76% of them in the United States. Only four decades later, the global automobile fleet is over 430 million, more than an eightfold increase. On average, the fleet has grown by about 9.5 million automobiles per year over

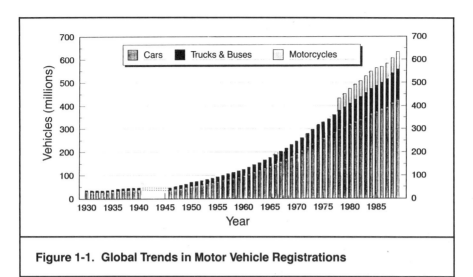

Figure 1-1. Global Trends in Motor Vehicle Registrations

this period. Simultaneously, as illustrated in Figure 1-1, the truck and bus fleet has been growing by about 3.6 million vehicles per year. Outside of the United States, the growth in automobiles has been especially high, rising from slightly under 13 million in 1950 to more than 270 million in 1988, a growth rate of more than 8% per year (MVMA 1991b, 35). Whereas the growth rate has slowed in the highly industrialized countries, population growth and increased urbanization and industrialization are accelerating the use of motor vehicles elsewhere. If the approximately 100 million two-wheeled vehicles around the world are included (growing at about 4 million vehicles per year over the last decade), the global motor vehicle fleet is now approximately 675 million. In 1950 almost 80% of the world's cars and trucks were on U.S. highways. By 1990 this figure had fallen to approximately 30% (see Figure 1-2).

Trends in World Motor Vehicle Production

Overall growth in the production of motor vehicles, especially since the end of World War II, has been equally dramatic, rising from about 5 million motor vehicles per year to almost 50 million. Between 1950 and 1989, production increased almost linearly from about 10 million vehicles per year to about 49.5 million per year, with approximately 1 million additional vehicles produced each year.

Over the past several decades, motor vehicle production has shifted away from North America. The first wave of competition came

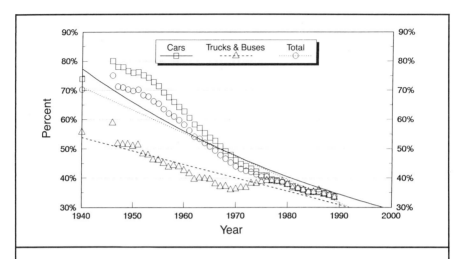

Figure 1-2. Global Trends in Motor Vehicle Registrations: Percent in the United States

from Europe, and by the late 1960s European production had surpassed that of the United States. Over the past two decades the car industry in Asia, led by Japan, has grown rapidly and now rivals that of both the United States and Europe.

As can be seen in Table 1-3, the motor vehicle manufacturing dominance of the United States and Germany and, to a much greater extent, that of the United Kingdom, has slipped over the past two decades. At the same time, the market share enjoyed by Spain, Korea, and especially Japan has grown dramatically. These rankings are based on the number of motor vehicles actually manufactured within the countries.

A Highly Concentrated Industry

Of the more than 49 million vehicles manufactured in 1989, over 70% were produced by the top ten manufacturers. The top fourteen produced 80% (see Table 1-4). Thirty other manufacturers made most of the rest. As a result of this market concentration, efforts to reduce the global climate impacts of motor vehicle use could, in principle, be achieved through improvements by a relatively few corporations. Of the top fourteen motor vehicle manufacturers, six were Japanese; three, American; two, West German; two, French; and one, Italian. (In this accounting, vehicles are counted by company, regardless of where

Table 1-3. Ranking of Western Motor-Vehicle-Producing Countries, 1965, 1975, 1985, and 1989 (Measured by Total Production Within the Country)

Country	1965	1975	1985	1989
United States	1	1	2	2
West Germany	2	3	3	3
United Kingdom	3	5	7	8
Japan	4	2	1	1
France	5	4	4	4
Italy	6	6	6	5
Canada	7	7	5	7
Australia	8	10	10	13
Spain	9	9	8	6
Sweden	10	11	11	12
Brazil	11	8	9	10
Mexico	12	12	12	11
Republic of Korea	13	13	13	9

Source: Automotive News (1986, 1990).

the vehicles are manufactured or assembled.) In 1989, North American companies manufactured 33% of all motor vehicles. Japanese companies placed a close second with 30%, and Western Europe third with 26%.

Japan's gains in nonpassenger (commercial) vehicle production since 1975 rival the country's gains in passenger car manufacturing. As a result, Japan is now the world's largest motor vehicle manufacturer (measured by the total number of vehicles manufactured within the country), ahead of the United States and Europe. (Countries can be ranked according to their motor vehicle production in two distinctly different ways. The first is based on the total number of vehicles actually manufactured within the borders of the country. By this measure, Japan is first. The second is based on the total number of vehicles manufactured by corporations headquartered within a country. According to this measure, U.S. manufacturers are still number one, largely because of overseas production.)

Trends in World Motor Vehicle Registrations

As for worldwide vehicle registrations, the long-term trends are sharply upward and are actually accelerating. Registrations of trucks

Table 1-4. Ranking of World Motor Vehicle Manufacturers, 1989 (Includes Vehicles Manufactured in Other Countries)

Manufacturer Rank	Production (millions of vehicles)	%	Cumulative %
1. General Motors (U.S.)	7.611	15.5	15.5
2. Ford Motor (U.S.)	6.047	12.3	27.9
3. Toyota (Japan)	4.278	8.7	36.6
4. Nissan (Japan)	3.003	6.1	42.7
5. Volkswagen (W. Germany)	2.880	5.9	48.6
6. Peugeot-Citroen (France)	2.688	5.5	54.1
7. Chrysler (U.S.)	2.209	4.5	58.6
8. Renault (France)	2.204	4.5	63.1
9. Fiat (Italy)	2.158	4.4	67.5
10. Honda (Japan)	1.812	3.7	71.2
11. Mazda (Japan)	1.487	3.0	74.2
12. Mitsubishi (Japan)	1.250	2.6	76.8
13. Suzuki (Japan)	0.868	1.8	78.6
14. Daimler-Benz (W. Germany)	0.783	1.6	80.2

Source: MVMA (1991b, 16).

and buses have been growing for the past two decades by about 4.2 million vehicles per year; motorcycles have grown at approximately the same rate, whereas car registrations have been growing almost three times as fast.

Europe (including Eastern Europe and the former Soviet Union) and North America each have about 30% of the world's motor vehicle population. The remainder is divided among Asia, South America, Africa, and Oceania (Australia, New Zealand, and Guam), in that order. North America has about 40% of the world's trucks and buses, followed closely by Asia and then Europe.

In terms of per capita motor vehicle registration for various regions, the United States, Japan, and Europe also account for the lion's share of the ownership and use of motor vehicles. Indeed, as illustrated in Figure 1-3, *the non-OECD countries of Africa, Asia (excluding Japan), and Latin America are home to more than four-fifths of the world's population, yet account for only about one-fourth of world motor vehicle registrations* (MVMA 1991b, 36–38)!

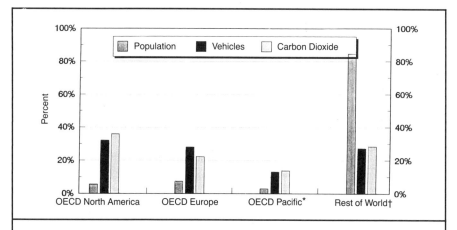

Figure 1-3. 1990 Global Shares of Population, Vehicles, and Carbon Dioxide

Notes:
* OECD Pacific = OECD countries of the Pacific, including Japan, Australia, and New Zealand.
† Includes much of Asia, Africa, and Latin America.

Where We Stand Today

Statistics on the global vehicle population today show wide disparities between regions of the world and between vehicle modes. For example, Figure 1-4 shows the per capita vehicle population for various regions of the world and illustrates that except for OECD countries, most of the world's people still live and work largely without motorized transport. As a result, as shown in Figure 1-5, the carbon dioxide emissions per capita from transportation are also widely divergent by region.

Different vehicle types also vary in their significance. For example, as illustrated in Figure 1-6, heavy-duty trucks represent less than 10% of the global fleet, but almost 20% of the annual kilometers driven and 25% of the CO_2 emissions from road transport. In the future these patterns will be increasingly important—that is, vehicle growth will inevitably be greater in most of the rest of the world than in the current highly industrialized regions, and vehicle modes that have tended to get less attention, such as heavy trucks and motorcycles, will be more and more important in terms of such problems as global warming.

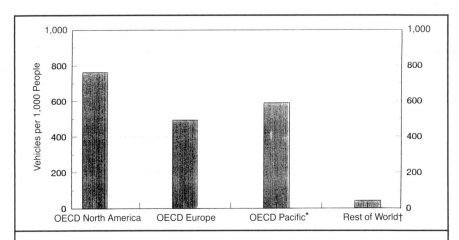

Figure 1-4. 1990 Global Distribution of Vehicles per Capita

Notes:
* OECD Pacific = OECD countries of the Pacific, including Japan, Australia, and New Zealand.
† Includes much of Asia, Africa, and Latin America.

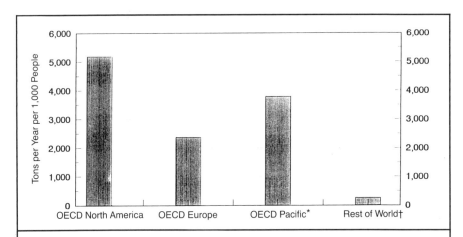

Figure 1-5. 1990 Global Variation in Transport Emissions of CO_2 per Capita

Notes:
* OECD Pacific = OECD countries of the Pacific, including Japan, Australia, and New Zealand.
† Includes much of Asia, Africa, and Latin America.

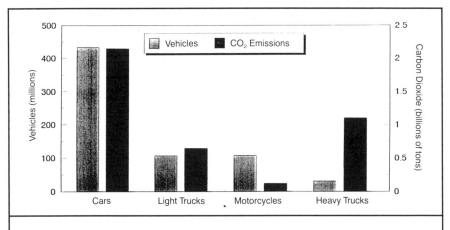

Figure 1-6. 1990 Global Distribution of Motor Vehicles and Carbon Dioxide

Future Trends in Motor Vehicle Registrations and Emissions

Worldwide, the number of motor vehicles is growing far faster than the global population—5.2% per year between 1960 and 1989 for motor vehicles, compared with 2.1% per year for population. Analysis of trends in global motor vehicle registrations reveals that the global fleet has been growing linearly since before 1970 and that each year for two decades an additional 16 million motor vehicles, not including two-wheeled vehicles, have been added to the world fleet. If this linear trend continues, the global vehicle population[5] will reach about 900 million by the year 2010.

Analysis of growth in registrations per capita yields an even higher estimate for the world motor vehicle fleet. Each year worldwide registrations grow by about 1.8 cars per thousand persons or 2.3 vehicles (cars plus trucks and buses) per thousand people, as shown in Figure 1-7. Motorcycles per capita over the last decade have been stable. If this trend were to continue until 2010, there would be 154 motor vehicles per 1,000 persons (excluding motorcycles), compared with 112 in 1990. If this figure is multiplied by the United Nations' (UN 1989) medium variant estimate for global population in 2010—7.2 billion—

---

[5] Not including two-wheeled vehicles.

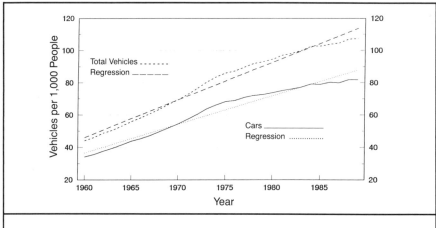

Figure 1-7. Global Trends in Motor Vehicles per Capita

the motor vehicle fleet will be an estimated 1.1 billion, almost double today's and about 20% greater than would result from the strictly linear projection.

Beyond four- (or more) wheeled vehicles, which dominate the fleet of vehicles in most of the industrialized world, motorcycles are an increasingly important vehicle mode in Asia, the area of the world with the most rapidly growing population. On a worldwide basis, the number of two-wheeled vehicles appears to be growing at about the same rate as the population—that is, the number of motorcycles per capita is staying approximately constant.

Underlying Factors Fostering Vehicle Growth

The growth in demand for motorized travel in recent decades is well understood. As urban areas populate and expand, land that is generally at the edges of the urban area and previously considered unsuitable for development is developed. The distance of these residential locations from the city center or other subcenters increases, increasing the need for motorized travel. Motorized travel, often in private vehicles, supplants traditional modes of travel, such as walking, various bicycle forms, water travel, and even mass transit. The need for private vehicles is reinforced as declining population densities with distances from urban centers reduce the economic viability of mass transit.

The evolution of the form of urban areas is influenced by the growth of income and accompanying increases in the acquisitions of private motor vehicles and changes in travel habits. As incomes rise, an increasing proportion of trips shifts, first to motorcycles and then, as income increases further, to private cars. *The trend toward private motorization is not inevitable but is also influenced by public policy toward land use, housing, and transportation infrastructure.* Although the proportion of middle- and upper-income households in developing and newly industrialized countries able to afford cars and motorcycles is lower than that in industrialized nations, the number of private vehicles still becomes very large as the middle- and upper-income groups grow in megacities in these developing countries. The number of vehicles and the levels of congestion in such megacities are comparable to or exceed those of major cities in industrialized countries. With the increase in motorized travel and congestion come increases in energy use, emissions, and air pollution (TDRI 1990).

If we focus on Southeast Asia, the region currently experiencing the most rapid growth in road vehicles, as an example, all projections of population trends indicate both rapid increases and increasing urbanization. In short, these trends generally add to the geographical spread of cities, both large and small, increasing the need for motorized transit to carry out a growing portion of daily activities. Further, when coupled with expanding economies as is more and more the case in Asian countries, a greater proportion of the urban population can afford personal motorized transportation, starting with motorcycles and progressing as soon as economically feasible to cars.

Trends in the Global Motor Vehicle Fleet

The underlying factors influencing vehicle population growth, especially population growth and economic development, have been weighted to make projections of the future vehicle population. In making these estimates, it was assumed that vehicle saturation, increased congestion, and increasing policy interventions by governments would restrain future growth, especially in highly industrialized areas. In spite of these factors, vehicles per capita are estimated to rise in all areas of the world.

In the past, the global vehicle fleet has been dominated by the highly industrialized areas of North America and Western Europe. Table 1-5 shows that this pattern is gradually changing, not because these areas have stopped growing, but because growth rates are accelerating in other areas. By early in the next century, based on current trends, the rapidly developing areas of the world (especially Asia, Eastern Europe, and Latin America) and the OECD Pacific region will have as many vehicles as North America and Western Europe do.

Table 1-5. Global Trends in Vehicle Populations, 1990–2010 (Base Case)[a]

Year	OECD North America	OECD Europe	Eastern Europe[b]	OECD Pacific[c]	Rapidly Developing Countries[d]	Rest of World[e]
1990	214,271,374	182,670,684	69,394,666	87,501,160	59,801,881	64,227,832
1995	231,557,420	203,429,878	80,513,525	101,188,083	83,561,406	76,282,516
2000	250,314,921	226,870,273	94,917,461	113,442,110	109,364,553	87,952,294
2010	289,737,440	272,123,778	127,079,087	134,629,665	177,569,654	119,109,543

Notes:
[a] Includes motorcycles, cars, trucks, and buses.
[b] Includes the republics of the former USSR.
[c] OECD Pacific = OECD countries of the Pacific, including Japan, Australia, and New Zealand.
[d] Includes rapidly industrializing countries that have taken steps to introduce state-of-the-art pollution controls on cars (Brazil, Chile, Hong Kong, Mexico, Singapore, South Korea, and Taiwan) and those with minimal pollution control programs (Indonesia, Malaysia, the Philippines, and Thailand).
[e] Includes much of Asia, Africa, and Latin America.

Table 1-6. Baseline Modal Split, 1990

Country	Cars	Light Trucks	Heavy Trucks	Motorcycles
OECD North America[a]	73.9%	19.8%	2.8%	3.5%
EC[b]	77.3%	9.0%	1.8%	12.0%
EFTA[c]	79.7%	7.8%	1.6%	11.0%
EE[d]	49.0%	16.7%	3.3%	31.0%
OECD Pacific[e]	48.9%	21.9%	7.3%	21.9%
RICA[f]	55.1%	12.9%	4.3%	27.8%
RICB[g]	19.3%	12.4%	4.1%	64.2%
Rest of world[h]	46.6%	15.0%	15.0%	23.3%

Notes:
[a] OECD North America = the United States and Canada.
[b] EC = European Community.
[c] EFTA = European Free Trade Association.
[d] EE = Eastern Europe and the republics of the former USSR.
[e] OECD Pacific = OECD countries of the Pacific, including Japan, Australia, and New Zealand.
[f] RICA = rapidly industrializing countries that have taken steps to introduce state-of-the-art pollution controls on cars (Brazil, Chile, Hong Kong, Mexico, Singapore, South Korea, and Taiwan).
[g] RICB = rapidly industrializing countries with minimal pollution control programs (Indonesia, Malaysia, the Philippines, and Thailand).
[h] Includes much of Asia, Africa, and Latin America.

The Baseline Modal Split

As noted earlier, there are significant differences in the vehicle mix in different regions of the world. Table 1-6 illustrates the modal split between cars, light trucks, heavy trucks, and motorcycles for eight regions of the world. It can be seen that cars and light trucks dominate the road vehicle category for the United States and Western Europe, but that two-wheeled vehicles and to a lesser extent heavy trucks are much more significant in the rest of the world.[6]

Other Key Inputs for Emissions Calculations

Annual Vehicle Growth Rates. Table 1-7 summarizes the annual vehicle growth rates for each region of the world. As the table shows, separate growth rates were estimated for each of four vehicle categories: cars, light-duty trucks (LDT), motorcycles (MC), and heavy-duty trucks and buses (HDT). Regions considered include the United States and Canada (US); the twelve member countries of the European Community (EC); the European Free Trade Association (EFTA); Eastern Europe and the republics of the former USSR (EE); the OECD countries of the Pacific, including Japan, Australia, and New Zealand (OECD Pacific); rapidly industrializing countries that have taken steps to introduce state-of-the-art pollution controls on cars (RICA); rapidly industrializing countries with minimal pollution control programs (RICB); and the rest of the world (ROW).

Emissions per Mile. Table 1-8 lists the emissions per mile for each region and vehicle type as summarized above. The emissions-per-mile rates for CO, HC, and NO_x in the base case were based on exhaust and evaporative emissions standards, fuel quality, maintenance practices, refueling controls, and inspection-and-maintenance program status and plans in each country in the region. For countries with none or very few pollution control strategies at present (RICB and ROW, primarily), it was estimated that they would generally adopt the same programs as the RICA countries after approximately a ten-year delay. Carbon dioxide emissions were based on vehicle fuel efficiency estimates for vehicles in the region as discussed below.

(Text continued on page 26)

---

[6] It is important to note that heavy trucks are driven much more than other vehicle types per year and are therefore responsible for a greater proportion of kilometers driven than Table 1-6, which is based on vehicle populations, would imply. Motorcycles are driven much less than other modes and therefore are responsible for proportionately less overall driving.

Table 1-7. Base Case Annual Vehicle Growth Rate

Vehicle Segment	U.S.	EC[a]	EFTA[b]	EE[c]	OECD Pacific[d]	RICA[e]	RICB[f]	ROW[g]
1989–1995								
Cars	1.5%	2.5%	2.0%	3.0%	4.0%	7.0%	7.0%	3.5%
LDT[h]	2.0%	2.5%	2.0%	3.0%	4.0%	7.0%	7.0%	3.5%
MC[i]	0.0%	0.0%	0.0%	3.0%	-1.0%	7.0%	7.0%	3.5%
HDT[j]	2.0%	2.5%	2.5%	3.5%	3.0%	5.0%	5.0%	3.5%
1995–2000								
Cars	1.5%	2.5%	2.0%	3.5%	3.0%	6.0%	6.0%	2.5%
LDT	2.0%	2.5%	2.0%	3.5%	3.0%	6.0%	6.0%	2.5%
MC	0.0%	0.0%	0.0%	3.0%	-1.0%	5.0%	5.0%	3.5%
HDT	2.0%	2.5%	2.5%	3.5%	2.5%	4.0%	4.0%	3.5%
2000–2010								
Cars	1.5%	2.0%	2.0%	3.5%	2.0%	5.0%	5.0%	3.0%
LDT	1.5%	2.0%	2.0%	3.0%	2.0%	5.0%	5.0%	3.0%
MC	0.0%	0.0%	0.0%	2.0%	0.0%	5.0%	5.0%	3.0%
HDT	2.0%	2.5%	2.0%	3.0%	2.0%	4.0%	4.0%	3.5%

Notes:
[a] EC = European Community.
[b] EFTA = European Free Trade Association.
[c] EE = Eastern Europe and the republics of the former USSR.
[d] OECD Pacific = OECD countries of the Pacific, including Japan, Australia, and New Zealand.
[e] RICA = rapidly industrializing countries that have taken steps to introduce state-of-the-art pollution controls on cars (Brazil, Chile, Hong Kong, Mexico, Singapore, South Korea, and Taiwan).
[f] RICB = rapidly industrializing countries with minimal pollution control programs (Indonesia, Malaysia, the Philippines, and Thailand).
[g] ROW = rest of the world, including much of Asia, Africa, and Latin America.
[h] LDT = light-duty trucks.
[i] MC = motorcycles.
[j] HDT = heavy-duty trucks.

Table 1-8. Emissions-per-Mile Rates

	NORTH AMERICA															
	CARS				LDT[a]				MC[b]				HDT[c]			
	CO	HC	NO$_x$	CO$_2$	CO	HC	NO$_x$	CO$_2$	CO	HC	NO$_x$	CO$_2$	CO	HC	NO$_x$	CO$_2$
BASE CASE																
1990	10.6	3.7	1.2	485	1.0	0.4	1.2	585	15.3	6.2	1.0	270	8.4	2.0	16.5	1,490
1995	5.9	1.5	0.9	462	1.0	0.4	0.9	554	15.0	4.3	1.0	270	7.7	1.7	9.6	1,490
2000	5.0	1.3	0.6	432	1.0	0.4	0.9	516	15.0	4.2	1.0	270	7.5	1.6	9.5	1,490
2010	5.0	1.2	0.4	361	1.0	0.4	0.9	430	15.0	4.2	1.0	270	7.4	1.6	8.5	1,490
2020	5.0	1.1	0.4	297	1.0	0.4	0.9	354	15.0	4.2	1.0	270	7.4	1.6	8.5	1,490
2030	5.0	1.1	0.4	249	1.0	0.4	0.9	296	15.0	4.2	1.0	270	7.4	1.6	8.5	1,490
2040	5.0	1.1	0.4	249	1.0	0.4	0.9	296	15.0	4.2	1.0	270	7.4	1.6	8.5	1,490
LOW EMISSIONS																
1990	10.6	3.7	1.2	485	1.0	0.4	1.2	585	15.3	6.2	1.0	270	8.4	2.0	16.5	1,490
1995	5.9	1.5	0.9	458	1.0	0.3	0.9	549	15.0	4.3	1.0	270	7.7	1.7	9.6	1,441
2000	3.5	1.2	0.5	418	1.0	0.3	0.9	499	15.0	4.2	1.0	270	7.5	1.6	7.7	1,310
2010	2.2	0.9	0.3	314	1.0	0.3	0.9	373	15.0	4.2	1.0	270	7.4	1.6	5.9	1,191
2020	2.0	0.9	0.2	203	1.0	0.3	0.9	241	15.0	4.2	1.0	270	7.4	1.6	5.7	1,083
2030	2.0	0.9	0.2	125	1.0	0.3	0.9	148	15.0	4.2	1.0	270	7.4	1.6	5.7	984
2040	2.0	0.9	0.2	125	1.0	0.3	0.9	148	15.0	4.2	1.0	270	7.4	1.6	5.7	895
	EUROPEAN COMMUNITY															
	CARS				LDT				MC				HDT			
	CO	HC	NO$_x$	CO$_2$	CO	HC	NO$_x$	CO$_2$	CO	HC	NO$_x$	CO$_2$	CO	HC	NO$_x$	CO$_2$
BASE CASE																
1990	56.3	6.6	3.2	415	1.0	0.4	1.9	485	15.3	11.9	1.0	222	8.4	2.0	17.0	1,110
1995	45.8	5.4	2.7	397	1.0	0.3	1.9	462	15.0	12.0	1.0	222	7.7	1.7	13.0	1,110
2000	26.2	3.9	1.4	372	1.0	0.3	1.7	432	15.0	12.0	1.0	222	7.5	1.6	12.0	1,110
2010	8.9	2.8	0.6	311	1.0	0.4	1.5	361	15.0	12.0	1.0	222	7.4	1.6	11.0	1,110
2020	6.1	2.6	0.4	256	1.0	0.4	1.1	297	15.0	12.0	1.0	222	7.4	1.6	10.0	1,110
2030	6.1	2.6	0.4	215	1.0	0.4	1.1	249	15.0	12.0	1.0	222	7.4	1.6	9.0	1,110
2040	6.1	2.6	0.4	215	1.0	0.4	1.1	249	15.0	12.0	1.0	222	7.4	1.6	9.0	1,110

Notes:
[a] LDT = light-duty trucks.
[b] MC = motorcycles.
[c] HDT = heavy-duty trucks.

Table 1-8. (continued)

EUROPEAN COMMUNITY (continued)															
CARS				LDT				MC				HDT			
CO	HC	NO_x	CO_2	CO	HC	NO_x	CO_2	CO	HC	NO_x	CO_2	CO	HC	NO_x	CO_2
LOW EMISSIONS															
1990 56.3	6.6	4.1	415	1.0	0.4	1.9	485	15.3	11.9	1.0	222	8.4	2.0	15.3	1,110
1995 45.8	5.4	2.7	393	0.9	0.3	1.9	458	15.0	12.0	1.0	222	7.7	1.7	12.0	1,110
2000 10.2	1.6	1.3	359	0.9	0.3	1.6	418	15.0	10.3	1.0	222	7.5	1.6	8.6	1,009
2010 2.8	0.8	0.3	271	1.0	0.3	1.0	314	15.0	4.6	1.0	222	7.4	1.6	5.9	917
2020 1.8	0.7	0.2	175	1.0	0.3	0.9	203	15.0	4.2	1.0	222	7.4	1.6	5.7	834
2030 1.8	0.7	0.2	107	1.0	0.3	0.9	125	15.0	4.2	1.0	222	7.4	1.6	5.7	758
2040 1.8	0.7	0.2	107	1.0	0.3	0.9	125	15.0	4.2	1.0	222	7.4	1.6	5.7	689

EUROPEAN FREE TRADE ASSOCIATION															
CARS				LDT				MC				HDT			
CO	HC	NO_x	CO_2	CO	HC	NO_x	CO_2	CO	HC	NO_x	CO_2	CO	HC	NO_x	CO_2
BASE CASE															
1990 45.0	5.5	3.0	415	1.0	0.4	1.7	485	15.3	11.9	1.0	222	8.4	2.0	15.3	1,110
1995 33.1	4.4	2.0	397	0.9	0.3	1.9	462	15.0	12.0	1.0	222	7.7	1.7	14.0	1,110
2000 20.6	3.4	1.2	372	0.9	0.3	1.7	432	15.0	12.0	1.0	222	7.5	1.6	13.0	1,110
2010 8.0	2.8	0.6	311	1.0	0.4	1.1	361	15.0	12.0	1.0	222	7.4	1.6	11.0	1,110
2020 6.1	2.6	0.4	256	1.0	0.4	1.1	297	15.0	12.0	1.0	222	7.4	1.6	10.0	1,110
2030 6.1	2.6	0.4	215	1.0	0.4	1.1	249	15.0	12.0	1.0	222	7.4	1.6	9.0	1,110
2040 6.1	2.6	0.4	215	1.0	0.4	1.1	249	15.0	12.0	1.0	222	7.4	1.6	9.0	1,110
LOW EMISSIONS															
1990 55.1	6.5	4.0	415	1.0	0.4	1.7	485	15.3	11.9	1.0	222	8.4	2.0	15.3	1,110
1995 33.1	4.4	2.0	393	0.9	0.3	1.9	458	15.0	12.0	1.0	222	7.7	1.7	13.0	1,110
2000 8.3	1.3	1.1	359	0.9	0.3	1.6	418	15.0	10.3	1.0	222	7.5	1.6	8.7	1,009
2010 2.6	0.7	0.3	271	1.0	0.3	1.0	314	15.0	4.6	1.0	222	7.4	1.6	5.9	917
2020 1.8	0.7	0.2	175	1.0	0.3	0.9	203	15.0	4.2	1.0	222	7.4	1.6	5.7	834
2030 1.8	0.7	0.2	107	1.0	0.3	0.9	125	15.0	4.2	1.0	222	7.4	1.6	5.7	758
2040 1.8	0.7	0.2	107	1.0	0.3	0.9	125	15.0	4.2	1.0	222	7.4	1.6	5.7	689

Table 1-8. (continued)

	EASTERN EUROPE[d]															
	CARS				LDT				MC				HDT			
	CO	HC	NO_x	CO_2	CO	HC	NO_x	CO_2	CO	HC	NO_x	CO_2	CO	HC	NO_x	CO_2
BASE CASE																
1990	99.0	10.0	3.3	415	1.0	0.4	2.1	485	15.3	11.9	1.0	222	8.4	2.0	17.0	1,110
1995	98.0	9.8	3.2	397	1.0	0.4	2.1	462	15.0	12.0	1.0	222	7.7	1.7	13.0	1,110
2000	80.6	8.1	3.6	372	1.0	0.4	2.0	432	15.0	12.0	1.0	222	7.5	1.6	12.0	1,110
2010	31.3	4.1	1.6	311	1.0	0.4	2.0	361	15.0	12.0	1.0	222	7.4	1.6	11.0	1,110
2020	9.7	2.8	0.6	256	1.0	0.4	1.6	297	15.0	12.0	1.0	222	7.8	1.6	10.0	1,110
2030	9.7	2.8	0.6	215	1.0	0.4	1.6	249	15.0	12.0	1.0	222	7.8	1.6	9.0	1,110
2040	9.7	2.8	0.6	215	1.0	0.4	1.6	249	15.0	12.0	1.0	222	7.8	1.6	9.0	1,110
LOW EMISSIONS																
1990	99.0	10.0	3.3	415	1.0	0.4	1.7	485	15.3	11.9	1.0	222	8.4	2.0	15.4	1,110
1995	98.0	9.8	3.2	393	0.9	0.3	1.9	458	15.0	12.0	1.0	222	7.7	1.7	13.5	1,110
2000	50.0	5.2	3.4	359	0.9	0.3	1.9	418	15.0	10.3	1.0	222	7.5	1.6	11.4	1,009
2010	6.1	1.1	0.6	271	1.0	0.3	1.1	314	15.0	4.6	1.0	222	7.4	1.6	6.1	917
2020	1.8	0.7	0.2	175	1.0	0.3	0.9	203	15.0	4.2	1.0	222	7.4	1.6	5.7	834
2030	1.8	0.7	0.2	107	1.0	0.3	0.9	125	15.0	4.2	1.0	222	7.4	1.6	5.7	758
2040	1.8	0.7	0.2	107	1.0	0.3	0.9	125	15.0	4.2	1.0	222	7.4	1.6	5.7	689

	OECD PACIFIC[e]															
	CARS				LDT				MC				HDT			
	CO	HC	NO_x	CO_2	CO	HC	NO_x	CO_2	CO	HC	NO_x	CO_2	CO	HC	NO_x	CO_2
BASE CASE																
1990	13.6	3.9	1.2	415	1.0	0.4	2.0	485	15.3	6.6	1.0	222	8.4	2.0	15.3	1,110
1995	10.7	3.3	1.0	397	0.9	0.3	1.9	462	15.0	6.0	1.0	222	7.7	1.7	12.7	1,110
2000	10.7	3.3	1.0	372	0.9	0.3	1.9	432	15.0	6.0	1.0	222	7.7	1.7	12.7	1,110
2010	9.1	3.0	0.8	311	1.0	0.4	1.5	361	15.0	5.9	1.0	222	7.4	1.6	10.9	1,110
2020	8.5	2.9	0.7	256	1.0	0.4	1.1	297	15.0	5.9	1.0	222	7.4	1.6	10.9	1,110
2030	8.5	2.9	0.7	215	1.0	0.4	1.1	249	15.0	5.9	1.0	222	7.4	1.6	10.9	1,110
2040	8.5	2.9	0.7	215	1.0	0.4	1.1	249	15.0	5.9	1.0	222	7.4	1.6	10.9	1,110

Notes:
[d] Includes the republics of the former USSR.
[e] OECD Pacific=OECD countries of the Pacific, including Japan, Australia, and New Zealand.

Table 1-8. (continued)

	OECD PACIFIC (continued)															
	CARS				LDT				MC				HDT			
	CO	HC	NO_x	CO_2	CO	HC	NO_x	CO_2	CO	HC	NO_x	CO_2	CO	HC	NO_x	CO_2
LOW EMISSIONS																
1990	13.6	3.9	1.2	415	1.0	0.4	1.7	485	15.3	6.6	1.0	222	8.4	2.0	15.3	1,110
1995	10.7	3.3	1.0	393	0.9	0.3	1.9	458	15.0	6.0	1.0	222	7.7	1.7	12.7	1,110
2000	6.2	1.5	0.8	359	0.9	0.3	1.6	418	15.0	4.2	1.0	222	7.5	1.6	11.3	1,009
2010	2.3	0.8	0.3	271	1.0	0.3	1.0	314	15.0	4.3	1.0	222	7.4	1.6	6.1	917
2020	1.8	0.7	0.2	175	1.0	0.3	0.9	203	15.0	4.2	1.0	222	7.4	1.6	5.7	834
2030	1.8	0.7	0.2	107	1.0	0.3	0.9	125	15.0	4.2	1.0	222	7.4	1.6	5.7	758
2040	1.8	0.7	0.2	107	1.0	0.3	0.9	125	15.0	4.2	1.0	222	7.4	1.6	5.7	689

RAPIDLY INDUSTRIALIZING COUNTRIES WITH MORE ADVANCED POLLUTION CONTROL PROGRAMS[f]

	CARS				LDT				MC				HDT			
	CO	HC	NO_x	CO_2	CO	HC	NO_x	CO_2	CO	HC	NO_x	CO_2	CO	HC	NO_x	CO_2
BASE CASE																
1990	—	11.9	3.2	415	1.0	0.4	1.7	485	18.3	13.2	0.9	222	8.4	2.0	15.4	1,110
1995	86.3	9.2	2.4	397	0.9	0.3	1.9	462	18.1	13.2	0.9	222	7.7	1.7	13.5	1,110
2000	43.8	6.1	1.5	372	0.9	0.3	2.0	432	18.1	10.2	0.9	222	7.5	1.6	12.9	1,110
2010	19.7	4.4	1.1	311	1.0	0.4	2.1	361	18.1	9.4	0.9	222	7.4	1.6	12.8	1,110
2020	17.2	4.1	1.0	256	1.0	0.4	2.1	297	18.1	9.4	0.9	222	7.4	1.6	12.8	1,110
2030	17.2	4.1	1.0	215	1.0	0.4	2.1	249	18.1	9.4	0.9	222	7.4	1.6	12.8	1,110
2040	17.2	4.1	1.0	215	1.0	0.4	2.1	249	18.1	9.4	0.9	222	7.4	1.6	12.8	1,110
LOW EMISSIONS																
1990	—	11.9	3.2	415	1.0	0.4	1.7	485	18.3	13.2	0.9	222	8.4	2.0	15.4	1,110
1995	86.3	9.2	2.4	393	0.9	0.3	1.9	458	18.1	13.2	0.9	222	7.7	1.7	13.5	1,110
2000	24.8	3.1	1.4	359	0.9	0.3	1.9	418	18.1	7.9	0.9	222	7.5	1.6	13.0	1,009
2010	4.1	1.1	0.4	271	1.0	0.3	1.1	314	18.1	5.1	0.9	222	7.4	1.6	6.2	917
2020	2.0	0.9	0.2	175	1.0	0.3	0.9	203	18.1	4.9	0.9	222	7.4	1.6	5.7	834
2030	2.0	0.9	0.2	107	1.0	0.3	0.9	125	18.1	4.9	0.9	222	7.4	1.6	5.7	758
2040	2.0	0.9	0.2	107	1.0	0.3	0.9	125	18.1	4.9	0.9	222	7.4	1.6	5.7	689

Notes:
[f] Includes Brazil, Chile, Hong Kong, Mexico, Singapore, South Korea, and Taiwan.

Table 1-8. (continued)

RAPIDLY INDUSTRIALIZING COUNTRIES WITH MINIMAL
POLLUTION CONTROL PROGRAMS[g]

	CARS				LDT				MC				HDT			
	CO	HC	NO_x	CO_2	CO	HC	NO_x	CO_2	CO	HC	NO_x	CO_2	CO	HC	NO_x	CO_2
BASE CASE																
1990	—	11.9	3.2	415	1.0	0.4	1.7	485	18.3	13.2	0.9	222	8.4	2.0	15.4	1,110
1995	—	11.4	3.3	397	0.9	0.3	1.9	462	18.1	13.2	0.9	222	7.7	1.7	13.5	1,110
2000	73.9	8.1	2.1	372	0.9	0.3	2.0	432	18.1	13.2	0.9	222	7.5	1.6	12.9	1,110
2010	24.5	4.7	1.2	311	1.0	0.4	2.1	361	18.1	9.5	0.9	222	7.4	1.6	12.8	1,110
2020	17.2	4.1	1.0	256	1.0	0.4	2.1	297	18.1	9.4	0.9	222	7.4	1.6	12.8	1,110
2030	17.2	4.1	1.0	215	1.0	0.4	2.1	249	18.1	9.4	0.9	222	7.4	1.6	12.8	1,110
2040	17.2	4.1	1.0	215	1.0	0.4	2.1	249	18.1	9.4	0.9	222	7.4	1.6	12.8	1,110
LOW EMISSIONS																
1990	—	11.9	3.2	415	1.0	0.4	1.7	485	18.3	13.2	0.9	222	8.4	2.0	15.4	1,110
1995	—	11.4	3.3	393	0.9	0.3	1.9	458	18.1	13.2	0.9	222	7.7	1.7	13.5	1,110
2000	71.7	7.0	3.1	359	0.9	0.3	1.9	418	18.1	10.9	0.9	222	7.5	1.6	13.0	1,009
2010	7.8	1.5	0.5	271	1.0	0.3	1.1	314	18.1	5.2	0.9	222	7.4	1.6	6.2	917
2020	2.0	0.9	0.2	175	1.0	0.3	0.9	203	18.1	4.9	0.9	222	7.4	1.6	5.7	834
2030	2.0	0.9	0.2	107	1.0	0.3	0.9	125	18.1	4.9	0.9	222	7.4	1.6	5.7	758
2040	2.0	0.9	0.2	107	1.0	0.3	0.9	125	18.1	4.9	0.9	222	7.4	1.6	5.7	689

REST OF THE WORLD[h]

	CARS				LDT				MC				HDT			
	CO	HC	NO_x	CO_2	CO	HC	NO_x	CO_2	CO	HC	NO_x	CO_2	CO	HC	NO_x	CO_2
BASE CASE																
1990	—	11.9	3.3	415	1.0	0.4	1.7	485	15.3	11.9	1.0	222	8.4	2.0	15.4	1,110
1995	98.0	9.8	3.2	397	0.9	0.3	1.9	462	15.0	12.0	1.0	222	7.4	1.7	13.5	1,110
2000	99.5	9.7	3.2	372	0.9	0.3	2.0	432	15.0	12.0	1.0	222	7.5	1.6	12.9	1,110
2010	24.5	4.7	1.2	311	1.0	0.4	2.1	361	18.1	9.5	0.9	222	7.4	1.6	12.8	1,110
2020	17.2	4.1	1.0	256	1.0	0.4	2.1	297	18.1	9.4	0.9	222	7.4	1.6	12.8	1,110
2030	17.2	4.1	1.0	215	1.0	0.4	2.1	249	18.1	9.4	0.9	222	7.4	1.6	12.8	1,110
2040	17.2	4.1	1.0	215	1.0	0.4	2.1	249	18.1	9.4	0.9	222	7.4	1.6	12.8	1,110

Notes:
[g] Includes Indonesia, Malaysia, the Philippines, and Thailand.
[h] Includes much of Asia, Africa, and Latin America.

Table 1-8. (continued)															
REST OF THE WORLD (continued)															
CARS				LDT				MC				HDT			
CO	HC	NO_x	CO_2	CO	HC	NO_x	CO_2	CO	HC	NO_x	CO_2	CO	HC	NO_x	CO_2
LOW EMISSIONS															
1990 —	11.9	3.3	415	1.0	0.4	1.7	485	15.3	11.9	1.0	222	8.4	2.0	15.4	1,110
1995 98.0	9.8	3.2	393	0.9	0.3	1.9	458	15.0	12.0	1.0	222	7.7	1.7	13.5	1,110
2000 62.0	6.4	3.0	359	0.9	0.3	1.9	418	15.0	10.3	1.0	222	7.5	1.6	13.0	1,009
2010 6.7	1.2	0.5	271	1.0	0.3	1.1	314	15.0	4.6	1.0	222	7.4	1.6	6.2	917
2020 1.8	0.7	0.2	175	1.0	0.3	0.9	203	15.0	4.2	1.0	222	7.4	1.6	5.7	834
2030 1.8	0.7	0.2	107	1.0	0.3	0.9	125	15.0	4.2	1.0	222	7.4	1.6	5.7	758
2040 1.8	0.7	0.2	107	1.0	0.3	0.9	125	15.0	4.2	1.0	222	7.4	1.6	5.7	689

Fuel Efficiency (Mpg) and Annual Mileage. Table 1-9 summarizes the miles per gallon and miles driven per year for each region and vehicle category considered. Fuel efficiency was the most difficult to estimate because there are so many confounding variables that can have an impact. For example, in the United States, the corporate average fuel economy (CAFE) standards increased significantly during the 1970s and early 1980s but have remained fairly flat since the mid 1980s, actually declining over the past few years. At the same time, sales of light trucks have increased substantially. (Since many of these light trucks tend to be used much like passenger cars and have much lower fuel efficiency than the cars they are replacing, overall light-duty vehicle efficiency gains are even less than it would appear.) *CAFE standards did not apply to heavy-duty vehicles, this category being subject only to a voluntary program.* Further, national legislation was modified to allow speed limits to climb to 65 mph, thereby further undercutting energy conservation since fuel consumption increases as highway vehicle speeds climb. During the last decade, the auto industry has been moving back toward the horsepower wars of the 1960s, substantially increasing power output and reducing 0 to 60 mph wide-open-throttle acceleration times over this period.[7] New-car fuel efficiency has also been declining in both Europe (Volkswagen 1990) and Japan (JMT 1990). *(Text continued on page 35)*

---

[7] In addition to hurting fuel economy, the greater horsepower and faster accelerations will likely increase the *actual* NO_x, HC, and CO emissions in use since the EPA emissions test procedure does not accurately reflect these new driving conditions.

Table 1-9. Fuel Efficiency (Mpg) and Annual Mileage

NORTH AMERICA

	MILES PER GALLON			MILES PER YEAR (BILLIONS)			
Cars	**LT**[a]	**MC**[b]	**HDT**[c]	**Cars**	**LT**	**MC**	**HDT**
BASE CASE							
1990 20.58131	17.06050	37	5.9	1,612	446	32	169
1995 21.60132	18.02382	37	5.9	1,736	493	32	186
2000 23.10337	19.34608	37	5.9	1,870	544	32	206
2010 27.65392	23.22930	37	5.9	2,171	631	32	251
2020 35.57740	28.20501	37	5.9	2,519	733	32	291
2030 40.12810	33.70760	37	5.9	2,648	770	32	306
2040 40.12810	33.70760	37	5.9	2,648	770	32	306
LOW EMISSIONS							
1990 20.58131	17.06050	37	5.9	1,612	446	32	169
1995 21.81369	18.19983	37	6.1	1,736	493	32	186
2000 23.91209	20.02108	37	6.7	1,870	544	32	206
2010 31.82314	26.76430	37	7.4	2,171	631	32	251
2020 49.24245	41.39539	37	8.1	2,519	733	32	291
2030 80.19410	67.39194	37	8.9	2,648	770	32	306
2040 80.19410	67.39194	37	9.8	2,648	770	32	306
LOW EMISSIONS/LOW GROWTH							
1990 20.58131	17.06050	37	5.9	1,612	446	32	169
1995 21.81369	18.19983	37	6.1	1,736	493	32	186
2000 23.91209	20.02108	37	6.7	1,780	518	31	196
2010 31.82314	26.76430	37	7.4	1,871	544	28	216
2020 49.24245	41.39539	37	8.1	1,967	572	25	227
2030 80.19410	67.39194	37	8.9	1,871	544	23	216
2040 80.19410	67.39194	37	9.8	1,871	544	11	216

Notes:
a LT = light trucks.
b MC = motorcycles.
c HDT = heavy-duty trucks.

Table 1-9. (continued)

				EUROPEAN COMMUNITY			
	MILES PER GALLON			MILES PER YEAR (BILLIONS)			
	Cars	LT	MC	HDT	Cars	LT	MC	HDT

	Cars	LT	MC	HDT	Cars	LT	MC	HDT
BASE CASE								
1990	24.1	20.6	45.0	9.0	1,294	154	83	82
1995	25.2	21.6	45.0	9.0	1,464	175	83	93
2000	26.9	23.1	45.0	9.0	1,656	198	83	105
2010	32.1	27.7	45.0	9.0	2,018	241	83	134
2020	38.9	33.6	45.0	9.0	2,230	266	83	156
2030	46.5	40.1	45.0	9.0	2,463	294	83	181
2040	46.5	40.1	45.0	9.0	3,492	417	83	256
LOW EMISSIONS								
1990	24.1	20.6	45.0	9.0	1,294	154	83	82
1995	25.4	21.8	45.0	9.0	1,464	175	83	93
2000	27.8	23.9	45.0	9.9	1,656	198	83	105
2010	36.9	31.8	45.0	10.9	2,018	241	83	134
2020	57.1	49.2	45.0	12.0	2,230	266	83	156
2030	93.0	80.2	45.0	13.2	2,463	294	83	181
2040	93.0	80.2	45.0	14.5	3,492	417	83	256
LOW EMISSIONS/LOW GROWTH								
1990	24.1	20.6	45.0	9.0	1,293.5	154.5	83.2	81.8
1995	25.4	21.8	45.0	9.0	1,463.5	174.8	83.2	92.5
2000	27.8	23.9	45.0	9.9	1,576.6	188.3	79.1	99.7
2010	36.9	31.8	45.0	10.9	1,741.6	208.0	71.5	115.7
2020	57.1	49.2	45.0	12.0	1,741.6	208.0	64.7	121.6
2030	93.0	80.2	45.0	13.2	1,741.6	208.0	58.5	127.8
2040	93.0	80.2	45.0	14.5	1,226.2	146.5	29.0	90.0

Table 1-9. (continued)

	EUROPEAN FREE TRADE ASSOCIATION							
	MILES PER GALLON				**MILES PER YEAR (BILLIONS)**			
	Cars	**LT**	**MC**	**HDT**	**Cars**	**LT**	**MC**	**HDT**
BASE CASE								
1990	24.1	20.6	45.0	9.0	152.4	15.3	8.8	8.2
1995	25.2	21.6	45.0	9.0	168.3	16.9	8.8	9.2
2000	26.9	23.1	45.0	9.0	185.8	18.7	8.8	10.4
2010	32.1	27.7	45.0	9.0	226.5	22.8	8.8	12.7
2020	38.9	33.6	45.0	9.0	262.9	26.4	8.8	15.5
2030	46.5	40.1	45.0	9.0	290.4	29.2	8.8	17.1
2040	46.5	40.1	45.0	9.0	290.4	29.2	8.8	17.1
LOW EMISSIONS								
1990	24.1	20.6	45.0	9.0	152.4	15.3	8.8	8.3
1995	25.4	21.8	45.0	9.0	168.3	16.9	8.8	9.2
2000	27.8	23.9	45.0	9.9	185.8	18.7	8.8	10.4
2010	36.9	31.8	45.0	10.9	226.5	22.8	8.8	12.7
2020	57.1	49.2	45.0	12.0	262.9	26.4	8.8	15.5
2030	93.0	80.2	45.0	13.2	290.4	29.2	8.8	17.1
2040	93.0	80.2	45.0	14.5	290.4	29.2	8.8	17.1
LOW EMISSIONS/LOW GROWTH								
1990	24	21	45	9	152	15	9	8
1995	25	22	45	9	168	17	9	9
2000	28	24	45	10	219	21	9	10
2010	37	32	45	11	205	21	8	12
2020	57	49	45	12	216	24	8	13
2030	93	80	45	13	216	24	7	13
2040	93	80	45	14	107	12	4	7

Table 1-9. (continued)

				EASTERN EUROPE[d]			
	MILES PER GALLON				MILES PER YEAR (BILLIONS)		
Cars	LT	MC	HDT	Cars	LT	MC	HDT
BASE CASE							
1990 24.1	20.6	45.0	9.0	346.5	121.5	92.8	64.6
1995 25.2	21.6	45.0	9.0	401.7	140.8	107.6	76.7
2000 26.9	23.1	45.0	9.0	477.1	167.2	124.7	91.1
2010 32.1	27.7	45.0	9.0	673.0	224.7	152.0	122.5
2020 38.9	33.6	45.0	9.0	861.4	287.7	167.9	156.8
2030 46.5	40.1	45.0	9.0	1,050.1	350.7	185.5	200.7
2040 46.5	40.1	45.0	9.0	2,505.4	836.7	372.2	478.9
LOW EMISSIONS							
1990 24.1	20.6	45.0	9.0	346.5	121.5	92.8	64.6
1995 25.4	21.8	45.0	9.0	401.7	140.8	107.6	76.7
2000 27.8	23.9	45.0	9.9	477.1	167.2	124.7	91.1
2010 36.9	31.8	45.0	10.9	673.0	224.7	152.0	122.5
2020 57.1	49.2	45.0	12.0	861.4	287.7	167.9	156.8
2030 93.0	80.2	45.0	13.2	1,050.1	350.7	185.5	200.7
2040 93.0	80.2	45.0	14.5	2,505.4	836.7	372.2	478.9
LOW EMISSIONS/LOW GROWTH							
1990 24.1	20.6	45.0	9.0	346.5	121.5	92.8	64.6
1995 25.4	21.8	45.0	9.0	401.7	140.8	107.6	76.7
2000 27.8	23.9	45.0	9.9	454.5	159.3	118.8	86.8
2010 36.9	31.8	45.0	10.9	581.8	194.2	131.2	105.8
2020 57.1	49.2	45.0	12.0	675.1	225.4	131.2	122.8
2030 93.0	80.2	45.0	13.2	745.8	248.9	131.2	142.5
2040 93.0	80.2	45.0	14.5	888.2	296.5	131.2	169.8

Notes:
d Includes the republics of the former USSR.

Table 1-9. (continued)

			OECD PACIFIC[e]				
	MILES PER GALLON			MILES PER YEAR (BILLIONS)			
Cars	LT	MC	HDT	Cars	LT	MC	HDT
BASE CASE							
1990 24.09035	20.58131	45	9	440.7921	203.2740	79.75553	177.6348
1995 25.17128	21.60132	45	9	536.2910	247.3139	75.84672	205.9274
2000 26.85649	23.10337	45	9	621.7083	286.7046	72.12947	232.9879
2010 32.07855	27.65392	45	9	757.8590	349.4913	72.12947	284.0110
2020 38.94978	33.57740	45	9	837.1478	386.0558	72.12947	321.5774
2030 46.54859	40.12810	45	9	924.7320	428.4458	72.12947	355.2215
2040 46.54859	40.12810	45	9	1063.546	490.4608	72.12947	408.5449
LOW EMISSIONS							
1990 24.09035	20.58131	45	9	440.7921	203.2740	79.75553	177.6348
1995 25.41989	21.81369	45	9	536.2910	247.3139	75.84672	205.9274
2000 27.79864	23.91209	45	9.9	621.7083	286.7046	72.12947	232.9879
2010 36.88674	31.82314	45	10.89	757.8590	349.4913	72.12947	284.0110
2020 57.09415	49.24245	45	11.979	837.1478	386.0558	72.12947	321.5774
2030 93.00055	80.19410	45	13.1769	924.7320	426.4458	72.12947	355.2215
2040 93.00055	80.19410	45	14.49459	1063.546	490.4608	72.12947	408.5449
LOW EMISSIONS/LOW GROWTH							
1990 24.09035	20.58131	45	9	440.7921	203.2740	79.75553	177.6348
1995 25.41989	21.81369	45	9	536.2910	247.3139	75.84672	205.9274
2000 27.79864	23.91209	45	9.9	592.1086	273.0545	68.55943	221.8423
2010 36.88674	31.82314	45	10.89	654.0563	301.6221	62.00392	245.0519
2020 57.09415	49.24245	45	11.979	654.0563	301.6221	56.07523	251.2476
2030 93.00055	80.19410	45	13.1769	654.0563	301.6221	50.71343	251.2476
2040 93.00055	80.19410	45	14.49459	372.7625	171.9017	25.09496	143.1920

Notes:
[e] OECD Pacific = OECD countries of the Pacific, including Japan, Australia, and New Zealand.

Table 1-9. (continued)

RAPIDLY INDUSTRIALIZING COUNTRIES
WITH POLLUTION CONTROL PROGRAMS[f]

	MILES PER GALLON				MILES PER YEAR (BILLIONS)		
Cars	LT	MC	HDT	Cars	LT	MC	HDT
BASE CASE							
1990 24.09035	20.58131	45	9	224.0836	53.91257	47.97992	46.68076
1995 25.17128	21.60132	45	9	314.2888	75.61517	67.29432	59.57779
2000 26.85649	23.10337	45	9	420.5893	101.1901	85.88650	72.48549
2010 32.07855	27.65392	45	9	685.0957	164.8281	139.9000	107.2962
2020 38.94978	33.57740	45	9	1014.109	243.9858	188.0139	158.8246
2030 46.54859	40.12810	45	9	1501.129	361.1586	252.6750	235.0992
2040 46.54859	40.12810	45	9	8454.514	2034.082	1010.588	2612.617
LOW EMISSIONS							
1990 24.09035	20.58131	45	9	224.0836	53.91257	47.97992	46.68076
1995 25.41989	21.81369	45	9	314.2888	75.61517	67.29432	59.57779
2000 27.79864	23.91209	45	9.9	420.5893	101.1901	85.88650	72.48549
2010 36.88674	31.82314	45	10.89	685.0957	164.8281	139.9000	107.8962
2020 57.09415	49.24245	45	11.979	1014.109	243.9858	188.0139	158.8246
2030 93.00055	80.19410	45	13.1769	1501.129	361.1586	252.6750	235.0992
2040 93.00055	80.19410	45	14.49459	8454.514	2034.082	1010.588	2612.617
LOW EMISSIONS/LOW GROWTH							
1990 24.09035	20.58131	45	9	224.0836	53.91257	47.97992	46.68076
1995 25.41989	21.81369	45	9	314.2888	75.61517	67.29432	59.57779
2000 27.79864	23.91209	45	9.9	401.1210	96.50625	81.87383	69.06699
2010 36.88674	31.82314	45	10.89	593.5751	142.8528	121.1932	92.82026
2020 57.09415	49.24245	45	11.979	797.9600	191.9822	147.7339	124.7426
2030 93.00055	80.19410	45	13.1769	1072.391	258.0081	180.0868	167.6437
2040 93.00055	80.19410	45	14.49459	1244.554	299.4289	198.9278	214.5981

Notes:
[f] Includes Brazil, Chile, Hong Kong, Mexico, Singapore, South Korea, and Taiwan.

Table 1-9. (continued)

RAPIDLY INDUSTRIALIZING COUNTRIES WITH LIMITED POLLUTION CONTROL PROGRAMS[g]							
MILES PER GALLON				MILES PER YEAR (BILLIONS)			
Cars	LT	MC	HDT	Cars	LT	MC	HDT
BASE CASE							
1990 24.09035	20.58131	45	9	39.18637	25.82057	55.16246	22.35701
1995 25.17128	21.60132	45	9	54.96091	36.21469	77.36820	28.53384
2000 26.85649	23.10337	45	9	73.55010	48.46343	98.74361	34.71578
2010 32.07855	27.65392	45	9	119.8053	78.94182	160.8429	51.38784
2020 38.94978	33.57740	45	9	195.1503	128.5879	216.1594	76.06656
2030 46.54859	40.12810	45	9	288.8701	190.3415	290.5002	112.5970
2040 46.54859	40.12810	45	9	2287.222	1507.090	1161.872	891.5237
LOW EMISSIONS							
1990 24.09035	20.58131	45	9	39.18637	25.82057	55.16246	22.35701
1995 25.41989	21.81369	45	9	54.96091	36.21469	77.36820	28.53384
2000 27.79864	23.91209	45	9.9	73.55010	48.46343	98.74361	34.71578
2010 36.88674	31.82314	45	10.89	119.8053	78.94182	160.8429	51.38784
2020 57.09415	49.24245	45	11.979	195.1503	128.5879	216.1594	76.06656
2030 93.00055	80.19410	45	13.1769	288.8701	190.3415	290.5002	112.5970
2040 93.00055	80.19410	45	14.49459	2287.222	1507.090	1161.872	891.5237
LOW EMISSIONS/LOW GROWTH							
1990 24.09035	20.58131	45	9	39.18637	25.82057	55.16246	22.35701
1995 25.41989	21.81369	45	9	54.96091	36.21469	77.36820	28.53384
2000 27.79864	23.91209	45	9.9	70.14560	46.22015	94.13025	33.07854
2010 36.88674	31.82314	45	10.89	103.8326	68.41711	139.3357	44.45480
2020 57.09415	49.24245	45	11.979	153.6976	101.2740	169.8495	59.74353
2030 93.00055	80.19410	45	13.1769	206.5567	136.1038	207.0456	80.29032
2040 93.00055	80.19410	45	14.49459	826.1359	544.3552	415.4915	321.1258

Notes:
g Includes Indonesia, Malaysia, the Philippines, and Thailand.

Table 1-9. (continued)

	THE REST OF THE WORLD [h]						
	MILES PER GALLON				MILES PER YEAR (BILLIONS)		
	Cars	LT	MC	HDT	Cars	LT	MC	HDT
---	---	---	---	---	---	---	---	---
BASE CASE								
1990	24.09035	20.58131	45	9	304.9820	101.4121	64.6254	268.4440
1995	25.17128	21.60132	45	9	362.2230	120.4458	76.75470	318.8273
2000	26.85649	23.10337	45	9	409.8221	136.2734	91.16050	378.6668
2010	32.07855	27.65392	45	9	550.7666	183.1401	122.5121	534.1469
2020	38.94978	33.57740	45	9	815.2692	271.0921	149.3415	753.4670
2030	46.54859	40.12810	45	9	1150.017	382.4022	182.0465	1012.596
2040	46.54859	40.12810	45	9	9105.635	3027.792	728.1057	5703.049
LOW EMISSIONS								
1990	24.09035	20.58131	45	9	304.9820	101.4121	64.6254	268.4440
1995	25.41989	21.81369	45	9	362.2230	120.4458	76.75470	318.8273
2000	27.79864	23.91209	45	9.9	409.8221	136.2734	91.16050	378.6668
2010	36.88674	31.82314	45	10.89	550.7666	183.1401	122.5121	534.1469
2020	57.09415	49.24245	45	11.979	815.2692	271.0921	149.3415	753.4670
2030	93.00055	80.19410	45	13.1769	1150.017	382.4022	182.0465	1012.596
2040	93.00055	80.19410	45	14.49459	9105.635	3027.792	728.1057	5703.049
LOW EMISSIONS/LOW GROWTH								
1990	24.09035	20.58131	45	9	304.9820	101.4121	64.6254	268.4440
1995	25.41989	21.81369	45	9	362.2230	120.4458	76.75470	318.8273
2000	27.79864	23.91209	45	9.9	390.2170	129.7544	86.84090	360.7238
2010	36.88674	31.82314	45	10.89	475.6724	158.1699	105.8585	461.7570
2020	57.09415	49.24245	45	11.979	639.2640	212.5671	116.9337	591.0880
2030	93.00055	80.19410	45	13.1769	818.3119	272.1039	129.1675	720.5330
2040	93.00055	80.19410	45	14.49459	3272.886	1088.295	259.2087	2043.039

Notes:
[h] Includes much of Asia, Africa, and Latin America.

Simultaneously, people are using private cars and light trucks to drive to work much more than in the past, with the result that public transit usage is down. This is true not only in highly industrialized countries in Western Europe and in the United States (MVMA 1991a), but even in the emerging countries of Eastern Europe (Walsh 1990). When considering the improvements in new-car fuel economy and the return of gasoline prices to pre-OPEC levels, the cost of fuel for driving in real terms is much lower in the United States today than at any time in the last two decades, further encouraging additional driving. Not surprisingly, annual vehicle miles traveled has been increasing across the United States by about 50 billion miles per year[8] and because the amount of driving is increasing faster than the improvement in mpg, annual fuel consumption continues to increase.

Taking account of these factors as well as a gradual increase in the cost of oil as global demand continues to grow, estimates were made for future vehicle efficiency as summarized in Table 1-9. Globally, it was estimated that new-car and light-truck mpg would gradually increase at approximately 2% per year from 1993 model year forward. Motorcycles and heavy trucks and buses are estimated to remain at current levels.

Global Vehicle Emissions Trends

Based on all currently adopted emissions requirements, projections of future emissions from vehicles around the world were carried out, with the results summarized in Tables 1-10 through 1-13. Based on a continuation of the strong motor vehicle control programs in the United States and Japan and the recent tightening of requirements in EC Europe, these estimates indicate that global CO, HC, and NO_x emissions will remain fairly stable throughout the next decade. Beyond that point, however, emissions of HC and NO_x will start to increase due to the projected continued growth in vehicle populations both in OECD countries and especially in other areas of the world where emissions controls are frequently minimal.

The CO_2 picture is even more bleak. Based on current worldwide trends, and even assuming a gradual increase in average mpg of the vehicle fleet, expected vehicle growth will cause continued increases in carbon dioxide emissions in all areas of the world. More than the other pollutants, for which technologies exist and are being applied to substantially lower emissions in at least some corners of the world and

---

[8] According to MVMA *Motor Vehicle Facts and Figures 1991*, annual average mileage actually increased an average of 75 billion miles per year during the period from 1985 to 1990.

Table 1-10. Global Trends in Motor Vehicle Emissions: Carbon Monoxide (tons/year)

Year	North America	OECD Europe	Eastern Europe[a]	OECD Pacific[b]	Rapidly Developing Countries[c]	Rest of World[d]
1990	21,496,854	90,279,287	40,078,892	9,806,144	36,357,799	42,559,806
1995	13,869,856	82,487,031	45,951,641	9,538,148	40,915,346	43,203,523
2000	13,196,254	54,669,969	45,318,637	10,748,497	31,009,323	49,650,794
2010	15,309,407	24,816,407	26,945,171	11,436,753	25,662,206	21,848,418

Notes:
[a] Includes the republics of the former USSR.
[b] OECD Pacific = OECD countries of the Pacific, including Japan, Australia, and New Zealand.
[c] Includes rapidly industrializing countries that have taken steps to introduce state-of-the-art pollution controls on cars (Brazil, Chile, Hong Kong, Mexico, Singapore, South Korea, and Taiwan) and those with minimal pollution control programs (Indonesia, Malaysia, the Philippines, and Thailand).
[d] Includes much of Asia, Africa, and Latin America.

Table 1-11. Global Trends in Motor Vehicle Emissions: Hydrocarbons (tons/year)

Year	North America	OECD Europe	Eastern Europe[a]	OECD Pacific[b]	Rapidly Developing Countries[c]	Rest of World[d]
1990	7,320,384	11,848,424	5,230,227	2,947,540	5,115,382	5,457,525
1995	3,533,675	10,944,192	5,941,814	2,929,095	6,163,866	5,545,195
2000	3,151,865	8,396,506	6,110,279	2,969,635	6,122,044	6,285,872
2010	3,625,149	8,553,896	5,336,115	3,611,647	7,454,737	5,166,728

Notes:
[a] Includes the republics of the former USSR.
[b] OECD Pacific = OECD countries of the Pacific, including Japan, Australia, and New Zealand.
[c] Includes rapidly industrializing countries that have taken steps to introduce state-of-the-art pollution controls on cars (Brazil, Chile, Hong Kong, Mexico, Singapore, South Korea, and Taiwan) and those with minimal pollution control programs (Indonesia, Malaysia, the Philippines, and Thailand).
[d] Includes much of Asia, Africa, and Latin America.

Table 1-12. Global Trends in Motor Vehicle Emissions: Nitrogen Oxides (tons/year)

Year	OECD North America	OECD Europe	Eastern Europe[a]	OECD Pacific[b]	Rapidly Developing Countries[c]	Rest of World[d]
1990	5,787,482	7,179,847	2,840,347	4,109,750	2,356,056	5,908,331
1995	4,190,988	6,621,918	2,968,121	4,041,708	2,696,917	6,346,989
2000	3,879,930	4,511,158	3,592,013	4,497,811	2,876,034	7,221,603
2010	4,031,779	3,709,953	3,349,325	4,775,000	4,046,886	8,732,197

Notes:
a Includes the republics of the former USSR.
b OECD Pacific = OECD countries of the Pacific, including Japan, Australia, and New Zealand.
c Includes rapidly industrializing countries that have taken steps to introduce state-of-the-art pollution controls on cars (Brazil, Chile, Hong Kong, Mexico, Singapore, South Korea, and Taiwan) and those with minimal pollution control programs (Indonesia, Malaysia, the Philippines, and Thailand).
d Includes much of Asia, Africa, and Latin America.

Table 1-13. Global Trends in Motor Vehicle Emissions: Carbon Dioxide (tons/year)

Year	North America	OECD Europe	Eastern Europe[a]	OECD Pacific[b]	Rapidly Developing Countries[c]	Rest of World[d]
1990	1,435,398,803	883,441,278	324,780,070	546,519,903	272,419,509	537,356,064
1995	1,499,927,299	957,616,830	367,323,179	630,530,938	361,365,185	628,068,122
2000	1,482,860,821	941,817,826	416,899,245	658,557,226	449,800,591	717,838,076
2010	1,583,193,340	1,076,627,436	507,021,799	763,650,725	640,434,593	944,504,411

Notes:
a Includes the republics of the former USSR.
b OECD Pacific = OECD countries of the Pacific, including Japan, Australia, and New Zealand.
c Includes rapidly industrializing countries that have taken steps to introduce state-of-the-art pollution controls on cars (Brazil, Chile, Hong Kong, Mexico, Singapore, South Korea, and Taiwan) and those with minimal pollution control programs (Indonesia, Malaysia, the Philippines, and Thailand).
d Includes much of Asia, Africa, and Latin America.

Table 1-14. Global Projections of Motor Vehicle Emissions: Carbon Monoxide (tons/year)

Year	Cars	Light Trucks	Motorcycles	Heavy Trucks
1990	223,357,376	1,260,248	8,168,139	7,793,019
1995	217,043,366	1,410,969	9,209,773	8,301,436
2000	183,131,401	1,623,464	10,464,134	9,374,474
2010	97,559,141	2,077,267	14,166,965	12,214,989

Table 1-15. Global Projections of Motor Vehicle Emissions: Hydrocarbons (tons/year)

Year	Cars	Light Trucks	Motorcycles	Heavy Trucks
1990	30,025,462	506,570	5,568,461	1,818,987
1995	26,309,692	529,987	6,387,750	1,830,407
2000	23,314,293	607,874	7,075,987	2,038,046
2010	22,084,536	798,924	8,227,297	2,637,515

Table 1-16. Global Projections of Motor Vehicle Emissions: Nitrogen Oxides (tons/year)

Year	Cars	Light Trucks	Motorcycles	Heavy Trucks
1990	11,049,831	1,995,856	481,970	14,654,156
1995	10,651,242	2,205,343	550,760	13,459,297
2000	8,387,873	2,517,257	619,217	15,054,203
2010	5,996,606	3,113,332	782,274	18,752,930

for which the issue is one of encouraging the more widespread use of these technologies, nowhere can one point to substantial progress yet with regard to carbon dioxide.

Tables 1-14 through 1-17 illustrate the trends in global emissions of CO, HC, NO_x, and CO_2 by vehicle type and provide some startling insights. First of all, not surprisingly, cars remain the dominant source of CO for the foreseeable future. However, motorcycles, most of which are two-stroke, are seen to be a significant contributor to HC emissions around the world, a fact that is largely ignored in the West

Table 1-17. Global Projections of Motor Vehicle Emissions: Carbon Dioxide (tons/year)

Year	Cars	Light Trucks	Motorcycles	Heavy Trucks
1990	2,140,563,394	648,810,244	115,235,655	1,095,306,335
1995	2,326,778,635	714,188,146	131,007,340	1,272,857,434
2000	2,287,475,047	764,561,988	147,578,254	1,468,158,497
2010	2,588,738,693	802,074,961	190,301,058	1,934,317,592

Table 1-18. Motor Vehicle Emissions Projections for North America: Carbon Monoxide (tons/year)

Year	Cars	Light Trucks	Motorcycles	Heavy Trucks
1990	18,884,987	501,193	542,431	1,568,242
1995	11,204,769	553,358	530,023	1,581,706
2000	10,361,043	610,952	530,023	1,694,236
2010	12,024,413	709,034	530,023	2,045,937

because of their small contribution in that region. With regard to NO_x emissions, heavy-duty trucks are a large and rapidly growing contributor, due to the minimal NO_x control in most regions of the world. And again, heavy trucks can be seen as a large and growing source of carbon dioxide as only minimal improvements in per-vehicle fuel efficiency are occurring with this category. By 2010, globally, cars will emit less CO_2 than other road vehicles.

North American Vehicle Emissions Trends

The trends in U.S. vehicle growth and emissions generally resemble global patterns. The number of registered motor vehicles in the United States has grown by an average of 4 million motor vehicles annually since 1970. If this linear trend continues, the U.S. fleet will total about 273 million motor vehicles in the year 2010, compared with 183 million in 1988.

Tables 1-18 through 1-21 illustrate North American trends in emissions of CO, HC, NO_x, and CO_2 by vehicle type and provide similar insights, especially with regard to trucks, which can be seen as a large and growing contributor to NO_x and CO_2, as only minimal improvements in per-vehicle fuel efficiency occur with this category.

Table 1-19. Motor Vehicle Emissions Projections for North America: Hydrocarbons (tons/year)

Year	Cars	Light Trucks	Motorcycles	Heavy Trucks
1990	6,531,650	201,460	221,227	366,047
1995	2,810,753	222,428	151,739	348,755
2000	2,390,096	245,579	149,257	366,933
2010	2,749,120	285,004	149,257	441,768

Table 1-20. Motor Vehicle Emissions Projections for North America: Nitrogen Oxides (tons/year)

Year	Cars	Light Trucks	Motorcycles	Heavy Trucks
1990	2,112,137	584,725	34,035	3,056,585
1995	1,682,627	504,532	34,389	1,969,439
2000	1,147,246	551,054	34,389	2,147,240
2010	1,004,027	646,473	34,389	2,346,891

Table 1-21. Motor Vehicle Emissions Projections for North America: Carbon Dioxide (tons/year)

Year	Cars	Light Trucks	Motorcycles	Heavy Trucks
1990	861,351,645	287,668,055	9,570,404	276,808,700
1995	884,104,200	300,633,524	9,570,404	305,619,172
2000	826,624,619	309,237,537	9,570,404	337,428,261
2010	863,411,047	298,888,722	9,570,404	411,323,167

Table 1-22 includes an additional vehicle category, aircraft, and illustrates that this is another sector deserving additional attention with regard to carbon dioxide emissions.

Summary, Analysis, and Policy Implications

The challenge of controlling motor vehicle emissions is truly daunting, and reducing carbon dioxide emissions—an important part of that strategy—will eventually require profound changes in global patterns

Table 1-22. Motor Vehicle Emissions Projections for North America: Carbon Dioxide (tons/year)

Year	Cars	Light Trucks	Motorcycles	Heavy Trucks	Aircraft
1990	861,351,645	287,668,055	9,570,404	276,808,700	261,828,440
1995	884,104,200	300,633,524	9,570,404	305,619,172	283,361,829
2000	826,624,619	309,237,537	9,570,404	337,428,261	302,873,717
2010	863,411,047	298,888,722	9,570,404	411,323,167	322,473,496

of energy supply and use. According to EPA estimates, "drastic cuts in emissions would be required to stabilize atmospheric composition." To simply stabilize atmospheric concentrations at existing levels will require reducing anthropogenic carbon dioxide emissions by 50% to 80% and freezing carbon monoxide and nitrogen oxides emissions at current levels (USEPA 1990c).

Motor vehicles, major direct and indirect sources of greenhouse gases, account for about 14% of global fuel-related carbon dioxide emissions, and these emissions are growing by about 2.4% per year. In the United States, motor vehicles remain a dominant source of CO, HC, NO_x, CO_2, and CFC emissions and the major consumer of oil. The recently enacted Clean Air Act and the Montreal Protocol should lead to significant progress in CO, HC, NO_x, and CFC emissions control. However, just to stabilize, much less reduce, CO_2 emissions will tax the nation's creativity and resources, and part of any strategy to control carbon dioxide emissions must be greatly improving new light-duty-vehicle fuel efficiency. Still, by itself, improved light-duty-vehicle efficiency can't get the job done if other vehicle categories are ignored and if vehicle use continues to grow. Indeed, the very real benefits from such improvements will eventually be canceled out by the impacts of more vehicles being driven more miles. Further, it should be increasingly clear that much more attention must be paid to countries other than the highly industrialized West as vehicle growth patterns indicate tremendous potential for further worsening in other parts of the world.

This does not mean that controlling U.S. auto CO_2 is a waste of time. The United States remains a major vehicle market served by every major manufacturer in the world. Reducing emissions in that market clearly will be beneficial both directly and indirectly. The design of vehicles sold in the developed countries will greatly influence the design of those sold elsewhere. If, for example, emissions controls or fuel economy requirements were tightened in the industrialized democracies, similar requirements would most likely be adopted in countries looking to export motor vehicles to the industrialized countries. By the same token, if requirements in the industrialized nations are weak, those throughout the rest of the world probably will be too.

Changes in new-car designs in the developed countries have impacts that extend far beyond the "useful life" of the vehicles. Once removed from service in industrialized countries, many older vehicles are exported to the developing world. The vehicle standards adopted in the industrialized nations thus will influence pollution emissions and fuel use in industrializing countries for many years to come.

Increasing vehicle use in the rest of the world indicates that controlling U.S. auto CO_2 emissions is hardly sufficient. Further, other emissions from autos must be controlled as well, an area in which the United States has and will continue to excel and that has clearly had a positive ripple effect around the world. In addition, other vehicle categories, especially heavy trucks and such high-growth transportation modes as aircraft should receive a great deal more attention than they have. This should not only entail improving per-vehicle emissions but exploring ways to shift from higher-energy-intensive modes of transport to less intensive modes, such as rail.

As we pursue these strategies, we must recognize that increasingly greater use of motor vehicles is inevitable in many less developed areas of the world. Therefore, it is reasonable to expect that emissions from vehicles in the United States and Europe, where per capita usage is so much higher, will need to be lowered even more than otherwise.

The four broad policy options outlined below should be explored as a possible foundation for a long-term transportation policy while gradually reducing the threats from petroleum-powered vehicles to the climate and air quality.

Reducing Vehicle Emissions of CO, HC, NO$_x$, and CFCs

The growth in the number and use of vehicles has largely canceled out the pollution reduction gains achieved so far, even though almost half of all new cars currently produced around the world are equipped with state-of-the-art emissions controls. But adopting the most technologically advanced controls for carbon monoxide, hydrocarbon, and nitrogen oxides on *all* vehicles throughout the world could at least temporarily restrain the growth in global emissions of these pollutants.

Various steps can be taken to reduce air pollution emissions from motor vehicles. These include incentives to remove older, higher-polluting vehicles from the road; tightening new-vehicle emissions standards for nitrogen oxides, volatile organic compounds, and carbon monoxide; developing and using cleaner fuels with lower volatility and fewer toxic components; enhancing inspection and maintenance (I&M) programs, including inspections of antitampering emissions-control equipment; and extending the useful life of pollution control equipment to the actual vehicle life. The potential overall impacts of tighter standards, enhanced inspection and maintenance, and extended useful life are especially significant because they help ensure that the benefits of clean-air technology will persist for the vehicle's full life.

During the last Congress, the 1990 Clean Air Act Amendments were adopted, which should lead to substantially cleaner vehicles in the future than would otherwise have been the case. The production of CFCs, the most potent greenhouse gases, will be drastically cut by the revised Montreal Protocol, adopted in June 1990. Thanks to the new international agreement, CFC production should cease by the year 2000. This landmark decision—a major first step toward controlling greenhouse gas emissions—provides a precedent for future negotiations and cooperation.

Future CFC releases could be greatly reduced by improving air conditioner seals and, especially, by changing work practices in repair shops. Eliminating the use of CFCs in automotive air conditioners or, in the short term, prohibiting unnecessary venting to the air, would protect the stratosphere from ozone depletion and reduce greenhouse warming. What may be needed over the long term is cradle-to-grave controls designed to eliminate CFC emissions from vehicles. A comprehensive CFC control strategy would require that hoses, seals, and fittings on air conditioners last for the vehicle's full life without leaking; limit repair of air conditioners to qualified, licensed facilities that use equipment designed to prevent leakage or venting of CFCs; and ban the sale of do-it-yourself kits to recharge auto air conditioners. A number of auto makers, including General Motors, Ford, Toyota, and Honda, have indicated their plans to install in each of their dealerships equipment that will capture the CFCs from motor vehicle air conditioners.

Improving New-Vehicle Fuel Efficiency

Over the next two decades, headway could be made in bringing carbon dioxide emissions from transportation under control by accelerating the global trend toward lower carbon dioxide emissions per vehicle. Moreover, experience gained during the 1970s and 1980s in the United States and Europe suggests that the dual goals of improved fuel efficiency (and therefore lower carbon dioxide emissions) and lowered pollution emissions are complementary rather than antagonistic. As a result, air pollution emissions could also be reduced at the same time.

Despite the recent countercurrents in the production of more fuel-efficient vehicles, major improvements in on-the-road new-vehicle efficiency are possible over the next fifteen to twenty years using technology that is now market-ready or nearly so (Bleviss 1988). So-called "concept" vehicles employing much of this advanced technology already exist (WRI 1990, 148–52). These improvements should not be limited solely to cars; as the above analysis indicates, they should include improvements especially in heavy-duty vehicles and aircraft as well.

The development of highly efficient vehicles should be supplemented by international efforts to create markets for highly efficient cars, trucks, and buses. Among the tools to bring this about are measures such as gas guzzler/gas sipper taxes on new vehicles, annual registration fees on all motor vehicles graduated according to fuel efficiency, mandatory fuel efficiency standards, and carbon taxes on fossil fuels. Higher fuel costs appear to play a significant role in encouraging more fuel-efficient vehicles.

A broad-based carbon tax on fossil fuels—already under consideration by several European countries—is an especially attractive means of encouraging efficiency because it would begin to make *all* fossil fuel prices reflect the climate risks and other environmental costs associated with each fuel. A carbon tax would be relatively easy to administer and could be adjusted upward or downward as more information on climate becomes available. Such a tax would encourage fuel users in all sectors of the economy, not just commuters and other drivers, to use energy more efficiently. It would also encourage the development and use of nonfossil energy sources, and the funds raised this way could be used to mitigate the impacts of global warming.

Technical Possibilities. For the present generation of vehicles, significant improvements in fuel consumption and pollution from vehicles in use seem feasible. Progress can be achieved by focusing first on the engine and transmission, on weight reductions, on aerodynamic improvements, and on increasing use of electronics.

Computer models and the actual construction of prototype automobiles with fuel economies in the range of 60–120 mpg have demonstrated that it is technologically possible to approximately double the average fuel economy of current automobiles without sacrificing interior space and while preserving adequate performance. Such large improvements are possible because of the multiplicative effects of improvements in the efficiency of the power plant and reductions in power requirements.

The energy efficiency of the propulsion system can also be improved by ensuring that the engine will be operated at its most efficient speed for each specific power demand at the wheels. This requires a transmission with a wide ratio range within which the ratio can be varied continuously or in relatively modest steps and with electronic controls or a system that indicates to the driver when to change the ratio (gear) for optimal fuel economy. Such transmissions have an additional energy efficiency benefit in that they make available the peak engine power at all road speeds and therefore make possible a reduction in unused engine peak power. In this case, the necessary technologies exist, but there is currently no great economic incentive to commercialize them.

Many different improvements are possible to reduce power requirements at the wheels, including continued reductions in weight (through materials substitutions) and aerodynamic drag. Unfortunately, some of the progress that has already been achieved in reducing power requirements has been offset by a shift toward more powerful engines that operate with poor efficiency in ordinary driving conditions (USEPA 1988).[9]

Other low-pollution and energy-efficient technologies appear feasible if encouraged by government regulatory or other incentives. These include two-stroke engines, gas turbines, hybrid vehicles with thermal and electric engines functioning together, and fuel cells using methanol or hydrogen.

Policy Tools to Bring About Low-Consumption/Low-Emission Vehicles. A variety of policy instruments should be considered to assure the introduction and acceptance of fuel-efficient technological advances in the marketplace. Among these are vehicle efficiency standards, economic instruments directed at vehicle and fuel manufacturers and consumers, and much more focused public information efforts. These economic instruments should strive to lower low-fuel-consumption vehicle taxes and concurrently increase the tax on high-consumption vehicles. They would likely include some combination of

• fuel taxes

• vehicle taxes related to size, weight, or fuel efficiency, both at time of sale and annually

---

[9] This report supports the conclusion that *the fuel efficiency wars of the late 1970s have been replaced by the horsepower wars of the 1980s.*

- road pricing and permanent barriers in some areas based on vehicle efficiency
- parking taxes and/or restrictions based on efficiency

The most effective policy would appear to be an integrated one that includes elements of both vehicle standards and economic instruments.

Increasing Transportation System Efficiency

Additional reductions in vehicular emissions can be achieved by reducing dependence on individual cars and trucks and by making greater use of van and car pools, buses, trolleys, and trains. Improving urban traffic management by installing synchronized traffic lights, reducing on-street parking, switching to "smart" roads, banning truck unloading during the day, and so forth can also improve transportation system fuel efficiency (OTA 1989).

Providing efficient, convenient, and affordable public transportation alternatives worldwide would produce multiple benefits. For every forty persons who get out of their cars and onto a bus for a 10-mile trip to work, some 50 to 75 pounds of carbon are not emitted to the air. Greater use of public transportation would reduce congestion, cut fatalities and injuries from traffic accidents, and greatly improve air quality. Fortunately, such transportation improvements can be phased in over time. For example, roadways initially dedicated to bus traffic can later be upgraded to light rail or heavy rail if circumstances warrant.

Developing Nonfossil Energy Sources for Transportation

Although technological improvements in petroleum-powered vehicles are essential to achieving short-term increases in the vehicle fleet's fuel efficiency, they will not—as this analysis makes clear—be sufficient for the long haul if the global vehicle fleet continues growing. For this reason, longer-term international efforts to develop new transportation energy sources that emit no carbon dioxide will have to be intensified as emissions are reduced. A program of research, development, demonstration, and, ultimately, the introduction of such vehicles should become a matter of high public priority for all the principal vehicle-producing nations.

The two energy sources that appear most attractive today to power the cars and trucks of tomorrow are electricity and hydrogen. Renewable technologies—such as hydroelectric plants, wind turbines, solar electric power plants, photovoltaic cells, oceanwave power plants, and geothermal plants—are potential electricity sources that emit no carbon dioxide. As for hydrogen, it can be obtained with electricity from water through electrolysis or, directly, through photoelectrochemical decomposition.

The principal obstacle to the widespread introduction of electric or hydrogen-powered vehicles is not so much the availability or cost of electricity from solar or other nonfossil energy sources. Rather, the obstacle is technical: providing adequate energy storage on board the vehicle itself.

Electric vehicles have traditionally been powered by lead-acid batteries, which are heavy and relatively short lived. Improved batteries with higher energy densities (such as the nickel-iron battery) look promising. Also attractive for use in electric vehicles are "ultracapacitors"—electricity storage devices now under development that promise to boost acceleration, double the range of today's electric vehicles, and extend battery life (Burke, Hardin & Dowgiallo 1990). Eventually, ultracapacitors could eliminate the need for batteries altogether.

The California Air Resources Board has also adopted regulations that will require that 10% of all new vehicles have zero emissions by the year 2003, a condition that can currently be met only by electric vehicles.

The emission of greenhouse gases from an electric vehicle depends on the emissions of the power plant that produces the electricity to charge it. If electric vehicles are charged by electricity from the expected mix of coal, oil, gas, nuclear, and hydro plants in the year 2000, greenhouse gas emissions per mile driven would fall by about 25%. Charging them with electricity made from coal, in contrast, could increase greenhouse gas emissions by 10% to 30% (OTA 1990, 20).

Currently, hydrogen can be stored in a vehicle using either metal-hydride storage tanks or specially insulated tanks for liquid hydrogen. Prototype hydrogen vehicles are being developed in Japan and Germany. Mercedes-Benz started testing hydrogen-powered vehicles as early as 1974 and has tested sedans, station wagons, vans, and small buses. The most promising means of storing hydrogen is in hydride tanks, where the hydrogen is absorbed by special metal powders (such as titanium-iron and magnesium-nickel) that have a strong attraction for hydrogen. The hydrogen is liberated from these compounds when the tank is heated.

Today's hydride tanks typically weigh about 800 pounds and store only the equivalent of 4 gallons of gasoline. As a result, present vehicles have driving ranges of only 75 miles. The development of commercial fuel cells, still at least a decade away, would greatly extend the driving range of hydrogen-powered cars, trucks, and buses. Fuel cells chemically convert hydrogen and oxygen into water and electricity and would effectively make the hydrogen vehicle a highly efficient electric vehicle. The pollution control benefits of this approach are clear. Vehicles powered by hydrogen emit only water vapor (also emitted by gasoline-powered vehicles) and trace amounts of nitrogen oxides, the latter easily controlled with existing technology.

While research and development on new vehicular energy sources goes on, carbon dioxide and pollution emissions in large metropolitan areas can be mitigated through the wider use of natural gas (methane) to power trucks, buses, and auto fleets. Light-duty vehicles powered by compressed natural gas emit about 15% less carbon dioxide per vehicle mile than comparable gasoline-powered vehicles and far less carbon monoxide and volatile organic compounds (Sperling 1988, 326). Methanol derived from natural gas also offers air pollution benefits.

References

Abrahamson, Dean E., ed. 1989. *The Challenge of Global Warming*. Washington, D.C.: Island Press.

ALA. 1989. *Health Effects of Ambient Air Pollution*. New York: American Lung Association. July.

Automotive News, Market Data Book Issues (1986, 1990).

Bleviss, Deborah L. 1988. *The New Oil Crisis and Fuel Economy Technologies*. Quorum Book.

Burke, A. F., J. E. Hardin, and E. J. Dowgiallo. 1990. "Application of Ultracapacitors in Electric Vehicle Propulsion Systems." Paper presented at 34th International Power Sources Symposium. June 25–28.

Ciborowski, Peter. 1989. "Sources, Sinks, Trends, and Opportunities." In *The Challenge of Global Warming*. Dean E. Abrahamson, ed. Washington, D.C.: Island Press.

Dasch, Jean Muhlbaier. 1992. "Nitrous Oxide Emissions from Vehicles." *Journal of Air Waste Management Association* 42 (1).

DeLuchi, M. A., et al. 1988. "Transportation Fuels and the Greenhouse Effect." *Transportation Research Record* 1175.

Japanese Ministry of Transport. 1990. Personal communication.

Khalil, M. A. K., and R. A. Rasmussen. 1988. "Carbon Monoxide in the Earth's Atmosphere: Indications of a Global Increase." *Nature* 245 (March).

Lubkert, Barbara, and Soizic de Tilly. 1987. "An Emissions Inventory for SO_2, NO_x, and VOC's in North-Western Europe." Air and Waste Management Association.

MacKenzie, James J., and Mohamed T. El-Ashry, eds. 1989. *Air Pollution's Toll on Forests and Crops*. New Haven: Yale University Press.

MVMA. 1991a. *MVMA Motor Vehicle Facts and Figures 1991*. Detroit: Motor Vehicle Manufacturers Association.

————. 1991b. *World Motor Vehicle Data, 1991*. Detroit: Motor Vehicle Manufacturers Association.

NAS. "Rethinking the Ozone Problem in Urban and Regional Air Pollution." National Academy of Sciences.

OECD. 1987. *OECD Environmental Data*. Paris: Organization for Economic Cooperation and Development.

OTA. 1989. *Advanced Vehicle/Highway Systems and Urban Traffic Problems*. Staff paper. Science, Education, and Transportation Program. U.S. Congress, Office of Technology Assessment. September.

————. 1990. *Replacing Gasoline: Alternative Fuels for Light-Duty Vehicles*. U.S. Congress, Office of Technology Assessment. September.

Sillman, Sanford, Jennifer A. Logan, and Steven C. Wofsy. 1990. "Sensitivity of Ozone to Nitrogen Oxides and Hydrocarbons in Regional Ozone Episodes." *Journal of Geophysical Research* 95:1837–1851.

Sperling, Daniel. 1988. *New Transportation Fuels: A Strategic Approach to Technological Change*. Berkeley and Los Angeles: University of California Press.

TDRI. 1990. "Energy and the Environment: Choosing the Right Mix." Research Report No. 7. The 1990 TDRI Year End Conference: Industrializing Thailand and Its Impact on the Environment. Bangkok. December.

UN. 1989. *World Population Prospects 1988*. Population Studies No. 106. New York: United Nations, Department of International Economic and Social Affairs.

UNEP. 1989. *Technical Progress on Protecting the Ozone Layer*. Refrigeration, Air Conditioning and Heat Pumps Technical Options Report, UNEP Technology Review Panel. July 30.

USDOE. 1990. *An Evaluation of the Relationship Between the Production and Use of Energy and Atmospheric Methane Emissions*. DOE/NBB-0088P. U.S. Department of Energy. April.

USEPA. 1986. *Air Quality Criteria for Ozone and Other Photochemical Oxidants*. Vol. 2. EPA/600/8-84/020bF. Washington, D.C.: U.S. Environmental Protection Agency. August.

————. 1987. *Regulatory Impact Analysis: Protection of Stratospheric Ozone*. Washington, D.C.: U.S. Environmental Protection Agency. December.

————. 1988. "How Industry Is Reducing Dependence on Ozone-Depleting Chemicals." Status report prepared by the Stratospheric Ozone Protection Program. Washington, D.C.: U.S. Environmental Protection Agency. June.

————. *Light Duty Automotive Technology and Fuel Economy Trends Through 1988*. Washington, D.C.: U.S. Environmental Protection Agency.

————. 1989. *The Potential Effects of Global Climate Change on the United States*. EPA-230-05-09-050. Washington, D.C.: U.S. Environmental Protection Agency. December.

————. 1990a. Update to "How Industry Is Reducing Dependence on Ozone-Depleting Chemicals." Status report prepared by the Stratospheric Ozone Protection Program. Washington, D.C.: U.S. Environmental Protection Agency.

————. 1990b. *National Air Quality and Emissions Trends Report, 1988*. EPA-450/4-90-002. Washington, D.C.: U.S. Environmental Protection Agency. March.

————. 1990c. *Policy Options for Stabilizing Global Climate*. Executive Summary Report to Congress. Washington, D.C.: U.S. Environmental Protection Agency. December.

Volkswagen. 1990. Personal communication.

Volz, A., and D. Kley. 1988. "Evaluation of the Montsouris Series of Ozone Measurements Made in the Nineteenth Century." *Nature* 332:240–43.

Walsh, Michael P. 1990. "Motor Vehicle Pollution in Hungary." Report prepared for the World Bank.

World Resources Institute (WRI). 1988. *World Resources 1988–1989*. New York: Basic Books.

————. 1990. *World Resources, 1990–1991*. New York: Oxford University Press.

Chapter 2

Trends in Transportation Energy Use, 1970–1988: An International Perspective

Lee Schipper, Ruth Steiner, and Stephen Meyers

P ersonal mobility and timely movement of goods have become increasingly important around the world, and energy use for transportation has grown rapidly as a consequence. Energy is used in transportation for two rather different activities: moving people, which we refer to as passenger travel, and moving freight. Whereas freight transport is closely connected to economic activity, much of passenger travel is conducted for personal reasons. In the Organization for Economic Cooperation and Development (OECD) countries, passenger travel accounts for around 70% of total transportation energy use. In contrast, freight transport accounts for the larger share in the former East Bloc and the less developed countries (LDCs).[1]

This chapter surveys international trends in the use of energy for transportation over the period 1970–1988. In our analysis, we focus on

---

An earlier version of this chapter appears in Schipper et al. 1992. The research presented in this chapter is part of a multiyear study that is being conducted by researchers at Lawrence Berkeley Laboratory, the University of California at Berkeley, and the University of California entitled "The Future of the Automobile in an Environmentally Constrained World." This research has been funded by the Stockholm Environment Institute, the U.S. Environmental Protection Agency, the U.S. Department of Energy, AB Volvo, Exxon USA, Nissan North America, Shell International Petroleum Company, and Shell Oil Company.

[1] The former East Bloc includes the former East Germany, the republics of the former USSR, Poland, the former Czechoslovakia, Hungary, Bulgaria, Rumania, the former Yugoslavia, and Albania. The former West Germany is, of course, included in the OECD. The LDCs include all countries outside the OECD and former East Bloc.

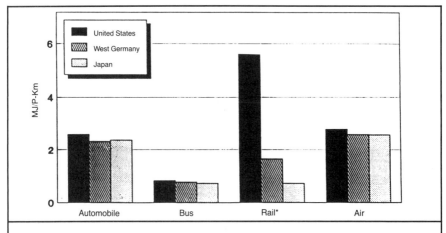

Figure 2-1. Energy Intensities by Mode of Travel in OECD Countries, 1988

* Electricity counted as primary energy.

three elements that shape transportation energy use: activity, which we measure in passenger-km (p-km) or tonne-km (t-km); modal structure (the share of total activity accounted for by various modes); and modal energy intensities (energy use per p-km or t-km). The modal structure of travel and freight transport is important because there are often considerable differences in energy intensity between modes. Figure 2-1 illustrates the 1988 average energy use per p-km of different travel modes in the United States, West Germany, and Japan. With the exception of rail in the United States, bus and rail travel had much lower energy intensity than did automobile and air travel.[2] What is perhaps surprising is that the energy intensity of air travel was only slightly higher than that of automobile travel. This reflects the much higher utilization of vehicle capacity in air travel and the large share of automobile travel that takes place in urban traffic (automobile energy intensity in long-distance driving is much lower than the average over all types of driving).

The aggregate energy intensity of travel or freight transport is shaped by the relative importance of different modes and modal energy intensities, which are determined by vehicle fuel intensity (energy per

---

[2] The high level of rail energy intensity in the United States is discussed in a later section.

km) and the utilization of vehicle capacity. An increase in the latter leads to a decline in modal energy intensity. Average vehicle energy intensity is shaped by the characteristics of old and new vehicles, the rate at which new vehicles replace old ones, and by factors that affect in-use energy intensity. These include vehicle maintenance, driving habits, and the operating environment. Traffic congestion increases idling time and the amount of distance covered at very low speed, both of which increase fuel consumption per km. Congestion is also a factor for airplanes, as crowded conditions at airports increase time spent circling. The quality of the transport infrastructure affects both mode choice and energy intensity. Quality factors that affect mode choice include the amount of time required for a trip and the level of amenity. Poor road quality, which is common in the LDCs, leads to higher energy intensity for vehicles that use the roads. Where roads are in bad condition, truck operators often choose heavy vehicles that can stand the punishment to which they are subjected.

This chapter is divided into separate sections on passenger travel and freight transport. Within each section we present discussions for the OECD countries, the LDCs, and the former East Bloc. Around 64% of total world transportation energy use in 1988 was accounted for by the OECD countries, which reflects the high level of automobile ownership and use. The shares of the LDCs and the former East Bloc were only 22% and 14%, respectively. Between 1970 and 1988, growth was much faster in the LDCs (5.1% per year) than in the OECD countries (2.4%) and the former East Bloc (2.0%) (Figure 2-2).

For the eight OECD countries considered in this study and the former Soviet Union, we have divided energy use as it appears in most statistics (disaggregated into road, rail, air, and water) into passenger travel and freight transport components. We were able to make this division by careful bottom-up analyses of data from each country. Data on p-km and t-km by mode were assembled from national transportation statistics. The data sources for the OECD countries are given in Schipper et al. (1992). The sources for the former Soviet Union are given in Schipper and Cooper (1991). Unless noted otherwise, the source of the data in all tables and figures is the above (ongoing) research projects.

We have not assembled a comparable data base for the LDCs. The analysis presented here relies on previous research (see Meyers 1988) and reports from various countries, as noted in the text. Because our research has looked more closely at the OECD countries, and because the available data are more detailed and reliable for these countries, the bulk of the discussion concerns them.

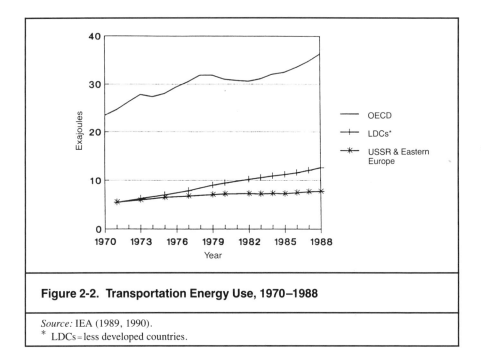

Figure 2-2. Transportation Energy Use, 1970–1988

Source: IEA (1989, 1990).
* LDCs = less developed countries.

Unless noted otherwise, we refer to domestic transportation only (that is, within national boundaries). We briefly cover international air travel but have not covered maritime freight transport. The statistics reported here refer to transport via motorized modes only. Walking and human- and animal-powered vehicles account for a significant amount of travel and freight transport in LDCs, and even a few percent of total p-km in Europe. Except where noted, energy use is measured in terms of final energy.[3]

Passenger Travel

People travel for a variety of reasons, including work commutes, on-the-job trips, shopping, social visits, and recreation. The number of trips people make in a given period is conditioned by their particular life situation and preferences, their income, the cost of travel, the amount of time available for travel, and the amount of time needed to accomplish various trips. The distance of various trips is affected by

---

[3] We primarily present energy use in Joules. 1 exajoule (EJ, 10^{18} Joules) = 0.948 quads = 23.9 Mtoe. 1 metajoule (MJ, 10^6 Joules) = 948 kBtu.

Table 2-1. Travel Energy Use and Activity in the OECD-8, 1988				
OECD-8	Energy Use (exajoules)	(%)	Activity (billion p-km)	(%)
United States	14.50	71	5,733	60
Japan	1.59	8	1,081	11
Europe-6	4.44	22	2,682	28
West Germany	1.36	7	659	7
United Kingdom	1.09	5	604	6
France	0.91	4	678	7
Italy	0.80	4	590	6
Sweden	0.19	1	103	1
Norway	0.09	0.4	48	0.5
TOTAL	20.53	100	9,495	100

the spatial relationship between origin/destination pairs, such as home/work or home/shopping. The choice of mode for a given trip is shaped by many factors, including the purpose and distance of the trip, availability and cost of modes, speed of modes, the quality of the travel experience, personal income, and preference. Some modes compete for certain types of travel, but not for others.

OECD Countries

We assembled data on travel activity and energy use by mode for eight OECD countries (OECD-8): the United States, Japan, the former West Germany, the United Kingdom, France, Italy, Sweden, and Norway. Together these eight countries account for over three-fourths of total OECD energy use for personal travel.[4] Among these eight, the United States accounted for 71% of total travel energy use in 1988 (Table 2-1). In our discussion, we focus on three entities: the United States, Japan, and an aggregate of the six European countries (Europe-6). The data include domestic travel only. In Western Europe, air travel between countries is about 60% greater than is total domestic air travel (Boeing 1991). Domestic air travel in Europe has grown faster than intra-Europe international travel, however, as travelers increasingly fly on routes for which rail or car were more common in the past.

---

[4] See Schipper et al. (1991) for further discussion of energy use in passenger travel in these countries.

Table 2-2. Growth in Travel Energy Use, Activity, and Aggregate Energy Intensity in the OECD-8, 1973–1988 (Total % Change)

OECD-8	Energy Use	P-Km	Aggregate Intensity
United States	13	38	−18
Japan	76	40	25
Europe-6	55	44	7
West Germany	56	33	17
France	50	46	3
United Kingdom	42	41	0
Italy	85	61	15
Sweden	37	39	−2
Norway	80	56	15
TOTAL	23	40	−13

Energy Use and Activity. Between 1973 and 1988, total energy use for personal travel grew by 13% in the United States, 55% in Europe-6, and 76% in Japan (Table 2-2). For all countries, growth in p-km was substantial (30%–40%). In the United States, a significant decrease in aggregate energy intensity dampened growth in energy use. In Japan, increased energy intensities contributed significantly to growth in energy use, whereas in Europe-6, intensity increased only slightly.

In the United States, the ratio of p-km to gross domestic product (GDP) declined between the early 1970s and the early 1980s but has remained about the same since 1982 (Figure 2-3). In Japan, domestic travel has grown more slowly than GDP since the early 1970s, whereas in Europe the two have increased at about the same rate. Travel increased in part because population grew. There was a decline in per capita travel after the 1973 oil embargo in the United States and to a lesser extent in Europe-6, but not in Japan (Figure 2-4). Per capita travel fell again in the United States during and after the 1979–1980 oil price rise, but not in Europe and Japan, where the increase in retail gasoline prices was proportionately smaller than in the United States. Between 1981 and 1988, however, per capita travel in the United States grew considerably. In all countries, leisure and vacation-related travel has been a major source of growth.

Per capita travel remains about twice as high in the United States as in Europe and Japan. Whereas one might think that the average trip

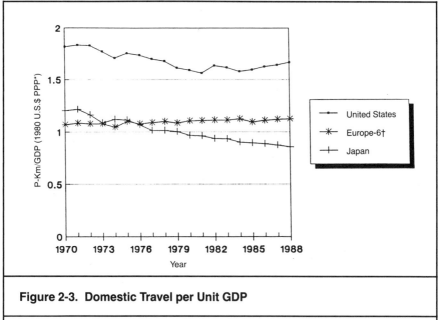

Figure 2-3. Domestic Travel per Unit GDP

Notes:
* PPP = purchasing power parity.
† The United Kingdom, West Germany, France, Italy, Sweden, and Norway.

covers a longer distance in the United States, given its geography, surveys suggest that this is not the case for automobile trips, which account for most travel. Rather, the number of trips per capita is higher in the United States than elsewhere.

Travel is affected by changes in disposable income, since people may take or curtail trips, or take longer or shorter trips, depending on their financial situation. The decline in per capita travel in the United States in the 1979–1981 period was due to effects of the recession on disposable income and business travel as well as to the influence of higher fuel prices. The change in highway vehicle-km per adult in the United States between 1960 and 1987 closely paralleled real disposable income per capita, corrected by a moderate fuel price elasticity of −0.1 (Ross 1989).

Change in Mode Shares. Between 1973 and 1988, the fraction of travel p-km accounted for by automobiles declined from 91% to 86% in the United States but increased from 43% to 53% in Japan, and from

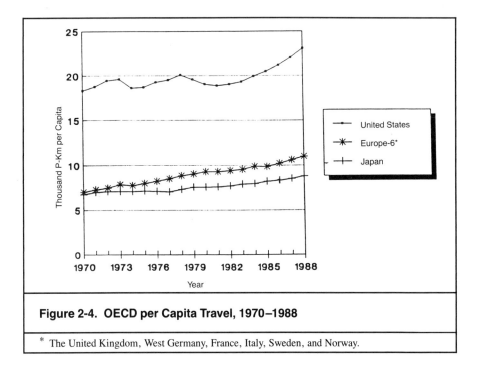

Figure 2-4. OECD per Capita Travel, 1970–1988

* The United Kingdom, West Germany, France, Italy, Sweden, and Norway.

79% to 82% in Europe-6 (Figures 2-5 through 2-7).[5] In the same period there was considerable growth in air travel in the United States. An increase in the share of air travel has also occurred in Japan and, to a lesser extent, Europe. (Again, much air travel within Europe is between countries and is not counted in the statistics we report here.) Air travel still accounts for a very small fraction of total travel, but growth in its share has major implications for energy use because it is more energy-intensive than other modes.[6] The volume of travel by rail and bus remained roughly constant in the United States, Japan, and Europe, but their shares of total travel declined considerably. They are

---

[5] We use the term *automobiles* to include "personal" light trucks (including vans and jeeps). Light trucks and similar vehicles are included only in the U.S. data, since such vehicles are not commonly used as passenger vehicles in Europe and Japan. For the United States, survey data indicate that the percentage of total light trucks used for personal business is 65%–75%.

[6] One reason why air travel accounts for a much higher fraction of total travel volume in the United States than in Japan and Europe is because destination points in the United States are so much farther apart (especially with major cities concentrated on the Atlantic and Pacific coasts).

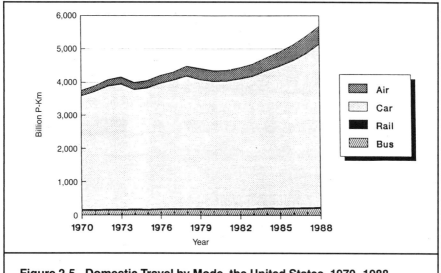

Figure 2-5. Domestic Travel by Mode, the United States, 1970–1988

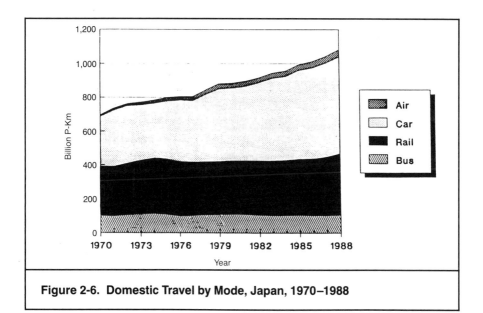

Figure 2-6. Domestic Travel by Mode, Japan, 1970–1988

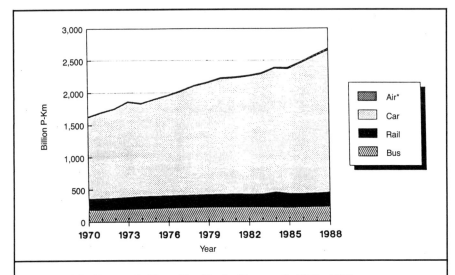

Figure 2-7. Domestic Travel by Mode, Europe-6, 1970–1988

Note: Europe-6 includes the United Kingdom, West Germany, France, Italy, Sweden, and Norway.
* Does not include international air travel.

still important modes in Japan but remain relatively insignificant in the United States.

Growth in the number of cars in use between 1973 and 1988 was considerable in Japan (from 15 to 31 million) and in Europe-6 (from 61 to 98 million). Even in the United States, where per capita ownership was already at the 1988 European level in 1970, the number of automobiles grew by 50% between 1973 and 1988. Increased car ownership has led to reduced use of bus and rail and higher overall travel as well (Webster et al. 1986).

Demographic and social factors have boosted car ownership. In the United States, the coming of age of the "baby boomers" caused a large growth in the driving age population. The percentage of eligible drivers with a driver's license also grew, in large part because of the movement of women into the labor force. In 1969, 39% of adult women were employed, and 74% of them had licenses. By 1983, 50% were employed, and 91% of them had licenses (Ross 1989).

Annual distance traveled per car has fluctuated in the United States but was about the same in 1988 as in 1970 (Figure 2-8). In Europe-6, there was a decline between 1970 and 1974, but there was a

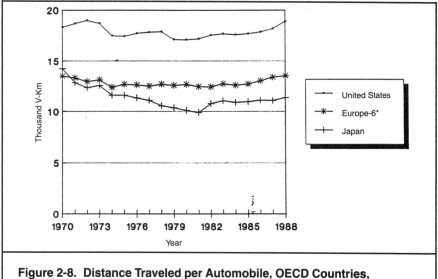

Figure 2-8. Distance Traveled per Automobile, OECD Countries, 1970–1988

* The United Kingdom, West Germany, France, Italy, Sweden, and Norway.

slight increase between 1974 and 1988 (mainly due to growth in the United Kingdom).[7] The average distance declined in Japan through 1981 because private cars, which are driven less distance than company cars and taxis, gradually accounted for a larger share of the total vehicle fleet, but it increased as private cars came to be driven more frequently and farther. Distance per car might have increased more had there not been growth in household ownership of second or even third vehicles, which tend to be used less than the primary car. In the United States, kilometers (km) per licensed driver increased between 1973 and 1988 more than did km per automobile.

Energy Intensities. The structural change described in the preceding section had only a modest net effect on aggregate travel energy intensity in the United States and Europe-6 but contributed significantly to an increase in intensity in Japan (Table 2-3).[8] In West Ger-

---

[7] The increase in the United Kingdom can be largely explained by the rise in the use of company-provided cars and taxation policies that favor use of company cars (Ferguson & Holman 1990).

[8] The method used to decompose change in aggregate energy intensity is rooted in the use of fixed-weight or Laspeyres indices. For further details see Schipper et al. (1991).

Table 2-3. Decomposition of the Change in Aggregate Travel Energy Intensity in the OECD-8, 1973–1988 (Total % Change)

OECD-8	Change in Aggregate Intensity	DECOMPOSITION Structure	DECOMPOSITION Intensity	DECOMPOSITION Interaction[a]
United States	−18	3	−15	−6
Japan	25	20	5	0
Europe-6	7	4	4	−1
West Germany	17	5	12	0
Sweden	−2	4	−2	−4
Norway	15	14	7	−6
France	3	2	2	−1
United Kingdom	0	5	−3	−2
Italy	15	4	13	−1
TOTAL	−13	4	−14	3

Note:
a Because the structural and intensity variables interact in a nonlinear fashion, the two effects do not sum to the total change in aggregate intensity.

many, which also had a sizable increase in aggregate energy intensity, most of the growth was due to an increase in modal energy intensities rather than to the structural change away from rail and buses.

AUTOMOBILES. Between 1973 and 1988, automobile energy use per p-km declined by 18% in the United States; increased in Japan, West Germany, Italy, and Norway; and remained about the same in the rest of Europe. A decline in the number of passengers per trip (partly due to a decrease in family size and increased numbers of cars per household) contributed to growth in energy intensity. In the United States, the average load declined from 2.2 persons per car in 1970 to 1.7 in 1983 and 1.5 in 1990. A decline also occurred in Japan (2.2 to 1.8), West Germany (1.7 to 1.5), Italy (2.0 to 1.7), and elsewhere in Europe.

Average fuel use per km fell more than did use per p-km. In the United States it declined by 29% between 1973 and 1988 (Figure 2-9). The fuel intensity of cars fell by 33% (to 12 liters/100 km, or 20 mpg), but this was balanced somewhat by an increase in the use of light trucks as passenger vehicles. The share of personal light trucks in total automobile vehicle-km increased from 9% to 18%. The fuel intensity

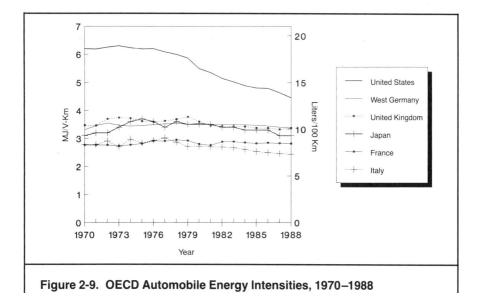

Figure 2-9. OECD Automobile Energy Intensities, 1970–1988

of light trucks fell by 19% (to 18 liters/100 km, or 13 mpg) but remained well above that of cars.[9]

In Europe and Japan, there was little change in automobile fleet fuel intensity. Although there were technical improvements in new cars that contributed to higher efficiency, this was counterbalanced by an increase in the size and power of automobiles and deterioration in operating conditions (more traffic congestion). In West Germany, for example, the fraction of all automobiles that had engine displacement of 1,500 cm^3 and above increased from 40% in 1973 to 60% in 1987, and the average horsepower rose from 59 to 77 (DIW 1991). By 1990, more than 80% of all cars sold in West Germany could reach 150 km/hr or greater, and 30% of them could surpass 180 km/hr. The average weight of an Audi 80 increased from 855 to 1,050 kg between 1970 and 1991, and that of an Opel Kadett from 685 kg in 1963 to 865 kg in 1991. The average size of engines in the United Kingdom and France also rose. In the United Kingdom, growth in use of company cars has contributed to an increase in car size (Potter 1991). As Figure 2-10 illustrates for the United Kingdom, the trend in Europe toward larger cars began in the 1960s.

---

[9] Some of the improvement for light trucks reflects a shift within the light-trucks category to smaller vans and pickup trucks.

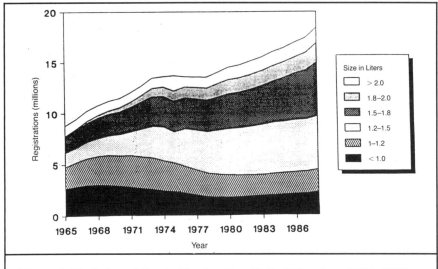

Figure 2-10. Automobiles by Engine Size, United Kingdom, 1965–1988

The turnover of the fleet had a different effect in the United States than in Europe and Japan. In the United States, the sales-weighted average fuel intensity of new automobiles (including all light trucks) declined by nearly 50% between 1973 and 1982 (Figure 2-11), so turnover of the stock strongly depressed fleet average fuel intensity. In Europe and Japan, the fuel intensity of new cars improved much less than in the United States, in part because it was already much lower in 1973, and in part because growth in vehicle size and power offset technical efficiency gains.[10] Test data show some decline in new-car fuel intensity since 1975 in several countries, but intensity has increased since 1982 in Japan and since 1985 in West Germany as average size and power have risen. The continued decline in France and Italy is partly due to growing penetration of diesel-fueled cars, which have lower fuel intensity than comparable gasoline-fueled cars.[11]

In the United States, a shift to smaller cars contributed only slightly to the decline in new-car fuel intensity after 1975. Average

---

[10] Because of the difference in testing procedures, and differences in calculating averages, we caution against comparing new-car fuel economy too exactly between countries. The trends over time within a country, however, give a valid picture for test performance, if not actual performance on the road.

[11] The diesel share of total automobiles (not only new ones) in France and Italy rose from 1% or less in 1970 to 12% and 14% respectively in 1988.

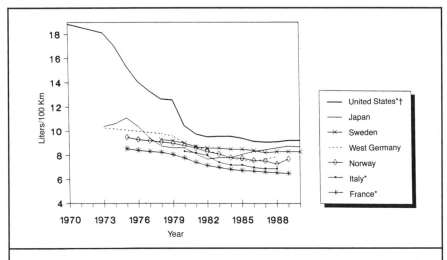

Figure 2-11. New-Automobile Fuel Economy, Test Values, OECD Countries, 1970–1990

Notes:
* Includes diesels.
† Includes light trucks.

interior volume hardly changed between 1978 and 1988. (Since 1980, compacts have gained share at the expense of subcompacts, but mid-sized cars have also lost share.) Most of the change came from a decrease in fuel intensity within each size class. The average power of new cars fell by 25% between 1975 and 1980, contributing to a decline in intensity, but has increased since 1982, pushing intensity upward (Heavenrich & Murrell 1990).

Fuel economy improvements have come from three main sources: propulsion system engineering, other elements of vehicle design, and performance trade-offs. In the United States, engineering improvements are exemplified by the remarkable 36% increase in power per unit of engine size between 1978 and 1987. The ratio of vehicle weight to interior volume was reduced by 16% in this period, and reductions in air drag and rolling resistance (through introduction of radial tires) also contributed to fuel economy improvement. Acceleration performance decreased in the 1980–1982 period, which contributed to a decline in fuel intensity, but acceleration performance has progressively improved since then.

The above discussion refers to passenger cars, but a significant factor in passenger travel statistics in the United States has been an increase in the popularity of light trucks for personal use. The share of light trucks (of which 65%–75% are for personal use) in total sales of light-duty vehicles rose from 19% in 1975 to 30% in 1988. Since light trucks have higher average weight and power than cars, this shift has somewhat balanced the decline in fuel intensity of new cars.

Worsening traffic congestion has pushed upward on the actual fuel intensity of the automobile fleet in most OECD countries. In the early 1980s, the U.S. Environmental Protection Agency (EPA) determined that vehicles in use achieved 15% lower fuel economy than the nominal vehicle rating based on the driving cycle test (Westbrook & Patterson 1989). Some observers believe that the discrepancy has grown to as much as 25% as a result of increasing urban congestion, increasing share of urban driving (the EPA rating assumes 55% of vehicle-km are urban), higher speeds on open highways, and higher levels of acceleration in actual use than in the test. It may also be the case that the average length of urban trips has decreased, and shorter trips use more fuel per km than longer ones (because the engine is cold for much of the trip).

In the 1970s, the reduction of highway speed limits in the United States dampened fleet fuel intensity. In West Germany, conversely, the lack of speed limits on expressways has contributed to demand for high-powered cars and high driving speeds. Although there are speed limits on motorways in the rest of Western Europe, relatively few drivers keep to these limits. Even when limits are observed, the fact that increasing numbers of cars are built to attain speeds in excess of 150 km/hr reduces the fuel economy of these cars at "ordinary" speeds (60–80 km/hr) (Dolan 1991).

AIR. Energy use per p-km in domestic air travel declined considerably in the United States, Western Europe, and Japan between 1973 and 1988 (Figure 2-12). The U.S. decline, a remarkable 50%, exceeded that of Europe and Japan.[12] An increase in load factor (passengers per available seats) contributed to the drop in energy intensity. In the United States, load factor rose from 54% of available seats in 1973 to 63% in 1988. Load factors also increased in Western Europe and Japan. (For example, Air France reports that its system load factor rose from 53% in 1973 to 62% in the late 1980s.)

Decline in energy use per seat-km was the major factor. New

---

[12] Data supplied by several European airlines confirmed that this trend is also seen in international travel. Indeed, the long-range aircraft used by European and Japanese airlines for intercontinental travel have significantly lower energy use per p-km than do smaller planes flown on domestic routes.

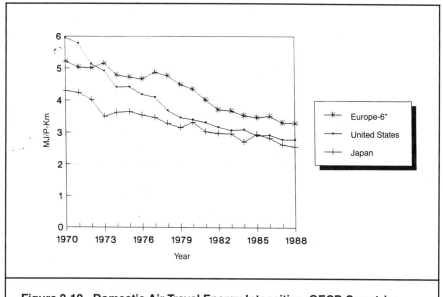

Figure 2-12. Domestic Air Travel Energy Intensities, OECD Countries, 1970–1988

* The United Kingdom, West Germany, France, Italy, Sweden, and Norway.

planes with significantly lower fuel intensity entered the fleets in large numbers. They were on average larger than those they replaced, and larger planes tend to use less energy per seat-km than smaller planes with comparable technology.[13] There was also considerable decline in fuel intensity in planes of a given size (Gately 1988). Technological changes included more fuel-efficient engines, improvement in aircraft structural efficiency (lighter airframes), and improved lift/drag performance. Airlines also retrofitted old planes with new engines (often for noise abatement reasons) and added seats. Lastly, airlines and airports instituted various operational improvements. As a result of these factors, energy use per seat-mile of U.S. jet aircraft declined by one-third between 1973 and 1988.

BUS AND RAIL. This category combines urban transit and intercity service, with the former being much more energy-intensive than the latter. Bus energy use per p-km increased in Western Europe and the

---

[13] For U.S. aircraft, available seats per plane increased from 111 in 1970 to 148 in 1980 and 161 in 1987.

United States and changed little in Japan between 1973 and 1988. In the United States, energy use per vehicle-km increased by nearly one-third for transit buses between 1973 and 1988, reflecting operation in increasingly congested conditions.[14] Energy use per p-km increased even more because of a decline in average load factor. In Western Europe, congestion and declining ridership due to rising acquisition and use of cars increased the intensities of bus travel. In the United Kingdom, there has been a shift to smaller buses (which use more energy per seat-km) since deregulation in 1986.

The energy intensity of rail travel declined slightly in Western Europe in the early 1970s but has changed little since then. Rail energy intensity in Japan, which is much lower than elsewhere because of high levels of ridership, has remained about the same since 1970. The intensity declined somewhat in the United States between 1976 and 1981 but has risen since then. The increase is due to the growth in urban rail as a share of total rail p-km as new fixed-rail systems have gone into service in several large metropolitan areas. Rail energy intensity is several times higher in the United States than in Europe and Japan (see Figure 2-1), in part because of the relatively large share of urban and commuter rail in total rail travel. These types of rail systems are more energy-intensive than intercity rail because there are more trains running more frequently at a lower average speed and with lower load factors (especially during nonpeak hours).

Effect of Fuel Prices on Intensity Trends. Although we have not performed a formal analysis of the impact of fuel price changes, some observations may be made. As shown in Figure 2-13, the increase in real gasoline prices in the 1970s was fairly modest in most countries.[15] Prices increased more in 1979–1981 but declined thereafter. In Western Europe and Japan, car buyers sought larger and more powerful cars, but the rise in prices and pressure from governments concerned about oil imports caused manufacturers to incorporate technical improvements that kept new-car fuel intensity from rising and, in fact, caused it to decline. The fall in real price after 1981–1982 had an

---

[14] School buses, which have low energy intensity because of their high load factor, constitute a significant portion of bus travel in the United States. The U.S. energy intensity would be higher if they were excluded.

[15] Prices from 1980 onward are taken from the International Energy Agency's quarterly publications, *Energy Prices and Taxes*. For the years before 1980, we used a compilation of prices carried out by Ms. Pat Baade of the U.S. DOE Energy Information Administration. Although these data were never officially published, they are well explained and referenced and map almost perfectly into the IEA series, which begin in 1978. Prices were converted to real local (1980) currency and then converted to U.S. dollars using 1980 purchasing power parities (PPP) as given by the OECD.

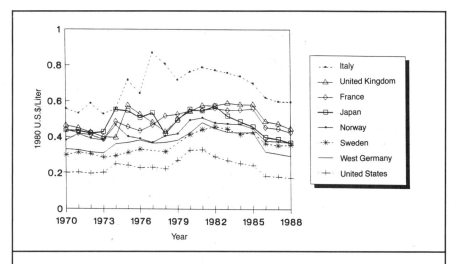

Figure 2-13. OECD Automobile Fuel Prices (Weighted Average of Gasoline and Diesel)

impact, however, especially in Japan, where new-car fuel intensity began to rise. In the United States, the impact of rising prices is difficult to judge, since the government's fuel economy standards were an influential intervention in the market (Greene 1990). The steady decline in real price since 1981 certainly contributed to lessened interest in fuel economy on the part of buyers. What is striking is that the real price of gasoline in 1988 in most countries was close to its 1970–1973 level.

International Differences in Travel Energy Intensities. Although aggregate travel energy intensity in the United States declined considerably between 1973 and 1988, at 2.5 MJ/p-km it remained much higher than in the other OECD countries. The 1988 energy intensity of other countries can be divided into three tiers. "Low intensity" (1.3–1.4 MJ/p-km) countries include Japan, Italy, and France. "Medium intensity" (around 1.8 MJ/p-km) countries include Norway, Sweden, and the United Kingdom; West Germany was "medium high" at 2.1 MJ/p-km.

Differences in aggregate travel energy intensity are due to variation in the modal structure of travel as well as to variation in modal energy intensities. Figure 2-14 shows the actual 1988 travel energy intensity in each country and what it would have been if each country

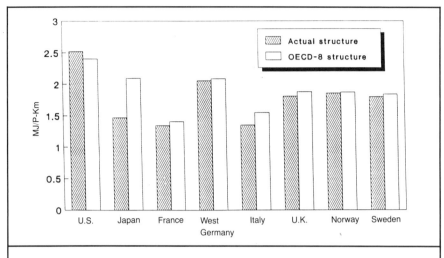

Figure 2-14. 1988 Travel Energy Intensity, Actual and OECD-8 Structure

Note: Travel energy intensity is measured using each country's own modal energy intensities.

had had a modal structure equal to the OECD-8 average. In this hypothetical case, the U.S. intensity declines and intensities in Western Europe increase slightly, whereas intensity in Japan increases considerably. The remaining differences between the countries are due to variation in the energy intensity of each mode, especially automobiles.

If each country had had a modal structure similar to that of Japan, but with its own modal energy intensity, total OECD-8 energy use for travel in 1988 would have been 11% lower than it actually was. If the U.S. modal mix were imposed on all eight countries, total energy use for travel would have been 7% higher than it actually was. (Japan and the United States have the lowest and highest shares of energy-intensive automobile and air travel of total travel.) The same experiments carried out in 1970 would have yielded 25% lower and 8% higher energy use respectively, indicating that the differences in modal mix have decreased over time.

Per capita energy use in automobiles is around three times as high in the United States as is the Europe-6 average. If U.S. automobiles in 1988 had averaged the same fuel intensity as European ones, the U.S. per capita value would have been about twice that of Europe-6 (Figure 2-15). If U.S. automobiles had been driven the same distance per year as European ones, U.S. energy use would have been about two and one-half times that of Europe. If both of the above had been the case,

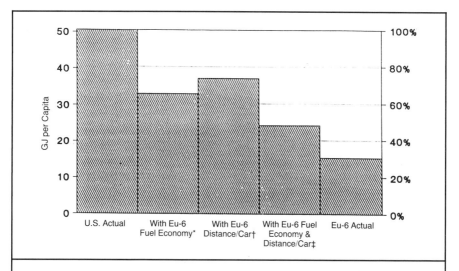

Figure 2-15. Per Capita Energy Use by Automobiles: Comparison of the United States and Europe-6 in 1988

Note: Europe-6 (Eu-6) includes West Germany, France, Italy, United Kingdom, Norway, and Sweden.
* U.S. energy use with Eu-6 fuel economy instead of U.S. fuel economy.
† U.S. energy use with Eu-6 travel (in distance/car) instead of U.S. distance/car.
‡ U.S. energy use with Eu-6 fuel economy and distance/car instead of U.S. fuel economy and distance/car.

the U.S. value in 1988 would have been only about 50% greater than that of Europe. The remaining difference is due to the higher level of automobile ownership per capita in the United States. Although the United States remains above Western Europe in terms of automobile fuel intensity, average distance, and ownership, the differences have narrowed. Whereas in 1973 automobile energy use per km was twice as high in the United States as in Europe-6, by 1988 it was only about 50% higher (see Figure 2-9); part of the difference is due to the popularity of light trucks in the United States.

Less Developed Countries

Lack of reliable data limits our ability to analyze change in travel energy use in the LDCs. On the activity side, complete data on p-km are either not available or of questionable accuracy. On the energy side, time-series disaggregation of transport energy use between travel and freight transport is rare and is more difficult to perform than in the

OECD countries because it is not uncommon for freight trucks in LDCs to use gasoline. In addition, in LDCs significant numbers of cars and trucks are used for both passenger travel and freight, often simultaneously.

Despite the lack of data, it is evident that per capita travel has increased considerably in the LDCs. Chinese data show growth in p-km per capita averaging nearly 11% per year between 1975 and 1988, but the 1988 level of 570 p-km per capita was still quite low even by LDC standards (ERI 1989).[16] In much wealthier South Korea, the data show a threefold increase from 970 to 3,200 p-km per capita between 1970 and 1987 (KEEI 1989). In Brazil, per capita road travel, which accounts for over 90% of estimated total travel, increased from 1,600 p-km in 1973 to 3,700 p-km in 1985 (Geller & Zylbersztajn 1991).

Buses and, in a few countries, rail, still account for a large majority of motorized travel in most LDCs. In South Korea, for example, the data show a decline in the shares of buses and rail between 1972 and 1987, but buses and rail still accounted for 60% and 24% of total travel in 1987, respectively, whereas cars (including taxis) accounted for only 14%. In China, rail still dominates travel, but its share of total p-km declined from 70% to 53% between 1970 and 1988, whereas the highway share increased from 23% to 41%. (The available data do not distinguish between buses and automobiles, but it is clear that buses account for a large share of total highway p-km, as ownership of private vehicles is very low.) In India, the share of road modes in total travel (78%) is larger than in China and has grown since the 1970s. In most countries, there has also been considerable growth in the number of cars (Figure 2-16).[17] In much of Asia, there has been rapid growth in mopeds and motorcycles. Lastly, domestic air travel has increased considerably in large countries in the past decade, in part because of lack of good highway or rail networks. In China, for example, the share of air in total travel grew from only 0.2% in 1970 to 3.4% in 1988.

The structure of travel in most LDCs shows a highly skewed pattern, with most people relying on bus, rail, or nonmotorized modes, while the wealthier use cars. Conventional and collective taxis (jitneys) are also important in most cities. Historically higher income and urbanization levels in Latin America and the Middle East have led to greater penetration of cars than in Asia and Africa. Business, govern-

---

[16] China's statistics on travel probably reflect the actual situation fairly well, since the number of cars is very low.

[17] The data are based on official vehicle registration statistics, as given in national sources. These overstate the actual number of cars in use in some cases.

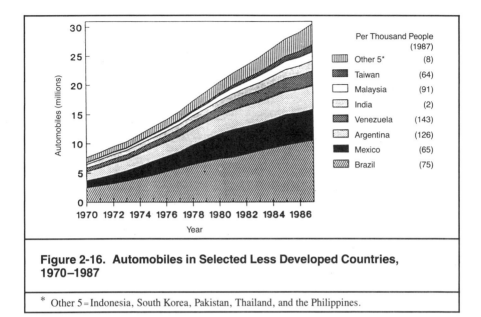

Figure 2-16. Automobiles in Selected Less Developed Countries, 1970–1987

* Other 5 = Indonesia, South Korea, Pakistan, Thailand, and the Philippines.

ment, and taxi operators own a considerable share of total automobiles in many LDCs.

Change in the energy intensity of travel modes in LDCs is difficult to assess. It is likely that the nominal energy intensity of new cars has declined in most LDCs in keeping with international trends in vehicle technology (Meyers 1988).[18] In Brazil, for example, the transition from gasoline- to ethanol-fueled cars has reduced average fuel intensity, since ethanol permits the use of engines with higher compression ratios. In addition, there has been reduction in the fuel intensity of both new gasoline- and new ethanol-fueled cars. Test data from manufacturers show a 10% reduction between 1983 and 1987 in the fuel intensity of new alcohol-fueled cars, which accounted for the majority of new cars sold in the mid-1980s. There has also been considerable improvement in automobile energy efficiency in India, where the protected industry historically produced very fuel-inefficient cars. The opening of the automotive industry to foreign collaboration played a major role in this change.

It is probable that in many if not most LDCs, the trend toward

---

[18] Compared with Western standards, cars in LDCs are smaller, less powerful, and less likely to have energy-intensive features, such as automatic transmission and air-conditioning.

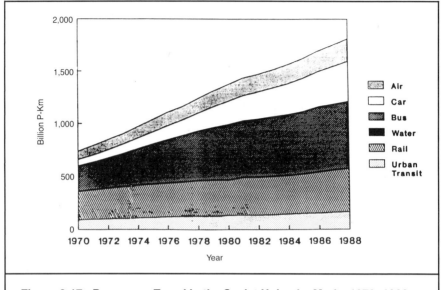

Figure 2-17. Passenger Travel in the Soviet Union by Mode, 1970–1988

higher efficiency of new cars has been countered by a gradual worsening of urban traffic conditions and, in some cases, a shift to larger, more powerful cars. Increasing congestion has probably had a similar effect on the energy intensity of buses.

Former East Bloc

Despite the huge size of the former Soviet Union, the level of per capita travel in 1988 (about 6,000 p-km) was half that of Japan, and one-third that of Western Europe. Growth in travel averaged 4.5% per year between 1973 and 1988, slower than the 7.5% per year between 1960 and 1973. Rail and bus dominate passenger travel (with 32% and 28% of total p-km in 1988, respectively), but automobile and air travel grew twice as rapidly as total travel, and thus increased their shares to 21% and 12% by 1987 (Figure 2-17).[19]

The growing shares of automobile and air travel have contributed to an increase in aggregate travel energy intensity. Since the early 1970s, however, the intensity of automobile travel has declined as

---

[19] Because of the deterioration of the economy of the former Soviet Union, passenger travel is likely to have changed over the last few years.

more small cars entered the fleet. If used under Western conditions, we estimated the energy intensity of the Soviet car fleet to be around 9 liters/100 km, or 26 mpg in 1988, which is not far above that of Western Europe.[20] But Soviet cars have considerably less power than Western ones. The actual on-the-road energy intensity of Soviet cars appears to be 11–12 liters/100 km (20–22 mpg) because of the poor quality of fuel, vehicle maintenance, roads, and parts.

The energy intensity of air travel in the former Soviet Union has declined by about 10% since the early 1970s, mainly because of an increase in aircraft size. Load factors were constant at nearly 100%. For this reason, the energy use per p-km of Soviet air travel is low compared with OECD countries, even though energy use per seat-km is about 50% higher than that of aircraft fleets in the West.

For Poland, the total level of travel appears to be around 6,000 p-km per capita, which is about where Western Europe was in 1970 (Leach & Nowak 1990). Domestic air travel is far less important in Poland than it was in the Soviet Union, but automobile travel is higher. The number of cars grew by nearly 13% per year between 1970 and 1987. At 110 cars/1,000 people, ownership was twice that of the Soviet Union.

International Air Travel

International air travel throughout the world increased nearly sixfold between 1970 and 1990—twice as much as world domestic air travel.[21] The share of international travel in total air travel rose from 30% in 1970 to 44% in 1990. The largest absolute growth in international air travel has been in trans-Atlantic travel, but the relative increase has been much larger for trans-Pacific and Europe-Asia travel (Figure 2-18). International travel within Asia (especially connections with Japan) has also grown significantly.

Most international travel markets are more competitive than domestic markets, so air carriers tend to use the newest, most efficient equipment on these routes. The longer distances of most international routes also favor use of more modern, larger aircraft. As a result, these routes tend to be less energy-intensive than domestic ones. In addition, longer flights are less energy-intensive than short ones because the fuel used in takeoff and ascent is a smaller share of overall fuel use.

---

[20] Large official cars account for a considerable share of the Soviet fleet. If they were removed, the average fleet intensity would be lower.

[21] Data in this section are from Boeing (1991).

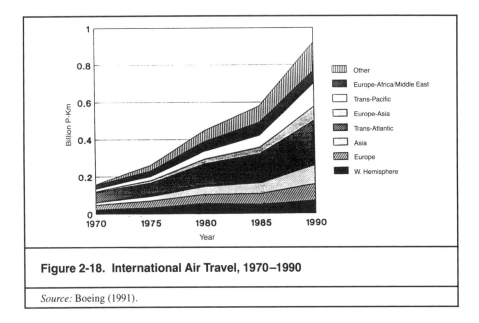

Figure 2-18. International Air Travel, 1970–1990

Source: Boeing (1991).

Freight Transport

The usual indicator of freight transport activity is tonne-km (t-km), which measures the weight of freight and the distance it is moved. (It does not consider the characteristics and value of the freight, however.) The distance of trips is shaped by the physical geography of a country, as well as by the geographic patterns of economic production and consumption. The total tonnage of freight shipped in a country depends on the magnitude and nature of agricultural, mining, and manufacturing output. As an economy evolves from economic output centered on agricultural and mining products to one in which manufactured goods predominate, the ratio of tonnage to GDP declines because manufactured goods have a higher value per tonne. Shipment of fuels for domestic use and export comprises a significant share of total freight t-km in many countries, so change in the mix of primary energy sources can affect freight transport.

The mode choice for freight shipments is strongly shaped by the type of freight to be moved. Mining and agricultural products, which have low value per tonne, are often transported via rail or water, both of which are much less energy-intensive than trucks. As economies develop, intermediate and final goods take on a greater share of freight. Since trucks offer greater flexibility for such shipments, they

Table 2-4. Freight Transport Energy Use and Activity in the OECD-8, 1988				
OECD-8	**Energy Use** **(exajoules)**	**(%)**	**Activity** **(billion t-km)**	**(%)**
United States	5.58	62	4,100	74
Japan	1.21	14	483	9
Europe-6	2.14	24	947	17
West Germany	.42	5	265	5
United Kingdom	.51	6	209	4
France	.53	6	171	3
Italy	.54	6	299	4
Sweden	.07	1	52	1
Norway	.06	1	53	4
TOTAL	8.93	100	5,530	100

tend to assume an increasing role in freight transport over time. Other factors affecting mode choice include the nature of the transport network (roads, rail, waterways), cost factors, the distance of trip, and time requirements.

The data reported in this section refer to domestic freight shipments. Fuel purchased by ships engaged in international commerce is counted as "marine bunkers" and is not included in national energy consumption.

OECD Countries

We organized data on freight transport energy use and activity by mode in the 1970–1988 period for eight OECD countries.[22] Among these eight, the United States accounted for 62% of total energy use in 1988 (Table 2-4). Europe-6 accounted for 24%, Japan for 14%.

Energy Use and Activity. Energy use for domestic freight transport increased by 40%, 33%, and 48% between 1973 and 1988 in the United States, Japan, and Europe-6, respectively (Table 2-5). Growth in total freight t-km was less than this, so aggregate intensity rose

---

[22] We have not included t-km shipped and energy used by oil and gas pipelines because of lack of time-series data for most countries. In the United States, the amount of natural gas shipped in pipelines in 1985 was estimated to be equal to around 7% of total freight t-km (Ross 1989).

Table 2-5. Growth in Freight Transport Energy Use, Activity, and Aggregate Energy Intensity in the OECD-8, 1973–1988 (Total % Change)

OECD-8	Energy Use	T-Km	Aggregate Intensity
United States	40	34	4
Japan	33	18	12
Europe-6	48	32	12
West Germany	17	24	−6
France	44	−2	46
United Kingdom	29	51	−14
Italy	134	77	32
Norway	43	34	7
Sweden	46	12	31
TOTAL	41	32	6

somewhat. Aggregate intensity rose considerably in Italy, Sweden, and France, where there was no change in activity and a large increase in intensity due to a substantial decline in the share of rail. The strong shift in the French primary energy mix away from oil contributed to both of these phenomena.

The ratio of freight activity to GDP has declined since the early 1970s in Japan, and since 1980 in the United States (Figure 2-19). There was essentially no change in Europe-6 between 1970 and 1988. Despite the decrease in the ratio in the United States, it remains around three times as high as in Western Europe or Japan. The sheer size of the United States is partly responsible for this high level. There is also considerable shipment of bulk materials (including grain and coal for export) over long distances. Another reason—also related to size—is that various types of freight activity that are international (and therefore not counted in domestic activity) for Europe and Japan take place domestically within the United States.

The ratio of total freight tonnage to GDP is probably falling in most countries, given the change in materials utilization that has taken place. West German data show a decline over time in the average number of tonnes per trip (DIW 1991). But there are more frequent small shipments in many cases, so total freight km likely grew faster than GDP.

Modal Structure. There has been a slight shift of freight t-km from rail to trucks and ships in the United States (Figure 2-20). In Japan and

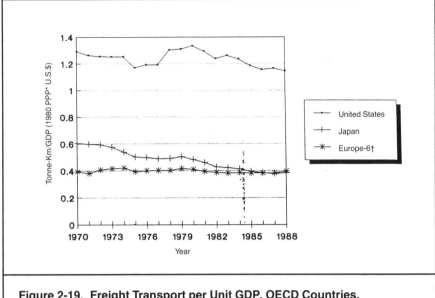

Figure 2-19. Freight Transport per Unit GDP, OECD Countries, 1970–1988

Notes:
* PPP = purchasing power parity.
† The United Kingdom, West Germany, France, Italy, Sweden, and Norway.

Europe, there was a major shift from rail to trucks. Between 1970 and 1988, the share of freight activity in trucks increased from 35% to 51% in Japan and from 54% to 63% in Europe-6 (Figure 2-21). The share of rail declined from 14% to 5% and 28% to 18%, respectively, during the same period. A large drop in the share of rail in France contributed strongly to the Europe-6 trend.

The increase in the role of trucks reflects change in the composition of freight toward products for which trucks have inherent advantages over competing modes. In addition, the growing use of "just in time" delivery in manufacturing has favored trucks.

Ships and barges are an important freight transport mode in the United States, where agricultural and mining products rely heavily on them, and in Japan, which has considerable interisland shipping. Ships are relatively less important in Europe, though there is considerable freight moved by ship between countries.

Energy Intensities. The structural change described in the previous section had a modest net effect on aggregate freight energy inten-

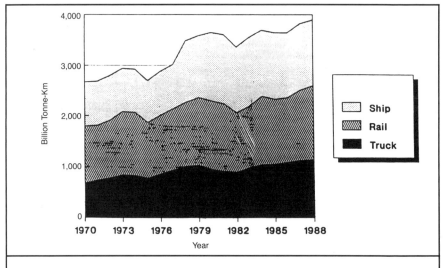

Figure 2-20. Freight Transport by Mode, the United States, 1970–1988

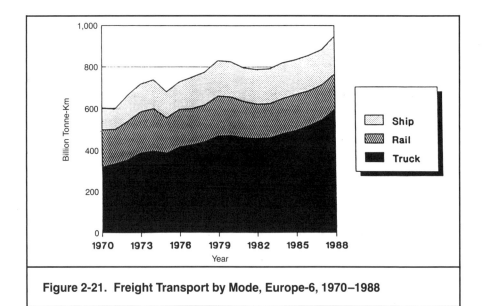

Figure 2-21. Freight Transport by Mode, Europe-6, 1970–1988

Note: Europe-6 includes the United Kingdom, West Germany, France, Italy, Sweden, and Norway.

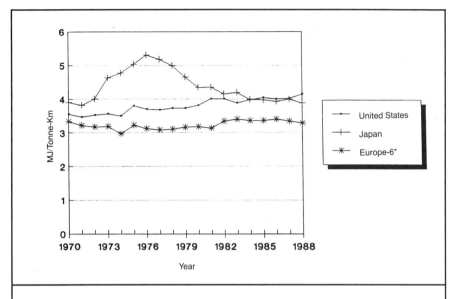

Figure 2-22. Truck Freight Energy Intensity, OECD Countries, 1970–1988

* The United Kingdom, West Germany, France, Italy, Sweden, and Norway.

sity in the United States between 1973 and 1988 but contributed significantly to an increase in industry in Japan and Europe-6. France and Italy had sizable increases in aggregate intensity because of increases in modal energy intensities and the structural shift from rail to trucks, whereas in Sweden the increase in aggregate intensity was largely due to an increase in modal intensity rather than structural change.

TRUCKS. The energy intensity of freight trucking (energy per t-km) increased by about 13% in the United States between 1973 and 1988 (Figure 2-22). It declined by 16% in Japan and increased slightly in Europe-6. In Japan, intensity rose through 1976 but fell sharply in the 1977–1980 period.

In the United States, the data show that average fuel use per km was the same in 1988 as in 1973 for both medium and heavy (tractor-trailer) trucks. Improvement in technical efficiency was apparently offset by increase in operating speeds on intercity highways and increasing traffic congestion in urban areas. The overall increase in energy per tonne-km was probably due to factors related to the operation of trucking fleets and the nature of freight carried. Despite deregulation of the

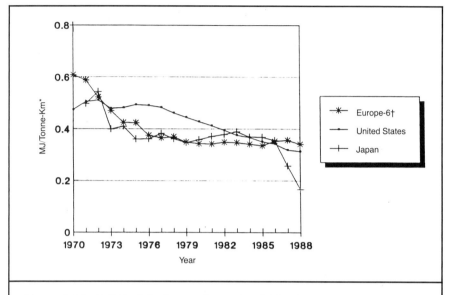

Figure 2-23. Rail Freight Energy Intensity, OECD Countries, 1970–1988

Notes:
* Delivered energy.
† The United Kingdom, West Germany, France, Italy, Sweden, and Norway.

trucking industry, there is evidence that there was an increase in empty backhauls, resulting in reduced tonnage per distance traveled (see Chapter 9 of this book). In addition, it appears that the weight carried per volume of truck capacity declined. One reason for this is increased packaging for many goods (packaging is lightweight but takes up truck capacity).

RAIL. Between 1973 and 1988, the final energy intensity of rail freight transport declined by 34% in the United States, by 26% in Europe-6, and by 58% in Japan, where rail activity fell considerably (Figure 2-23). Electrification accounts for part of the decline in Japan and Europe. (The efficiency of a diesel locomotive is 20%–25%, that of electric traction 90%, so replacement of diesel by electricity causes a significant decline in final energy intensity.) Other factors were the use of stronger locomotives and the trend to cutting unprofitable lines, which presumably supported smaller trains with less than full loads. The large decline in Japan in the 1987–1988 period was apparently due to a radical restructuring of the rail industry (Kibune 1991).

Table 2-6. Decomposition of the Change in Aggregate Freight Transport Energy Intensity in the OECD-8, 1973–1988 (Total % Change)

OECD-8	Change in Aggregate Intensity	DECOMPOSITION Structure	DECOMPOSITION Intensities	DECOMPOSITION Interaction
United States	4	3	1	0
Japan	12	30	-13	-5
Europe-6	12	13	-2	1
West Germany	-6	15	-20	-1
Sweden	31	4	27	0
Norway	7	15	-5	-3
France	46	22	18	6
United Kingdom	-14	1	-12	-3
Italy	32	15	14	3
TOTAL	6	8	-2	0

Decomposing Change in Freight Energy Intensity. Between 1973 and 1988, aggregate freight transport energy intensity increased by 4% in the United States and by 12% in Japan and Europe-6 (Table 2-6). Structural change toward trucks contributed strongly to the increase in Japan, more than offsetting decline in energy intensities. It accounted for all of the aggregate intensity increase in Europe-6.

Japan, West Germany, and the United Kingdom had a net decline in modal energy intensities. The United States showed little change, since the increase in intensity for trucks was offset by decreases in other modes. In Europe-6, the countries averaged out to almost no change. France, Italy, and Sweden had increases in the modal intensity of trucks, which more than offset decreases in the intensity of other modes.

Developing Countries

Energy use for freight transport has risen significantly in the LDCs.[23] In China, the ratio of freight tonne-km to GDP declined slightly between 1978 and 1988, perhaps reflecting some lightening of economic output. Data for South Korea show little change in the ratio between 1970 and 1987. Brazilian data, on the other hand, show a sig-

---

[23] The data sources for China, South Korea, and Brazil are the same as those given in the section on passenger travel.

nificant increase between 1973 and 1985; greater transport of agricultural and mineral products from the Amazon region may have played a role. The modal structure of freight transport in LDCs varies across countries and over time, depending on the composition of economic output and national geography. China and India have extensive (but outmoded and overburdened) rail networks. Both countries have considerable shipment of grains, coal, and other mineral products for domestic consumption. Rail has historically dominated freight transport in both, though the share of trucks has increased since the 1970s. Chinese data show the share of road transport in total tonne-km rising from 6% in 1978 to 13% in 1988. Ships have also become more important in China and accounted for the same share (42%) as rail in 1988.

Except for China and India, most LDCs have not built extensive rail networks.[24] Much of the freight is moved by truck or, in some countries, via ship. Where the manufacturing sector has grown rapidly, the share of trucks in freight transport has risen also. In South Korea, for example, the share of trucks increased from only 11% in 1970 to 48% in 1987, whereas rail declined considerably in share.

Growth in the share of trucks leads to an increase in the aggregate energy intensity of freight transport. Data from South Korea show a 13% increase in this indicator even for the short period from 1983 to 1987. In Brazil, on the other hand, the data show a decline in the share of trucks from 62% in 1973 to 54% in 1985, and an increase in the share of ships. Since the latter have much lower energy intensity than trucks, this shift contributed to a decline in aggregate freight transport energy intensity.

Lack of data makes it difficult to assess how the energy intensity of particular freight transport modes has changed in LDCs. However, for trucks, two factors have contributed to a decline in energy intensity. One is a shift from gasoline- to diesel-fueled trucks. The other is an increase in the share of heavy trucks, which tend to use less energy per t-km than medium or light trucks. In Brazil, the fraction of diesel-fueled trucks increased from about 50% of the fleet in 1973 to over 85% by 1985, whereas the fraction of heavy and semiheavy trucks rose from 15% to 28%. In India, the transition from gasoline- to diesel-fueled trucks is nearly complete, whereas in China most trucks still use gasoline. Trucks in India are larger than those in China, but are often

---

[24] In part this reflects the colonial history and its ending during a period when highways were preferred over railways. The small size of internal markets also made construction of rail networks less attractive.

overloaded, which leads to high energy use per km. In both countries, technological improvement affecting the fuel efficiency of gasoline and diesel trucks has been minimal. Poor road conditions in these countries and others contribute to high fuel intensity.

The energy intensity of rail transport has declined in India because of increasing use of diesel and electric locomotives in place of inefficient coal-fueled steam locomotives, but the efficiency of diesel and electric locomotives has not improved very much. In China, steam trains are still predominant, though a growing use of diesel locomotives has reduced energy intensity.

Former East Bloc

Relative to economic activity, the level of freight transport in the former Soviet Union was very high because of the dominance of heavy raw materials and energy. Pipeline shipment of oil and gas (a substantial amount of which was destined for export) accounted for one-third of total tonne-km in 1988. (Even if we exclude pipeline transport for comparability with OECD countries, the Soviet level was still high.) In addition, the lack of real markets meant that materials and goods were often shipped long distances because of the way the "buying" and "selling" ministries exchanged.

Pipeline shipment of oil and gas accounted for most of the growth in total freight transport after 1974 (Figure 2-24). The increase in other transport modes averaged only 2% per year between 1973 and 1987, compared with 6% per year between 1965 and 1973. This reflects the slowing of the Soviet economy. Excluding gas pipelines, rail accounted for around two-thirds of freight tonne-km. Trucks accounted for only 7%, in part because of the relative unimportance of consumer goods and the lack of deliveries of these goods to consumer outlets.

Because of the dominance of rail, the aggregate energy intensity of Soviet freight transport was low relative to Western European levels. The energy intensity of each mode is close to levels in the West; this is not due to high vehicle efficiency, however, but rather to the importance of large shipments of bulk materials. The intensity for trucks fell, mainly because of an increase in the share of diesel trucks. Rail energy intensity (final energy) has also decreased, first through replacement of coal traction by oil, then through electrification.

The pattern in Poland is quite different from that in the former Soviet Union. Total freight transport in Poland reached only 4,250 t-km per capita in 1987, far below the level of the Soviet Union but close to that of West Germany (Leach & Nowak 1990). Compared with West Germany, however, Poland has a high level of t-km per

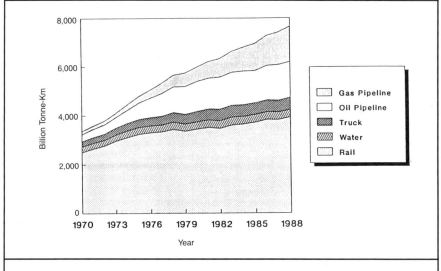

Figure 2-24. Freight Transport in the Soviet Union by Mode, 1970–1988

GDP, in part because coal shipments are very important. Three-quarters of domestic freight is hauled by rail, a share that has remained stable since the late 1970s. In part this reflects the importance of coal for domestic use and export. The fuel intensity of trucks is considerably higher than in Western Europe.

Conclusion

Per capita travel has increased throughout the world as personal mobility has grown and business links have expanded. In all regions there has been a shift in modal structure toward automobiles and airplanes, though the share of these modes is much lower in the former East Bloc and the LDCs than in the OECD countries. This shift has caused growth in the aggregate energy intensity of travel. The energy intensity of automobile travel declined considerably in the United States but changed little in Western Europe and Japan, where growth in vehicle size and power offset technical efficiency gains. In the former East Bloc and the LDCs, the extent of any decrease in automobile energy intensity is difficult to jduge, but it appears to have been modest. In contrast to automobiles, the energy intensity of air travel fell dramatically in all of the major OECD countries.

Freight transport per unit GDP declined somewhat in the United

States and Japan but changed little in Western Europe and (probably) the former East Bloc. In the LDCs, trends in the ratio have differed between those countries for which we have historical data. As in passenger travel, there has been a shift toward a more energy-intensive structure, in this case from rail to trucks, whose flexibility and convenience provide advantages for moving many manufactured products. In contrast to automobiles, there has not been much decline in truck energy intensity, at least in the OECD countries. In some LDCs, the shift from gasoline to diesel trucks has reduced energy intensity somewhat. There has been more decline in the energy intensity of rail freight transport, though some of this is also a result of fuel switching.

The combination of growth in activity, structural change toward more energy-intensive modes, and a relatively modest (in most cases) decline in modal energy intensities has led to a considerable growth in transportation energy use throughout the world. Since oil products account for almost all transport energy use, this growth has been the key factor pushing upward on world oil demand. It has also contributed to the rise in global CO_2 emissions.

Our intention in this paper has been to shed light on past trends. A discussion of the future outlook for transportation energy use is presented elsewhere.[25] An important difference between the period covered here and the next decade or two is that increase in world oil prices is expected to be modest. This means that there will be little incentive to improve efficiency to save money. On the other hand, environmental problems are more pressing than in the past at local and global levels, and the transportation system is approaching or already in crisis in many cities. Strategies that improve the energy efficiency of vehicles can reduce some of these problems, but making changes with respect to transport activity and modal structure will be required in order to move toward a system that is sustainable in the long run.

References

Boeing Commercial Airplane Group. 1991. *Current Market Outlook: World Market Demand and Airplane Supply Requirements.* Seattle.

DIW (Deutsches Institut für Wirtschaftsforschung). 1991. *Verkehr in Zählen.* Bonn, Germany: Bundesminister für Verkehr.

Dolan, K. 1991. "Tomorrow's Clean and Fuel-Efficient Automobile: Opportunities for East-West Cooperation. A Summary of the Berlin Conference, March 25–27, 1991." Paris, France: OECD

---

[25] See Chapters 8, 9, and 10 in Schipper et al. (1992).

Environment Directorate, and Berkeley: Lawrence Berkeley Laboratory.

ERI (Energy Research Institute). 1989. Sectoral Energy Demand in China. Beijing.

Ferguson, M., and C. Holman. 1990. *Atmospheric Emissions from the Use of Transport in the UK*. Vol. 1. London: Earth Resources Research.

Gately, D. 1988. "Taking Off: The U.S. Demand for Air Travel and Jet Fuel." *Energy Journal* 9 (4): 63–88.

Geller, H. S., and D. Zylbersztajn. 1991. "Energy Intensity Trends in Brazil." *Annual Review of Energy*. Vol. 16.

Greene, D. L. 1990. "CAFE OR PRICE?: An Analysis of the Effects of Federal Fuel Economy Regulations and Gasoline Price on New Car MPG, 1978–89." *Energy Journal* 11 (3): 37–57.

Heavenrich, R., and J. Murrell. 1990. *Light-Duty Automotive Technology and Fuel Economy Trends Through 1990*. Ann Arbor, Mich.: U.S. Environmental Protection Agency.

IEA (International Energy Agency). Annual issues, 1980–1988. *Energy Prices and Taxes*. Paris, France.

———. 1989. *World Energy Statistics and Balances 1971–1987*. Paris, France.

———. 1990. *World Energy Statistics and Balances 1985–1988*. Paris, France.

KEEI (Korea Energy Economics Institute). 1989. *Sectoral Energy Demand in the Republic of Korea*. Seoul, South Korea.

Kibune, H. 1991. Japan Institute of Energy Economics, Tokyo. Private communication.

Leach, G., and Z. Nowak. 1990. "Cutting Carbon Dioxide Emissions from Poland and the United Kingdom." Draft Research Report. Stockholm, Sweden: The Stockholm Environment Institute.

Meyers, S. 1988. *Transportation in the LDCs: A Major Growth in World Oil Demand*. Lawrence Berkeley Laboratory Report LBL-24198. Berkeley.

Potter, S. 1991. "Company Car Report." Milton Keynes, England: The Open University, Energy and Environment Research Unit.

Ross, M. 1989. "Energy and Transportation in the United States." *Annual Review of Energy* 14:131–171.

Schipper, L., and S. Meyers, with R. Howarth and R. Steiner. 1992. *Energy Efficiency and Human Activity: Past Trends, Future Prospects*. Cambridge: Cambridge University Press.

Schipper, L., and R. C. Cooper. 1991. *Energy Use and Conservation in the USSR: Patterns, Prospects, and Problems*. Lawrence Berkeley Laboratory Report LBL-29831. Berkeley.

Schipper, L., R. Steiner, P. Duerr, F. An, and S. Strøm. 1992. "Energy Use in Passenger Transport in OECD Countries: Changes between 1970 and 1987." *Transportation* 19:25–42.

Webster, F. V., P. H. Bly, R. H. Johnson, N. Pauley, and M. Dasgupta. 1986. "Changing Patterns of Urban Travel. Part 1. Urbanization, Household Travel, and Car Ownership." *Transport Reviews* 6 (1): 49–86.

Westbrook, F., and P. Patterson. 1989. "Changing Driving Patterns and Their Effect on Fuel Economy." Paper presented at the 1989 SAE Government/Industry Meeting, Washington, D.C. May 2.

Chapter 3

The Effects of Transportation Sector Growth on Energy Use, the Environment, and Traffic Congestion in Four Asian Cities

Mia Layne Birk and Peter Reilly-Roe

Meeting transport needs in developing countries is increasingly becoming a challenge. Traditionally, this challenge has been met by massive investment in road infrastructure accompanied by a sharp increase in road vehicles, both cars and trucks. For example, from 1985 to 1991, 81% of World Bank urban transportation loan approvals to developing countries were for road building and maintenance, whereas only 7% were for traffic management, 7% for bus system improvements, and 5% for technical assistance and other measures. No loans were approved during that period for rail systems or pedestrian and nonmotorized transport facilities (Philips 1991, 66–67). The rapid growth in the vehicle fleets of many developing countries has put tremendous pressure on the available infrastructure. Between 1984 and 1988, the Korean vehicle fleet grew 30% per year; the Kenyan fleet, 26%; the Chinese fleet, 14%; the Brazilian fleet, 11%; and the Thai fleet, 12%. In contrast, the United States vehicle fleet grew only 2% per annum during that period, and the British fleet grew 3% (Faiz et al. 1990, vii).

This traditional development path has led to painful problems for many cities around the world. The transport sector often accounts for over 25% of developing countries' total energy consumption, constraining their ability to use foreign exchange export earnings for needs other than petroleum (USDOE 1987, 40). Many developing countries spend over 15% of their export earnings on imported oil, and in 1987, twelve developing countries spent over 50% of their earnings on this commodity (World Bank 1987b, 218–219).

Rapid transportation system growth has caused severe environmental damage in many urban areas, especially by deteriorating local air quality with road vehicle emissions, such as hydrocarbons, nitrogen oxides, carbon monoxide, and particulates. Furthermore, traffic congestion has become so aggravated in many developing-country cities that severe economic losses result from the productive time wasted in commuting. The tourism industry, which many developing countries rely on for foreign exchange earnings, has been hurt in congested cities, such as Mexico City and Bangkok; potential tourists have been staying away to avoid the pollution and congestion, and tourists in the cities have not been able to do as many things as they would like.

To minimize the negative impacts of transportation development, countries require new solutions that simultaneously enable them to meet transport needs and address energy, environmental, and economic constraints. The precise mechanisms for accomplishing this task vary from country to country. Among the strategies needed, though, are improving the efficiency of individual vehicles, switching to alternative and cleaner fuels, improving the telecommunications systems, maximizing the efficiency of existing transportation systems, and increasing emphasis on the more energy-efficient, environmentally positive modes of transport, such as mass transit and nonmotorized transport. Finally, emphasis must be placed on comprehensive land use planning to design effective, efficient transport systems equipped to handle future changes.

Four case studies undertaken by the International Institute for Energy Conservation (IIEC) highlight the issues described above. This chapter reflects the current progress of these studies, which are designed to illustrate the problems encountered in meeting transportation needs in a range of environments, and the potential solutions to overcoming these barriers.

Options Tailored to Each City

The four cities that are the focus of this chapter—Bangkok, Thailand; Surabaya, Indonesia; Varanasi, India; and Islamabad, Pakistan—were selected because each is representative of a different level of infrastructure development. Bangkok typifies those cities that have highly developed road transport systems and are experiencing crises in their transportation sectors over high levels of energy use, pollution, and traffic congestion. Other such cities include Mexico City, Mexico; São Paulo, Brazil; Lagos and Ibadan, Nigeria; Manila, the Philippines; Seoul, South Korea; and Jakarta, Indonesia.

Surabaya typifies those urban regions that are growing rapidly in transport infrastructure but which have not yet reached the pollution and congestion levels of a city like Bangkok, although they are proceeding rapidly along this path. Semarang and Bandung, Indonesia; Jaipur, India; and Chiang Mai, Thailand, all share similar characteristics.

Varanasi is representative of smaller cities whose transport sectors are still dominated by traditional, nonmotorized transport modes but which are expected to increasingly use motorized modes in the future; since these cities are in their transportation infrastructure infancy, good planning can help them avoid the transport-related problems now suffered by highly motorized cities. Many cities throughout the developing world fall into this category.

Finally, Islamabad is similar to Varanasi in its level of transportation infrastructure, but it is a new city, built in the 1960s, whose development has been carefully planned and managed. Islamabad's planned development provides a comparison to the unstructured, unmanaged growth of Varanasi. More details of each city's transportation sector will be provided below.

As Bangkok, Surabaya, Islamabad, and Varanasi each has a unique transport system, solutions tailored to each city are necessary. For each of the cities studied, local teams have been working to relate the present and future traffic levels to air pollution and energy consumption. Each team has been collecting available data on national transportation activity and energy use; their city's urban development history and present state; the city's transportation system, including road infrastructure, vehicle fleet, and both passenger and freight transport demand; refinery structure, fuel production, and quality; the urban transport energy demand; and urban transport emissions, air quality, and public health. The teams have been using this information to outline the main transportation, energy, and environmental issues and available options for mitigating the negative impacts of transportation growth in each of their cities. Such options may include improved vehicle technology, improved vehicle operations, better traffic management, enhanced and necessary new infrastructure, land use and urban development policies, government policy and institutional changes, and the use of cleaner and alternative fuels. Finally, at the end of these ongoing studies, each team will conclude with a series of feasible actions tailored to their city's needs, and will attempt, where possible, to quantify the monetary cost of such actions and their likely effects on the city's air quality and energy use.

Bangkok

Bangkok, Thailand, a city of close to 10 million people, is characterized by one of the world's most congested transport systems. The speed of travel by vehicles on main city roads at any hour, day or night, is typically less than 10 kilometers per hour (*Bangkok Post* 1990b, 20; *Washington Post Health Magazine* 1991, 13). Officials estimate that a typical motorist spends a total of forty-four days a year just idling in standstill traffic (*Bangkok Post* 1990d, 20).

The road network, while extensive compared to those of many other developing-country cities, cannot handle the travel demand. An additional twenty thousand to thirty thousand new vehicles *per month* are being added to the already saturated network (*Bangkok Post* 1990a, 16). The government has reacted by pouring money into road building, with each new section of road becoming congested shortly after it is built. According to estimates by the Japanese International Cooperation Agency, the city will need to spend about U.S.$100 billion over the next seventeen years just to maintain present levels of traffic congestion (*Bangkok Post* 1991d, 20). Even if Bangkok were to invest that amount of money or more, it is critical that the city also invest in managing the demand for road space and restraining the growth in the vehicle population. If demand management is not included as an investment priority, the growth in population and vehicle fleet will overwhelm even the largest of infrastructure investments. Furthermore, the Thai government recently relaxed many vehicle importation restrictions, which, although making more efficient cars more available, will likely cause the vehicle fleet to grow even faster.

Bangkok's buses cover an extensive route system. Certain lanes running counter to traffic flow are designated for buses, but the bulk run with traffic without separation. The buses, often overloaded and poorly maintained, add to the city's traffic woes by stopping frequently to pick up passengers, thus disrupting traffic by pulling in and out. Residents also use river boats and rail for transport. Overloading of river and rail modes, traditionally less crowded and relatively quicker than anything on the roads, is increasingly prevalent. The fact that more residents are choosing to use rail and river has had no noticeable impact on road congestion.

The government has so far concentrated many of its efforts to improve the system on detailed studies of the potential use of such ideas as traffic management; bus system expansion and improvement; restricting access to certain areas; road pricing; and the building of new roads, highways, and light rail. Of these options, road and highway building has thus far received the bulk of investment commitments. Because projects have been proposed to clients in various government departments who have differing agendas, many worthy projects actually compete with each other and are conflicting, rather than complementary. For example, two much discussed mass-rail-transit projects—called the Skytrain and Hopewell projects—would, in certain spots, both run rail tracks along the same route. The construction of these lines, which are also proposed to run along the same line as an elevated highway, will disrupt traffic in parts of the city for years to come. Furthermore, they will cost the city billions of dollars. Finally, the level of travel demand in Bangkok, as high as it is, has been suppressed by all the problems; residents avoid the roads whenever possible. Because travel demand is lower than it would be in the absence of major congestion, these projects can significantly relieve congestion in the short run only.

The overloading of Bangkok's road space is worsened by other factors as well. For example, in Bangkok children do not necessarily attend schools in their neighborhood, nor are they provided with a school bus system. Thus, during school months, traffic is noticeably worse because parents or chauffeurs drive each child to a school that may be across town.

Automobile fuels in Thailand are either leaded gasoline or diesel. However, the government of Thailand recently mandated that unleaded fuel be available nationwide before 1993, and small quantities are now available. Furthermore, it also mandated that all new cars be equipped with catalytic converters as of January 1, 1993.

Well over 50% of the vehicle population in Bangkok consists of two- and three-wheeled vehicles. Most of the three-wheeled motorized vehicles, known as *tuk-tuk*s, are fueled by propane, also called liquid petroleum gas (LPG), a cleaner-burning fuel in general than gasoline. However, *tuk-tuk*s still emit smog-causing white smoke and contribute to noise pollution.

Nonmotorized transport currently has a mixed role in Bangkok. There are plenty of sidewalks crowded with pedestrian traffic, although it is rather unpleasant to walk because of the vehicle emissions and noise. On the other hand, few people bicycle because it is dangerous and unhealthy due to the congestion and air pollution, and there are no separated paths for bicycles and bicycle-carts.

Bangkok's congestion has resulted in serious economic losses. Had the person-hours wasted in traffic been put to productive use, the city's gross regional product could have grown annually by one-tenth more, officials estimate (*Bangkok Post* 1990c, 20; *Nation* 1990, Sec. 6, 1).

The environmental problems caused by the transport system are well documented. The city is encased in a thick layer of choking smog directly resulting from vehicle emissions. At least 1 million of Bangkok's residents received treatment in 1990 for smog-related respiratory problems, such as emphysema and asthma (*Bangkok Post* 1990e, 11; *Washington Post Health Magazine* 1991, 13). Blood lead levels in traffic police from leaded gasoline emissions are far in excess of levels considered dangerous in the United States. Noise levels from traffic soar well past safe limits at many times during the day; tests show traffic police have varying losses of hearing (*Washington Post Health Magazine* 1991, 13).

Finally, fuel consumption by vehicles idling in traffic in Bangkok amounts to about U.S.$1.4 million *per day* (*Bangkok Post* 1990d, 20). Thailand imports the bulk of the oil it uses, which accounts for 66% of energy demanded in the country (TDRI 1990, 11). As the transportation sector alone consumes over 50% of that oil, the fuel lost because of congestion adds substantially to the already significant oil import bill, leaving less foreign exchange for development uses.

Surabaya

Surabaya is located east of Jakarta on the island of Java and has a population of approximately 2.5 million people. Its population is projected to increase to 4.5 million in the next twenty years. Its transport sector is also congested and contributes significantly to air pollution and energy consumption in the city, but the situation is relatively good compared with that of Bangkok. However, it is apparent to city planners that, if the present urban growth rates and development trajectory continue without change, Surabaya will very likely have a Bangkok-like transportation crisis within the decade.

Like Bangkok's, Surabaya's mass public transport consists of a bus system, with minibuses and taxis as well. Currently, about 20% of Surabaya's citizens rely on the bus system, which seems to serve the population quite well. However, the expanding population will need an expanded system.

The main flow of traffic in Surabaya is on one north-south corridor that connects the port to the main business areas. There are also a number of main roads connecting the east and west portions of the city. Traffic has been routed so that most streets run one way. These streets are, for the most part, nonparallel and lengthy. Thus, except if one is traveling directly north or south, Surabaya's one-way traffic system makes it difficult to avoid long, winding, inefficient routes. This problem is further complicated by the lack of road direction signs, traffic management, and proper signalization.

*Becak*s, or human-powered bicycle-taxis, are still a common mode of transport in the city. The government of Indonesia is actively discouraging this transport mode as outdated and a traffic impediment. In 1989, the government went so far as to confiscate some 100,000 *becak*s and throw them into the sea. Although a slow-moving bicycle pulling a cart containing several people across six lanes of rapidly moving traffic is indeed an impediment, *becak*s bring many more positive impacts to Surabaya than negative. For example, they provide employment for thousands of drivers, who often act as caretakers and low-cost chauffeurs for schoolchildren and elderly people. *Becak*s are a perfect mode of transport for short-distance errands and light-goods movement. And of course, they use no fossil fuels and are nonpolluting. Legally, *becak*s are not supposed to be on the main roads at all, but since very few intersections exist where they can cross main roads to get to the secondary routes, they have little choice. Thus making this mode more safe and less disrupting of motorized traffic flows while maintaining it as a main feature of Surabaya's system should be actively encouraged.

Conspicuously absent in Surabaya are crosswalks for pedestrians. This is partly because of a lack of traffic signals, which also means that there are few break points at which pedestrians and *becak*s can avoid crossing several lanes of fast-moving traffic. Crossing the street is thus a dangerous undertaking. The city government is reportedly considering providing some pedestrian bridges over the main roads.

Like Bangkok's, Surabaya's school system is nonlocal, and thus traffic problems increase during school months. Since *becak* drivers often transport children to school when their schools happen to be close to home, a neighborhood school system would mean more use of nonmotorized modes and less motorized traffic.

A positive impact on Surabaya's traffic congestion is that government and commercial workers have differing beginning and ending work hours from Monday to Friday. Thus, the rush hours in the morning and evening are not as hard felt, since fewer workers are on the road during one time period. At Saturday midday, when both the government and commercial sectors finish work at the same time and combine with shopping traffic, traffic is noticeably worse. In contrast, Bangkok experiences nonstop peak traffic flow.

The air pollution levels in Surabaya are noticeable, but not nearly as overpowering as Bangkok's. For example, carbon monoxide, hydrocarbon, and nitrogen oxide levels in Bangkok are almost three times those of Surabaya; lead and particulate levels are at similarly disparate levels. The use of leaded fuel and the lack of pollution control equipment on cars contribute significantly to air pollution in Surabaya, as in Bangkok, and Surabaya's motor vehicle population is also increasing rapidly. According to 1985 World Bank figures, Surabaya's total motor vehicle population (cars, trucks, buses, and motorcycles) is growing about 10% per year (World Bank 1987a, 40).

Indonesia has begun to experiment with compressed natural gas (CNG) as an alternative to diesel and gasoline in taxis in Jakarta. Gas supplies recently discovered in east Java will soon be connected by pipeline to Surabaya; thus the prospect for CNG use in transport in Surabaya is promising.

Indonesia, an oil-exporting country, presently has not concentrated on decreasing the rate of growth of oil demand, although it could clearly earn more from oil sales if it did not use so much in its transport sector. Furthermore, Indonesia's oil production capacity is likely to remain stable or decline. Thus, at present oil consumption rates, Indonesia could become an oil-importing country within the decade (USDOE 1987, 11).

Islamabad

Islamabad, the capital of Pakistan, has a population of about 350,000 people. The Pakistani government decided to move the capital from Karachi in the 1950s and subsequently built Islamabad on an unpopulated site. The city was officially inaugurated as the capital in 1962. The government has carefully orchestrated and managed Islamabad's development according to a master plan that lays the city out much like a grid.

A much older, more typical Asian city, Rawalpindi, with a population of 2–3 million, is about 25 kilometers from Islamabad and supplies much of Islamabad's work force. There is an effective bus system running between Islamabad and Rawalpindi, but no bus system to speak of within Islamabad itself. According to Islamabad's master development plan, Rawalpindi and Islamabad are to eventually merge into one physical area but still be governed by distinct municipal administrations. If the pressure of Rawalpindi's rising population reaches Islamabad, the city will find itself in need of a more public transit–oriented design.

With a car population of 35,000–50,000, there is very little traffic in Islamabad, and no noticeable air pollution. However, the vehicle population is expanding, and travel times are longer today than a decade ago because of more traffic. The residential areas are suburban in nature, located some distance from the business and commercial areas. Due to the lack of public transit and the long travel lengths between business and residential areas, traveling by car is a near necessity. Islamabad is characterized by wide, long, paved streets that would be perfect for nonmotorized traffic use, but very few people ride bicycles or walk to get around, possibly because distances between destinations are so long.

Pakistan is an oil-importing country that could greatly benefit from improved transportation system energy efficiency. The National Energy Conservation Centre (ENERCON) has already initiated a program to decrease fuel consumption losses from poor vehicle maintenance. The program focuses on providing automobile tune-ups and improving public awareness of the improved vehicle economy one gets from a well-tuned vehicle. ENERCON reports energy efficiency improvements of 5% to 6% and emissions reductions of 50% for both carbon monoxide and hydrocarbons.

The fuels used in vehicles in Islamabad, as in most Asian countries, are leaded and very polluting. Experimentation with compressed natural gas as a vehicle fuel for personal automobiles has begun in earnest in Islamabad; the one CNG filling station also handles conversions of automobiles to CNG usage and has a waiting list of several months for conversion requests.

Varanasi

Varanasi, or Banaras, as it is more commonly referred to, is an ancient city of close to 1 million people. It is one of India's religious and spiritual centers, with thousands of people coming each day from all over the world to make pilgrimages. In contrast to Islamabad, it is a more typical Asian city with no planned or managed growth. Its population is growing rapidly, and the transportation system is already tremendously congested. However, the traffic is primarily made up of nonmotorized transport modes.

Varanasi's congestion stems from a total lack of traffic management. In fact, there is not one traffic signal in the entire city. The police are supposed to manage the traffic flow, especially at the city's many circular intersections, but in reality, the police have little, if any, effect on traffic flows. Compared with a traffic situation like Bangkok's, however, the bottleneck points are much less unpleasant. The reason for this is that the vehicle fleet is dominated by nonmotorized modes of transport: bicycles, bicycle-rickshaws (a bicycle pulling or pushing a cart with two to five people or goods), pedestrians, and animal-powered carts. Thus there is little air pollution, although dust levels are quite high. And since the vehicles are mostly small and maneuverable, it is possible to get through.

In addition to the nonmotorized transport modes, there are many three-wheeled motorized vehicles known as *bajaj*s, and many motorcycles and motor scooters. Although the fleet of two- and three-wheeled motorized vehicles is expanding slowly, the automobile population, currently minuscule, is expanding rapidly.

Varanasi is situated along the west bank of the Ganges River, and its shape resembles three concentric crescents. The first crescent, which borders the Ganges for a distance of several kilometers and radiates out from the river about a kilometer, is very densely populated and consists of a complex web of narrow, cobblestone streets. This area is literally impenetrable by vehicles other than bicycles; thus this ancient first crescent will be preserved no matter how much the motor vehicle fleet grows. The second crescent surrounds the first and is less dense. Its road network of narrow streets flowing to the north, south, and west is crowded with bicycle-rickshaws, bicycles, ox-carts, *bajaj*s, motorcycles, motor scooters, and cows and pedestrians. The third crescent is a relatively low-density area, with wider streets that are more crowded with buses, trucks, and autos. The trucks mainly pass along the city edges carrying freight, and the buses mainly bring loads of visitors coming for a two- or three-day pilgrimage.

Because the second crescent, really incorporating the bulk of the city's road space, is largely used by a nonautomobile fleet and is already congested, the impact to traffic levels in Varanasi of an enlarged private auto population will be enormous. The opportunity exists, however, for the government to design a system that, for example, could have public buslines connecting the outer and inner edges of the city. Automobiles could be restricted from the more dense areas of Varanasi. In other words, at this stage in its development, good land use planning taking into consideration the changing modal mix and the growing population could mitigate the negative effects of a rapidly expanding automobile fleet.

Fuel consumption for a city like Varanasi, with its low motorized-vehicle usage, is not a significant problem at present. Again, however, a rapidly enlarging automobile fleet may change the city's fuel consumption level considerably. For India, which imports a considerable amount of oil already, increasing levels of fuel consumption in growing cities throughout the country will be a major problem.

Challenges Faced

Although the analysis of the effects of these four cities' growing transportation systems on energy use, the environment, and traffic congestion is not yet complete, it is clear that common challenges are faced by all four cities. These challenges are not meant to be taken as conclusions from the case studies; rather they are meant to illustrate the problems faced by the study teams during their work thus far.

Urban Population Pressure

Bangkok, Surabaya, Islamabad, and Varanasi vary significantly in population, area, land use, degree of motorization, road infrastructure, and in other important respects, such as economic wealth and industry. However, the cities do have one common factor shared with many other cities in developing countries—a rapid rate of population growth. This is due partly to natural growth of the urban population and partly to migration of people from rural areas. Population growth produces one of the greatest challenges for those responsible for the provision of transportation and other municipal services, such as water, sewage treatment, and land development. Coping with population growth is a tough challenge for any city of any size in any part of the world.

The usual result of rapid population growth is that, at best, only a part of the necessary services are provided or planned for. In larger cities, such as Bangkok, the typical consequences of spiraling, unexpected population growth are the springing up of high-density shanty towns housing a migrant population for whom inadequate public transport services are provided and an overloaded urban road system for major portions of the urban area. Development along highways leading to the city occurs as the demand for housing and employment in the city surpasses construction and economic activity. This results in population concentration away from the job markets, and long, congested commute trips. A transportation system incapable of satisfying travel demand thus develops in these cities.

Although rising levels of congestion may suppress travel demand to a degree, the cost of congestion is high in terms of wasted time, increased pollution, and expensive energy use. When congestion reaches a level as high as Bangkok's, any new section of highway will likely fill up shortly after it is opened. This has been the experience in Bangkok with the road projects implemented so far.

Another consequence of rapid population growth is often a rapidly growing vehicle fleet, especially in cities where incomes are also rising rapidly, like Bangkok or Surabaya. The absorption of a rapidly growing population of private motorized vehicles, including two-, three-, and four-wheelers, presents a series of challenges, opportunities, and adverse impacts. For a city like Surabaya to provide enough road, parking, and traffic control for the growing vehicle population without becoming a Bangkok is a practical impossibility in terms of cost. While private vehicle owners enjoy the flexibility of private vehicles in providing relatively fast, convenient transportation (at least where the vehicle stock is small), the costs to a city in terms of congestion, pollution, energy consumption, noise, safety, and visual impairment are overwhelming.

The experience of Bangkok represents the worst-case scenario of the consequences of poorly managed urban growth. The fact is, however, that it is difficult for any city, no matter what the population base, to cope with population growth. As the case study teams are discovering, meeting transportation needs requires a comprehensive, well-coordinated program of measures, affecting all areas of transportation, that plans for the future needs of an expanded population. Dealing with problems as they arise is not adequate. All major players, including all levels of government, private interests, and citizens, should be involved in reaching a consensus on the best program for each city.

Planning Deficiencies

A second apparent fact from the four-city analysis is that the crisis-proportion problems of a Bangkok can be avoided if cities begin a comprehensive planning process early on. A smaller city has the potential to avoid future problems and even grow into a viable bigger city through good transit-oriented land use planning that sets the context for a logical and affordable transportation system. A larger city can also benefit from good planning that tackles all problems simultaneously.

For each city, the large low-income population, which cannot afford private transportation, must have low-cost access to the areas of the city in which they can find employment. This usually means formal or informal bus or minibus services, or bicycling and walking where distances are sufficiently short. Thus land use planning should, for example, establish adequate public transport choices, then restrict development to occur along the public transport routes so that citizens will always be within public transport access of their daily needs. Small "nodes" of commercial activity along transport lines could be set up to which citizens could walk from a public transport stop. Modes such as Surabaya's *becak*s could provide a link to the public bus system by bringing people to bus stops or the commercial "node" in their neighborhood, in addition to servicing local neighborhood errands.

Transit-oriented land use planning is, at present, neglected as a solution in many cities for a number of reasons. First, there are often very few trained staff with a clear mandate to concentrate on future planning with energy use and environment in mind, especially at the municipal level. In fact, one difficulty throughout the assessment process has been finding people with such expertise to work with the local study teams. Second, there may be competition between government agencies; priorities thus get muddled. An example is Bangkok, where more than twenty different government departments all have responsibility for some aspect of the city's transportation system. In Indonesia, municipal funding for transport development is decided at the national level and funneled through the provincial government to the city. The national and provincial governments thus retain control over city-level interests in transport planning and often have a completely different set of priorities than the city. Competing interests may also play a negative role. For example, in many developing-country cities, police operate the traffic signals, a practice decided for political reasons to generate employment. This is clearly not the most efficient or effective way to operate traffic signals. Third, politically vested interests may override land use considerations. In Bangkok, solving the transport crisis is probably the number-one national political issue, leading the executive cabinet to form a committee to coordinate the various departments' ideas. The result was that the previous premier,[1] for political reasons, tended to opt for the more splashy, large capital investment projects, overriding the decision-making power of his transport planners (who were not coordinated in their strategies in any case). For land use planning to be properly considered, cities must become responsible for all aspects of their development, especially in the transport sector.

Lack of Information and Awareness

A third area of concern for local governments evident from the four assessments is that each city faces a lack of good information about how to go about implementing a transport system or a comprehensive land use plan that minimizes energy waste, environmental degradation, and congestion while responding to population growth pressures. Again, this has been apparent in the four case studies; each team has

---

[1] Former premier Chatichai Choonhaven was overthrown in a bloodless coup in February 1991.

been struggling to find useful information and has had difficulty analyzing and using it themselves.

When it comes to air pollution, for example, it is just as important to make improvements to two- and three-wheeled vehicles as to four-wheeled vehicles. Technology is available to reduce this problem at low cost. However, research has shown a lack of awareness of this need. Good information, presented in a form that governments unfamiliar with the vehicle industry can use as a basis for program selection and design, is essential. For instance, it would be useful to have a manual describing the different ways that an emissions standards program for new vehicles could be set up, with details of costs and government resource needs. The relationship between new-vehicle standards and fuel quality and pricing structure should be included. A similar manual could be written for a vehicle inspection program. Furthermore, a manual detailing the elements needed to implement a comprehensive, transit-oriented land use plan would be a major aid to solving the information gap problem.

Provision of good information should also be coordinated with raising public and government awareness of the environmental and energy use impacts of transportation. For example, Bangkok's introduction of unleaded fuel into society should be accompanied by an education campaign that explains the difference between leaded and unleaded fuel, the impacts of each on people's health, and the benefits of using unleaded fuel.

Another important aspect in the information and awareness gap is lack of equipment and operational training. As an example, an operating chassis dynamometer to determine accurate fuel consumption and emission measurements does not yet exist in any Southeast Asian country, so that awareness of the need for reduction of energy use and emissions is very low. Governments have no basis from which to make related regulations.

Conflict with National, International, and Industry Priorities

From the challenges sketched above, it is clear that city governments face an ominous task. One can also see that there are a number of factors affecting cities and their energy use and environment that are outside the jurisdictional boundaries of local government. As mentioned earlier, national and provincial interests have often superseded municipal priorities in a given city's development and have thus been counterproductive. And national governments have been weak in such areas as setting national fuel economy or emissions standards, fuel pricing, and setting tax and tariff policies favorable to more fuel-efficient cars.

An important national-level factor affecting cities is motor vehicle design and fuels. Decisions on these are often abrogated to the vehicle and fuel suppliers, whose objectives are naturally profit maximization. National governments are beginning to realize that their intervention is necessary if they are to address the growing energy and environmental impacts of urban transportation. For new vehicles, fuel economy and emissions control standards are important, as is attention to fuel specifications and quality. For existing vehicles, the main issues are the improvement of maintenance and operating practices. These problems cannot usually be solved by governments alone, and so some cooperative or advisory arrangements with industry are necessary.

In addition to the need for national government and industry involvement in transport decision making, there is a need for international involvement. Vehicle assemblers in many developing countries themselves do not have access locally to equipment they need to meet national government fuel economy or emissions standards. Local vehicle assemblers can therefore not be required to comply with fuel economy or emissions regulations in the same way that companies are regulated in Organization for Economic Cooperation and Development (OECD) countries. One way around this type of problem is to involve the headquarters of multinational vehicle and fuel suppliers in coming up with workable solutions as part of a comprehensive aid strategy endorsed by donor agencies. Involving vehicle and fuel suppliers' headquarters is perhaps the best way to approach fuel economy or emissions standards for new vehicles, especially if the manufacturer's headquarters are at the leading edge of emissions control and fuel economy technology, but the local assembly operation is producing vehicles with little or none of this technology.

Conclusion

The four city studies, although not complete, reveal tough challenges faced by cities of all sizes. They must find a way to provide low-cost transport services while coping with the impacts of urban population and private vehicle fleet growth. This challenge is common to cities in all stages of growth.

For each option available to address this challenge, each city will face trade-offs in terms of costs and benefits. For example, Surabaya's one-way traffic system was intended to benefit residents through improved circulation and increased average speeds. However, the costs of this system may have overwhelmed the benefits: the lack of signals has left pedestrians with no place to cross the street, travel times have increased because of the difficulty in navigating through the maze of one-way streets, and the viability of nonmotorized transport modes has decreased sharply. Another example is in Bangkok, where the addition of some new roads and a new light-rail system may benefit the city by alleviating some of the congestion and raising travel speeds. However, the costs of these particular infrastructure additions will include an enormous capital outlay for the city, as well as construction disruptions for years to come. And with the present rate of vehicle fleet growth, these additions will probably not improve the situation unless a comprehensive plan is enacted that affects traffic and growth in all sectors of the city and includes an environmental action plan to improve vehicle emissions and decrease vehicle usage. In sum, it is important to realize that each option recommended by a study team may entail drawbacks and problems in its implementation; thus each study team is attempting to find the combination of measures that will produce the fewest number of drawbacks and the greatest number of pluses.

Since the material for this chapter was originally presented as a paper at the Asilomar Conference on Transportation and Global Climate Change in mid-1991, the IIEC Assessment of Transportation Growth in Asia has been completed. The case studies for the four cities were published in November 1992. Despite the clear differences between these cities, striking similarities in growth trends were found, as well as common features in terms of fuel quality, vehicle technology, policies, institutional structures, and land use patterns. These similarities are detailed in IIEC's final report from the case studies, *Moving Toward Integrated Transport Planning: Energy, Environment, and Mobility in Four Asian Cities*, published in March 1993.

Many options were analyzed by each city to improve their transport system development: land use planning (designing the urban layout to be more amenable to public and nonmotorized transport and to improve citizens' access to needed services); switching to more energy-efficient transport modes (e.g., public and nonmotorized transport); improving the efficiency of the existing transport system (through such measures as traffic management, pricing mechanisms, vehicle movement restrictions, and improved telecommunications systems); building more transport infrastructure (particularly that diverts traffic from city centers); improving the efficiency of individual vehicles (through both technological innovations and improved driving handling and maintenance); and switching to cleaner-burning and alternative fuels. To steer transport system development toward a sustainable future, each city requires an integrated program comprised of a combination of these options.

Although the teams were able to generally assemble a recommended plan of options, the quantitative tools to truly compare the options were found to be lacking. Hence, *Moving Toward Integrated Transport Planning* calls for a new approach to transport planning. The new integrated transport planning approach would view citizens' access to needed urban services as the highest priority, rather than mobility for individual vehicles. To do this, the new approach would require consideration of a wide variety of options to improve access to transport services and would incorporate long-range environmental, energy use, and social impact analyses into all considerations. Finally, to accomplish a radical reorientation of transport trends, an institutional restructuring must come about in many places to ensure control over and implementation of the best available options.

For copies of these reports, contact IIEC at 750 First Street N.E., Suite 940, Washington, D.C. 20002 (telephone 202-842-3388, or fax 202-842-1565).

References

Bangkok Post. 1990a. April 10.

———. 1990b. April 15.

———. 1990c. August 1.

———. 1990d. August 15.

———. 1990e. November 17.

Faiz, Asif, Kumares Sinha, Michael Walsh, and Amiy Varma. 1991. *Automotive Air Pollution: Issues and Options for Developing Countries.* 1990. Washington, D.C.: World Bank. August.

The Nation (Thailand). 1990. April 6.

Philips, Michael. 1991. *The Least-Cost Path for Developing Countries: Energy Efficient Investments for the Multilateral Development Banks.* Washington, D.C.: International Institute for Energy Conservation. September.

TDRI. 1990. *Energy and Environment: Choosing the Right Mix.* Bangkok: Thai Development Research Institute. December.

USDOE. 1987. *Patterns of U.S. Energy Demand.* Washington, D.C.: U.S. Department of Energy, Policy, Planning, and Analysis, Director of Policy Integration. August.

Washington Post Health Magazine. 1991. May 7.

World Bank. 1987a. Staff Appraisal Report #6605-IND, for the Regional Cities Urban Transport Project. Washington, D.C.: World Bank. April.

———. 1987b. *World Development Report.* Washington, D.C.: World Bank.

Chapter 4

Designing Incentive-Based Approaches to Limit Carbon Dioxide Emissions from the Light-Duty Vehicle Fleet

Robin Miles-McLean, Susan M. Haltmaier, and
Michael G. Shelby

Carbon dioxide (CO_2) is one of the major greenhouse gases emitted in the United States,[1] and the light-duty vehicle fleet is responsible for approximately one-third of U.S. CO_2 emissions. This chapter analyzes in detail three incentive-based policy options that would stabilize or reduce emissions of CO_2 from the combustion of gasoline in cars and light trucks: gasoline taxes, a gas guzzler tax/gas sipper rebate program, and an oil import fee. In each case the goal is to reduce such light-duty vehicle emissions to their 1989 level by the year 2000, then maintain that level through 2010.

Two of these policy options—the gasoline tax and the oil import fee—would be revenue producing. Several methods were considered for applying the resulting revenues: reducing the federal deficit, a revenue-raising approach; reducing personal and corporate income taxes, a deficit-neutral approach; and reducing the employer-paid portion of payroll taxes, also a deficit-neutral approach. The *relative* merits of the policy options are the same regardless of the method chosen to handle the

---

This chapter summarizes a large body of work whose principal investigators are the authors plus Roger Brinner, Joyce Yanchar, Bernard Campbell, William Veno, Mary Novak, and David Kelly. For a more extended discussion of issues presented here, see DRI/McGraw-Hill 1991.

[1] CO_2 emissions currently account for 54% of the U.S. contribution to global warming. By 2010, this figure is predicted to rise to 68%. See Cristofaro & Scheraga 1991.

revenues.[2] Here we present the results of recycling revenues via the third method, the employer-paid portion of payroll taxes, which was found to have the smallest overall negative impact on the economy.

For the gas guzzler tax/gas sipper rebate program, a tax/rebate schedule is constructed to be revenue-neutral; the amount of the guzzler taxes is designed to offset the amount of the sipper rebates. For this reason, the macroeconomic impacts are assumed to be negligible.

Methodology

Econometric models of macroeconomic activity and energy demands—estimated within the context of a more detailed analysis of the U.S. transportation sector—are used to analyze the impacts of carbon emission control policies. For the two revenue-producing measures, the required level of tax or import fee needed to stabilize light-duty emissions is determined, absent macroeconomic feedback, using a vintage capital stock model of the U.S. transportation sector (see Figure 4-1).

In this section, we describe the transportation sector model in more detail. This model is premised on the notion that the demand for motor fuels is derived from the demand for travel and consumers' preferences toward particular vehicles, assuming a fixed-budget constraint. Consumers determine the level of travel as well as the vehicle stock composition through their purchase decisions. The projection of segment mix and domestic versus import shares is a function of demographics and the future-product plans, pricing, and distribution strategies of individual manufacturers. These projections define the stock composition and associated efficiency characteristics. In combination with a projection of vehicle usage patterns as a function of population, income, and costs of driving, the level of fuel consumption is determined for each of four vehicle categories (passenger cars and light-, medium-, and heavy-duty trucks).

Estimating Miles per Gallon

Two alternative methods are employed to estimate the responsiveness of stock average miles per gallon to carbon emission control policies. First, an econometric approach estimates new-vehicle mpg as a function of demographics and real fuel prices. An engineering approach that draws on work done by Energy and Environmental Analysis

---

[2] It is not the purpose of this chapter to address the issue of revenue recycling. A detailed look at the macroeconomic consequences of the three approaches to revenue recycling can be found in Brinner et al. 1991.

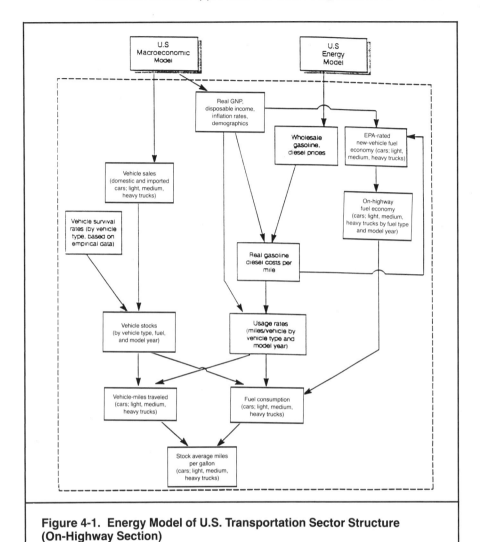

Figure 4-1. Energy Model of U.S. Transportation Sector Structure (On-Highway Section)

(EEA), Inc., of Arlington, Virginia, is incorporated in a model constructed explicitly for this project to validate our econometric estimate of mpg responsiveness. EEA provided us various technology cost curves for each of fourteen segments (seven size categories, for imports and domestics) that give the cumulative cost of adding fuel-saving technologies using only those technologies that are already available in existing car lines or prototypes.

The engineering model examines the cost to manufacturers of installing fuel-saving technologies and the incentives for consumers to switch market segments with higher gasoline prices or gas guzzler taxes. It was found that mpg is slightly less responsive to gasoline price changes in the engineering model than in the econometric model. This difference can be attributed to a "technological drift" captured in the econometric analysis: a gain of roughly 0.5 mpg per year is generated, independent of gasoline price movements. This "drift" may be explained by the introduction of corporate average fuel economy (CAFE) standards in 1978. Others looking at the issue have tested CAFE standards and have found such standards to be significant (see Greene 1989).

Key Assumptions

There are two key decisions employed in the engineering/economic methodology: (1) the choice of a payback period and associated discount rate and (2) how to model segment shift. The discounting assumptions commonly adopted by EEA are used in this analysis: new-car buyers generally consider only the taxes/penalties that accrue in the first four years of vehicle ownership, discounting them by 10%. New-car buyers generally trade their vehicles after approximately four years and would be unconcerned about penalties in subsequent years.

Some analysts argue for a "superrational" consumer who considers the most likely future path of oil prices in his or her new-vehicle purchase decision. In a situation of rising prices, buyers might therefore be inclined to buy more fuel-saving technology than could be justified solely by today's prices. If this is true, the four-year payback and 10% discount rate are too conservative, and a more fuel-efficient vehicle stock would result from a given policy change.

As noted, we assume a fixed-budget constraint in determining the segment mix of new-vehicle purchases: the more drivers spend on fuel, the less they spend on purchasing a vehicle. This constraint is roughly analogous to assuming unitary elasticity for transportation expenditures. There is both empirical and theoretical evidence supporting our fixed-budget constraint. In the 1960s, consumers spent 9.6% of their budget on motor vehicles and motor fuels; twenty years later (that is, in the 1980s), after two significant oil price shocks, the figure was still 9.6%. Furthermore, in the years that gasoline prices rose significantly, the figure was as likely to decline as to increase. Finally, varying the elasticity in this analysis—to as low as 0.6 and as high as 1.4—does not change any of our findings more than 1 mpg in either direction.

Table 4-1. Estimates of EPA-Rated Domestic New-Car Mpg Under Various Gasoline Prices in the Year 2000

Real Gasoline Price (1989$/gallon)	Econometric (mpg)	Engineering (mpg)
$1.30	29.3	29.3
$1.50	30.7	29.8
$1.70	32.0	30.0
$1.90	33.1	32.3
$2.10	34.1	33.1
$2.30	34.9	35.0
$2.50	35.6	36.0

Although the assumption that consumers economize on other transportation spending to offset changes in fuel prices seems reasonable, it is not known how consumers economize. They may buy cheaper, more fuel-efficient vehicles, or they may hold onto vehicles longer. Our methodology "forces" economizing by buying less expensive cars, thereby overstating to some extent the mix-shift implication of rising fuel prices or registration taxes.

It is important to emphasize that the majority of the fuel savings projected in this study comes from adoption of fuel-efficient technology (segment mix savings amount to no more than 18% of total savings or more than 4% of total consumption of gasoline). If we are overestimating these savings, it is a small number. Even relaxing our assumption of unitary elasticity does not significantly affect the findings. For example, assuming that consumers offset only half the incremental cost of a tax/subsidy scheme at the point of purchase (rather than 100%), fuel consumption by 2000 would differ by less than 2%.

Contrasting Projections from Each Approach

Even for the most extreme gas price assessed (a real gasoline price of $2.50 per gallon in 1989 dollars in 2000), the difference in predicted fuel economy between the two approaches was just 0.4 mpg, or roughly 1%. An appraisal of future mpg standards that is rooted in historical analysis of aggregate, fleetwide figures yields an mpg answer remarkably similar to one that focuses on future technological responses implemented at a segment level and the resulting mix shift (see Table 4-1).

Base Case Projections

Although the ultimate target is fuel consumption, not fuel efficiency, a reduction in consumption and associated CO_2 emissions cannot come solely from a reduction in vehicle miles traveled (VMT). Since demand for travel is expected to grow as a result of rising income and population, vehicle fuel efficiency must improve to stabilize or reduce fuel consumption. How significant the improvements must be depends on one's projection of gasoline consumption in the absence of policy changes.

The base case forecast, assuming no policy changes, calls for motor gasoline consumption by cars and trucks to increase at an average rate of about 0.5% per year between 1989 and 2010, slower than the 1.6% growth rate in the 1985–1989 period. The future growth in gasoline consumption is based on a projection of 1.7% per year growth in combined VMT for cars and light trucks and an increase in domestic U.S. Environmental Protection Agency (EPA)–rated new-car mpg[3] from the current 27 mpg to 33.5 mpg by 2010.

Due to the fixed carbon content of gasoline and the absence of tail-pipe carbon control technologies, near-term reductions in light-vehicle CO_2 emissions are tied to reductions in gasoline usage. Discussions about personal transportation and potential greenhouse gases often use the terms *fuel consumption* and *fuel efficiency* interchangeably. Although the two interact, fuel efficiency increases do not guarantee corresponding reductions in fuel consumption. This analysis focuses on the final objective—how to influence fuel consumption. Of the three policies, gasoline taxes and gas guzzler tax/gas sipper rebate programs influence only gasoline consumption, whereas an oil import fee is broader based, raising the price of oil across all sectors—transportation, industrial, utility, and residential/commercial.

Gasoline Taxes

Given the linear relationship between fuel consumption and the emissions of CO_2 (each gallon of gasoline burned releases 19.7 pounds of CO_2), a cents-per-gallon gasoline tax is equivalent to a cents-per-pound pollution (carbon) fee. Moreover, this tax is levied on those who pollute (that is, consume gasoline) and is directly proportional to their emissions. Because the gasoline tax essentially taxes pollution di-

---

[3] EPA currently estimates on-road new-car efficiency at 15% less than the mpg rating found in testing. Phil Patterson of the Department of Energy and Fred Westbrook of Camden Corporation hypothesize that this "shortfall" will increase to 30% by the year 2010. Within this analysis, the 15% shortfall is used in all years and all cases.

rectly, it is the most economically efficient of the two transportation-only policies.

A gasoline tax encourages individuals to reduce usage, buy more fuel-efficient vehicles, and better maintain their cars. The key difference between gasoline taxes and efficiency tax/rebates is that gasoline taxes encourage a reduction in VMT; it is the only policy option considered here that increases the social cost of driving each additional mile.

Although the elasticity of VMT with respect to gasoline prices is small, the CO_2 emission reduction benefits from lower VMT are realized immediately over the whole vehicle stock. Efficiency tax/rebates, in contrast, work only on new-car purchase decisions, and their benefits show up slowly because of the size of the stock relative to the number of vehicles purchased in a given year. For example, in 1990, 14.3 million new cars and light trucks were purchased out of a combined stock of 191.5 million vehicles, or 7.5%.

Impacts of Higher Gasoline Taxes. To reduce CO_2 emissions from light-duty vehicles to 1989 levels by 2000 and hold them there, our analysis estimates that the federal gasoline tax (in 1989$) must rise from $0.09 per gallon in 1989 to $0.40 per gallon by 2000 and $0.50 per gallon by 2010. Between 1989 and 2010, the total retail price of gasoline (in 1989$) grows on average 3.2% per year, from $1.06 per gallon in 1989 to $2.06 per gallon (or $5.57 per gallon in nominal dollars) by 2010 (see Figure 4-2).

With the gasoline taxes designed to be "fiscally neutral" via cuts in the employer-paid portion of payroll taxes, the net impacts on gross national product (GNP), inflation, interest rates, and other economic concepts from baseline levels are minimal. In fact, due to the recycling of the revenues, cumulative GNP over the twenty-year period is slightly higher compared with the baseline. Measured in terms of cumulative discounted real GNP losses per discounted ton of CO_2 reduced, there is close to a $30/ton gain (see Table 4-2).

Higher gasoline prices affect new-vehicle efficiency most strongly in the first ten years of the forecast. EPA-rated new-car mpg rises from 27.8 mpg in 1989 to 32.3 mpg by 2000 and 36.3 mpg by 2010 (see Table 4-3). The projected new-car mpg figures are the econometric estimate of the needed efficiency, not the engineering estimate (see Table 4-1).

Higher prices initially dampen growth in VMT, the product of the number of vehicles on the road and the average number of miles traveled per vehicle. Although average usage remains below the baseline throughout the forecast period, the number of cars and light-duty

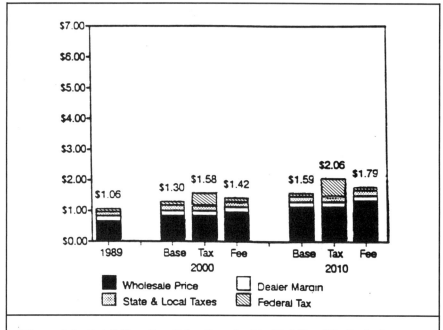

Figure 4-2. Retail Gasoline Price Required to Stabilize CO$_2$ Emissions from Light-Duty Vehicles (1989$/gallon)

Table 4-2. Cumulative Economic Impacts of Stabilizing CO$_2$ Emissions, 1991–2010 (Difference from Base)

Taxes and Fees	Real GNP (bil $)	CO$_2$ Emissions (mil tons)	Real GNP Loss/Ton Reduction ($/ton)	Oil Imports (mil bbls)	Real GNP Loss/Bbl Reduction ($/bbl)
Gasoline tax					
0% discount rate	56	−1,791	−31	−4,199	−13
3% discount rate	34	−1,258	−27	−2,949	−11
Oil import fee					
0% discount rate	105	−1,767	−59	−7,654	−14
3% discount rate	51	−1,242	−41	−5,323	−10

Table 4-3. New-Car EPA-Rated Mpg Required to Stabilize CO$_2$ Emissions			
Scenario	1989	2000	2010
Base case	27.8	30.2	33.5
Gasoline tax		32.3	36.3
Gas guzzler/gas sipper		33.0	37.1
Oil import fee		30.3	34.7

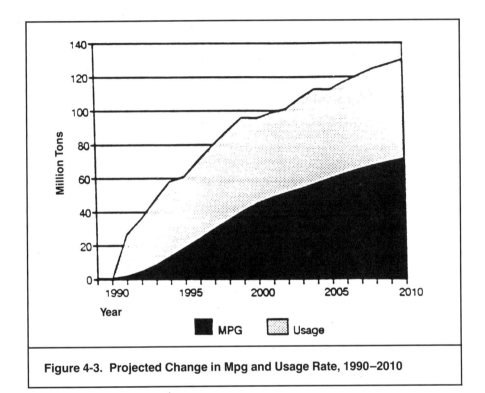

Figure 4-3. Projected Change in Mpg and Usage Rate, 1990–2010

trucks rises above the baseline in the second half of the forecast period because of the positive long-term impact on GNP in this scenario. Growth in total VMT returns to baseline levels after 2000, implying that a rising proportion of the savings in CO$_2$ emissions from holding gasoline consumption constant is coming from higher mpg (see Figure 4-3).

The taxes necessary to maintain constant CO$_2$ emissions forestall

Table 4-4. Projected Change in Passenger Car Segment Mix, 1989–2000 (%)

Car Segment	1989	PROJECTION TO 2000		
		Base Case	Gasoline Tax	Gas Guzzler/ Gas Sipper
Luxury	8.5	11.4	10.9	10.0
Full-size	8.4	7.1	6.5	5.8
Intermediate	23.7	18.6	18.3	16.4
Compact	26.1	31.0	27.3	32.5
Sportscar	6.5	9.8	9.2	8.6
Subcompact	24.4	18.7	22.9	22.5
Minicar	2.4	3.6	4.9	5.7

Table 4-5. Projected Change in Light-Truck and Import Share of Vehicle Mix, 1989–2000 (%)

Vehicle Segment	1989	PROJECTION TO 2000		
		Base Case	Gasoline Tax	Gas Guzzler/ Gas Sipper
Passenger cars	68	65	66	68
Light-duty trucks	31	35	34	32
Domestic	67	56	54	54
Imports	33	44	46	46

much of the projected base case shift into larger cars and largely arrest a twenty-year trend favoring light trucks over passenger cars (see Tables 4-4 and 4-5). In addition, the import car share is higher than the base case by 2000 as a result of the relatively stronger performance of imports in the smaller-vehicle classes.

Holding gasoline consumption constant through 2010 reduces U.S. oil import dependency by 2 percentage points compared with the base case, resulting in an average annual reduction in the oil import bill of $10 billion. The annual trade account improves by a somewhat smaller amount, $4 billion to $9 billion, in part because of the rise in the share of imported cars.

Gas Guzzler Tax/Gas Sipper Rebate

Gas guzzler taxes—paid by buyers of the most fuel-thirsty vehicles—already are imposed in the United States. But the present tax applies to less than 2% of sales, and the manufacturer, not the consumer, pays that tax. Although consumers do see the tax listed on the car's sticker price, they do not have to pay the fee directly and can finance the tax as part of their purchase.

The gas guzzler/gas sipper rebate program envisioned in this analysis would be applied at the time of purchase and be paid by the consumer as a separate fee based on the vehicle's relative miles-per-gallon (mpg) ratings. To the extent that consumers have a high discount rate for up-front capital costs (as suggested by purchasing patterns for fuel-efficient technologies in other sectors, such as appliances), a direct fee that cannot be financed will have a greater impact than the current gas guzzler tax.

The gas guzzler tax/gas sipper rebate program affects fuel consumption quite differently than does a gasoline tax because it targets fuel efficiency, not fuel consumption. The principal advantage of an incentive/disincentive that tangibly affects purchase decisions is that it will lead to a more fuel-efficient vehicle stock more quickly and at less cost than any other mechanism.

But there also can be perverse effects on usage and new-car sales. All else being equal, increased fuel efficiency makes it cheaper to drive, which increases VMT.[4] Furthermore, the program would encourage new cars to incorporate more fuel-efficient technologies, raising the average price of new cars, which could discourage new-vehicle purchases. These perverse effects occur because the efficiency tax/rebate scheme does not force consumers to equate the marginal social cost of pollution reduction with the value of the corresponding reductions.

Higher new-car prices also would encourage segment shifts into smaller-vehicle classes. Such segment shifts could raise the share of imports in new-vehicle sales, partially offsetting the trade benefits of

---

[4] Two studies of this effect concluded that the elasticity of gasoline demand with respect to vehicle efficiency was in the -0.7 to -0.8 range. That is, a 10% improvement in efficiency would result in a 7% to 8% reduction in gasoline consumption. Therefore, 20% to 30% of the potential reduction in consumption would be offset by an increase in miles driven. A more recent analysis by David Greene of Oak Ridge National Laboratory suggests that this rebound effect has been declining over time and could be as small as 5% in recent years. In this analysis, DRI used an elasticity of -0.915, implying a rebound effect of 8.5%. See Blair et al. 1984; Mayo & Mathis 1988; Greene 1992.

reduced oil imports. By design, both a gasoline tax and a guzzler/sipper scheme would achieve the same target reduction in CO_2 emissions and thus lower oil imports by an equal amount. But because a gas guzzler tax/gas sipper rebate scheme meets the target solely through efficiency gains, it is likely to cause a larger segment shift than a gasoline tax that operates on both efficiency and miles traveled.

Determination of a Tax/Subsidy Program. A tax/subsidy schedule is determined using a four-step approach. First, the target new-car average mpg figures needed to stabilize CO_2 are calculated via repeated solutions of the U.S. transportation sector model. Second, the schedule of gas guzzler taxes necessary to achieve the goals is quantified by iterative solutions of manufacturer and consumer responses to such taxes.

Using EEA's technology cost curves, manufacturers are assumed to add technology until the cost associated with adding one more technology exceeds the tax savings that would accrue as a result of adding this technology. For instance, if the program imposed a $75-per-mpg tax (from some base fuel-efficient standard), all technologies that cost less than $75 per mpg improvement (according to EEA) are adopted.

The consumers' response is based on the assumption of a fixed-budget constraint: to the extent that drivers spend more on registration taxes, they will spend less on the purchase prices of the vehicles. Once the new segment mix is determined, we are able to estimate a sales-weighted, EPA-rated mpg value that explicitly incorporates technical feasibility and expected changes in consumer behavior. This provides a first estimate of the tax schedule necessary to achieve the goal. However, the marginal benefit from buying a vehicle with one extra mpg falls as mpg rises, all other things being equal. The third step refines the simulations to provide different mpg penalties across the vehicle range, based on a mean calculated in the first estimate of the tax schedule. This refinement often yields a new mean and slight shifts in the overall schedule. The process concludes once the schedule provides consumers and manufacturers with the correct signals *and* achieves the mpg goals.

The fourth step adds the gas sipper rebates to the penalty schedules to make the program revenue-neutral. This step estimates the number of vehicles sold into each segment, ascribes an average penalty or subsidy to each segment, and iterates until subsidies equal penalties, while maintaining the marginal penalties determined in step three.

Impacts of a Tax/Subsidy Program. The penalty/subsidy schedule that achieves the needed new-car mpgs is shown in Table 4-6. The pen-

Table 4-6. Gas Guzzler/Gas Sipper Tax Schedules to Achieve Needed New-Car Mpgs (1989$)

Penalty/ Subsidy	Marginal Penalty	NEW-CAR MPG 1993	2000
(395)	53	45	50
(341)	54	44	49
(286)	55	43	48
(230)	56	42	47
(173)	57	41	46
(115)	58	40	45
(56)	59	39	44
4	60	38	43
65	61	37	42
128	63	36	41
193	65	35	40
260	67	34	39
329	69	33	38
400	71	32	37
472	72	31	36
546	74	30	35
621	75	29	34
699	78	28	33
781	82	27	32
868	87	26	31
960	92	25	30
1,055	95	24	29
1,154	99	23	28
1,259	105	22	27
1,364	105	21	26
1,469	105	20	25

alties/subsidies average $75 per mpg (in 1989$). In 1993, the highest penalty ($1,469) applies to 20-mpg cars, and the largest subsidy ($395) is given to buyers of 45-mpg cars. By 2000, these figures rise to 25 and 50 mpg, respectively. The marginal penalty ranges from $53 for the highest-mpg car to $105 for the lowest-mpg car.

Since the efficiency tax/rebate program is revenue-neutral, its costs must be measured in terms of the different vehicle characteristics that consumers are able to choose from compared with those in an unconstrained marketplace. The cost of the program is the value of the vehicle's attributes—for example, performance—that consumers forego. Directly comparing the costs of this approach with those of a gasoline tax is difficult. But we can look at the differences in new-vehicle efficiencies that would be required to stabilize CO_2 emissions by 2000.

Gasoline consumption, CO_2 emissions, and oil imports all decline by the same magnitudes in this scenario as under a gasoline tax. But, without the disincentive of higher gasoline taxes, vehicle miles traveled grow faster than in the gasoline tax scenario so that the reduction in gasoline consumption must come from better mpg alone.

In addition, the necessary efficiency gains would have to be realized well before the target date, since a gas guzzler tax/gas sipper rebate program affects only new-vehicle purchases, and the ratio of such purchases to the vehicle stock is less than 10% in any given year. EPA-rated new-car mpg must rise to 33.0 mpg by 2000 and 37.1 mpg by 2010 to hold CO_2 emissions at the 1989 level in this case, compared with 32.3 mpg and 36.3 mpg, respectively, in the gasoline tax case (see Table 4-3).

Adoption of fuel-efficient technologies does not, by itself, achieve the mpg targets, so the segment mix of vehicles sold would have to shift. To hold CO_2 constant by 2000, 80% of the reduction would be achieved by adopting fuel-efficient technologies that would add about $300 to the price of a vehicle; the remaining 20% would be achieved by mix shift.

A similar reversal of the projected base case trend toward larger cars that is observed in the gasoline tax case would occur in this scenario, leading to the same increase in import share as in the gasoline tax case. But the share of light-vehicle sales accounted for by light-duty trucks would not grow very much above the 1989 level by 2000 (see Tables 4-4 and 4-5). Since the reduction in gasoline consumption, by design, is the same with both a gasoline tax and a gas guzzler tax/gas sipper rebate program and the increase in the share of imported vehicles is projected to be the same with both policy options, the impacts on the U.S. trade balance are similar.

Oil Import Fee

An oil import fee is broader based than either of the other two policy options in that it raises the price of imported oil in all uses. Since the transportation sector represents nearly 65% of total oil use, this option will provide strong incentives to reduce transportation fuel use. However, an oil import fee will raise oil prices and affect oil consumption in other sectors throughout the economy.

Like a gasoline tax, an oil import fee taxes pollution directly. But, unlike a gasoline tax, an oil import fee may provide the wrong long-term incentive in other sectors to switch from oil to more carbon-intensive fuels. For example, burning coal releases approximately 20% more CO_2 than burning an equivalent amount of oil, whereas burning natural gas releases approximately 30% less carbon.

The broad-based nature of the oil import fee also causes more inflation than a gasoline tax. An oil import fee sends price increases rippling through a wide variety of markets, including transportation fuels, home heating oil, and electricity, and influences the prices of energy-intensive goods and services as producers pass through the higher costs to consumers.

Compared with the other policies examined, the oil import fee directly stimulates investment in mining and petroleum structures, partially offsetting investment cutbacks in other sectors, as the oil price received by domestic producers rises to the after-tax imported price. The additional investment enables the United States to meet more of its domestic energy needs from domestic supplies, further reducing U.S. dependence on imported oil.

On a balance-of-trade basis, the inflationary effect of an import fee would show up in U.S. export prices for energy-intensive goods and services, resulting in a loss of U.S. competitiveness that could partially offset the savings in oil imports. And, to the extent that lost U.S. exports would be replaced by energy-intensive exports from other countries, the emissions reductions in the United States would be offset by emissions increases elsewhere. With a transportation-only policy, there is less likely to be an export of carbon emissions since personal mobility cannot readily be traded across national boundaries.

Impacts of an Oil Import Fee. In the oil import fee scenario, the objective was to achieve the same path of emissions reductions as in the gasoline tax case. Since the target was to stabilize gasoline-based CO_2 emissions at 1989 levels by 2000, the import fee needed to rise faster in the first ten years of the forecast period than after 2000. The initial fee in 1991 was set at $2.88 in 1989$ ($3.10 in nominal dollar terms). To stabilize emissions, the import fee (in 1989$) had to rise to $5.66 by 2000 and $8.40 by 2010. By 2010, the fee raised the price of crude oil 24% above the base case.

As with a gasoline tax, an oil import fee depresses macroeconomic activity in the short term, although the inflation offset provided by the payroll tax reduction softens the negative economic effect. In the longer term, interest rates are higher (and the economy's supply potential lower) than in the base case. Real GNP drops only 0.2% in the near term and rises 0.5% above the baseline by 2005 and thereafter. On a discounted dollar-per-ton basis, there is a slight gain to the economy that is approximately the same as with a gasoline tax (see Table 4-2).

By 2010, total energy consumption is nearly the same as in the gasoline tax case, about 2% lower than the baseline. Reduced transportation sector demand accounts for about two-thirds of the decline, whereas the residential and commercial sectors together account for 17%. Lower industrial consumption contributes another 11%, and the utility sector the remaining 5%.

Overall, CO_2 emissions from coal combustion are 2% higher, emissions from natural gas are 1% lower, and emissions from oil are 5.5% lower than the base case. In the gasoline tax case, even though all of the reduction comes from lower oil consumption, there is no increase in CO_2 emissions from coal so that CO_2 emissions from oil consumption are only 4% lower than the base case.

If the goal were to reduce oil imports for energy security reasons, then the oil import fee would be a better tool than a gasoline tax because of its broad base. Since the prices of all oil products rise with a fee, the reductions in oil consumption could come from the places where fuel substitution is easiest. For a given level of oil savings, the cost to the economy would be lower with a fee than with a tax on gasoline since the demand for gasoline is relatively inelastic.

But the goal is a reduction in carbon emissions, and the substitution of coal for oil in the industrial and electric utility sectors has a cost in terms of CO_2 emissions. Furthermore, users of oil can avoid the fee not only by fuel switching, but also by reducing usage, increasing efficiency, or some combination of the three. Therefore, there is not much incentive to introduce less carbon-intensive technologies. For example, in the gasoline tax case, new-car EPA-rated mpg rose 8% above the baseline figure by 2010. In the fee case, new-car mpg is only 3.5% higher (see Table 4-3).

Because oil consumption must be lowered by more than in the other cases to account for the rise in coal consumption, the oil import savings are larger. Oil import savings with the import fee rise to 1.5 million barrels per day by 2010, almost twice the 0.8 million barrels per day that are saved in the gasoline tax and gas guzzler/gas sipper cases. In spite of the greater savings in oil imports, the resulting improvement in the trade account is about the same size as in the gasoline tax case because of the energy-related rise in export prices.

Conclusions

Incentive-based policies can be designed to reduce CO_2 emissions with small overall long-term costs to the U.S. economy. The broad-based nature of the oil import fee is a disadvantage when used as a proxy for a carbon tax because it encourages substitution into coal, a higher-carbon fuel. Of the transportation-only policies, a gasoline tax is preferable to a gas guzzler tax/gas sipper rebate program because a gasoline tax is directly proportional to the level of emissions.

Although the guzzler/sipper approach leads to a more fuel-efficient vehicle stock more quickly and at less cost than other options, it has perverse effects on usage and, by extension, fuel consumption. The guzzler/sipper scheme also has the largest impact on segment mix and import car share. Although it is difficult to quantify the costs associated with the loss of consumer utility from driving more fuel-efficient cars, there could be negative trade implications from a rise in the import car share.

To reduce emissions of carbon dioxide from fossil fuel combustion, a policy that taxes carbon emissions directly will have smaller long-term costs than other options. In this analysis, a gasoline tax is such a policy.

References

Blair, Roger, et al. 1984. "The Impact of Improved Mileage on Gasoline Consumption." *Economic Inquiry*. April.

Brinner, Roger, et al. 1991. "Optimizing Tax Strategies to Reduce Greenhouse Gases Without Curtailing Growth." *Energy Journal* 12 (4).

Cristofaro, Alex, and Joel Scheraga. 1991. "Policy Implications of a Greenhouse Gas Budget." *Forum for Applied Research and Public Policy*. Fall.

DRI/McGraw-Hill. 1991. "An Analysis of Public Policy Measures to Reduce Carbon Dioxide Emissions from the U.S. Transportation Sector." Prepared for the U.S. Environmental Protection Agency, Office of Policy, Planning and Evaluation, Energy Policy Branch. January.

Greene, David. 1989. "CAFE or Price." *Energy Journal* 11.

————. 1992. "Vehicle Use and Fuel Economy: How Big Is the Rebound Effect?" *Energy Journal* 13 (1).

Mayo, John W., and John E. Mathis. 1988. "The Effectiveness of Mandatory Fuel Efficiency Standards in Reducing the Demand for Gasoline." *Applied Economics* 20 (Feb.): 211–19.

Chapter 5

IC Engines and Fuels for Cars and Light Trucks: 2015

John L. Mason

ersuasive national reasons exist for increased U.S. attention to
vehicular fuel economy. These include balance of payments,
energy security, and concern about the impact of atmospheric
carbon dioxide (CO_2) build-up on global climate change. Passenger
cars and light trucks, together called light vehicles, are the largest
energy-using segment of the U.S. transportation fleet, being responsible in 1989 for 92% of the energy consumed in domestic transportation
and 25% of the total U.S. energy consumption (Davis & Morris 1992,
2-12, 2-13).

This chapter explores the limits of engine fuel economy obtainable
with internal combustion (IC) engines, both gasoline and diesel, of the
type in use today in light vehicles. Competitive combustion engine
types, such as gas turbine and Stirling, are not covered. The title not-
withstanding, this chapter contains no predictions with respect to what
will happen by the year 2015. Rather, the purpose is to indicate what
could be done technologically by 2015 if the market and economic
conditions were right.

Customer wants and attitudes are an important ingredient of the
vehicle marketplace, as are the overall economic situation and the regulatory environment. Vehicle manufacturers' perceptions of customer
wants and attitudes therefore influence the direction and rate of engine
improvement. It is no secret that today's U.S. car and light-truck customers are not vitally interested in fuel economy. Figure 5-1 illustrates
this point by comparing attitudes toward fuel economy in two different
vehicular market areas: heavy-duty (commercial) vehicles and light
vehicles.

For highly utilized commercial vehicles, such as heavy trucks and

Commercial-vehicle customers

- must make a profit
- must live with price competition
- see fuel consumption as an element of cost
- value fuel economy

Light-vehicle customers

- see fuel cost as low and affordable
- typically put fuel economy fourth or fifth on their want list

Figure 5-1. Fuel Economy as Seen by International Commercial-Vehicle and U.S. Light-Vehicle Customers

large jet aircraft, the cost of fuel is a substantial part of vehicle operating cost. Wherever there is price competition for transportation services, commercial users are forced to pay close attention to all costs, and so engine fuel economy becomes an important design objective. Certainly in theory and to a degree in practice, international commercial engine designers and users evaluate fuel economy improvements in terms of their cost of incorporation and their net value to the user over the vehicle life.

With light vehicles in the United States, the situation is different. Figure 5-2 shows that the total cost of driving a passenger car in the United States in 1989 was about 36 cents per mile, of which about 5 cents, or 14%, was spent for gasoline and oil. In 1975, gasoline and oil amounted to 26% of the 40-cents-per-mile total cost (Davis & Morris 1992, 2-37). As long as fuel prices remain low, the majority of light-vehicle owners will not be motivated to care much about the fuel economy of the vehicles they buy.

Much of the recent research and development on IC engines has been directed toward low emissions. For the foreseeable future, emission legislation is likely to continue to have great influence on the design of IC engines. Consideration of alternative fuels will also continue to be largely emission driven. The light-vehicle IC engine will likely face competition from battery-electric propulsion systems, especially in emission-plagued regions. California has already mandated a 2% market share of newly sold zero-emission vehicles (battery-electric vehicles or those with equivalent emissions) by model year 1998, and 10% by model year 2003 (Lents & Abe 1992, 3).

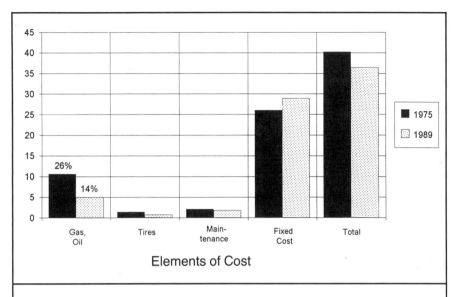

Figure 5-2. Passenger-Car Operating Costs, 1975 and 1989 (Cents/Mile—1988$)

Source: Davis & Morris (1992, 2–37).

This chapter first discusses ideal and actual engine cycles and the differences between them, which will narrow with time. A look at selected IC engine technologies and the prospects for their improvement follows. The final section presents conclusions and recommendations.

Ideal and Actual Engine Cycles

Figures 5-3 and 5-4 show pressure-volume (PV) diagrams for three air-standard ideal cycles: (1) the constant-volume cycle, (2) the limited-pressure cycle, and (3) the constant-pressure cycle. The constant-volume cycle is associated with spark ignition (SI) engines. The limited-pressure and constant-pressure cycles are associated with diesel engines.

Ideal cycles define the upper limit of achievable efficiency of real SI and diesel engines. They give some indication of the dependence of real engine performance on compression ratio. By comparison with real engines, they give some indication of where to look for efficiency improvements.

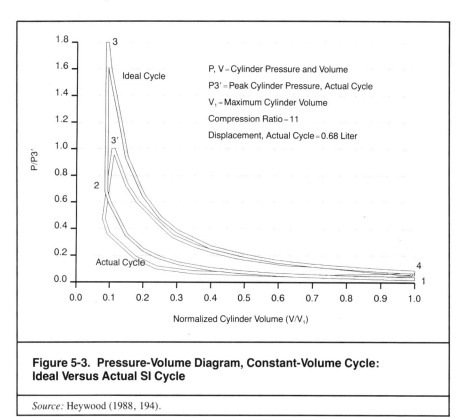

Figure 5-3. Pressure-Volume Diagram, Constant-Volume Cycle: Ideal Versus Actual SI Cycle

Source: Heywood (1988, 194).

Besides the constant-volume ideal cycle, Figure 5-3 shows for comparison an indicator diagram of an actual 0.68-liter engine (Heywood 1988, 194). The two cycle diagrams of Figure 5-3 have the same compression ratio, 11. For the ideal constant-volume cycle, isentropic compression takes place between point 1 (bottom center, BC) and point 2 (top center, TC), followed by constant-volume heat addition at TC between points 2 and 3, simulating combustion in real engines. This is followed by an isentropic expansion between points 3 and 4. The final step, from point 4 to point 1 of the ideal cycle, is heat removal, simulating blowdown followed by exhaust in real engines. The real indicator diagram has a lower peak pressure than does the ideal cycle. The latter is assumed to be adiabatic.

In Figure 5-4 for the limited-pressure ideal cycle, steps 4–1 and 1–2 are the same as for the ideal constant-volume cycle of Figure 5-3. The compression ratio in the cycles of Figure 5-4 is 18, a representative number for diesel cycles. Step $2–3_{LP}$ (limited pressure) is constant-

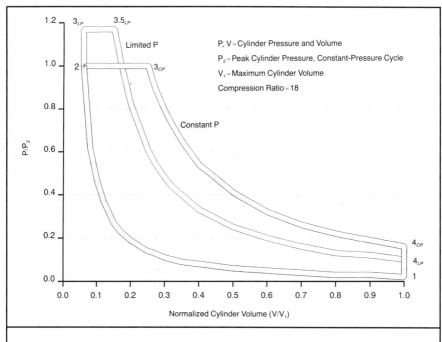

Figure 5-4. Pressure-Volume Diagram: Limited- and Constant-Pressure Cycles

Source: Heywood (1988, 174).

volume heat addition (combustion) up to a limiting pressure, point 3_{LP}. This is followed by completion of heat addition (combustion) at constant pressure, in step 3_{LP}–3.5_{LP}.

The constant-pressure cycle, also shown in Figure 5-4, differs from the limited-pressure cycle only in having all of its combustion at constant pressure, between points 2 and 3_{CP}.

Figure 5-5 shows energy conversion efficiency (η) defined as power output per unit (HV * fuel flow) versus compression ratio (r_c) for the three ideal cycles: constant volume, limited pressure, and constant pressure. For all three cycles, η depends on r_c and specific heat ratio (k). For the constant-volume ideal cycle, η is a function of only these two variables:

$$\eta = 1 - \frac{1}{r_c^{k-1}}$$

The specific heat ratio k is 1.4 for air at room temperature. If one value

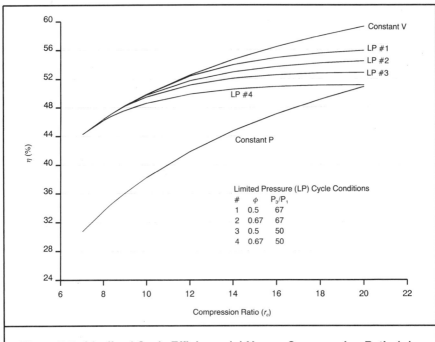

Figure 5-5. Idealized Cycle Efficiency (η) Versus Compression Ratio (r_c)

Source: Heywood (1988, 175).

is to be used for k for SI engines, the recommended value is 1.3, for both compression and expansion (Heywood 1988, 173). For the other two cycles, additional independent variables are necessary to define η, and the equations are more complex than the above. The equations defining η for the limited-pressure and constant-pressure cycles are given in most IC engine texts (Ferguson 1986, 75–77).

For the limited-pressure cycle, η may be given as a function of r_c, k, and two additional dimensionless variables, $\alpha = (P_{3LP}/P_1)$, and $\beta = (HV\ \phi/RT_1)$, where

P_{3LP} = upper limiting pressure in cycle
P_1 = pressure at point 1 in cycle
T_1 = absolute temperature at point 1 in cycle
HV = fuel (lower) heating value
R = gas constant for air
ϕ = fuel-air equivalence ratio

To show the effect of these two added independent variables, Figure 5-5 has four curves for the limited-pressure cycle, made up of combinations of two values of $\alpha = (P_{3LP}/P_1)$, 50 and 67, and two values of the fuel-air equivalence ratio, ϕ, 0.50 and 0.67.

For the constant-pressure cycle, η is a function of r_c, k, and $\beta = (HV \, \phi/RT_1)$. In Figure 5-5, η is plotted versus r_c for $\phi = 0.67$, which is below the maximum allowable smoke-limiting ϕ for diesel engines (Heywood 1988, 492).

Figure 5-5 shows that the constant-volume cycle has the highest energy conversion efficiency of the three ideal cycles shown, at all compression ratios. In the ideal cycle, combustion is assumed to take place instantaneously at TC. In real SI engines, the duration of combustion is about $30°$ to $40°$ of crank travel (more or less independent of engine rpm) so that combustion takes place both before and after TC (Ferguson 1986, 211–15). Anything that would reduce burn time and yet maintain stable combustion would get the SI engine a little closer to the ideal of constant-volume combustion. More important, reduced burn time would reduce the potential for knock, and thereby enable operation at higher compression ratios than are practical today. With today's production engines and fuels, the knock limit on compression ratio is of the order of 9 to 10 (Heywood 1988, 492). The potential for compression ratio improvement of SI engines, and the obstacles thereto, will be covered in the next section.

In diesel engines, the knock phenomenon does not limit compression ratio. Practical compression ratios of 16 to 18 and higher are routine. Fuel injection and ignition in the diesel engine are such that a good part of the combustion takes place near TC, with the remainder taking place after TC during the expansion stroke. This timing of the combustion event fits the relatively efficient limited-pressure ideal cycle better than the constant-pressure ideal cycle (Obert 1973, 144).

Figure 5-5 shows that limited-pressure ideal-cycle energy conversion efficiency increases with increasing $\alpha = (P_{3LP}/P_1)$. Limitations to α are those imposed by diesel engine structural weight and cost, especially with turbocharging.

The limited-pressure ideal cycle also shows an energy conversion efficiency increase with decreasing ϕ. (The magnitude of the dependence on ϕ decreases with increasing $\alpha = (P_{3LP}/P_1)$. If α is high enough, the limited-pressure ideal cycle approaches the constant-volume cycle, which has no dependence on ϕ.) At any given rpm, the power output of diesel engines is reduced by reducing fuel flow without throttling airflow, therefore by reducing ϕ. This means that diesel engines operate at part load with no cycle-derived loss mechanism.

Recapping, to achieve high ideal-cycle efficiency in the SI engine,

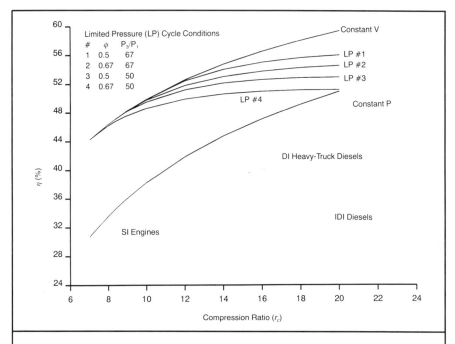

Figure 5-6. Peak Efficiency of IC Engines Versus Compression Ratio (r_c)

Source: Duret, Ecomard, & Audinet (1988); Heywood (1988, 797); Robbins & Salter (1974); Thomson et al. (1987).

we aim for high compression ratio; to achieve high ideal-cycle efficiency in the diesel engine (which already has high compression ratios), we aim for high $\alpha = (P_{3LP}/P_1)$.

Figure 5-6 shows the energy conversion efficiency (η) of several vehicular IC engines, calculated from the point of lowest specific fuel consumption (sfc) for each engine. Both gasoline and diesel engines are shown. The bounding ideal-cycle curves are carried over from Figure 5-5 for reference.

The SI and diesel engines have a number of imperfections and limitations in common. Loss mechanisms in two categories cause the engines to deviate from the matching ideal cycles shown in Figures 5-5 and 5-6. The loss mechanisms can be grouped into two categories:

Category 1. Those affecting the indicated performance of the real engine, and causing it to deviate from the indicated performance of the corresponding ideal cycle:

- heat transfer from the burning and expanding gases to the cooled cylinder wall

- nonoptimal timing of release of combustion heat

- exhaust gas blowdown losses

- incomplete combustion, including that resulting from cylinder-to-cylinder and cycle-to-cycle variations

- leakage

Category 2. Those that together make up the difference between indicated and brake (actual) SI engine performance:

- rubbing friction

- pumping losses (affected by pressure losses in the inlet and exhaust valves, by turbocharging, and by other factors)

- power to drive accessories

The size of the losses in the two categories should give some idea of the potential for efficiency improvement. The category 1 losses, representing the difference between the energy conversion efficiencies of the ideal and actual indicated cycles, typically were found to be 11 percentage points (53% ideal efficiency, less 42% actual efficiency) and 17 percentage points (53% ideal efficiency, less 36% actual efficiency) by testing of two representative SI engines (Caris & Nelson 1959; Kerley & Thurston 1962). By rule of thumb, the indicated real-cycle efficiency is about 80% of the ideal-cycle efficiency. This would correspond closely to the 11% loss quoted above.

Category 2 losses have been obtained from engine data as a percentage of real indicated mean effective pressure (IMEP) for 1.6-liter engines, SI and diesel (Heywood 1988, 713). At 1800 rpm and 6 bar brake mean effective pressure (BMEP), they were found to be 15% of IMEP for the SI engine and 16% of IMEP for the diesel. Not surprisingly, percentage losses were much higher at part load than at full load. At 1800 rpm and 2 bar BMEP (about 25% of rated power), the category 2 losses were 42% of IMEP for the SI engine and 38% of IMEP for the diesel. The high losses for the SI engine include pumping losses because of throttling.

The above losses would be consistent with an SI engine at compression ratio 12, with 53% ideal efficiency, about 40% actual indicated efficiency, and about 34% brake energy conversion efficiency. A diesel with a compression ratio of 16 to 20 would have an ideal efficiency of 55% to 56%, an indicated efficiency of 44% to 45%

(taking the diesel category 1 loss as 11 percentage points, per rule of thumb) and a brake energy conversion efficiency of 37% to 38%. These efficiencies are not far from the best efficiencies of today's light-vehicle engines.

Technology Improvement Possibilities

Alternative Fuels

This section describes ways in which IC engine technology may be improved. Topics include alternative fuels, various engine cycles, part-load fuel economy, and other mechanical technologies and devices.

Three of the leading-candidate alternative fuels for IC engines are ethanol, methane, and methanol. Hydrogen, also proposed as an alternative fuel, is not covered in this chapter. Hydrogen produces no CO_2 and has other attractive features as an automobile fuel. Hydrogen also has drawbacks, chief of which is cost.

The interest in alternative fuels for the sake of emissions reduction is well known. The issue to be addressed here is whether these fuels can also be used to improve IC engine energy conversion efficiency.

Alternative fuels can be used in two ways. The first is to retrofit existing SI engines to convert them to the new fuel. This could be a way to get low-emission performance into the existing fleet without waiting years for the fleet to turn over. However, the impact on engine fuel economy would be minimal. Typically, the result would be a simple one-for-one trade of gasoline Btu's for alternative fuel Btu's.

The second way to use an alternative fuel is to design a new engine tailored to the advantages of the specific alternative fuel. Each of the candidate alternative fuels has the potential for high octane ratings compared with commercially available gasolines, as illustrated in Table 5-1.

The estimated knock-limited SI engine r_c in Table 5-1 was derived from the rule of thumb of 1 allowable ratio increase for every 5 points increase in research octane number (RON) above gasoline (Heywood 1988, 478). Obviously, this rule provides only a rough order-of-magnitude estimate. Even a two-ratio increase (from 9 to 11) will show a good improvement in operating efficiency. A goal of 12 is suggested for an SI engine designed for an alternative fuel. This is ambitious but should be achievable.

Mixing of one of the alcohols into gasoline may be desirable as a low-level octane improver but does not appear to have the potential to get much above 10 in compression ratio.

Table 5-1. Estimated Compression Ratios for Gasoline and Three Alternative Fuels

Fuel	Res. Oct. No.	Estimated r_c
Gasoline	95	9
Methanol	106	11
Ethanol	107	11
Methane	120	14

Source: Heywood (1988, 915).

Some of the problems that could be expected in use of alternative fuels for SI engines (not all applicable to all fuels) are (1) cost of the fuel itself and of a new fuel infrastructure, (2) on-board storage problems, (3) ignition problems, (4) refueling time and complexity, (5) materials compatibility, and (6) with some fuels, possibly safety. Alternative-fuel research and development must resolve these problems if alternative fuels are to be accepted in light-vehicle engines.

With regard to operation at increased compression ratio, practical problems exist, such as the sensitivity of high-compression engines to knock-inducing internal deposits that accumulate in service.

Diesel Engines

In the United States and worldwide, the direct-injection (DI) diesel engine is dominant in heavy-duty vehicles. Peak energy conversion efficiencies of 40% were reported in production engines in the United States as long ago as the 1970s (Robbins & Salter 1974). The best engines in use today are about two points better (Okino, Okada & Abe 1985; Schittler 1985). Unlike the SI engine, the diesel, being unthrottled, has excellent part-load fuel economy.

Outside the United States, small indirect-injection (IDI) diesel engines are used in light vehicles, with peak energy conversion efficiencies typically in the range of 34% to 35% (Grandinson & Hedin 1982). Besides exhaust emissions, the diesel engine has some well-known drawbacks that have made it unattractive to the U.S. automobile user. Included are weight, cost, noise, exhaust smoke and odor, the time required to start the engine at low temperatures, and lackluster transient performance.

The most important obstacle to the use of the diesel engine in U.S. light vehicles is regulated exhaust emissions, especially particulates and NO_x. Existing NO_x reduction catalysts will not work in the excess oxygen that is present in diesel exhausts. The low temperature of diesel engine exhausts at part load (500° F and lower) is also a negative with respect to catalyst function.

With regard to diesel engine emissions, it is predicted that the best efforts of engine technologists will not provide technology that would permit an untreated emissions-compliant diesel for the U.S. light-vehicle market. (This is the author's subjective opinion, based as much on estimates of the future of emissions legislation in the United States as on technical factors, such as the chemistry of combustion in the diesel engine.) If this is the case, the only way to use the diesel in the light-vehicle market is to develop and apply emerging exhaust emission treatment technologies. These will be needed for commercial diesels in any event. They include

- regenerable particulate traps (Stiglic 1990).

- zeolite catalytic converters for NO_x reduction, together with exhaust treatment with chemical injectants such as ammonia. This approach has been tested in Germany, on a commercial vehicular diesel (Lepperhoff, Hüthwohl & Pischinger 1992).

- exhaust gas recirculation for NO_x reduction. A U.S. industry consortium is now investigating this possibility for commercial vehicular diesels.

The above investigations are all in the feasibility stage. If feasible, their cost-effectiveness as applied to light-vehicle diesels would still have to be established.

Other work can be done to improve the acceptability of the diesel engine to light-vehicle users, but the essential problem to be solved is regulated emissions. If the emissions work is successful, the diesel should be a candidate for use in a portion of the 3.9 million light trucks that are sold annually in the United States (Davis & Morris 1992, 3–7).

Two-Stroke Engines

The two-stroke engine has inherent advantages of compactness and simplicity. Two-stroke engines require their cylinder charge air to be supplied at a positive pressure relative to the engine exhaust, because the charge air has to be able to scavenge the engine cylinder of exhaust gas near the end of the expansion stroke.

In the form used in small outboard and similar engines, the scavenging air is provided through the crankcase, which is pressurized by downward stroke of the piston. The scavenging air contains a carbureted mixture of fuel and oil. The result is an inevitable loss of some fresh charge by short-circuiting from the engine inlet to the exhaust port. The unburned fuel and oil swept out with the charge result in excessive hydrocarbon exhaust emissions and fuel consumption.

This problem may be avoided by direct injection of fuel into the engine cylinders and use of a conventional lubrication system. The charge air then contains no hydrocarbons. A small loss of charge air is tolerable, as long as it does not contain fuel and oil. (Direct injection can of course be applied to four-stroke engines but does not fill the critical need that it does for a two-stroke engine, as just described.)

A number of organizations are said to be working on direct-injection stratified-charge (DISC) two-stroke engines (*Automotive News* 1991). One has reported a novel laboratory engine in the 1-liter class with air-pressurized direct fuel injection, a compression ratio of 7.88, and a peak energy conversion efficiency of 32% (Duret, Eco-mard & Audinet 1988).

One favorable outcome of the DISC development would be an engine with stable combustion at very low equivalence ratios (ϕ), so that, like the diesel, it could operate all the way down to idle without being throttled. Avoidance of throttling losses is one of the better ways of improving part-load fuel economy of an SI engine.

Turbocharging

Turbocharging boosts power output of an IC engine by raising the inlet air density. In many turbocharger applications, there is also a measurable (but not large) favorable impact on fuel consumption, in that the turbocharger creates a positive pressure differential across the engine. That is, the inlet manifold pressure is greater than the exhaust manifold pressure. This is a reversal of the pumping power loss that detracts from the energy conversion efficiency of a naturally aspirated engine cycle.

By boosting power output, a turbocharger can give to a small-displacement SI engine a level of performance close to that of a large-displacement, naturally aspirated engine of the same rated horsepower. The turbocharged small-displacement SI engine will have a substantial edge in fuel economy over the large, naturally aspirated engine but will probably cost more.

Turbocharging is used in the great majority of heavy-commercial-vehicle diesel engines. Turbocharging is also popular with light-vehicle diesels (in countries where diesels are used in light vehicles) to get a level of performance for the diesel that is competitive with SI engines. Maximum turbocharger boost pressure for vehicular diesel engines typically ranges from 1 to 3 atmospheres gauge, depending on the application.

Issues have been raised about the applicability of turbochargers to SI engines in light vehicles. These issues will now be explored. Only about 1% to 2% of the U.S. SI light-vehicle fleet is turbocharged. One reason for this is the limited turbocharger boost and/or reduced compression ratio necessary in an SI engine to avoid knocking. With today's fuels, the light-vehicle SI engine maximum boost pressure is typically 0.5 to 0.8 atmospheres gauge. (Compare this with the diesel boost figures given above.)

Also, to avoid knocking, a turbocharged SI engine is typically designed with retarded spark timing and/or with a compression ratio reduced by as much as 1 below the compression ratio of a comparable naturally aspirated engine run with the same fuel (Dertian, Holiday & Sanburn 1979, 9; Allen & Rinschler 1984, 29). Following are two ways (usable together) of recouping any reduction in r_c:

1. *Charge air cooling (intercooling).* This provides a further increase in charge air density beyond that obtainable from turbocharging alone. Charge air cooling is also a direct way of reducing knock tendency of a turbocharged SI engine because decreased charge air temperature correlates directly with decrease in knock.

2. *Water injection into or immediately upstream of the engine inlet air.* Like charge air cooling, this reduces cylinder air temperature and therefore directly reduces knock tendency. Water injection was successfully used in an early turbocharger application (Lewis, Burrell & Ball 1962, 5). Engine compression ratio was 10.5, albeit on premium fuel. Water consumption was 0.13 to 1.3 gallons per thousand miles. The water injection system worked well. Drawbacks were the complication of another expendable fluid, and possibly the consequence of running out of water. Today, electronic controls could be used to mitigate these problems, and logistic concerns could be relaxed by combining reservoirs with that of the all-but-universal windshield washer.

A naturally aspirated SI engine responds almost instantaneously to transient power demands. In a turbocharged engine, it takes time following an increase in throttle position for the turbocharger rotor to accelerate and provide air at increased boost pressures. The time required is known as turbocharger lag. Much has been done in recent years to reduce its magnitude, mostly by good attention to detail in matching of the turbocharger to the engine, and in turbocharger installation.

A somewhat high-tech way to improve engine transient response is the use of lightweight ceramics in the turbocharger turbine rotor, instead of the usual nickel-based alloy, to reduce rotor inertia. Ceramic turbochargers have performed reliably since their introduction in the mid-1980s. They have been sold by the thousands in the United States and by the hundreds of thousands in Japan.

Other mechanical improvements are available to improve turbocharger transient response. These include use of ball bearings and variable turbine nozzles.

There has been concern about the impact on transient emissions of the turbocharger thermal mass, primarily after a cold start. Catalyst performance suffers until the exhaust system comes up to temperature. The turbocharger turbine end is part of the exhaust system, and it contributes to the exhaust system's thermal mass. A straightforward approach to this problem is the reduction of turbocharger hot-end thermal mass. Use of ceramics in the turbocharger hot end is a step in this direction.

Part-Load Fuel Economy

A weakness of the SI engine is its use of throttling and consequent loss in fuel economy at part load. The latter is a most important operating regime for light vehicles.

One approach to elimination of the throttle is stratified-charge combustion, in which the unthrottled fuel-air mixture is leaned out as load is reduced. This was discussed above under "Two-Stroke Engines"; as noted there, stratified charge could be used in four-stroke engines as well.

The so-called Miller cycle is a conceptual approach to improvement of SI engine part-load fuel economy (Heywood 1988, 275). At part load, the inlet valve is closed early, before the completion of the intake stroke. The charge is expanded during the remainder of the intake stroke and then compressed normally. In this way, the mass of the charge is reduced just as it is in a throttled engine—but without the throttling loss.

Implementation of the Miller cycle would require fast-acting intake valves with continuously variable actuation timing. Even though the Miller cycle is not recommended as a practical approach for the immediate future, it is mentioned here because it is conceptually interesting and promising, and is one of the few known direct approaches to the SI part-load throttling problem.

Another way of improving part-load fuel economy, applicable primarily to the diesel, is the variable-compression-ratio (VCR) piston (Ashley 1990). Originally proposed for large diesels, the VCR piston has recently been evaluated by a European automotive manufacturer. The VCR piston contains an internal actuator that varies the effective height of the piston. When the diesel engine is lightly loaded, the VCR piston is actuated so that the compression ratio is at a maximum, for good part-load fuel economy. As load increases, the VCR piston is actuated to reduce the compression ratio and avoid excessive cylinder pressures. Thus the introduction of variable geometry permits part-load operation at a compression ratio that is higher—and more efficient—than would otherwise be possible.

The VCR piston might also be used in SI engines to allow increased compression ratio at part load, up to the knock limit.

Other Mechanical Technologies and Devices

About 10% to 15% of the energy input to an IC engine is lost in mechanical and accessory friction and related losses. Following are some mechanical improvements aimed at reducing these losses.

Ceramic Engine Materials for Low-Heat-Rejection Diesel Engines. About 25% of the fuel-heating value of a current-production diesel is rejected to the engine coolant (Heywood 1988, 674). Experimental low-heat-rejection diesel engines have been built and tested using ceramic hot parts. To date, durability and general cost-effectiveness have not been demonstrated. Lubricating oil effectiveness and durability at high temperatures are questionable. In spite of the difficulties, there is potential for improvement here. To exploit fully the benefits of a successful low-heat-rejection engine, turbocompounding would be necessary. Turbocompounding offers the potential of recovering some of the exhaust blowdown energy losses that are built into the ideal-engine cycles of Figures 5-3 and 5-4. Turbocompounding therefore is a way to raise the baseline efficiency of the ideal-engine cycles.

Low-Heat-Rejection SI Engines. Low-heat-rejection SI engines would be less attractive than a low-heat-rejection diesel, because in the SI engine low-heat rejection would raise the temperature of the unburned gases and increase the tendency of the engine to knock.

Ceramic and Metal Matrix Composite Materials for Weight Reduction. Engine weight reduction improves vehicular fuel economy. Reduction in weight of reciprocating or other internal moving parts decreases internal engine structural loads. For example, valves and other parts of the valve assembly that move during valve actuation are now being made in ceramic rather than metal to reduce the power required of the valve actuation mechanism.

Multivalve Engines, Variable Valve Timing. Four-valve engines increase valve area and tend to improve volumetric efficiency at rated speed and power; therefore they tend to increase the power rating itself. At low speed, the reduced flow through four valves may lead to insufficient turbulence to get good combustion. One manufacturer has approached this problem by means of a variable valve-opening scheme, in which only one of the two inlet valves in each cylinder is opened at low rpm. At high rpm, both valves are open. Good mixing of fuel and air is obtained at low engine rpm, by maintaining high air velocity and swirl formation as a result of the reduced valve-open area. The result is stated to be improved combustion efficiency, with rapid and stable combustion at equivalence ratios as low as 0.6.

Summary

This summary contains numerical projections of engine energy conversion efficiency, together with recommendations for research and development.

Projections

From Figures 5-5 and 5-6, the peak energy conversion efficiencies of today's best light-vehicle SI and diesel engines are about equal, at 34% to 35%; heavy-vehicle diesels are at 42% to 43%; and the corresponding ideal-cycle energy conversion efficiencies are 56% for the SI engine and 53% for the diesel. (These are based on an assumed compression ratio r_c of 12 for SI and 20 for diesel.) The difference between actual and ideal performance gives a theoretical improvement potential of about 21 percentage points for the SI engine and about 18 percentage points for the light-vehicle diesel. If the technology to realize one-third of this potential could be achieved in the next twenty-plus years, and this appears reasonable, there could be engines of either type, SI or diesel, with peak energy conversion efficiencies in the range of 40% to 42% by 2015.

Recommendations for Research and Development

The following research and development (R&D) is recommended as promising improved fuel economy of light-vehicle engines:

1. High-compression-ratio four-stroke SI engines should be optimized for fuel economy and low exhaust emissions, tailored to the alternative fuels ethanol, methane, and/or methanol.
   Basis: There would be a clear gain if the present SI engine compression ratio of 8 to 9, achievable with today's regular fuels,

could be increased to about 12, which appears possible with combined use of alternative fuels and possibly other measures. Alternative fuels are clearly going to be used in quantity at some time in the future, and R&D on how to use them most efficiently should be cost-effective.

2. Small two-stroke direct-injection stratified-charge (DISC) SI engines should be further developed to get low exhaust emissions and superior fuel economy, with emphasis on part-load fuel economy, together with the other attributes necessary for a commercially successful light-vehicle engine.
   Basis: The two-stroke SI engine is compact, light, and simple compared with the four-stroke engine. The fuel economy and exhaust emissions of this engine in its current simplest (crankcase-scavenged) commercially available form are not acceptable for automotive use. The DISC engine offers potential for operating unthrottled, therefore of having good part-load fuel economy. Recent work on DISC engines appears encouraging.

3. Exhaust aftertreatment of commercial and light-vehicle diesel engines, including development of new catalysts and chemical injectants, is necessary to reestablish this fuel-efficient engine in the U.S. light-vehicle market.
   Basis: The diesel engine is the most fuel-efficient vehicular engine in use today. Its major shortcoming is emissions. Current diesel engine emissions work is focused on heavy-duty diesels. Because of the potential fuel economy gain from use of the diesel engine in light vehicles, this work needs to be intensified and expanded in scope.

4. Turbocharging should be reevaluated as one of the more promising readily available ways of improving SI engine fuel economy.
   Basis: A small turbocharged SI engine can give very good fuel economy, combined with transient performance approaching that of a large naturally aspirated engine. This requires a low-inertia turbocharger and good integration of the turbocharger into the engine flow path.

5. The technologies outlined above under the headings "Part-Load Fuel Economy" and "Other Mechanical Technologies and Devices" should be pursued, with the exception of the Miller cycle, which needs further evaluation.
   Basis: Even though the IC engine is very mature, there is still room for further mechanical progress in the form of detailed improvements, many of which are made possible by new materials.

References

Allen, F. E., and G. Rinschler. 1984. "Turbocharging the Chrysler 2.2 Liter Engine." Society of Automotive Engineers Paper 840252. Warrendale, Pa.

Ashley, C. 1990. "Variable Compression Pistons." Society of Automotive Engineers Paper 901685. Warrendale, Pa.

Automotive News. 1991. June 17.

Caris, D., and E. Nelson. 1959. "A New Look at High-Compression Engines." Society of Automotive Engineers Transactions 67:112–24.

Davis, S., and M. Morris. 1992. *Transportation Energy Data Book*. 12th ed. Oak Ridge National Laboratory Report ORNL-6710. Oak Ridge, Tenn.

Dertian, H. H., G. Holiday, and G. Sanburn. 1979. "Turbocharging Ford's 2.3 Liter Spark-Ignition Engine." Society of Automotive Engineers Paper 79-0312. Warrendale, Pa.

Duret, P., A. Ecomard, and M. Audinet. 1988. "A New Two-Stroke Engine with Compressor-Air Assisted Fuel Injection for High-Efficiency Low-Emissions Applications." Society of Automotive Engineers Paper 880176. Warrendale, Pa.

Ferguson, C. R. 1986. *Internal Combustion Engines*. New York: John Wiley & Sons.

Grandinson, A., and I. Hedin. 1982. "A Turbocharged Engine for a Growing Market." Institution of Mechanical Engineers Paper C119/82. London.

Heywood, J. 1988. *Internal Combustion Engine Fundamentals*. New York: McGraw-Hill.

Kerley, R. V., and K. Thurston. 1962. "The Indicated Performance of Otto-Cycle Engines." Society of Automotive Engineers Transactions 70:5–37.

Lents, J. M., and C. Abe. 1992. "Measures to Promote Zero-Emission Vehicles in Southern California." Institution of Mechanical Engineers Paper C389/469. Fisita Congress, London.

Lepperhoff, S., S. Hüthwohl, and F. Pischinger. 1992. "Catalytic Reduction of NO_x in Diesel Exhaust." IMechE paper C389/329. London.

Lewis, J., G. Burrell, and F. Ball. "The Oldsmobile F-85 Jetfire Turbo Rocket Engine." Society of Automotive Engineers Paper 531B. Warrendale, Pa.

Obert, E. 1973. *Internal Combustion Engines and Air Pollution*. New York: Harper-Collins.

Okino, M., K. Okada, and M. Abe. 1985. "Isuzu New 8.4L Diesel

Engine." Society of Automotive Engineers Paper 850258. Warrendale, Pa.

Robbins, G., and C. Salter. 1974. "Mack's New Intercooled Diesel Maxidyne 300." Society of Automotive Engineers Paper 740622. Warrendale, Pa.

Schittler, M. 1985. "MWM TBD 234 Compact High-Output Engines for Installation in Heavy Equipment and Military Vehicles." Society of Automotive Engineers Paper 850257. Warrendale, Pa.

Stiglic, P. 1990. "Emission Testing of Two Heavy-Duty Diesel Engines Equipped with Exhaust Aftertreatment." Society of Automotive Engineers Paper 900919. Warrendale, Pa.

Chapter 6

Vehicle Efficiency and the Electric Option

Paul B. MacCready

T he word *efficiency* for an automobile is usually assumed to relate to technological factors and to be quantifiable by terms such as miles per gallon (mpg) or gallons per passenger-mile. However, when exploring the limits to efficiency from the broader view of this country's surface transportation future, we realize that the practical limits may relate more to manufacturing, economic, social, environmental, and political (both U.S. and global) factors than to technological ones.

To put technological efficiency in perspective, this chapter begins with the topic of our overall transportation energy/environment goals—goals that include decreasing oil consumption. Some dominant nontechnological items that help or hinder strategies aimed at reaching these goals are considered. Next, the technological side is treated, first from the standpoint of the fundamental energies needed to transport people, and then from the standpoint of practical vehicles. For technological, cost, and pollution reasons, electric and hybrid vehicles turn out to be attractive candidates for the vehicle fleet after the year 2000.

To decrease oil consumption, consumers, who are strongly motivated by cost, must be brought into the solution. Yet with vehicles at their present efficiency level and with gasoline so cheap, the consumer has little economic incentive to pay for further efficiency or to curtail his or her fuel purchases. Vehicle efficiency will help us achieve transportation energy/environment goals, but it is only one of many factors.

The Goals

Figure 6-1 shows the goals I have chosen for our transportation energy/ environment situation in the year 2005. Other people will pick a differ-

---

- Substantially decrease U.S. reliance on oil imports, especially from the Mideast. (Decrease to 25%–50% of 1989–1990 value. Exact goal to be clarified in 1993 on basis of study considering technology, environment, security, and economics.)

- Substantially decrease release of greenhouse gases in the United States and globally. (Decrease to less than 1990 values. From intensified studies of pollutant effects on climate, reassess urgency in 1995 and adjust target. Note that all fossil fuels are implicated, not just automobile fuel.)

- Substantially decrease release of local pollutants. (Decrease by a factor of 5 from 1990 vehicles.)

Key Conditions for 2005 Goals

- That the transportation energy/environment goals be met while permitting the increasing number of U.S. consumers to continue to have adequate and affordable personal mobility.

- That the viability of the automotive and energy industries be maintained.

Figure 6-1. U.S. Transportation Energy and Environment Goals for 2005

---

ent year and different quantities, but their goals must still include mention of fuel sources, local and global pollution consequences, and the health of our industries associated with personal mobility. The important thing is that goals must be put forth, and accepted, if rational decisions about strategies for reaching the goals are to be made. These strategies must integrate the changing technological and nontechnological factors.

In the United States we have a tendency to avoid setting clear goals—except in simple, obvious situations: winning World War II, setting foot on the moon before the end of the 1960s, wiping out polio, and so forth. The more factors that must be included, the tougher the task of specifying a goal. Unfortunately, a comprehensive transportation energy/environment goal cannot be simplified to one sentence or a motto. Many people and institutions are working toward technological and political improvements that move us toward an intuitively sensed goal, but while working toward how to get there we resist specifying where "there" is. It is a manifestation of the "ready, fire, aim" habits we all share.

Vehicle efficiency is not a goal, but part of a strategy. If some inexpensive, inexhaustible, nonpolluting energy source were to emerge to substitute for gasoline (if cold fusion had worked out), we could ignore efficiency and concern ourselves only with safety, economy, convenience, marketability—and traffic. In the United States, big efficiency gains over the past decade (for new cars, cutting gasoline consumption per mile to half) have not decreased our dependence on foreign oil. We're importing more all the time. And all the while, our low energy costs, on which our habits are based, keep us consuming about twice as much oil per person and per unit of gross national product as do those efficient producers and exporters Germany and Japan. Improved efficiency is beneficial, but it is not the answer.

Consequences of the Goals

The goals shown in Figure 6-1 cannot be achieved solely by combining evolutionary development of existing automobile technology with conventional consumer habits, even under strong regulatory pressures. Rather, in addition to evolutionary development, some revolutionary technology seems required, plus some revolutionary action to institute change in consumer incentives, choices, and habits.

If some highly efficient or alternatively fueled vehicle were to emerge from technological advances, it would help achieve the goals shown in Figure 6-1 only if such vehicles became so widely used that they caused the retirement of large numbers of older conventional vehicles. Adding a zero-pollution vehicle to the fleet does not by itself decrease oil consumption and pollution; getting rid of a polluting low-mpg car that is used regularly does. Regulatory pressures can help stimulate the use of new, improved vehicles and the retirement of obsolete vehicles, but major adoption of the new cars requires that they compete well in the minds of users when judged on safety, cost, performance, convenience, comfort, and style.

Turning a satisfactory new-technology demonstrator into a mass-produced, mass-distributed, and widely applied vehicle takes a long time and a major investment. The investment on the part of a manufacturer can be justified only if the ground rules are clarified and fixed. The ground rules involve future regulatory incentives and pressures, taking into consideration the future price of the dominant fuel, gasoline. Government, industry, and consumers are all in this together, and together can achieve the 2005 goals.

Many people assume that car companies design the cars of the future and deserve criticism if later hindsight shows that what gets built does not fully meet society's needs. Actually, we customers are the real designers of future cars, through the purchase selections we make today and have made in the past, and through the regulations and subsidies and incentives that we apply through our elected officials. The manufacturers respond to our dictates. We should be proud of the cars we've selected into existence so far; they are a good starting point for the cars that fit the different energy and environmental constraints in the future.

The Comparative Economics of Airplanes and Cars

The marketplace has applied selection pressures that have caused the evolution of wonderful aircraft that are extremely efficient from the standpoint of fuel use. Airliners and business aircraft operate in an economic arena in which the vehicles (which are not mass produced and are rarely sitting idle and not earning money) are expensive. It makes sense to pay the high price for strict requirements of aerodynamic efficiency and structural lightness, as well as engine efficiency, when the vehicle will be carrying hundreds of passengers many hours each day. Fuel represents a big part of the operating cost of aircraft. They use a lot. And the large amount of fuel needed to fly long distances limits an aircraft's payload capacity. Thus efficiency has high priority over cost and exterior styling.

Cars must be mass produced to permit low cost, and styling has a large effect on automobile sales, whereas fuel efficiency has a smaller effect. Over the last decade, pressures to control local pollutants have stimulated efficiency improvements that also help with the global pollutant CO_2. Regulatory pressures have also played a role in improving automobile efficiency. But all in all, the marketplace, which designs cars by selection, has been saying to manufacturers that it is better to put efficiency at as low a priority as regulations permit in order to save a bit in initial cost. A look at the unstreamlined underside of any car shows that the manufacturers have responded rationally to these "instructions."

Cars can be designed and built with the airplane philosophy—that is, with wonderful energy efficiency—but they will be so expensive that few will be purchased and used. Thus, these elegant cars will have negligible societal value. A challenge for future cars is to try to adopt the philosophy of design and manufacturing of aircraft without sacrificing mass-production economy and vehicle reliability and simplicity. But the cultures of airplanes and cars are very different: cars will adopt little from airplane technology unless customers, by their dollar votes, demand it.

	Cost
Year	(1989$)
1989	$1.00 ($3.00 in Europe)
1969	$2.00
1949	$3.00
1929	$4.00

Table 6-1. Gasoline Cost at Pump for Average New Car to Travel 25 Miles

Consequences of the Cost of Fuel

With gasoline in the United States at about $1.25 a gallon, cheaper than bottled water, the incentives for the purchaser of a car to vote for economy are not strong. Fuel cost per mile, considering gasoline price, inflation, and improved car efficiency, is about as low as it has ever been. Table 6-1, prepared in 1989 but still generally valid, shows representative numbers.

Actually, when we pay for a gallon of gas at the pump, we also acquire an additional debt that may be as much as $2.00—the externalities. These represent primarily the military and economic costs of our addiction to Mideast oil, the costs associated with global and local pollution, and the costs of tying our economy to a nonreplenishable resource (one for which U.S. supplies are especially limited). There is no way to get general agreement about quantifying the externalities. The main point is that the externalities are large and mean that our fuel may actually be costing the country, and the world, something more like the $2.50–$5.00 per gallon that is charged the consumer in all other advanced countries. But there are benefits too. This fuel has powered the rise of civilization for most of this century.

Obviously, a substantial extra tax on gasoline (phased in, say, over ten years) would start affecting the purchase decisions of car buyers, and the average cars of the future would become more efficient without any other pressures. But such a tax is deemed politically unacceptable in the United States, so we are left trying to achieve our goal by a mix of technology and regulations, incentives, and penalties. A fundamental problem is that these relate primarily to the vehicle, not directly to our real focus, the fuel, the way a fuel tax would.

I suspect that if we adopt clear goals for 2005, with political leadership following voters' desires, some new tax policy may turn out to be politically feasible. But until there is some such tax, we must do as well as possible without this direct solution. The feasibility of a tax

Table 6-2. Total Annual Costs for a Typical Car One to Three Years Old, 1991		
Category	Cost (1991$)	%
Gasoline	$ 600	13.3
Depreciation	1,300	28.9
Interest on capital	1,000	22.2
Insurance	900	20.0
Maintenance, service, misc.	400	8.9
License, registration	300	6.7
TOTAL	$4,500	100.0

will depend on what we do with the tax money—eliminate the national debt, provide no-fault insurance, and so forth—and how we compensate for its regressive aspects.

We now want society, the sum of purchasers, to buy high-mpg cars. But society is the sum of individuals, ourselves, who have a sense of how little we pay for gasoline and hence tend to select mostly the more powerful, larger, lower-mpg vehicles. The motives of the individual are not in parallel with those of society.

Total annual costs for a typical car one to three years old divide approximately as shown in Table 6-2. These figures will vary widely with the type of car, and where and how much it is operated, but the main point still emerges: gas is only a small part of total car cost (here 13.3 percent). The capital-related costs—depreciation, interest, and insurance—are all larger. Cars are selected mostly for style and function, not fuel economy. When cars become still more efficient, your fuel cost will be even less significant and will represent no reason to curtail driving.

Power Used by the Vehicle

Figure 6-2 illustrates the consumption of the energy from gasoline in an average of highway and urban driving cycles. The figure ignores the secondary factors of bearings and appliances and is a bit generous in the amount of mechanical energy that actually becomes available. Under high power, the engine efficiency may rise to 30%, but this high power is rarely used and, for our typical driving, which includes idling, the number is closer to 15% than the 18% shown. But the main

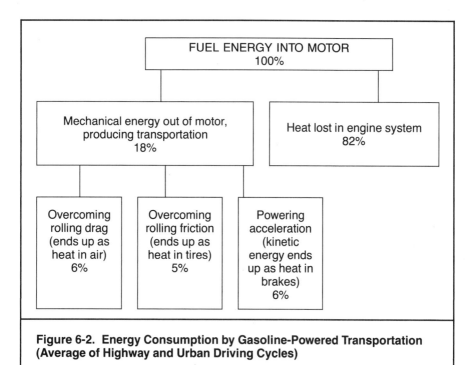

Figure 6-2. Energy Consumption by Gasoline-Powered Transportation (Average of Highway and Urban Driving Cycles)

point is that some one-third of this mechanical energy goes into air drag (it is more like three-fourths at steady highway speeds), one-third goes into rolling friction, and one-third goes into heating the brakes to decelerate the car and delete its kinetic energy (more in the urban cycle). Obviously, cars would use less fuel if the aerodynamics were improved, if lower weight and better tires gave less tire drag, and if lower weight saved some braking loss (regenerative braking could eliminate a big part of this loss). All such improvements would initially cost a bit, and whether they might alter safety or marketability would have to be considered.

If gas were expensive, or if regulations put equivalent pressures toward efficiency, there would be obvious areas for improvement. For a user who operates primarily on the highway at high speeds, aerodynamic improvements provide the big benefit. This drag could be cut in half, compared with that of many old and some new cars, while retaining desirable packaging, safety, and styling. But aerodynamics mean much less in the urban cycle, where speeds are low and the kinetic losses from deceleration dominate. A lighter car cuts kinetic losses proportionally. The only practical regenerative braking scheme that has emerged is with the battery-powered car. This can now recover nearly two-thirds of the kinetic energy, and perhaps a bigger percentage with future technology, but the kinetic energy is proportionally greater because of increased weight from batteries (weight that also hurts tire drag).

Realistic strategies for dealing with fuel efficiency need to be based on some assessment of representative magnitude of the dominant factors that determine mpg—the use of energy to propel the car, and the efficiency of generation of that energy. For the energy a car uses, one convenient way of assessing magnitudes is to put energy in terms of the equivalent potential energy of height×weight needed to propel the vehicle a mile. Assuming a particular weight, height alone becomes a quantity for comparison. Later we deal with the efficiency of converting fuel to the mechanical energy that drives the wheels, and that must equal the equivalent potential energy. Assume a typical modern car, weighing 3,500 lb (3,200 lb empty weight, plus two passengers), with tires having a 0.007 rolling-friction coefficient, and the aerodynamic drag area being a low 7.5 ft² (25 ft² frontal area, 0.3 drag coefficient).

The tire drag for the selected car is 0.007 of the weight, and the energy needed for 1 mile of movement is this drag times 5,280 feet, which is the same as the vehicle weight times 37.0 feet of height. Thus, a vehicle with wheels having a rolling-drag coefficient of 0.007 would maintain speed in a vacuum (no air drag) by coasting down a slope of 37.0 feet per mile; equivalently, on a horizontal surface, to move the car a mile against wheel drag would take the same energy as lifting the car 37.0 feet. This height is independent of weight.

The aerodynamic drag in pounds for the selected drag area is, at sea level, $19.3 \times 10^{-3} \, v^2$, when v is in mph. Thus, at 30 mph, the drag is 17.4 lb; at 15 mph, it is 4.3 lb; and at 60 mph, it is 69.5 lb. For a 3,500-lb vehicle, a slope of 26.2 feet in a mile would maintain the steady 30-mph speed, if there were no rolling friction. For 15 mph, the height would be 6.6 ft; for 60 mph, it would be 105.0 ft. A vehicle twice as heavy would have to be lifted only half as high to provide the same energy, and the same fuel would have to be consumed in doing the lifting.

If a vehicle (of any weight), moving at 60 mph, were to be stopped abruptly by the brakes, if a 3% correction is made for the rotating kinetic energy of wheels and engine, the kinetic energy wasted would be equivalent to a height loss of 125.2 ft (31.3 ft for 30 mph, 7.8 ft for 15 mph). These figures are summarized in Table 6-3.

Table 6-3. Kinetic Energy Lost in Abrupt Vehicle Stops (One Stop per Mile)			
	KINETIC ENERGY LOST (ft height/mile)		
Source of Loss	15 mph	30 mph	60 mph
Rolling friction	37.0	37.0	37.0
Aerodynamic drag	6.6	26.2	105.0
Subtotal, steady motion	43.6	63.2	142.0
(Horsepower, steady motion)	1.8	5.1	22.8
TOTAL	7.8	31.3	125.2

Table 6-3 shows that at low speeds, rolling friction is the dominant term. Tire drag coefficients can be lowered, perhaps to 0.005, but at some sacrifice in ruggedness, smooth ride, and ability to hold the road. For reference, racing-bicycle tires are under one-half of these numbers, and steel train wheels on steel tracks are one-tenth of these numbers. Lower weight benefits rolling friction, proportionally, and similarly benefits kinetic loss.

At high speeds, aerodynamic drag is especially important, and even at a slow 30 mph it cannot be neglected. Some recent cars have demonstrated that this drag can be lowered substantially from even the rather low value assumed here, while still permitting appealing styling. The manufacturing of the more streamlined vehicles becomes more expensive, more like building airplanes, and service convenience may be inhibited.

Kinetic loss can be large in some driving cycles, which emphasizes the value of finding some practical way to provide regenerative braking. The energy consumed in one stop from 60 mph is almost as much as the energy to propel the car a mile at 60 mph.

One conclusion to draw is that the best vehicle for the urban driving cycle (which in many locations is becoming the gridlock cycle) may be a rather different vehicle from the one used primarily for high-speed driving with few stops. The customer usually wants a single vehicle to cover all driving conditions. Current compromise vehicles do the jobs moderately well, and future vehicles can be expected to handle the compromise better. The customer will be offered choices that emphasize one type of driving more than the other, but the vehicle will handle the other type adequately.

Power from the Fuel

The gasoline engine for our assumed 3,500-lb-gross-weight vehicle (ignoring accessories) needs at least 100 horsepower to provide good acceleration and hill-climbing capability, but in steady level motion needs only one-fourth of that at 60 mph, one-twentieth at 30 mph, and one-fiftieth at 15 mph. But at these low powers, it is relatively inefficient—and, at idle, it has zero efficiency. It may average 15% efficiency over a typical mixture of driving situations, as compared with 30% at the rarely used high power. There are a number of approaches to improving the basic efficiency of internal combustion engines (ICEs), and the efficiency in the way they are used, that may eventually produce something like a fifth more efficiency in the high-power region and percentagewise even more improvements at low and varying power. Also, the lighter and smaller-sized ICEs of the future will permit further weight savings throughout the whole vehicle, which will mean that less power will be needed from the engine for hill climbing and acceleration.

The ICE may use fuels other than gasoline, such as methanol, ethanol, compressed natural gas (CNG), diesel, propane, or hydrogen. Some are attractive from the standpoint of being available in the United States, being potentially in unlimited supply, and producing fewer pollutants at the local or global level. However, if taxes and subsidies are eliminated, these alternative fuels are more expensive than gasoline and, in the case of pressurized CNG or hydrogen, more difficult to carry. The more efficient the basic vehicle, the less mechanical energy it needs, and so the more feasible these alternatives become.

Electric and Hybrid Vehicles

From the considerations of the previous two sections, the benefits and limitations of electric vehicles can be seen. A battery-powered car provides its mechanical energy with good efficiency over a wide range of driving conditions, readily provides substantial regenerative braking, produces zero local pollution, and can be quiet. However, Table 6-4 shows the main problem: the energy from an available lead-acid cell is only about 1% of the energy derived with an ICE from the same weight of gasoline. The weight and cost of a large battery are troublesome. The concept behind the GM Impact battery-powered car, now being tailored for mass production, was to emphasize efficiency (aerodynamic and rolling drag) so much that a vehicle emitting zero local pollution with satisfactory performance for many market niches could exist in spite of the compromises dictated by existing batteries.

Table 6-4. Useful Energy: Height to Which Energy Source Can Lift Its Own Initial Weight

Fuel Source	Height (mi)
Gasoline	1,000
Lead-acid battery	10
Rubber band	0.5

Lead-acid battery performance (power, energy, and cycle life) is adequate now only for limited applications. It will certainly improve in the future. Many other battery technologies are receiving intensive research and development, including sodium-sulfur, nickel-iron, nickel-zinc, nickel-cadmium, nickel–metal hydride, and lithium-polymer, as well as batteries using consumable fuel, such as aluminum-air and zinc-air (with possible recharge capability). Every battery approach has its potential benefits and its problems. Picking the eventual winner at this time is unlikely, so prudence dictates that research on many options continue. Certainly significant improvements will emerge as time goes on.

Hybrid vehicles show promise of high efficiency. They convert chemical fuel on-board (say, by an ICE) to electricity to power the electric-drive motor or to charge the battery. The ICE can be operated at a constant power where its efficiency is optimized near the 30% value and good pollution control is maintained. With varying rpm, high efficiency can even be obtained with an ICE over a wide range of powers. Hybrids could use other energy sources as well: perhaps gas turbines, fuel cells using hydrogen, or ICEs using fuels other than gasoline. There are inefficiencies in going into and out of battery storage, and the added weight of a large battery produces a penalty from tire drag and kinetic losses, but there is a big benefit from regenerative braking in stop-and-go driving. The electric-motor system can be highly efficient at both high and low power. The net consequence is that, from a fuel economy standpoint, the hybrid looks especially attractive for low speeds and stop-and-go driving, and moderately attractive even at high speeds. There are many variations of hybrid to consider. The characteristics of the auxiliary power unit and the battery are important system elements for selecting the relative amounts of power from each to deliver to the wheels or drive motor at any particular moment.

If saving fuel is important, or minimizing pollution, the battery-powered vehicle has a future, and the hybrid, which overcomes severe range limitations, looks eventually like a good bet. These electric-powered vehicles now require expensive battery and electrical systems, and until there has been considerable development, experience, and time-consuming production investment, and until mass production takes place, they cannot be expected to cost the manufacturer as little as the standard gasoline cars that have been evolving for a century. Eventually they probably will.

In the meantime, even when exploring the viability of electric-drive vehicles, the competition from today's best gasoline-powered vehicles must always be considered. In the short run, any economical, efficient car that causes a customer to discard an old car puts society ahead. In the long run, I think electric-drive hybrid cars will win because they are likely to be better all around for the customer. A practical battery car is the first step toward this revolution in transportation technology.

Final Comments

Achieving a reasonable transportation energy/environment goal by 2005 requires a mixture of strategies that include (1) attention to both gasoline and alternative fuels—especially methanol, ethanol, CNG, and hydrogen—with consideration given to nonforeign sources, replenishability, CO_2 benefits, and local pollution benefits; (2) for mechanical-drive, electric-drive, and hybrid vehicles, attention to energy conversion devices beside the standard ICEs—including improved ICEs, variations such as two-cycle, rotary, or gas turbines—and hydrogen fuel cells; and (3) attention to overall efficiency of safe, marketable vehicles. The real costs of the various fuels will have some bearing on their use, but as vehicles continue to get more efficient, the cost of fuel will become less important to the customer. If more desirable alternative fuels become cheaper than the real cost of gasoline, considering externalities that are not applicable to the alternatives, and if cars are adapted to meet customers' needs using these alternative fuels, the future is bright.

The technologies either exist already or can be seen coming in the near future for achieving reasonable 2005 goals, through doing more with less (that is, efficiency) and doing it with energy that is more societally desirable. Harnessing the combined consumer-government–automobile manufacturer–energy industry into a team to use these technologies represents the much greater part of the challenge.

Chapter 7

The USDOE Vehicle Propulsion Research and Development Program

John J. Brogan and Sek R. Venkateswaran

The major issues of concern about the U.S. transportation sector are well known: rising energy consumption, excessive petroleum dependence, air pollution, and large economic impacts. Increasing concerns over greenhouse gas accumulation, especially carbon dioxide (CO_2), and global climate change could lead to the imposition of controls on greenhouse gas emissions from the transportation sector. Greenhouse gas emissions in the United States are closely related to energy use. U.S. CO_2 emissions, which represent about 20% of the global total, originate almost exclusively from fossil fuel combustion (OTA 1991). Of the energy-using sectors, transportation is one of the largest contributors to CO_2 emissions. In the United States and other industrially developed countries, emissions from highway vehicles (including emissions from feedstock recovery, processing, and distribution) account for about 25% of the total CO_2 emissions from use of all fossil fuels (DeLuchi 1990; OTA 1991). It is apparent that any CO_2 reduction program must address vehicles, especially automobiles and light trucks, which account for over 60% of transportation energy use (Davis & Hu 1989).

This chapter focuses primarily on automobile (and light-truck) CO_2 emissions and the potential for their reduction. However, it is important to recognize that, in addition to CO_2, methane (CH_4), nitrous oxide (N_2O), and chlorofluorocarbons (CFCs) also play potentially important roles in the greenhouse effect. It has been estimated that each of the greenhouse gases made the following contribution to global warming in the 1980s: CO_2, 55%; CFCs, 24%; CH_4, 15%; N_2O, 6% (OTA 1991).

Significant long-term reductions in transportation sector emissions of CO_2 can be achieved by increasing vehicle fuel efficiency and by using selected alternative fuels, especially nonfossil fuel–based electricity for hydrogen and electric vehicles (DeLuchi 1990). In a recent assessment of steps to reduce greenhouse gases, the U.S. Congress Office of Technology Assessment (OTA) concluded that the two main opportunities for reducing transportation's contribution to global warming are measures to increase the energy efficiency of light-duty vehicles and measures to encourage urban passengers to drive less (OTA 1991).

A broad range of options are potentially available to improve vehicle fuel efficiency and at the same time increase fuel flexibility and reduce polluting emissions. For example, a variety of renewable and nonrenewable resources can be converted into a range of transportation fuels to replace today's petroleum-based fuels. These fuels can be produced, stored, and distributed in different ways and used to power a variety of conventional and advanced propulsion systems in the different end-use sectors. Within any given area (such as fuels or engines), no single option has yet emerged as clearly superior based on currently available information. For automobiles, the conventional gasoline-powered engine is continuously undergoing improvements and remains a competitive option. Each alternative has its own technical, economic, or environmental advantages and drawbacks; potential market niches; time horizon; and proponents. It is therefore necessary to pursue multiple options and strategies based on near- to long-term priorities, available resources, and the results of past and current public- and private-sector initiatives.

The U.S. Department of Energy (DOE) is undertaking a balanced program of near-, mid-, and long-term research in transportation technologies, with highway vehicles as the primary target. The National Energy Strategy developed by DOE emphasizes expanded efforts to develop these advanced transportation technologies (USDOE 1991). On the demand side, DOE is pursuing a portfolio of technology options that includes advanced high-temperature heat engines as well as batteries and fuel cells for electric and hybrid vehicles. These activities are aimed at improving vehicle efficiency by 40% to 60% and enabling widespread use of alternative fuels by 2010 without restricting consumer choice of vehicles. Supporting programs emphasize the development of an advanced materials-technology base to provide industry with the capability to produce new, reliable, and cost-effective

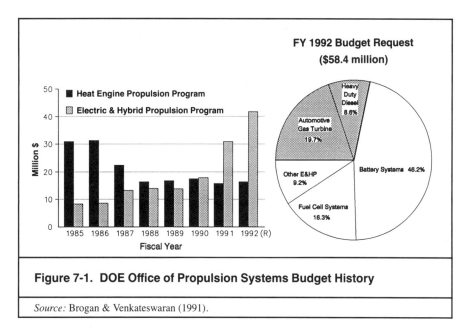

Figure 7-1. DOE Office of Propulsion Systems Budget History

Source: Brogan & Venkateswaran (1991).

components for advanced heat engines and to reduce the weight of vehicle structures. On the energy supply side, DOE research activities are aimed at eliminating barriers to the widespread adoption of alternative fuels, particularly the barriers of high production costs and inadequate technology for the use of these fuels. A primary objective is the commercial introduction of cost-effective, domestically produced biofuels, such as ethanol.

This chapter discusses the conventional spark-ignition (SI) engine as well as several advanced technologies that are being developed under the DOE program as fuel-efficient, fuel-flexible, and low-emission alternatives. They include the ceramic gas turbine and electric technologies, and electric-hybrid approaches based on batteries, fuel cells, and heat engines. For each option, the technical characteristics and related prospects for automotive use are presented, along with the status of DOE technology development efforts. The 1985–1992 funding history of DOE's Heat Engine and Electric and Hybrid Propulsion programs as well as a breakdown of the fiscal year 1992 budget request submitted to Congress are shown in Figure 7-1. The lower funding levels for the Heat Engine Program beginning in fiscal year 1988 partly reflect the winding down and termination of development efforts for the automotive Stirling engine.

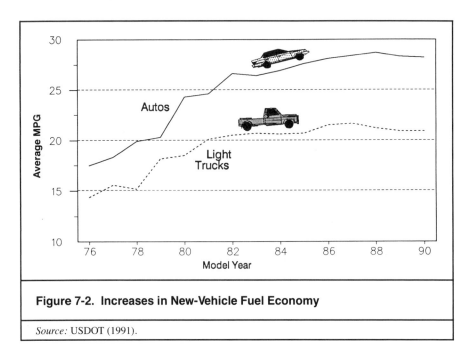

Figure 7-2. Increases in New-Vehicle Fuel Economy

Source: USDOT (1991).

Four-Stroke/Two-Stroke SI Engines

For automobiles, the conventional four-stroke gasoline-fueled engine has been continuously improved and remains a formidable competitor to advanced alternatives. In the foreseeable future, upgrading of the conventional SI engine and vehicle fuel efficiencies will remain a primary means of limiting CO_2 emissions from the transportation sector. As shown in Figure 7-2, the fuel economy of light-duty vehicles has substantially improved since the early 1970s. In addition to increases in powertrain efficiency, however, some of these improvements have been due to reductions in the average size and weight of the vehicles. Since 1982, the rate of improvement in new-vehicle fuel economy has leveled off. It is also interesting to note that, despite the fuel economy improvements, overall fuel consumption for light-duty vehicles continues to rise—mainly because of continuing dramatic increases in total vehicle miles traveled. Further increases in conventional vehicle fuel economy are likely to occur because of improvements in powertrain efficiency (intake valve control, overhead camshafts, roller followers, lower friction, fuel system upgrades, electronic control of transmission shifts, continuously variable transmission, and so forth); reduction in vehicle weight (through materials selection); lower drag coefficient; improvements in lubricants and tires; and more efficient accessories (Amann 1990b). A recent announcement by two leading Japanese car manufacturers claimed 10% to 20% improvements in fuel economy of small automobiles without performance penalties, achieved through lean-burn engine technology. Other Japanese engine developers (at the Nippon Clean Engine Lab. Co.) have reported on performance and combustion characteristics of a unique direct-injection stratified-charge engine, with single-cylinder tests indicating thermal efficiencies in excess of 40% with gasoline and methanol (Kato & Onishi 1990). These are mentioned as a few examples of considerable world-wide research and development (R&D) activities on SI engines.

Currently, there is also strong worldwide interest and developmental activity among major auto manufacturers on two-stroke-cycle engines. These engines have long been used for two-wheelers and light marine applications to take advantage of their high power/weight ratio and smaller size. Orbital Engine Company's two-stroke engine for automotive applications is claimed to demonstrate low emissions that meet current and proposed U.S. standards with good fuel economy. A key element of the engine that helps to achieve low emissions is its computer-controlled, air-assisted, direct-injection system. Auto industry estimates of further improvements are less optimistic than Orbital's with one company estimating 5%–8% potential improvement in engine efficiency as compared with the current four-stroke engines and a 10%–13% improvement in the overall fuel economy of small passenger cars with a two-stroke-cycle engine (Fleming 1990). There are several issues related to lubrication, emissions, durability, and so forth that need to be resolved before two-stroke-cycle engines find their way into automotive applications. In the final analysis, two-stroke engines may prove practical for small cars and/or as the range extender in battery-powered electric hybrids.

Gas Turbine Engines

The gas turbine engine has attracted automotive industry attention for over four decades and, for many reasons, is a promising candidate technology for automotive use. It offers the potential for high fuel economy when operating temperatures are increased beyond what is possible with all-metal turbines using ceramics. It should deliver smooth, quiet power with expected low exhaust emissions (without aftertreatment), multifuel capability, high reliability, low maintenance, compactness, low parts count, and low weight.

DOE's automotive gas turbine program is designed to build upon federal and industrial R&D that has been conducted on gas turbine engines for automotive applications for the last fifteen years. The primary technical challenges facing the program include the continued development of the following:

- reliable, high-temperature, structural ceramic components to enable operation at turbine inlet temperatures of 2,500° F without cooling—a key requirement for achieving the 30% fuel economy improvement goal of the current program

- low-emission, fuel-flexible combustor technology

- efficient heat recovery and management (regenerator/recuperator technology)

- high-efficiency, small turbomachinery

- high-temperature bearings and lubrication

- scale-up of ceramic fabrication processes for large-scale production of components cost-effectively

From 1980 until mid-1987, automotive gas turbine development activities were supported by DOE under the Advanced Gas Turbine (AGT) Program. The AGT Program successfully demonstrated the use of advanced ceramics for hot-section components of an automotive gas turbine. The two prime contractors, Allison Gas Turbine Division (of General Motors) and Garrett Auxiliary Power Division (of Allied-Signal), designed, fabricated, and successfully tested (to near-design conditions) two different ceramic turbine engines: the Allison AGT 100 and the Garrett AGT 101. The program showed that further knowledge and improvements were needed to develop the technology base for producing high-temperature structural-ceramic components capable of operation at 2,500° F. Consequently, the AGT Program was followed by the Advanced Turbine Technology Applications Program (ATTAP) to address this key requirement. ATTAP's major milestone is a 300-hour durability demonstration of the hot-section ceramic components in AGT test-bed engines at temperatures up to 2,500° F under typical cyclic automotive conditions.

Over the last ten years, considerable technical progress in specific areas has been achieved by the DOE gas turbine program. Ceramic regenerator systems have been developed, as well as high-efficiency small turbomachinery designs. Ceramic components have been developed to increase the operating temperatures from 1,700° F to over 2,300° F. In fact, hot-rig testing of the automotive gas turbine has been initiated at turbine temperatures in excess of the 2,500° F design goal.

The turbine rotor remains the critical component because of the high-temperature, high-stress environment in which it operates, in addition to its geometric complexity and susceptibility to impact damage. Two ceramic rotors have operated for over 1,200 hours at up to full speed and at temperatures ranging from 2,000° F to 2,543° F. The potential for very low emissions has been experimentally demonstrated. Additionally, costs for fabrication of ceramic components have been reduced from tens of thousands of dollars for R&D components to hundreds of dollars for small development quantities.

Several critical issues still need to be addressed to advance the automotive gas turbine technology to a stage at which industry can make a decision to proceed with commercial-product development. Continued technology development is needed to resolve the remaining problems with ceramics, combustor, regenerator and seals, and lubrication. The ability to sustain 2,500° F peak turbine inlet temperatures during the engine's operational life (about 3,500 hours for 100,000 vehicle-miles) must be proven in engine bench tests, with final performance testing in on-the-road vehicles. Emissions compliance, alternative-fuel capability, fuel economy improvements, performance, and reliability also need to be demonstrated through vehicle tests. Intensive planning is currently in progress within DOE to establish priorities and to determine the extent of continued government support for automotive gas turbine technology development, system development, and vehicle demonstration activities beyond ATTAP.

Battery-Powered Electric Vehicles

Electric vehicles (EVs) have considerable potential to reduce greenhouse gas emissions, especially in geographical areas where the contribution of fossil fuels to the electric-power-generation fuel mix is relatively low. Depending on the efficiency of the EV relative to the conventional gasoline-fueled vehicle and the electric-power-generation fuel mix, the impact of EVs can range from a moderate reduction in emission of greenhouse gases to their nearly complete elimination (for example, with the use of nuclear, hydroelectric, or solar power for recharging batteries) (DeLuchi 1990).

The DOE Electric Vehicle Program supports R&D, testing, and evaluation to assist industry in developing an advanced EV technology base that will accelerate the commercialization of these vehicles. Funding for the DOE program has increased sharply over the recent past (see Figure 7-1), from $8.4 million in 1985 to $31 million in 1991. The overall technical objective is to support development of EVs in the areas of performance, drivability, cost, and user convenience to

Table 7-1. Status of DOE Battery Technology Development, 1979–1990

Battery	SPECIFIC ENERGY (Wh/kg)			SPECIFIC POWER (W/kg)			CYCLE LIFE TO 80% DOD (cycles)		
	1979	1990	Goal	1979	1990	Goal	1979	1990	Goal
Lead-acid	42^c	53^m	56	75^c	104^m	79	250^c	130^m	450
Nickel-iron	40^m	50^m	56	100^m	108^m	79	1,000^m	1,100^m	1,125
Zinc-bromine	20^m	55^b	75	15^m	88^b	79	10^m	142^b	600
Lithium aluminum–iron sulfide	100^c	96^m	100	45^c	86^m	106	286^c	130^m	600
Sodium-sulfur	110^c	96^m	100	25^c	130^c	106	N/A	261^m	600
Iron-air	N/A	70^c	100	N/A	90^c	106	N/A	120^c	600

Source: Barber (1990).
Note: DOD = depth of discharge; c = cell data; m = module data; b = battery data; N/A = not available.

levels comparable to those found in conventional internal-combustion-engine vehicles. One of the driving forces behind the sharply increased DOE budget and growing surge of auto industry interest in EVs is the requirement mandated by the State of California for the gradual introduction of zero-emission vehicles starting in 1998. Currently, only EVs meet such qualification. Other states appear to be following the example set by California.

Battery technology remains a critical barrier to large-scale commercializing of EVs. Suitable batteries are needed with enough energy storage capacity to provide a reasonable vehicle range between rechargings, sufficient power to achieve the acceleration needed for the particular transportation applications, and reasonable energy density, so as to minimize the use of energy for just moving the battery mass.

For several years, DOE has awarded major R&D contracts to industry for development of various advanced battery technologies, including lead-acid, nickel-iron, lithium aluminum–iron sulfide, sodium–metal chloride, sodium-sulfur, zinc-bromine, and iron-air battery technologies. In addition, basic research has been aimed at understanding electrochemical phenomena and examining electrochemical and metallurgical interactions that influence battery performance and life. Table 7-1 summarizes the progress made in the development of advanced cells, modules, and batteries between 1979 and 1990, as well as target performance criteria that will have to be specifically achieved for practical EV applications. It is expected that at least one of the high-temperature batteries, most likely the sodium-sulfur battery, could be ready for production by 1998. A summary of progress in electric-vehicle propulsion and battery technology is provided in Burke 1990.

In January 1991, the big-three U.S. auto manufacturers announced the formation of a research consortium (the United States Advanced Battery Consortium, USABC) to develop and evaluate advanced battery technologies for use in the next generation of EVs, which would have significantly increased range and performance. The premise in organizing the consortium was that there is no clear advanced battery choice today, and identification and development of the most promising alternative is beyond the resources of any single manufacturer or technology group. The consortium offers a collective, efficient, and economical way to proceed with this task. The consortium will seek to establish the capability necessary for a U.S. advanced battery-manufacturing industry and to accelerate the market potential of EVs. USABC is not intended, however, to be a joint vehicle-research or joint battery-production organization. R&D will be conducted by battery manufacturers and other nonmember parties under contract to the consortium. The current consensus is that the sodium-sulfur, lithium-polymer, and lithium–metal disulfide battery technologies are the best candidates for development. Nickel–metal hydride and zinc-air are also being evaluated as potential candidates for the midterm requirements. Preliminary results from the research are expected by 1994. In July, the Electric Power Research Institute agreed to join the consortium to represent the electric-utility industry and to provide funding at a level equivalent to the average of the automotive partners in the consortium. Contract negotiations are ongoing between DOE and the consortium as to shared funding arrangements.

Along with battery technologies, DOE is also supporting research and development of integrated electric-vehicle propulsion systems to ensure that the electric-power-storage subsystem characteristics are carefully matched with those of the propulsion subsystem. The recently concluded ETX-II program successfully characterized and demonstrated an integrated single-shaft, alternating-current (AC) propulsion system and sodium-sulfur battery system operating in a Ford Aerostar test vehicle. Under the follow-on Modular Electric Vehicle Program (MEVP), the Ford Motor and General Electric companies are under contract to develop an advanced modular AC powertrain applicable to a broad range of vehicle types and sizes and suitable for mass production. The best features of the technology developed in earlier programs will be combined. MEVP performance goals are shown in Table 7-2. This effort will culminate with the delivery of three proto-

Table 7-2. Modular Electric Vehicle Program (MEVP) Performance Goals

Category	Goal
Range on federal urban driving cycle	>150 mi (240 km)
Acceleration 0–50 mph (0–80 km/h)	<15 sec
Gradeability limit	30%
Top speed	70 mph (112 km/h)
Energy consumption	0.32 kWh/mi (0.20 kWh/km)
Automotive acceptable driveability	
Source: Brogan & Venkateswaran (1991).	

type EVs with 50-, 75-, and 100-hp propulsion units by 1994. Subsequently, industry is expected to proceed with commercial development with no further government involvement.

The DOE program also supports field testing and evaluation of new EV technologies at the Idaho National Engineering Laboratory. In addition, EVs are currently being used at nine different sites that are operated on a cost-shared basis by fleet operators within utility companies, engineering schools, DOE laboratories, and government agencies. As routine daily missions are performed, vehicle performance is evaluated, and engineering and operational data are collected and disseminated to industry on EVs, batteries, and other components.

Heat Engine/Battery Hybrid Vehicles

The concept of a hybrid vehicle arose from the combined need for all the advantages of electric propulsion plus full-performance capability comparable to that of conventional (internal-combustion-engine) vehicles. Numerous hybrid-propulsion schemes have been explored worldwide (Burke 1990). Heat engines and battery electric drives, for example, can be combined in various series and parallel configurations to provide motive power to the wheels. In the short term, one of the most promising approaches appears to be the series combination of an electric-battery system with a relatively small heat-engine generator that almost always operates at a fixed speed and power level (independent of vehicle speeds) near its peak efficiency and provides for range extension by on-board battery recharging. The preferred strategy with such a system is to use the battery with charge from the utility network as much as possible and the heat engine only when the battery is depleted. In practice, the heat engine operates in an on-off mode, being turned on when the battery reaches a preset discharge level. In the near term, such hybrids will likely use lead-acid batteries, followed by advanced batteries as they become available. As for heat engines, in the near term commercially available off-the-shelf four-stroke SI engine generator sets can be utilized. One drawback is that these gensets are not usually optimized for fuel economy or emissions. In the mid to long term, two-stroke- or four-stroke-cycle SI engines, followed by Stirling engines and ceramic gas turbines, are likely high-efficiency heat engine candidates for hybrid vehicles.

The technology for near-term heat engine/battery hybrids has been demonstrated, and its commercial development will be left to industry. However, DOE continues to monitor domestic and foreign developments in hybrid vehicles as well as industry improvements in batteries, powertrains, engines, motors, and so forth for their potential use in future hybrid systems. In-house studies of energy storage systems have been conducted in the past, and flywheels, hydraulic accumulators, and small range-extender heat engines have been evaluated for possible use in hybrid vehicles.

Published reports indicate that heat engine/battery hybrid vehicles based on the range-extender concept are under evaluation by several manufacturers worldwide, including General Motors (GM) (Wyczalek 1991) and Volkswagen AG (Kalberlah 1991). A small number of individual hybrid vehicles have been built that demonstrate the feasibility of this concept. A notable example is GM's HX3 hybrid-concept car, which combines an electric-powered vehicle (in which thirty-two lead-acid batteries with 13-kWh capacity drive two 60-hp AC induction motors) with a 906-cc, three-cylinder, four-stroke gasoline engine generator for range extension. The internal-combustion engine runs at its optimum speed of 2500 rpm for high efficiency and low emissions. A 10-gallon fuel tank gives the HX3 a range of about 300 miles. The concept car is aerodynamically designed with extensive use of lightweight materials and composites. It appears that GM has no current plans to produce the HX3 hybrid. The potentially higher cost of hybrids, compared with that of EVs, is a concern that would have to be addressed through technology improvements.

Fuel Cell/Battery Hybrid Vehicles

Over the longer term, improvements in fuel cell technologies could make possible the successful commercialization of energy-efficient, fuel-flexible, ultra-low-emission hybrid vehicles with virtually unlimited range (through rapid refueling) and the ease of use offered by present automobiles. Although originally developed for other uses, such as power generation for electric utilities and space applications, specific fuel cell technologies have advanced to the stage at which their potential role in transportation applications has been established and developmental needs identified. The DOE program is aimed at the development of two such technologies for transportation propulsion: the phosphoric acid and the proton exchange membrane (PEM) fuel cells. Fuel cell R&D will be aimed at automobile, bus, and van applications and at developing the capability of fuel cells to use methanol, ethanol, and natural-gas fuels.

A major project is to develop a hybrid system combining a methanol-fueled phosphoric acid fuel cell, battery, and electric-drive propulsion for a thirty-foot urban bus. Expected performance benefits include 50% greater fuel economy than in existing diesel buses, noise level reductions of 10 to 20 db, and more than a 90% reduction in exhaust emissions compared with diesel buses. The proof-of-feasibility phase of this technology has been successfully completed with the building of two 25-kW fuel cell/battery systems and their subsequent evaluation in a laboratory. In the next phase, a full-sized fuel cell/battery propulsion system will be integrated into a test-bed bus to demonstrate proof of concept. Track testing and field evaluation of this test-bed bus will also be carried out. These efforts are expected to provide the technology base needed to proceed to field testing of a small fleet of prototype buses. The fuel cell development program is cosponsored by the U.S. Department of Transportation and the South Coast Air Quality Management District in Los Angeles, California.

A second major effort is focused on PEM fuel cells. This technology has the potential to provide the high power densities needed for automotive applications and such additional advantages over the phosphoric acid fuel cells as reduced size and weight, faster start-up, better transient response, increased reliability, and potentially lower cost. DOE's PEM fuel cell program is aimed at developing this technology to provide a 70% to 80% increase in fuel economy over conventional gasoline-powered vehicles, comparable range and performance, substantially reduced noise, and near-zero emissions. Additional research will be needed on improved membrane technology and better catalyst distribution to reduce noble-metal loadings and increase power densities of the fuel cell system. Research is also being conducted to develop nonplatinum catalysts and lower-cost membranes to provide substantial reductions in the cost of PEM fuel cells.

In early September 1990, DOE awarded a contract to Allison Gas Turbine Division of General Motors for research and development of PEM fuel cells for automotive propulsion. Allison is subcontracting work to Ballard Power Systems, Dow Chemical Company, Los Alamos National Laboratory, and the General Motors Research Center. The target for the development team is to produce a hybrid system with high power density and a useful life of five years and 2,500 cycles to a 40% depth of discharge. This multiyear, cost-shared contract includes the conceptual design of a PEM-based propulsion system; component R&D; and the integration and testing of a complete, methanol-fueled, 10-kW PEM fuel cell system. The expected outcome of this effort is a demonstration of the feasibility of PEM fuel cells for transportation. If the results are favorable, subsequent phases will establish proof of feasibility by means of a 25-kW brassboard system, followed by a full-scale 50-kW propulsion system to be evaluated in the laboratory and in test-bed vehicles.

The DOE program is also developing advanced reformer technology to improve the competitiveness of fuel cell–powered vehicles by reducing system size, cost, and start-up time, and increasing transient-response capability. The program will also lead to vehicles with greater fuel flexibility—capable of operating on reformed methanol, ethanol, or natural gas.

Other Engine Alternatives

Other automotive engine alternatives also have been considered over the years in addition to those discussed above (Brogan & Venkateswaran 1991). The Rankine (steam) engine was extensively investigated during the 1970s and eliminated because of poor fuel economy. Development of an automotive Stirling engine was terminated by DOE in 1989 mainly because the test results showed no substantial gains over the SI engine. However, it is again being considered as a candidate heat engine for hybrid vehicles. Whereas the diesel engine is well entrenched in the heavy-duty field, the passenger-car diesel has not fared well with U.S. consumers despite its attractive fuel economy. Diesels for light-duty trucks, however, retain a firm market niche. DOE has an active low-heat-rejection diesel engine R&D program focused on heavy-duty transport.

Possibilities for the Future

It is apparent from the above discussion that several propulsion alternatives are available that may potentially increase automobile fuel efficiency, improve fuel flexibility, and reduce emissions. To predict the future as to which of these alternatives will successfully enter the automotive market is very difficult, especially in the face of changing regulations on fuel economy, emissions, and safety. While the

Table 7-3. Automotive Propulsion Possibilities for the Future	
Time Frame	**Propulsion System**
Near term (1991–1995)	4-stroke SI engine Hybrid (2- *or* 4-stroke SI engine/battery)
Midterm (1996–2000)	4-stroke SI engine Electric (battery) Hybrid (2- *or* 4-stroke SI engine/battery)
Long term (>2000)	4-stroke SI engine Electric (battery) Ceramic gas turbine Advanced hybrid (gas turbine/battery) Advanced hybrid (PEM fuel cell/battery)

development of alternative propulsion technologies is proceeding, the SI engine continues to show its versatility and adaptability to meet more stringent regulations. It remains a tough competitor to other alternatives and will remain in service for the foreseeable future.

Table 7-3 lists some future possibilities for the appearance of alternative automotive power plants on our roadways. As we move from near term to long term, the number of possibilities increases as advances result from work now in progress. The conventional SI engine appears in every time frame. In the near term (five years or less), heat engine/battery hybrid vehicles could appear on our roadways. Additionally, small two-stroke- or four-stroke-cycle SI engines could find use as range extenders for the hybrids. In the midterm (five to ten years), EVs with advanced batteries might appear, perhaps in some hybrid configuration with two-stroke SI or possibly Stirling engines. In the long term (beyond ten years), electric and hybrid vehicles incorporating advanced fuel cells and batteries appear possible, as do gas turbine-powered vehicles. Expanded R&D on batteries in conjunction with the industry-led consortium could significantly advance the commercialization of EVs and hybrids. For the gas turbine, commercialization will depend to a large extent on whether ceramics can be used throughout the hot sections of the engine. In brief, the fate of the turbine appears almost totally dependent on the success of the jointly funded (industry/government) ongoing development activities for advanced ceramic materials. Recent successes in the ceramics program have boosted confidence that this can be achieved.

Potential Impacts of Advances in Vehicle Technology on Energy Use and CO_2 Emissions

The potential impacts of expected advances in vehicle technology on automobile energy use and CO_2 emissions have been quantified by comparative analysis. The analysis focuses on several major automobile fuel efficiency improvements expected to emerge from DOE's and some of industry's developmental efforts. They include changes in powertrain (engine and drivetrain) efficiency and in vehicle characteristics, such as weight and aerodynamic drag. These changes to the automobile are likely to result from

- advances in four-stroke SI engines due to ongoing industry efforts

- introduction of advanced propulsion alternatives from DOE/industry programs

- use of alternative fuels

- introduction of lightweight structural materials (from a new DOE initiative on lightweight transportation materials and ongoing industry efforts), combined with improved materials selection on the part of auto manufacturers

- improvements in aerodynamic design

The fuel energy requirements (Btu/mi) and CO_2 emissions (gm/mi) are estimated for a midsized automobile (with the powertrain options listed in Table 7-3) over the Federal Urban Driving Schedule (FUDS). A total of ten powertrain options are analyzed: two in the near term, three in the midterm, and five in the long term. In the case of electric propulsion, the fuel energy requirements and CO_2 emissions are estimated at the electricity-generating power plant. For each powertrain option that requires on-board fuel, the use of gasoline, methanol, compressed natural gas, or hydrogen as the fuel is analyzed. Hydrogen is considered as an acceptable fuel for the SI engine (with appropriate modifications) and provides the potential for increased thermal efficiency (Amann 1990a). However, hydrogen is analyzed as a fuel alternative only in the long term since its earlier availability and use as an automotive fuel is not considered likely.

For each time frame and powertrain/fuel combination, the primary vehicle characteristics (weight, drag coefficient, frontal area, rolling resistance) and powertrain characteristics (engine power output, component efficiencies, accessory load, and so forth) are specified. The vehicle and powertrain specifications for the mid and long term reflect several likely improvements in vehicle technology and design as compared with those of the near term (Burke 1990; Cheng 1988; Mintz & Vyas 1990; OTA 1991; Santini et al. 1989; USDOE 1990). The vehicle and powertrain characteristics specified for the analysis, and the results of the analysis, are discussed below.

It is important to note at the outset that this analysis is essentially limited in scope and is aimed primarily at quantifying the extent to which energy use and CO_2 emissions can be reduced *at the vehicle level* as improvements in vehicle design and propulsion technology are introduced. The emissions estimates presented here include only CO_2 produced from the direct combustion of the fuel on board the vehicle or at the electricity-generating power plant (in the case of EVs). CO_2 emissions associated with processing, transportation, and distribution of fuels, and emissions of other greenhouse gases (CH_4, N_2O), are not considered, and results of this analysis are not intended to be used as a basis for selecting between fuels or powertrain options. In this respect, this analysis does not attempt to duplicate other, more comprehensive assessments that have considered the entire fuel cycle, emissions of greenhouse gases other than CO_2, and a wider range of assumptions to account for the many uncertainties regarding the future (DeLuchi 1990; OTA 1991; Santini et al. 1989).

Vehicle Characteristics

Table 7-4 summarizes the automobile range and weight characteristics for each alternative powertrain/fuel combination analyzed. In specifying the characteristics of vehicles with advanced powertrain options, it is assumed that DOE's mid- and long-term program goals for advanced heat engines, batteries, and fuel cells will be met. A gasoline SI engine–powered, midsized automobile is used as the baseline vehicle in each time frame. The estimated impact of various powertrain and fuel options on vehicle weight is shown for each case.

For the near term, the baseline vehicle (with gasoline SI engine) is representative of a popular midsized automobile currently available on the market. The 3,000-lb curb weight of this baseline vehicle in the near term is reduced by 10% and 20% to 2,700 and 2,400 lb, respectively, in the mid and long term to reflect the possible availability of new, lightweight structural materials and improved materials selection on the part of auto manufacturers (Mintz & Vyas). The resulting vehicle weights (including a 300-lb payload) for each alternative powertrain/fuel combination are shown in Table 7-4. The vehicle range is maintained at 250 miles, with the exception of the heat engine/battery hybrid vehicle in the near term (220 miles) and the electric vehicle in the midterm (200 miles). In both of these cases, the range is limited

Table 7-4. Vehicle Characteristics of Midsized Automobile with Alternative Powertrain and Fuel Combinations

| | ON-BOARD FUEL | | | | | | | |
| | Gasoline | | Methanol | | CNG | | Hydrogen | |
Powertrain	Range (mi)	Wt. (lb)	Range (mi)	Wt. (lb)	Range (mi)	Wt. (lb)	Range (mi)	Wt. (lb)
Near term								
4-stroke SI	250[a]	3,300[a]	250	3,300	250	3,500	NA[b]	NA
Hybrid (heat engine/ battery)[c]	220	4,200 (900)	220	4,200 (900)	220	4,300 (900)	NA	NA
Midterm[d]								
4-stroke SI	250	3,000	250	3,000	250	3,200	NA	NA
Electric (battery)	Range = 200 mi; Vehicle wt. = 4,250 lb (1,500 lb)							
Hybrid (heat engine/ battery)[c]	250	3,750 (750)	250	3,750 (750)	250	3,850 (750)	NA	NA
Long term[d]								
4-stroke SI	250	2,700	250	2,700	250	2,825	250	3,050
Electric (adv. battery)	Range = 250 mi; Vehicle wt. = 3,140 lb (690 lb)							
Ceramic gas turbine	250	2,450	250	2,450	250	2,550	250	2,700
Adv. hybrid (gas turbine/ battery)[d]	250	3,030 (330)	250	3,030 (330)	250	3,100 (330)	250	3,130 (330)
Adv. hybrid (PEM fuel cell/ battery)	NA	NA	250	3,000 (300)	250	3,080 (300)	250	3,070 (300)

Note: Vehicle urban driving range and corresponding test weight (including 300-lb payload) were used in estimation of fuel energy use and CO_2 emissions. Where applicable, battery weight is provided in parentheses. Other significant assumptions about vehicle include rolling resistance coefficient = 0.008; frontal area = 22.3 sq. ft.; aerodynamic drag coefficient = 0.33 (near term), 0.3 (midterm), 0.25 (long term).

[a] Represents popular midsized automobile that is currently available with 19-mpg fuel economy. A 13-gallon fuel tank is assumed for 250-mile range (base case for the entire analysis).

[b] NA = not analyzed.

[c] Series hybrid vehicle, with small heat-engine generator (gen-set) to extend range, with gen-set electrically coupled to drivetrain.

[d] Use of advanced lightweight structural materials and improved materials selection on the part of auto manufacturers is assumed to reduce vehicle curb weight by 10% and 20% in the mid and long term, respectively, without compromising safety or passenger and trunk space.

Table 7-5. Battery Characteristics and USDOE Battery Consortium Goals

Characteristic	Near Term (lead-acid)	Midterm (sodium-sulfur)	Long Term
Specific energy (Wh/kg)	28	100	200
Specific peak power (W/kg)	125	175	400
Cycles @ 80% DOD	~350	~600	1,000

Source: U.S. Advanced Battery Consortium (per. comm. 1991).
Note: DOD = depth of discharge.

by the battery weight. In specifying vehicle weight and powertrain capabilities, a certain degree of functional and performance equivalence is maintained to the extent that the weight of the vehicle minus the powertrain and fuel systems is kept the same for all vehicles within each time frame. With methanol, CNG, and hydrogen fuels, this implies loss of trunk space to accommodate increased fuel tank volumes. Peak power-to-weight ratios are also maintained, although in the case of the near-term and midterm hybrid vehicles and the midterm EVs, there is some loss of performance because of battery weight constraints.

The weight of the methanol-fueled vehicles is kept the same as that of the gasoline-fueled vehicles in all cases. The added weight due to increased methanol fuel volume is canceled by a weight reduction through engine downsizing to give gasoline-equivalent performance. In the case of CNG and hydrogen vehicles, fuel is stored on-board at 3,000 psi in fiberglass-wrapped aluminum cylinders and at 6,000 psi in Kevlar-wrapped cylinders, respectively. Compared with gasoline, fuel system weight (and volume) is higher with CNG and hydrogen to provide the 250-mile range. The gasoline, CNG, and hydrogen engines are assumed to weigh the same.

The weight of batteries for the electric and hybrid powertrains is based on specific energy (Wh/kg) and specific peak power (W/kg) values that reflect current lead-acid batteries and DOE battery consortium midterm and long-term goals (see Table 7-5). In Table 7-4, the extra weight of EVs is primarily attributable to the batteries (and supports) minus a weight reduction for the EV powertrain, which is lighter than the SI engine powertrain. The near-term hybrid (range-extender) vehicle uses lead-acid batteries and a small, off-the-shelf, four-stroke SI engine generator (which is electrically coupled to the drivetrain) to sustain the vehicle beyond battery-only range. In the long-term hybrid vehicle, the SI engine is replaced by a ceramic gas turbine. The hybrid

Table 7-6. Four-Stroke SI Engine Efficiencies (%)

Powertrain	Gasoline	ON-BOARD FUEL Methanol	CNG	Hydrogen
Near term				
4-stroke SI (stand-alone)[a]	16.0	17.6	16.0	NA[b]
4-stroke SI (hybrid)[c]	21.1	23.2	21.1	NA
Midterm				
4-stroke SI (stand-alone)[a]	16.8	19.3	18.5	NA
4-stroke SI (hybrid)[c]	23.2	26.7	25.5	NA
Long term				
4-stroke SI (stand-alone)[a]	17.6	20.8	19.4	21.1

Notes:
[a] Average engine efficiency over Federal Urban Driving Schedule (FUDS).
[b] NA = not analyzed.
[c] Maximum efficiency.

vehicles have a lower battery weight than do EVs but have the added weight of the heat engine generator and on-board fuel systems.

The weight of the PEM fuel cell system for the long-term hybrid vehicle was based on DOE's long-term PEM fuel cell program goals: a 75-kg stack weight and a 50-kg reformer weight for a 20-kW continuous-power (60-kW peak-power) fuel cell system. Despite the extra weight of hydrogen fuel storage, the hydrogen-fueled PEM fuel cell vehicle is about the same weight as the CNG or methanol fuel cell vehicles, since it does not require a reformer.

Powertrain Characteristics

The average engine efficiency over the FUDS for the near-term baseline vehicle (with current technology, gasoline, four-stroke SI engine) is 16%, based on EPA test data for midsized automobiles. For the near-term hybrid vehicle, the gasoline-fueled engine generator is set to always operate at its maximum efficiency point (21.1%, based on data for a commercially available product). Table 7-6 shows the efficiency values for the SI engines in the conventional stand-alone and hybrid configurations for each alternative fuel. It is assumed that the average efficiency of the baseline four-stroke SI (gasoline) engine will increase conservatively by 5% and 10% over current values in the mid and long term, respectively. Significantly larger improvements in the efficiency of automotive SI engines are possible over the mid to long term as a result of ongoing industry development efforts worldwide in several

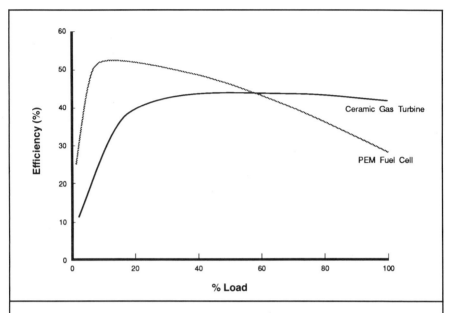

Figure 7-3. Projected Efficiency Characteristics: Ceramic Gas Turbine and PEM Fuel Cell Systems

Source: Allison Gas Turbine Division of General Motors.

areas, such as two-stroke-cycle engine, lean-burn engine, direct-injection stratified-charge engine, and so forth. However, the prospects for their use beyond selected niches is not clear. The efficiency of methanol, CNG, and hydrogen-fueled SI engines is set at 10%–20% above those of corresponding gasoline engines, as shown in Table 7-6. These values reflect achieved efficiency levels and projections reported in literature (DeLuchi 1989, 1990; Santini et al. 1989). The drivetrain efficiency is set at 85% in all cases. Finally, the peak power output of the stand-alone engines in the near-, mid-, and long-term time frame are specified as 100, 90, and 80 hp, respectively.

For the long-term options, the analysis used DOE projections of efficiency characteristics for the ceramic gas turbine (in stand-alone and hybrid configurations) and PEM fuel cell systems. These projections are for automobiles that may become available beyond the year 2000. The efficiency-versus-load characteristics are shown in Figure 7-3 and indicate maximum-point efficiencies of 43.5% for the ceramic gas turbine and 52% for the PEM fuel cell (with hydrogen as fuel).

Table 7-7. Electric-Powertrain-Component Efficiencies (%)			
Component	Near Term	Midterm	Long Term
Drivetrain	85	85	90
Motor and controller	85	90	90
Battery	75	75	80
Charger	90	90	90

Methanol and CNG reformer efficiencies are 90% and 80%, respectively.

The electric-powertrain-component efficiencies for the near, mid, and long term are shown in Table 7-7. Improvements in electric drivetrain, motor and controller, and battery efficiencies are projected from near term to long term. For the electric and hybrid automobiles, 10% regeneration is assumed over the full range of the urban driving cycle.

Estimates of Energy Use and CO_2 Emissions

A simplified calculation procedure is used to estimate the vehicle fuel energy requirements over the urban driving cycle. The power required at the driving wheels (on a level road) is calculated for second-by-second increments over the FUDS on the basis of the vehicle weight, drag coefficient, frontal area, and rolling-resistance coefficient, combined with the specified velocity-time profile and required acceleration.

In the case of the heat engine–powered vehicles, the required power at the wheels is adjusted with the drivetrain efficiency and an average accessory load to obtain the engine output. A check is performed to ensure that the engine output required does not exceed the available maximum. When the vehicle is at rest, the engine output is set to the idling value. Finally, the fuel energy input to the engine for each second of the driving cycle is calculated from the required engine output and efficiency. The engine efficiency is specified either as an average value over the FUDS (for the SI engines) or as efficiency-versus-load curves (for the ceramic gas turbine and PEM fuel cell).

In the case of electric vehicles, to calculate the power required at the electrical charging outlet, the level-road load power is adjusted for 10% regeneration, an average accessory load, and the efficiencies of the drivetrain, motor and controller, battery, and charger. The outlet power is transferred back to the fuel input at the electrical power plant on the basis of the transmission and distribution efficiency (95%) and the power plant efficiency (34%).

In the case of the heat engine/battery hybrid vehicles, a combination of the above procedures for heat engine and electric vehicles is used to estimate on-board vehicle and power plant fuel energy requirements. In the near term, it is assumed that 50% of the driving energy to the wheels comes from electrical outlet power (through charging the batteries) and 50% from the heat engine generator. In the mid to long term, as battery-only range of the vehicle is increased, the contribution of electrical outlet power is increased to 60%. The hybrid heat engine is assumed to always operate at its maximum efficiency point. In the case of the fuel cell/battery hybrid, all the vehicle energy requirements are supplied by the on-board fuel, with the battery being charged by the fuel cell and in turn supplying peaking power requirements.

In all cases, the fuel energy requirement is summed over the 7.5-mile FUDS and the average (per mile) value calculated. The average CO_2 emissions (in gm/mi) for each alternative powertrain/fuel combination are obtained directly from the fuel energy use. In the case of the SI engines, a 2-gm CO_2/mi contribution from burning of lubricating engine oil is also included (DeLuchi 1990). The carbon content of the various fuels (used on board the vehicle or at the power plant) and the power generation fuel mix for the United States are specified as notes to Table 7-8. For this analysis, it is assumed that all fuel carbon is directly oxidized to CO_2, even though this is not entirely accurate. Some of the carbon leaves the tailpipe or power plant stack as carbon monoxide, methane, nonmethane hydrocarbons, or soot, each of which has its own greenhouse gas impacts.

The estimated fuel energy requirement and CO_2 emissions at the vehicle and/or electricity generation power plant for each of the alternative powertrain/fuel combinations analyzed are presented in Table 7-8. The estimates are presented as a fraction of the base case values—6,550 Btu/mi and 480 gm CO_2/mi for the near-term vehicle with a gasoline, four-stroke SI engine. The base case represents current technology. Within each time frame, the energy use estimates primarily reflect the differences in automobile weight and powertrain efficiencies associated with each powertrain/fuel combination. The energy use estimates also reflect increasing use of lightweight structural materials and improved aerodynamic design of the vehicles over time. The CO_2 emissions estimates, in addition, reflect the carbon content of each fuel.

In the near term, heat engine/battery hybrids based on off-the-shelf SI engine generators and lead-acid batteries offer some fuel efficiency and CO_2 emissions benefits (see Table 7-8) over the conven-

Table 7-8. Average Automobile Fuel Energy Use and CO_2 Emissions with Alternative Powertrain and Fuel Combinations (Fraction of Base Case Values)

| | ON-BOARD FUEL | | | | | | | |
| | Gasoline | | Methanol | | CNG[a] | | Hydrogen[a] | |
Powertrain	Energy Use[b]	CO_2[c]	Energy Use[b]	CO_2[c]	Energy Use[b]	CO_2	Energy Use[b]	CO_2[c]
Near term								
4-stroke SI	1.0[d]	1.0[d]	0.91	0.82	1.04	0.75	NA[e]	NA
Hybrid (heat engine/battery)	0.87	0.79	0.83	0.72	0.89	0.68	NA	NA
Midterm								
4-stroke SI	0.88	0.88	0.77	0.70	0.84	0.61	NA	NA
Electric (battery)[f]	Energy use = 0.81				CO_2 = 0.68			
Hybrid (heat engine/battery)	0.72	0.65	0.69	0.59	0.71	0.57	NA	NA
Long term								
4-stroke SI	0.77	0.77	0.65	0.59	0.72	0.52	0.69	0.01
Electric (adv. battery)[f]	Energy use = 0.57				CO_2 = 0.47			
Ceramic gas turbine	0.48	0.48	0.48	0.43	0.48	0.35	0.49	0
Adv. hybrid (gas turbine/battery)	0.45	0.40	0.45	0.39	0.46	0.37	0.46	0.29
Adv. hybrid (PEM fuel cell/battery)	NA	NA	0.38	0.35	0.44	0.32	0.35	0

Notes:

a CNG and compressed hydrogen gas stored on board vehicle at 3,000 psi and 6,000 psi, respectively (DeLuchi 1989). Hydrogen is not considered as a near- or midterm fuel for automobiles.

b For midsized automobile over Federal Urban Driving Schedule (FUDS). See Tables 7-3 through 7-6 for assumptions on vehicle and powertrain characteristics. Assumes current U.S. generation fuel mix in near term (54% coal, 4% oil, 9% gas, 33% nuclear and renewable), and North American Electric Reliability Council projections for post-1995 period in mid and long term (55% coal, 7% oil, 7% gas, 31% nuclear and renewable) (EPRI 1989).

c Includes only CO_2 emissions from fuel combustion (and burning of engine oil) on board vehicle or at electricity generation power plant. Other greenhouse gases are not considered. CO_2 emissions based on complete oxidation of fuel carbon content of 20 mg/Btu for gasoline, 18 mg/Btu for methanol, 14 mg/Btu for CNG, 26 mg/Btu for coal, and 21 mg/Btu for oil (Marland & Pippin 1991; OTA 1991).

d Base case values are 6,550 Btu/mile and 480 gm CO_2/mi, representing current-technology gasoline-fueled, 4-stroke SI engine in a popular midsized automobile (19-mpg urban fuel economy).

e NA = not analyzed.

f For electric vehicles, fuel energy use and CO_2 emissions are estimated at electricity generation plant.

tional SI engine. However, costs of the hybrids are initially expected to be higher and performance lower, reflecting the limitation of current battery technology.

In the midterm, the availability of improved batteries (such as sodium-sulfur) is expected to make electric passenger cars with at least a 200-mile range feasible. However, the still significant battery weight penalty associated with these midterm EVs (see Table 7-4) could limit the energy use and CO_2 emissions benefits as compared with conventional gasoline-fueled SI engines. Midterm hybrid vehicles, incorporating sodium-sulfur batteries and small SI engine generators optimized for fuel economy and emissions, could show significant reductions in energy use and CO_2 emissions (see Table 7-8) along with more competitive range and performance characteristics.

In the long term, substantial reductions in energy use and CO_2 emissions could become possible with the introduction of advanced batteries from consortium-led efforts, and the ceramic gas turbine and PEM fuel cell systems for automotive use. As compared with the gasoline SI engine–powered vehicle in the long term, the advanced EV shows a 26% reduction in energy use and a 39% reduction in CO_2 emissions, whereas the gasoline-fueled ceramic gas turbine vehicle shows a 38% reduction in both energy use and CO_2 emissions, and the gasoline-fueled hybrid (gas turbine/battery) shows a 42% reduction in energy use and a 48% reduction in CO_2 emissions. The greatest benefits are offered by the hydrogen-fueled PEM fuel cell/battery hybrid vehicle, which shows a 55% reduction in energy use and zero CO_2 emissions from the vehicle.

Although the specific estimates of energy use and CO_2 emissions shown in Table 7-8 are subject to a host of assumptions, the magnitude of the overall trend is unmistakable. And although this chapter has focused on energy use and CO_2 emissions, fuel cell and ceramic gas turbine engines also hold the potential to substantially reduce regulated pollutants (carbon monoxide, nitrogen oxides, and hydrocarbons). This can be seen in Figure 7-4, which compares the projected emissions performances of fuel cells and advanced gas turbine vehicles with U.S. standards.

It is also useful to compare the overall vehicle efficiency values calculated for the various powertrain/fuel combinations analyzed. Overall vehicle efficiency is calculated from the fuel input (at vehicle/power plant) to the road. For four-stroke SI engine–powered vehicles, overall efficiency varies from almost 11% with gasoline in the near term to 14% with methanol and hydrogen in the long term. In contrast, the overall vehicle efficiency is around 18% for both the ceramic gas turbine vehicle and the advanced electric vehicle in the long term. The

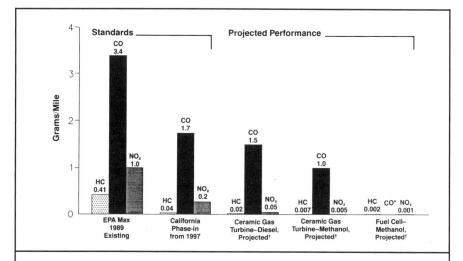

Figure 7-4. Regulated Emissions for Passenger Cars: Standards and Projected Performance

Source: Brogan & Venkateswaran (1991).
* Less than 2 ppm.
† The ceramic gas turbine and fuel cell have low levels of particulates and smoke.

corresponding value for the methanol-fueled, PEM fuel cell vehicle is 25%. The hybrid configuration of the fuel cell vehicle allows peak power requirements to be met by a battery, whereas the fuel cell system is sized to meet only average power requirements. This allows the fuel cell to operate at a significantly higher efficiency level over the urban driving cycle than the stand-alone gas turbine engine, which is sized to meet peak power requirements. In the case of the gas turbine/battery hybrid vehicle, the overall vehicle efficiency is higher (at 22%) than with the stand-alone gas turbine, since the hybrid heat engine operates at its maximum efficiency level.

A cursory look at the impact of alternative fuels on energy use and CO_2 emissions shows that methanol-fueled vehicles generally exhibit the lowest average energy use for each powertrain option. This is as expected since these vehicles are not penalized by the higher fuel system weight requirements of CNG and hydrogen vehicles (to maintain range). In addition, methanol-fueled SI engines are projected to be more efficient than gasoline- or CNG-fueled engines. With respect to fuel carbon content, hydrogen has the obvious advantage, followed by CNG, which is a relatively low-carbon fossil fuel.

Conclusions

The DOE Vehicle Propulsion R&D Program is aimed at jointly exploring alternative-propulsion-system candidates with industry and supporting R&D as necessary to accelerate commercialization of the better technologies. The successful introduction of advanced propulsion technologies (and alternative fuels) into the automotive marketplace will provide a pathway to improved fuel economy, fuel flexibility, and lower emissions (including those of greenhouse gases) for the nation's automobile fleet. These advanced technologies are also generally applicable to the light-truck market. Expanded R&D on batteries, in conjunction with the industry-led consortium, and on advanced fuel cells is likely to significantly accelerate the commercialization of EVs and hybrids. Recent successes in ceramic materials development have boosted confidence that a viable automotive gas turbine engine can be developed.

A scenario was projected for the future appearance of alternative automotive power plants on our roadways, and a comparative analysis was performed of several alternative powertrain/fuel combinations in a midsized automobile. The analysis indicates a substantially large potential for reducing automobile energy use and related CO_2 emissions through improvements to the conventional four-stroke SI engine, introduction of advanced heat engine, electric, and electric-hybrid alternatives, combined with reduction in the weight of vehicle structures (through new lightweight materials) and vehicle design improvements. In the best case, the fuel energy use (6,550 Btu/mi) and CO_2 emissions (480 gm CO_2/mi) for a current-technology midsized automobile with gasoline-fueled SI engine could be potentially reduced (in the long term) to as low as 2,300 Btu/mi and zero emissions of CO_2 with a PEM fuel cell/battery hybrid vehicle fueled by hydrogen. In the long term, the ceramic gas turbine–powered vehicle, and electric and hybrid vehicles based on advanced batteries and the gas turbine, could also provide almost equally large reductions in automobile energy use and CO_2 emissions. These projections, however, assume that long-term DOE program R&D goals for the ceramic gas turbine, batteries, and fuel cells can be achieved and that advanced lightweight structural materials will become available to reduce vehicle weight without compromising safety or functionality.

When comparing alternative fuels purely on the basis of CO_2 emissions from fuel combustion (on board the vehicle/at the power plant), hydrogen is, as expected, the preferred fuel, followed by CNG. Hydrogen is, however, the least developed for use as an automotive fuel and presents major problems with respect to production, storage and distribution infrastructure, utilization, and cost. In addition to the compressed-hydrogen-gas storage considered in this chapter, liquid hydrogen and metal hydride storage alternatives present performance advantages as well as assorted problems (DeLuchi 1989).

The level of CO_2 emissions associated with electric vehicles depends on the fuel mix used for electrical power generation. Increased use of electricity generated from renewable or nuclear energy would reduce CO_2 emissions, whereas use of power from fossil fuels could lead to increases. The current U.S. mix of almost 70% fossil fuel power does provide some benefits. Nevertheless, a fair comparison of the alternative fuels (including electricity) for vehicle propulsion should consider CO_2 emissions from processing and distributing the fuel (which depends on the source) and the emissions of greenhouse gases other than CO_2. Those considerations, however, are beyond the scope of this analysis.

Finally, it is important to note that the results presented here are subject to a host of assumptions about vehicle, fuel, and powertrain characteristics, many of which are projections for the future and subject to debate and uncertainty. These results are meant to be viewed as one cross-section of a more comprehensive parametric study that would be required to account for uncertainties in several critical assumptions, such as powertrain component efficiencies, materials availability, and so forth. Efforts will be continued to refine and expand the analysis in order to set up a fair and consistent framework for establishing future vehicle propulsion technology trends and to ascertain the potential for reducing automotive energy use and emissions.

References

Amann, C. A. 1900a. "The Passenger Car and the Greenhouse Effect." Paper presented at the International Fuels and Lubricants Meeting and Exposition, Tulsa, Okla., October 22–25. Society of Automotive Engineers (SAE) Paper 902099.

————. 1990b. *Technical Options for Energy Conservation and Controlling Environmental Impact in Highway Vehicles.* General Motors Research Laboratories Publication GMR-6942. February.

Barber, K. F. 1990. "An Overview of the Electric and Hybrid Vehicles R&D Program at the U.S. Department of Energy." Paper presented at the 10th International Electric Vehicle Symposium, Hong Kong, December 3–5.

Brogan, J. J., and S. R. Venkateswaran. 1991. "U.S. Department of Energy's Perspective on Fuel-Efficient and Low Emission Propulsion Technology Options for Automobiles." Paper presented at the

International Conference on Tomorrow's Clean and Fuel-Efficient Automobile: Opportunities for East-West Cooperation, Berlin, March.

Burke, A. F. 1990. "Electric Vehicle Propulsion and Battery Technology, 1975–1995." Paper presented at the 25th Intersociety Energy Conversion Engineering Conference, Reno, Nev., August.

Cheng, H. C. 1988. *Potential Reductions in the U.S. CO₂ Emissions in 1995 and 2010 by Technology Improvements in Electricity Generation and Transportation Sectors.* Brookhaven National Laboratory Report. Upton, N.Y. April.

Davis, S., and P. Hu. 1989. *Transportation Energy Data Book.* 10th ed. Oak Ridge National Laboratory Report ORNL-6565. Oak Ridge, Tenn. September.

DeLuchi, M. A. 1989. "Hydrogen Vehicles: An Evaluation of Fuel Storage, Performance, Safety, Environmental Impacts, and Cost." *International J. Hydrogen Energy* 14 (2): 81–130.

———. 1990. "State-of-the-Art Assessment of Emissions of Greenhouse Gases from the Use of Fossil and Non-Fossil Fuels, with Emphasis on Alternative Transportation Fuels." University of California Report. Davis, Calif. June.

Electric Power Research Institute. 1989. "Electric Van and Gasoline Van Emissions: A Comparison." Technical Brief, Customer Systems Division. Palo Alto, Calif.

Fleming, R. D. 1990. "Status of Spark Ignition Two-Stroke Cycle Engine Technology for Automotive Applications." U.S. Department of Energy Report. Washington, D.C. September.

Kalberlah, A. 1991. "Electric Hybrid Drive Systems for Passenger Cars and Taxis." Paper presented at the Society of Automotive Engineers (SAE) International Congress and Exposition, Detroit, Mich., February/March. SAE Paper 910247.

Kato, S., and S. Onishi. 1990. "Direct Injection Stratified Charge Engine by Impingement of Fuel Jet (OSKA): Performance and Combustion Characteristics." Paper presented at the Society of Automotive Engineers (SAE) International Congress and Exposition, Detroit, Mich., February/March. SAE Paper 900608.

Marland, G., and A. Pippin. 1991. "United States Emissions of Carbon Dioxide to the Earth's Atmosphere by Economic Activity." *Energy Systems and Policy* 14:101–118.

Mintz, M. M., and A. D. Vyas. 1990. *Forecast of Transportation Energy Demand Through the Year 2010.* Center for Transportation Research, Argonne National Laboratory, Report ANL/ESD-9. Argonne, Ill. November.

Santini, D. J., M. A. DeLuchi, A. Vyas, and M. Walsh. 1989. "Greenhouse Gas Emissions from Selected Alternative Transportation Fuels Market Niches." Paper presented at the 1989 Summer National Meeting of the American Institute of Chemical Engineers, August.

U.S. Congress, Office of Technology Assessment. 1991. *Changing by Degrees: Steps to Reduce Greenhouse Gases*. Office of Technology Assessment Report OTA-O-482. Washington, D.C. February.

USDOE. 1990. *Assessment of Costs and Benefits of Flexible and Alternative Fuel Use in the U.S. Transportation Sector. Technical Report Four: Vehicle and Fuel Distribution Requirements*. Office of Policy, Planning and Analysis Report DOE/PE-0095P. Washington, D.C. August.

————. 1991. *National Energy Strategy: Powerful Ideas for Tomorrow*. 1st ed. Washington, D.C.: U.S. Department of Energy. February.

USDOT. 1991. "Summary of Fuel Economy Performance." National Highway Transportation Safety Administration Report. June.

Wyczalek, F. A. 1991. "GM Electric Vehicle Technology in the 1990s." Paper presented at the 26th Intersociety Energy Conversion Engineering Conference, Boston. August.

Chapter 8

Solar Hydrogen Transportation Fuels

Joan M. Ogden and Mark A. DeLuchi

oncerns about global warming, urban air quality, acid deposition, and energy supply security are motivating increased interest in low-polluting alternative transportation fuels. Hydrogen
is a high-quality, exceptionally clean fuel that has been demonstrated
in experimental cars, buses, trucks, and airplanes (Buchner 1984;
Buchner & Povel 1982; DeLuchi 1989; Feucht, Holzel & Hurwich
1988; Furuhama 1988; Protosenko 1988; Schucan 1990; Schwarz
1990; Sperling 1989). With today's hydrogen internal-combustion-
engine vehicles, the only pollutants are nitrogen oxides (NO_x), which
can be controlled to low levels. With hydrogen fuel cell vehicles,
which could be developed over the next several years, even NO_x emissions would be eliminated. If hydrogen is produced from renewable
resources, via water electrolysis using solar, wind, or hydroelectric
power or via gasification of renewably grown biomass, it would be
possible in principle to produce and use transport fuel on a large scale
with greatly reduced greenhouse gas emissions and very little local
pollution (Ogden 1991; Winter & Nitsch 1988).

In this chapter we analyze the prospects for producing hydrogen
transportation fuel from renewable resources. We first review the technologies for producing hydrogen from renewables and describe several
base case renewable hydrogen production systems. We then estimate
hydrogen production costs, based on current technology and projections for the near term (1990s) and the long term (post 2000 with
mature technologies widely employed so that economies of scale are

The authors would like to thank Eric Larson and Robert Williams for useful discussions.
This work was supported by the National Renewable Energy Laboratory and the U.S. Environmental Protection Agency.

fully exploited).[1] Potential resources for producing hydrogen from solar, wind, hydropower, and biomass are estimated, and environmental aspects of renewable hydrogen systems are considered. We discuss hydrogen transportation technologies, with an emphasis on fuel cell vehicles now under development. Hydrogen fuel cell vehicles are particularly interesting because they could combine the best features of electric-battery vehicles (zero emissions, high efficiency, quiet, long life) with the convenience and flexibility of gasoline vehicles (fast refueling time, long range) and could potentially serve a larger fraction of the market than battery-powered electric vehicles (Nesbitt, DeLuchi & Kurani 1991). The life-cycle cost of automotive transportation for a fuel cell vehicle fueled with solar hydrogen is compared with other alternatives, such as gasoline internal-combustion-engine vehicles, methanol fuel cell vehicles, and battery-powered electric vehicles. Emissions of greenhouse gases and other pollutants are estimated for various alternatives. Finally, we discuss a strategy for developing renewable hydrogen transportation systems.

Technologies for Producing Hydrogen from Renewable Resources

In this section we describe technologies for producing hydrogen from renewable resources, focusing on technologies that could be employed over the next ten to twenty years. To facilitate comparison between technologies, the levelized cost of hydrogen production is calculated using a consistent set of economic assumptions (see the chapter appendix). Cost and performance of various technologies are given in Tables 8-1 through 8-9, and hydrogen production costs are summarized in Table 8-10.

Solar-Powered Water Electrolysis

In solar-powered electrolysis systems, a source of renewable electricity—such as solar photovoltaics, solar thermal power, wind, or hydro power—is connected to an electrolyzer, which splits water into its constituent elements, hydrogen and oxygen. The hydrogen can be used on-site, compressed for storage, or transmitted via pipelines to distant users. A solar photovoltaic electrolytic hydrogen system is diagrammed in Figure 8-1.

---

[1] To facilitate comparison between technologies we have calculated levelized production costs (in constant 1989 U.S.$) using a consistent set of economic assumptions. (See the chapter appendix for assumptions and cost equations.)

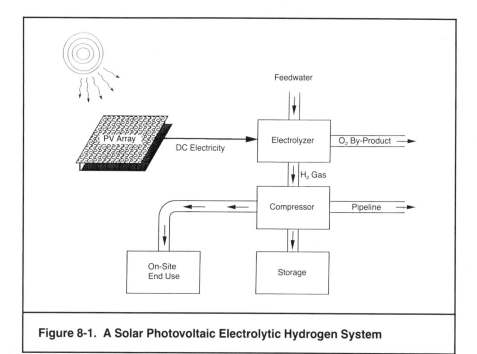

Figure 8-1. A Solar Photovoltaic Electrolytic Hydrogen System

Solar-Electric Technologies. Several sources of renewable electricity could be used to power electrolyters.

HYDROELECTRIC POWER. Hydroelectricity is a mature, commercial electricity-generation technology. At sites where excess off-peak power is available, hydro power can be very inexpensive, making it attractive for electrolytic hydrogen production. To estimate hydrogen costs, we assume that off-peak hydro power would be available at 2–4 cents/kWhAC, for eight hours per day (Stuart 1991).

WIND POWER. There have been dramatic improvements in wind technology over the past ten years, and today about 1600 MW of wind power is installed around the world. At present, the installed system capital cost is about $1,100/kW for 100- to 200-kW wind turbines. Over the next few years, costs are projected to drop to about $1,000/kW for 340-kW turbines with variable speed drives (Lucas et al. 1990; Smith 1991). Beyond the year 2000, costs could drop further to $750–$850/kW (Cohen et al. 1989; Hock, Thresher & Cohen 1990; Smith 1991; USDOE 1990) (see Table 8-1).

At a typical "good" site (with an average wind power density of 350 W/m²), we calculate that for 1990 technology, the cost of electric-

Table 8-1. Cost and Performance of Wind Power Technologies

Cost and Performance	1990[a]	Near Term[b]	Post 2000[c]
Total installed cost ($/kWp)	1,100	1,000	750
Turbine output (kW)	100	340	1,000
Turbine diameter (m)	17.5	33	52
Availability	90%	95%	95%
Annual O&M costs, including retrofits (cents/kWhAC)	1.5	1.1	0.6
Rent on land (cents/kWh)	0.3	0.3	0.3
System lifetime (years)	25	30	30
Annual average capacity factor[d]			
Wind power density = 350 W/m²	0.132	0.202	0.273
Wind power density = 500 W/m²	0.205	0.288	0.390
Wind power density = 630 W/m²	—	0.362	0.490
AC electricity cost (cents/kWh)[e]			
Wind power density = 350 W/m²	14.3	7.0	4.0
Wind power density = 500 W/m²	8.3	5.2	3.3
Wind power density = 630 W/m²	—	4.5	2.6

Notes:
[a] Cost and performance estimates are for US Windpower 100-kW models (Smith 1991). See also Cohen et al. (1989).
[b] Costs are estimated for mid-1990s wind turbine technology based on the US Windpower 33-meter-diameter variable-speed-drive model (Smith 1991). See also Lucas et al. (1990).
[c] Costs and performance projections for advanced wind turbines are from studies by the Solar Energy Research Institute. See Hock, Thresher & Cohen (1990) and Appendix F of Idaho National Engineering Lab (1990).
[d] The annual average capacity factor is given for three levels of average wind power density (350, 500, and 630 W/m² of swept rotor area), measured at the rotor hub height. With present wind turbines, the hub height is typically 30 meters, and the average wind power density is 350 W/m² in class 4 wind regions and about 500 W/m² in class 5–6 wind regions. With near-term technology, it should be possible to extend the height to 50 meters. In this case, the average power density would be 350 W/m² for a class 3 region, about 500 W/m² for a class 4–5 region, and 700 W/m² for class 6 regions. Class 3, 4, and 5 wind resources are widely found throughout the world; class 6 is less common.
[e] Levelized electricity costs are calculated in constant 1989 U.S.$ using the equations in the chapter appendix and the economic assumptions in appendix Table A-1.

ity would be about 14.3 cents/kWhAC (see Table 8-1). At an "excellent" site (with a wind power density of 500 W/m²), the cost of electricity would be about 8.3 cents/kWh. Recent operating experience and design studies have indicated that advanced airfoils, innovative drive controls, drivetrain improvements, and site-dependent optimization strategies could improve the efficiency of energy capture at little or no extra cost (Hock, Thresher & Cohen 1990). As these technical improvements are incorporated into the next generation of wind turbines in the early to mid-1990s, the cost of electricity should drop by several cents/kWh. For example, with the introduction of variable-speed drive technology, which is now being commercialized by US Windpower, costs of electricity should fall to 7 cents/kWh for a good site and 5.2 cents/kWh for an excellent site. In the longer term, electricity costs could reach 2.6–4 cents/kWh. Wind technology is modular, with little economy of scale beyond typical wind turbine sizes of 50–300 kW.

SOLAR THERMAL ELECTRIC. In solar thermal-electric systems, solar radiation is converted into high-temperature heat by collecting sunlight over a large-area "collector" and focusing it onto a smaller-area "receiver." The heat is then used to power an electric generator. To better match utility electric-demand profiles, the heat can be stored for later use, or a supplemental fuel (generally natural gas) can be used to provide extra heat when needed. For efficient operation, solar thermal systems require direct sunlight. With central-receiver and parabolic-dish designs, tracking systems must be used to follow the sun. Several types of solar thermal-electric systems have been developed (DeLaquil 1991; DeLaquil et al. 1993; USDOE 1990) (see Table 8-2).

Parabolic-trough collectors concentrate solar radiation ten to one hundred times, by focusing sunlight onto a central pipe containing oil. The heated oil (at 300°–400° C) is used to produce steam, which powers a steam turbine generator. The overall efficiency of converting sunlight to electricity is about 13%–17%. A natural-gas burner provides supplemental heat when sunlight is inadequate to meet demands. Parabolic-trough systems are commercially available at $2,800–$3,500/kW and produce electricity at a cost of 12–16 cents/kWh. A total of about 350 MW of solar thermal-electric parabolic-trough systems are already installed, mostly in California. With improvements, capital costs are projected to drop to $2,000–$2,400/kW, and electricity costs to about 8–12 cents/kWh (see Table 8-2).

In *central-receiver systems*, an array of movable flat-plate heliostats focuses sunlight on a central-receiver tower, with a concentration of 300–1,500 times, and heats a working fluid to 500°–1,500° C. Steam is raised in a heat exchanger to power a steam turbine, and typically some heat is stored for later use. Efficiencies for these systems are about 8%–15% but are projected to reach 10%–16%. Capacity factors with storage would be 25%–40% at present but could reach as high as 55%–63%. Central-receiver systems have been demonstrated in several 1–10 MW pilot projects, although the technology has not yet

Table 8-2. Cost and Performance of Solar Thermal-Electric Technologies

PARABOLIC-TROUGH SYSTEMS

	1990	Near Term	Post 2000
Capital cost ($/kW)	2,800–3,500	2,400–3,000	2,000–2,400
Peak capacity (MWe)	80	80	160
Annual energy efficiency solar mode	13%–17%	13%–17%	13%–17%
Method for enhanced load matching	—————	natural-gas firing	—————
Fraction of kWh from gas	25%	25%	25%
Solar capacity factor	22%–25%	18%–26%	22%–27%
O&M cost (cents/kWh)	1.8–2.5	1.6–2.4	1.3–2.0
System lifetime (years)	30	30	30
AC electricity cost (cents/kWhAC)[a]	11.6–16.0	9.8–16.6	8.0–11.6

CENTRAL-RECEIVER SYSTEMS

	1990	Near Term	Post 2000
Capital cost ($/kW)	3,000–4,000	2,225–3,000	2,900–3,500
Peak capacity (MWe)	100	200	200
Annual energy efficiency solar mode	8%–15%	10%–16%	10%–16%
Method for enhanced load matching	—————	thermal storage	—————
Solar capacity factor	25%–40%	30%–40%	55%–63%
O&M cost (mills/kWh)	1.3–1.9	0.8–1.6	0.5–0.8
System lifetime (years)	30	30	30
AC electricity cost (cents/kWhAC)[a]	9.7–20.0	6.8–12.3	5.4–7.6

PARABOLIC-DISH SYSTEMS

	1990	Near Term	Post 2000
Capital cost ($/kW)	3,000–5,000	2,000–3,500	1,250–2,000
Peak capacity (MWe)	3	30	300
Annual energy efficiency solar mode	16%–24%	18%–26%	20%–28%
Method for enhanced load matching	—————	solar only	—————
Solar capacity factor	16%–22%	20%–26%	22%–28%
O&M cost (mills/kWh)	2.5–5.0	2.0–3.0	1.5–2.5
System lifetime (years)	30	30	30
AC electricity cost (cents/kWhAC)[a]	17–38	10.2–22.0	6.1–12.2

Source: Adapted from USDOE (1990).
Note: It is assumed in all cases that the system lifetime is thirty years, the price of natural gas is $3/GJ, and that nonfuel O&M costs are 2 cents/kWh.
[a] Levelized electricity costs are calculated in constant 1989 U.S.$, using the equations in the chapter appendix and the economic assumptions of appendix Table A-1, and assuming a southwestern U.S. location.

been commercialized. To reach economies of scale, the system capacity must be at least 100–200 MW. With present technology, the system capital cost would be about \$3,000–\$4,000/kW, which, according to our calculations, would result in an electricity cost of about 10–20 cents/kWh. In the near term, capital costs could drop to perhaps \$2,000–\$3,000/kW, resulting in an electricity cost of 7–12 cents/kWh. In the longer term, with higher-capacity factor and more storage, the electricity cost could drop to 5.4–7.6 cents/kWh.

Parabolic dishes achieve high concentration (1,000–2,000 times) and temperatures of over 1,500° C. The system consists of an array of parabolic dishes, each of which tracks the sun and focuses light onto a receiver at the focal point of the dish. Electricity is produced either by using a small Stirling engine at each dish, or by having the receiver heat a working fluid that is then piped to a central location to produce steam and electricity. Efficiencies for these systems are about 16%–24% and could reach 20%–28%. No storage is used, but supplemental heat can be generated to match a utility electric-demand profile, as with parabolic-trough systems. Parabolic-dish systems have been demonstrated in several projects. Individual dishes with Stirling engines have performed well (at efficiencies of up to 29%), but systems with circulating fluids have been plagued by difficulties in the heat transfer process. Stirling/dish systems are modular and can produce electricity at small size (5–25 kW). In the near term, these systems are projected to cost \$3,000–\$5,000/kW, with electricity costs of 17–38 cents/kWh. In the longer term, costs of \$1,250–\$2,000/kW and 6–12 cents/kWh are projected.

Parabolic-trough systems are the simplest and most developed solar thermal-electric technology, but central-receiver and parabolic-dish/Stirling designs could reach higher efficiencies and lower costs in the long term. Parabolic-trough and central-receiver systems would have to be large (100–200 MW) to reach economies of scale. Parabolic-dish systems could be much smaller (tens of kilowatts for each unit).

SOLAR PHOTOVOLTAICS. Solar photovoltaic (PV) technologies, which convert sunlight directly into electricity, are advancing rapidly (Hubbard 1989; Zweibel 1990). In recent years, the annual production of PV modules has been growing at about 30% per year, with over 40 MW manufactured in 1990. PV power is already economically competitive on a life-cycle cost basis for applications at remote sites far from a utility grid, such as charging batteries, pumping water, and small-scale (<20 kW) power generation. PV systems require little maintenance. They are modular and can be built as small as a few kilowatts. As costs decrease during the 1990s, PVs should start to become competitive for residential power and central-station peaking power. Unlike solar thermal-electric systems, some PV systems can be used in cloudy areas that have only limited direct sunlight.

Various types of solar cells have been developed based on crystalline, polycrystalline, and amorphous materials. Commercially available crystalline solar cells are made by growing single-crystal cylindrical ingots of silicon or other materials and sawing them into circular wafers 100–200 microns thick. Commercially available polycrystalline solar cells are made by casting silicon into rectangular blocks, which are sawed to form individual solar cells. Crystalline solar cells are more efficient than other technologies—efficiencies of 35% have been achieved with laboratory crystalline solar cells—but are more expensive to manufacture. Polycrystalline cells are less efficient—the best laboratory cells are 17% efficient, and commercial modules are 12% (Zweibel 1990)—but less costly to manufacture.

Over the past ten years, thin-film solar cells using amorphous silicon, polycrystalline materials, and crystalline silicon have been developed. Thin-film solar cells typically are 1–5 microns in thickness, as compared with 100–200 microns for grown crystalline silicon or cast polycrystalline materials, and as a result use much less material. They can be manufactured more simply, by various processes that directly deposit the solar cells on glass or ceramics. Although thin-film solar cells are less efficient than other solar-cell materials (the best laboratory cells are now about 16% efficient, and modules are about 6%–8% efficient), they have the potential to reach much lower mass-production costs.

To produce power, solar cells are connected to form modules. In flat-plate modules, solar cells are encapsulated between layers of glass. Concentrator modules use plastic Fresnel lenses to concentrate sunlight from a large area onto a small-area cell. Modules can be mounted in fixed arrays, or tracking arrays can be used to follow the sun. Tracking arrays capture more of the sun's radiation, and are required for concentrators, but are more expensive and complex than fixed, flat-plate systems.

Large (>5 MW) PV systems today cost about $4,000–$9,000/kW installed and produce PV electricity for 14–35 cents/kWh (see Tables 8-3 and 8-4). As the efficiency of solar-cell materials improves and manufacturing processes are scaled-up and refined, the cost of PV systems is expected to drop to $1,500–$3,500/kW in the 1990s, with DC electricity costs of 6–14 cents/kWh. By the early part of the next century, thin-film solar-cell or concentrator systems could cost $500–$1,100/kW, with DC electricity costs of 2.2–4.4 cents/kWhDC.

Table 8-3. Cost and Performance of Solar Photovoltaic Modules

Solar PV Technology	PV MODULE EFFICIENCY (%)			PV MODULE MANUFACTURING COST ($/m²)		
	1990	Near Term	Post 2000	1990	Near Term	Post 2000
FLAT-PLATE MODULES						
Thin films						
Amorphous silicon[a]	6	8–10	12–18	100	70	30–55
CuInSe₂[b,c]	10	10	15	200	75–200	45
CdTe[b,d]	8	10	15	200	75–200	45
Thin-film silicon[b]		16			50	
Polycrystalline[b]	13		17	250–400		170–340
Crystalline[b]	15		20	500–800		200–400
CONCENTRATOR MODULES[e]	20	25	35	300–700	200	150

Notes:
[a] From Carlson (1989, 1990).
[b] From Zweibel (1991) and Barnett (1991).
[c] CuInSe₂ = copper indium diselenide.
[d] CdTe = cadmium telluride.
[e] Estimates for concentrators are from Boes (1991).

Electrolysis Technology. The technology of water electrolysis is well established, and several types of electrolyzers have been developed (Carpetis 1984; Dutta, Block & Port 1990; Fein & Edwards 1984; Hammerli 1984, 1990; Hug et al. 1990; IEA 1991; Leroy & Stuart 1978; Steeb et al. 1990; Stuart 1991; Winter & Nitsch 1988).

Alkaline water electrolysis is a mature, commercially available technology. An aqueous electrolyte (generally 30% potassium hydroxide [KOH] in water) is used, with nickel or nickel-alloy electrodes. Electrolysis cells are configured so that the electrodes are either in "bipolar" mode, in which each electrode has two polarities and is both an anode and a cathode, or in "unipolar" mode, in which each electrode has only one polarity and is either an anode or a cathode. Unipolar electrolyzers operate at atmospheric pressure and are slightly less expensive than bipolar electrolyzers, which can operate up to 3 MPa (450 psia). Most industrial electrolysis systems today are used to produce very pure hydrogen for chemical applications, and are only 10 to 100 kW. A few plants larger than 10 MW have been installed near

Table 8-4. Cost and Performance of Large Solar Photovoltaic Systems

	1990	Near Term	Post 2000
Balance of system costs ($/m²)			
Fixed, flat-plate	50–80	37–55	37
1-axis tracking		75	75
2-axis tracking		125	100
Balance of system efficiency[a]	85%	89%	89%
System lifetime (years)	30	30	30
Annual O&M costs			
Fixed, flat-plate ($/m²/yr)	1.2	0.5	0.5
1- or 2-axis tracking ($/kWh)	0.01	0.01	0.01
Indirect costs (% of capital cost)	33%	25%	25%

TOTAL INSTALLED SYSTEM COST ($/Wp)

	1990	Near Term	Post 2000
Flat-plate systems			
Thin films	3.9–4.4	1.5–3.5	0.5–1.1
Polycrystalline	3.6–5.8		1.7–3.2
Crystalline	5.7–9.2		1.7–3.2
Concentrator systems (2-axis tracking)	4.3–7.4	1.9	1.1

COST OF ELECTRICITY ($/kWhDC[b])

	1990	Near Term	Post 2000
Flat-plate systems			
Thin films	0.16–0.21	0.061–0.14	0.022–0.044
Polycrystalline	0.14–0.22		0.071–0.13
Crystalline	0.22–0.35		0.068–0.13
Concentrator systems (2-axis tracking)[c]	0.17–0.28	0.085	0.055

Note: Costs are given for large (>5 MW) PV systems. PV system costs (except long-term balance-of-system costs for fixed flat-plate systems) are from Zweibel (1990). Long-term balance-of-system costs ($37/m²) are from R. Matlin (1990) and Candelario et al. (1991).
[a] Equal to DC system efficiency divided by module efficiency.
[b] Levelized cost of DC electricity (in $/kWhDC) in the southwestern United States, with average annual insolation of 271 W/m². If AC power were produced instead of DC power, the power-conditioning equipment would add an extra $150/kW. The balance-of-system efficiency for an AC system would be 85% rather than 89% because of energy losses in the inverter, which is assumed to be 96% efficient. The cost of power would be about $0.006/kWh greater than the costs shown here.
[c] Estimates for concentrators are from Boes (1991).

Table 8-5. Cost and Performance of Advanced Alkaline Electrolyzers

| | ELECTROLYZER TYPE | | | |
| | BIPOLAR[a] | | UNIPOLAR[b] | |
	Present	Future	Present	Future
Rated power (MWe)	10	100	10	100
Pressure (MPa)	3	3	0.1	0.1
Temperature (° C)	90	160	70	70
Type of diaphragm	asbestos	$CaTio_3$-Cermet	asbestos	synthetic
Rated current density (mA/cm²)	200	450	134	250
Maximum operating current density (mA/cm²)	267	600	168	333
Rated voltage (V)	1.86	1.7	1.9	1.74
Efficiency at rated current density				
(HHV)	73%	90%	73%	90%
(LHV)	62%	76%	62%	76%
Efficiency of rectifier	96%	98%	96%	98%
Feed water (liters/GJ H_2 HHV)	63	63	63	63
Cooling water (m³/GJ H_2 HHV)	2.5	2.5	2.5	2.5
Capital costs: ($/kWAC) (including rectifier, building)	600	330	600	400
Capital costs for DC plant ($/kW)			474	274
Annual O&M costs (% of capital costs, including feed and cooling-water costs and regeneration of KOH)	4%	4%	2%	2%
Lifetime (years)	20	20	20	20

Notes:
[a] Estimates for bipolar technology are from Nitsch et al. (1990) for near-term electrolysis technology. At present, bipolar electrolyzers have 73% efficiency (HHV), operate at 90° C, and have capital costs of $600/kWAC.
[b] Estimates for unipolar technology are for commercially available technology at large scale. From Craft (1985); Hammerli (1984); Leroy & Stuart (1978); Stuart (1991).

sources of low-cost hydroelectricity (Hammerli 1984). Electrolysis is a modular technology with no significant-scale economies above sizes of 2–10 MW (Fein & Edwards 1984). Cost and performance data and projections for large alkaline-electrolysis systems are summarized in Table 8-5.

Two other types of electrolyzers are in earlier stages of development. *Solid-polymer-electrolyte (SPE)* electrolyzers could offer higher current density and higher efficiency (up to 90%) than alkaline electro-

Table 8-6. Current and Projected Costs for Solar Electricity (cents/kWh)

Technology	1991	Near Term	Post 2000
Wind			
(630 W/m²)	—	6	3.5
(500 W/m²)	11.1	6.9	4.4
(350 W/m²)	19.0	9.3	5.3
Solar thermal electric (SW U.S.)	11–16	11–16	5.5–7.8
Solar PV (SW U.S.)	14–35	7–16	2.2–4.4 (DC)
			3.2–5.4 (AC)
Hydropower (off-peak)	2–4	2–4	2–4

Note: We have shown here the production cost of intermittent electricity at the generation site with no storage. Levelized electricity costs are calculated in constant 1989 U.S.$ for the economic assumptions in chapter appendix Table A-1, using the equations in the chapter appendix. (See Tables 8-1–8-4 for details.) For wind power, the annual average wind power density at hub height is shown in parentheses.

lyzers but, at present, require expensive membrane electrolyte materials and platinum catalysts for stable operation. Current research is focused on finding lower-cost electrolyte materials and catalysts. *High-temperature electrolysis* could offer significantly lower electricity consumption per unit of hydrogen produced, because some of the work of water splitting would be done by heat. However, the operating temperature of 900°–1,000° C creates many as-yet-unsolved material and fabrication problems. Over the next ten to twenty years, alkaline electrolysis is likely to remain the technology of choice for solar electrolysis systems (Stuart 1991; Winter & Nitsch 1988).

If an intermittent power source such as wind or solar is used, the electrolyzer plant, and the electrodes particularly, must be designed to tolerate variable operation. At present there is only limited experience with PV-powered electrolyzers (Hammerli 1990; Hug et al. 1990; Lehmann 1990; Metz 1985; Steeb et al. 1990) and none with wind or solar-thermal-electric-powered electrolyzers. Although there have been no intractable problems with PV electrolysis experiments to date, the long-term performance and reliability of electrolysis systems under intermittent operation is not well known. Several electrolyzer manufacturers and research groups are now studying these issues (IEA 1991).

Solar Electricity Costs. In the near term (1990s), off-peak hydropower would offer the lowest electricity costs. By the year 2000, the cost of wind power could be less than 4 cents/kWh, and in the longer term, both solar PV and wind look attractive (see Table 8-6).

Solar-Electrolytic Hydrogen Systems. In Tables 8-7 and 8-8 we describe base case post-2000 solar-electrolytic hydrogen systems based on wind and PV. The calculated production cost of hydrogen from PV would be $12–$19/GJ, equivalent to about $1.5–$2.5/gallon of gasoline. Wind-electrolytic hydrogen is estimated to cost $13–$21/ GJ, or $1.7–$2.7/equivalent gallon of gasoline. For comparison, hydrogen from off-peak hydropower costing 2–4 cents/kWh would cost $12–$19/GJ, and hydrogen from solar-thermal electricity, based on post-2000 projections, would cost $22–$30/GJ (see Table 8-10).

Hydrogen from Biomass Gasification

Hydrogen also can be produced by gasifying at high temperatures biomass feedstocks such as wood chips and forest and agricultural residues. The gasifier output, consisting mainly of hydrogen, carbon monoxide, and methane, can then be reformed and shifted to produce a mixture of hydrogen and carbon dioxide. The carbon dioxide is then removed, leaving hydrogen.

Biomass gasifiers have been demonstrated at the laboratory and pilot-plant scale. Several biomass gasifiers under development in the United States, mainly for methanol production, are probably suitable for hydrogen production as well. All the equipment needed for converting the gasifier output to hydrogen—methane reformers, shift reactors, CO_2 removal technology, and pressure-swing-adsorption technology for hydrogen purification—is commercially available and widely used in the chemical-process industries.

Table 8-9 gives cost and performance data for a biomass hydrogen plant processing 1,650 dry tonnes of biomass per day and using the Battelle Columbus Laboratory gasification technology (Larson & Katofsky 1992). The cost of biomass hydrogen produced at 1,000 psia would be $6.2–$8.8/GJ, assuming a biomass feedstock cost of $2–$4/ GJ. Biomass hydrogen plants would exhibit considerable economies of scale, and at smaller plant sizes, hydrogen costs could be significantly higher.

Summary: Production Cost of Hydrogen from Renewable Resources

The cost of producing hydrogen from various renewable and fossil sources is summarized in Table 8-10 for present, near-term, and post-2000 technologies. As this table shows, the cost of renewable hydrogen is projected to decrease markedly over the next ten to twenty years.

At large scale (for plants producing 50 million standard cubic feet [SCF] of hydrogen per day), biomass hydrogen would cost about

Table 8-7. Post-2000 Wind-Electrolytic Hydrogen System Parameters

HORIZONTAL AXIS WIND TURBINE[a]	
Turbine capacity	1,000 kW
Turbine diameter	52 m
Hub height	50 m
Total installed-system cost	$750/kWpeak
Annual O&M cost	$0.005/kWhAC
Land rent	$0.003/kWhAC
System lifetime	30 years
System availability	95%
Turbine spacing/turbine diameter	5×10
Hectares/MWe	16
Efficiency of coupling to electrolyzer[b]	94%
Spacing losses	25%
ATMOSPHERIC PRESSURE UNIPOLAR ELECTROLYZER[c]	
Rated voltage	1.74 volts
Rated current density	250 mA/cm^2
Maximum operating current density	333 mA/cm^2
Efficiency at maximum operating voltage	85%
Rectifier cost	$130/kWACin
Rectifier efficiency	96%
Installed AC plant capital cost at maximum operating-current density	$371/kWACin
Electrolyzer annual O&M cost	2% of capital cost
Electrolyzer lifetime	20 years
TOTAL WIND/ELECTROLYSIS SYSTEM CAPITAL COST	$1,461–$1,592/kW H$_2$ out

Notes:
[a] Costs and performance for wind systems are from Cohen et al. (1989); Hock, Thresher & Cohen (1990); INEL (1990); Lucas et al. (1990).
[b] It is assumed that the wind system produces AC power, which is then rectified to DC for use in electrolysis. AC losses from the wind tower to the electrolyzer are assumed to be 6% (Winter & Nitsch 1988).
[c] Electrolyzer operating characteristics and costs are based on currently available unipolar technology. It is assumed that the rectifier is sized for maximum current density (Hammerli 1984; Leroy & Stuart 1978; Pirani & Stuart 1991; Stucki 1991). The maximum current density is taken to be 1.25 times the rated current density (Steeb et al. 1990; Winter & Nitsch 1988).

Table 8-7. (continued)

WIND RESOURCE

Annual average wind power density W/m² (power per unit of area swept by turbine)	630	350
Levelized cost of wind electricity (cents/kWh)	3.5	5.3
Levelized cost of wind hydrogen ($/GJ)	17.8	27.7

Table 8-8. Post-2000 PV Electrolytic Hydrogen System Parameters

THIN-FILM PV MODULES, TILTED, FIXED FLAT-PLATE ARRAY (>10 MWp)[a]

PV module efficiency	12%–18%
PV module manufacturing cost	$30–$55/m²
Area-related balance-of-system cost	$37/m²
Balance-of-system efficiency	89%
PV system efficiency	10.7%–16.0%
PV annual O&M cost	$0.5/m²/yr
PV system lifetime	30 years
PV system indirect-cost factor	25%
PV system capital cost	$522–$1,077/kWDC
Efficiency of coupling to electrolyzer[b]	93% (direct connection)
Cost of coupling to electrolyzer	negligible

SOLAR RESOURCE

Annual average insolation SW U.S.	271 W/m²
Land area required in SW U.S.	
10.7% efficient PV system	1.87 hectares/MWe
16.0% efficient PV system	1.25 hectares/MWe

Notes:

[a] Projected efficiencies and manufacturing costs for thin-film PV modules are from Carlson (1990) and Zweibel (1990). Area-related balance-of-system costs are based on conceptual designs for large fixed, flat-plate arrays and are from Matlin (1990) and Ogden & Williams (1989). Balance-of-system efficiency for a DC system is derived from USDOE estimates (USDOE 1987). Operation and maintenance costs are projections based on field experience from EPRI (Conover 1989) and SMUD (Shusnar et al. 1985). Indirect costs of 25% are assumed based on Sandia experience with fixed, flat-plate arrays (Noel et al. 1985; Zweibel 1990). PV system lifetime of thirty years is taken from USDOE year 2000 goals (Zweibel 1990).

[b] PV/electrolyzer coupling efficiencies are based on small experimental systems (Metz & Piraino 1985; Steeb et al. 1990).

Table 8-8. (continued)

ATMOSPHERIC PRESSURE UNIPOLAR ELECTROLYZER[c]

Rated voltage	1.74 volts
Rated current density	250 mA/cm^2
Maximum operating current density	333 mA/cm^2
Efficiency at maximum operating voltage	85%
Installed DC plant capital cost at maximum operating current density	$231/kWDCin
Electrolyzer annual O&M cost	2% of capital cost
Electrolyzer lifetime	20 years

COST AND PERFORMANCE OF PV HYDROGEN SYSTEM

System efficiency (H$_2$ HHV)/insolation	8.4%–12.7%
TOTAL CAPITAL COST	$954–$1,654/kWH$_2$ out

ENERGY COSTS

Module efficiency	18%	12%
Module manufacturing cost	$30/m^2	$55/m^2
Levelized cost of DC electricity (cents/kWh)	2.2	4.4
Levelized cost of PV hydrogen ($/GJ)	11.6	19.1

Notes:
c Electrolyzer operating characteristics and costs are based on currently available unipolar technology. It is assumed that no rectifier is needed (Steeb et al. 1990). The maximum current density is taken to be 1.25 times the rated current density (Steeb et al. 1990; Winter & Nitsch 1988).

Table 8-9. Cost and Performance Data for Production of Hydrogen from Biomass

Dry tonnes biomass per day	1,650
Biomass energy input (GJ/h)	1,382
External electricity input (MWe)	18.2
Thermal conversion efficiency GJ-hydrogen out/GJ-energy in (biomass + elec)	70%
Plant lifetime (years) ˙	25
Plant capacity (factor)	90%
Total investment cost (10^6 $)	137
Working capital (10^6 $)	10.1
Land (10^6 $)	2.05
Cost of biomass ($/GJ)	2–4
Variable operating costs excluding biomass (10^6 $/year)	9.24
Biomass costs (10^6 $/year)	21.8–43.7
Fixed operating cost (10^6 $/year)	7.20
Levelized costs ($/GJ)	
Capital	1.71
Labor, maintenance, chemicals	1.15
Purchased electricity	0.81
Biomass	2.57–5.15
TOTAL LEVELIZED COSTS	6.24–8.82

Source: Based on the Battelle Columbus Laboratory gasification technology (Larson & Katofsky 1992).

Table 8-10. Current and Projected Production Costs of Hydrogen ($/GJ)

	1991	Near Term	Post 2000
RENEWABLE SOURCES			
Electrolytic hydrogen (for plants producing 0.5 million SCF/day) (180 GJ)[a] from:			
Solar PV (SW U.S.)	54–121	29–57	12–19
Wind			
(630 Wm²)			18
(500 Wm²)	59	36	23
(350 Wm²)	102	49	28
Solar thermal (SW U.S.)	45–60	37–63	22–30
Off-peak hydroelectricity[b]	12–19	12–19	12–19
Hydrogen from biomass gasification[c]			
Large plant (50 million SCF/day)			6.2–8.8
FOSSIL SOURCES			
Hydrogen from steam reforming of natural gas[d]			
Large plant (100 million SCF/day)	6.1–8.1	6.1–8.1	8.1–10.1
Small plant (0.5 million SCF/day)	11–14	11–14	14–17
Hydrogen from coal gasification[e]			
Large plant (100 million SCF/day)	8	8	8
Medium plant (25 million SCF/day)	13	13	13

Note: Levelized hydrogen production costs are given in constant 1989 U.S.$.
[a] A hydrogen plant producing 180 GJ/day could provide enough energy to fuel about 1,000 fuel cell fleet vehicles, each traveling 48,000 km/yr.
[b] Assuming that off-peak hydroelectricity at existing sites costs 2 to 4 cents/kWh.
[c] Assuming that the biomass feedstock costs $2 to $4/GJ.
[d] Assuming that natural gas costs $2 to $4/GJ in the 1990s and $4 to $6/GJ beyond the year 2000, which is the range projected for the year 2000 for industrial and commercial customers.
[e] Costs for hydrogen from coal gasification are based on the steam-iron process (Gregory et al. 1980), assuming coal costs $1.78/GJ, which is the projected cost for the year 2000.

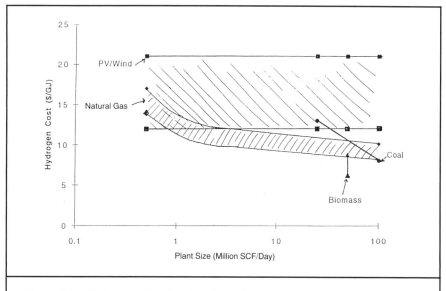

Figure 8-2. Hydrogen Production Cost Versus Plant Size (1990$)

$6.2–$8.8/GJ to produce, making it the least expensive method of renewable hydrogen production (DeLuchi, Larson & Williams 1991; Larson & Katofsky 1992; Phillips 1990). Electrolytic hydrogen from wind, solar PV, or off-peak hydropower would cost about twice as much, $12–$21/GJ. However, because of their modular nature, electrolytic hydrogen systems could be employed at much smaller scale than biomass gasifiers.[2] At small scales of production—which one would expect at the beginning of a transition to hydrogen, or if environmental constraints limited the size of any one production area—hydrogen from biomass might not enjoy any cost advantage over hydrogen from PV or wind electrolysis.

Projected costs for renewable hydrogen would be comparable to those of hydrogen produced from fossil feedstocks. At large scale, biomass gasification could compete with steam reforming of natural gas or coal gasification, and at the small scale, steam reforming of natural gas would cost about as much as wind or PV electrolysis (see Figure 8-2).

---

[2] PV or wind electrolyzers would have little scale economy above sizes of 0.5 million SCF of hydrogen per day (enough to fuel a fleet of about 1,000 fuel cell vehicles), and electrolytic hydrogen would probably be less expensive than biomass hydrogen up to plant capacities of several million SCF/day.

Delivering Hydrogen Transportation Fuel

Once hydrogen is produced, it must be stored, transported, distributed, and delivered to the vehicle in the desired form. Here we estimate the cost of delivering gaseous hydrogen for use in fuel cell vehicles (based on post-2000 projections for PV, wind, and biomass hydrogen systems), including costs of hydrogen compression and storage at the production site (which would be necessary to level the output of PV or wind electrolyzers), pipeline transmission (if required), local distribution costs, and filling station costs. Because components of gaseous hydrogen delivery systems (compressors, compressed-gas storage systems, pipelines) exhibit considerable economy of scale, costs are calculated for three system sizes (see Table 8-11):

1. *A 10-MW PV or wind hydrogen electrolysis "demonstration" system* supplies transportation fuel for a centrally refueled fleet of 1,000 fuel cell cars. Hydrogen is compressed for storage in aboveground compressed-gas cylinders. Hydrogen fuel cell fleet vehicles with compressed-gas storage are refueled on-site from high-pressure cascades. Compression adds about $2.4/GJ, storage about $1.4/GJ, and filling station equipment $2.5/GJ, so that delivery adds a total of about $6/GJ to the cost of hydrogen.

2. *A 750-MW "city supply" system* produces hydrogen fuel for 300,000 fuel cell vehicles. Here hydrogen could be produced via PV or wind electrolysis or biomass gasification. For intermittent systems, hydrogen is compressed to 750 psia and stored in underground rock caverns to level the plant output. Compression and storage would not be required for biomass plants, which would operate continuously. Hydrogen is fed into a city gas network and piped a short distance to about one hundred filling stations for passenger cars. Here scale economies reduce compression costs to $1.4/GJ and storage costs to $1.0/GJ, but local-distribution costs of $0.5/GJ and filling station costs of $5.2/GJ must be added, so that delivery adds about $8/GJ to the cost of hydrogen.

3. *A 75-GW "solar export" PV hydrogen system* produces fuel for long-distance pipeline transmission to serve 30 million fuel cell vehicles. Hydrogen is stored in depleted gas fields or aquifers, compressed to 1,000 psia for pipeline transmission 1,000 miles. Local distribution to filling stations occurs at the end of the pipeline. Here, scale economies further reduce storage costs, but long-distance pipeline costs must be added, so that delivery adds about $8/GJ to the hydrogen cost.

Table 8-11. Delivered Cost of Hydrogen Based on Post-2000 Projections

	SYSTEM					
	DEMONSTRATION (10 MWp)		CITY SUPPLY (750 MWp)			SOLAR EXPORT (75 GWp)
	PV	Wind	PV	Wind	Biomass	PV
CAPITAL COSTS						
	(million $)		(billion $)			(billion $)
Power system	5–11	7.5	0.4–0.8	0.6	0.14	40–80
Electrolyzer	2.3	3.7	0.17	0.28		17
Compressor	0.43	0.41	0.02	0.02		1.0
Storage	0.73	0.97	0.04	0.04		1.1
Pipeline	—	—	—	—		1.9
Filling station	0.5	0.5				
TOTAL	9.2–14.8	13.1	0.6–1	1.0	0.14	60–100
CONTRIBUTIONS TO HYDROGEN COST ($/GJ)						
Power system	7.0–14.2	12.8	7.0–14.2	12.8	6.2–8.8	7.0–14.2
Electrolyzer	4.5	6.4	4.5	6.4		4.5
Compression	2.4	2.2	1.4	1.4		1.4
Hydrogen storage	1.4	1.6	1.0	1.0		0.3
Pipeline (1,000 mi)	—	—	—	—		0.4
Local distribution	—	—	0.5	0.5	0.5	0.5
Filling station	2.5	2.5	5.2	5.2	5.2	5.2
COST OF HYDROGEN TO CONSUMER AT FILLING STATION						
($/GJ)	17.8–25.0	25.5	19.6–26.8	27.3	11.9–14.5	19.3–26.5
($/gallon gasoline)	2.32–3.27	3.34	2.55–3.49	3.56	1.55–1.89	2.52–3.46
BREAK-EVEN GASOLINE PRICE WITH TAX						
($/gallon)	1.28–1.54	1.56	1.34–1.61	1.63	1.06–1.16	1.33–1.60
LAND USED BY POWER SYSTEM						
	(hectares)		(km^2)			(km^2)
	12–19	47–160	9–14	35–120	367	900–1,400

Table 8-11. (continued)						
	SYSTEM					
	DEMONSTRATION (10 MWp)		**CITY SUPPLY (750 MWp)**			**SOLAR EXPORT (75 GWp)**
	PV	**Wind**	**PV**	**Wind**	**Biomass**	**PV**
ENERGY DELIVERED PER YEAR						
	(GJ)		**(GJ)**			**(EJ)**
	66,000	76,000	5 million	7 million		0.5
VEHICLES FUELED						
	1,000[a]		300,000			30 million[b]

Note: Costs and performance for PV and wind electrolysis systems (1989$) are taken from Tables 8-7 and 8-8. Hydrogen costs are based on the higher heating value.
[a] For fleet vehicles with efficiency equivalent to 60 mpg gasoline, driven 48,000 km per year.
[b] For passenger vehicles with efficiency equivalent to 60 mpg gasoline, driven 16,000 km per year.

The total delivered cost of PV or wind hydrogen is about $18–$27/GJ (a cost of energy equivalent to about $2.3–$3.6/gallon of gasoline) and would be approximately independent of production scale. For biomass hydrogen produced in a "city supply" system, delivered costs would be $12–$15/GJ ($1.6–$1.9/gallon gasoline equivalent).

Environmental and Resource Issues

Unlike fossil fuels, which are unevenly distributed around the world, renewable hydrogen can be generated almost anywhere. Using one or more indigenous renewable resources, it would be possible, in principle, to produce large quantities of hydrogen in most parts of the world (see Table 8-12). However, the contributions of various renewable sources of hydrogen to future energy supply will depend not only on the theoretically available resource base (see Table 8-12), but on the land area and water required (see Table 8-13), as well as on other environmental effects of large-scale renewable energy development and production.

Electrolytic Hydrogen from Hydropower

In theory, the global potential for electrolytic hydrogen from hydropower could be significant.[3] However, hydropower systems require

---

[3] If half of all technically usable hydropower were dedicated to hydrogen production, it would be possible to produce 28 EJ of hydrogen per year (an amount of energy equal to about one-fourth the present annual global oil production).

| | ELECTROLYTIC HYDROGEN SOURCE | | | Biomass H$_2$ Produced on 10% of Forest, Woods, Cropland |
Region	Technically Usable Hydro (EJ H$_2$/yr)	Total Wind Potential (EJ H$_2$/yr)	PV on 1% Land Area (EJ H$_2$/yr)	(EJ H$_2$/yr)
Africa	9.1	257	128	18
Asia	15.5	68	103	21
Australia	1.1	75	47	5
North America	9.1	308	94	17
South/Central America	11.0	122	77	24
Europe + former USSR	10.6	366	130	24
TOTAL	56.3	1,196	579	113

Table 8-12. Potential Resources for Renewable Hydrogen Production

Source: Ogden & Nitsch (1993).

large amounts of land and water (see Table 8-13) and can have adverse environmental and social impacts. Moreover, resources are geographically limited to good sites (many of which are already developed). These factors will limit hydropower to a fraction of the technically usable potential, and the global contribution of hydropower to a hydrogen energy system would be relatively small. Still, because of its low cost, off-peak hydropower at existing sites might offer an opportunity to help launch electrolytic hydrogen as an energy carrier.

Biomass Hydrogen

Today, energy could be derived from a variety of biomass feedstocks, including residues from the agricultural and forest products industries, urban wastes, and wood derived from better management of existing commercial forests. In the future, bioenergy plantations might be developed, using fast-growing trees or energy crops. Biomass is likely to be used for generating electricity before it is used for making transportation fuels. By the time biomass hydrogen could be produced on a large scale, many of the currently available feedstocks, such as residues or urban wastes, might already be committed to fueling electric plants. Depending on the demand for fuel and the available resources, it might become necessary to develop biomass plantations to produce biomass transportation fuels on a large scale (DeLuchi, Larson & Williams 1991; Johansson et al. 1993).

Table 8-13. Land and Water Requirements per Unit of Hydrogen Energy Production

	Land Requirements hectares/MWe, peak	m²/(GJ/yr)	Water Requirements liters/GJ (HHV)
Electrolytic hydrogen from:			
PV[a]	1.3	1.89	63
Solar thermal electric[b]	4.0	5.71	63
Wind[c]	4.7–16	6.3–33	63
Hydroelectric[d]	16–900	11–500	>>63
Biomass hydrogen[e]	—	50	37,000–74,000

Notes:

a It is assumed that a fixed, flat-plate PV system is used, with array spacing so that one-half of the land area is covered by arrays. The efficiency of the PV array is assumed to be 15%; the DC electrolyzer efficiency is taken to be 80%, based on the higher heating value of hydrogen; and the coupling efficiency between the PV array and the electrolyzer is taken to be 96%. Annual energy production is given for a southwestern U.S. location with average annual insolation of 271 Watts/m². Water requirements are for electrolyzer feedwater.

b Land use is estimated for a parabolic-trough system, assuming that the efficiency (percentage of the solar energy falling on the collector area that is converted to electricity) is 10%, and that one-fourth of the land area is covered by collectors. (Land use per MW would be similar for central-receiver or dish systems.) An electrolyzer with AC efficiency of 79% is used, and the coupling efficiency of the solar thermal-electric plant and the electrolyzer is assumed to be 96%. Annual energy production is given for a southwestern U.S. location with average annual insolation of 271 Watts/m². Water requirements are for electrolyzer feedwater only. If wet cooling towers were used for cooling the steam turbine condensers, there would be substantial water losses. The steam turbine would also consume some water during operation.

c It is assumed that an array of 33-meter-diameter 340-kW wind turbines is used. For areas with a unidirectional or bidirectional wind resource (as in some mountain passes), the wind turbine spacing could be 1.5 diameters in the direction perpendicular to the prevailing wind and 10 diameters in the direction parallel to the prevailing wind (Smith 1991) without interference losses. In this case, the land use would be 4.7 hectares/MW of electric power. For areas with more variable wind direction (such as the Great Plains), the spacing would be 5 diameters by 10 diameters, with a land use of 16 hectares/MWe. An electrolyzer with an AC efficiency of 79% is used. Coupling efficiency between the wind turbine and the electrolyzer is assumed to be 96%. The wind turbine capacity factor is assumed to be 26%, corresponding to a class 4 site, with hub height of 50 meters. Water requirements are for electrolyzer feedwater.

d Land use for hydroelectric power varies greatly depending on the location. The range shown is for large projects in various countries (WEC 1980). Water requirements are for electrolyzer feedwater only. Evaporative losses at the reservoir would probably be much greater than feedwater consumption, depending on the site.

e It is assumed that biomass productivity of 15 dry tonnes/hectare/year is achieved, and that the biomass has a higher heating value of 19.38 GJ/dry tonne. The energy conversion efficiency of biomass to hydrogen via gasification in a Battelle Columbus Laboratory gasifier is assumed to be 70.0%. Water use is based on a rainfall of 75–150 cm/year needed to achieve a biomass productivity of 15 dry tonnes/hectare (Hall et al. 1993).

Table 8-13. (continued)

LAND REQUIREMENTS TO PRODUCE HYDROGEN EQUIVALENT
IN ENERGY TO 10^6 KM^2

	PRESENT				PROJECTED WORLD NON-ELECTRIC FUEL DEMAND (IPCC)[f]	
	U.S. light-duty vehicles if powered by fuel cells (4.8 EJ)	U.S. Oil (34 EJ)	World Oil (115 EJ)	World Fossil Fuel (300 EJ)	2025 (286 EJ)	2050 (289 EJ)
PV	0.008	0.079	0.268	0.700	0.667	0.674
Wind	0.13	0.87	2.9	7.7	7.3	7.4
Biomass	0.23	2.2	7.6	19.8	18.9	19.0

Global land area = 137 million km^2

U.S. land area = 7.8 million km^2

Notes:
[f] Projections are from the IPCC accelerated-policy scenario (IPCC 1990).

The global potential for hydrogen production from biomass plantations could be substantial (see Table 8-12). However, land and water requirements would be huge, much larger than for solar or wind electrolysis systems (see Table 8-13). To produce an amount of hydrogen equivalent in energy to global oil use today (115 EJ/yr), an amount of land equal to about 10% of the total land area presently committed to forest, woodland, and cropland would have to be developed as biomass plantations, assuming that an average productivity of 15 dry tonnes of biomass per hectare per year could be achieved.

In addition to land requirements, the large-scale production of biomass for energy gives rise to a range of other environmental concerns, including erosion, the adverse consequences of the use of herbicides and fertilizer, the potential loss of biological diversity (Hall et al. 1993; Miles & Miles 1992), and high water consumption. These environmental criteria will eliminate particularly sensitive or unique lands from consideration as potential biomass resources and will govern the development and managemement of the lands that are suitable. Careful and creative development and management techniques will be needed to satisfy stringent environmental constraints.

Although the land requirements for biomass plantations would be large, there are vast areas of currently unproductive agricultural or deforested land that might be reclaimed for bioenergy. For example, if all the degraded lands in developing countries suitable for reforestation (nearly 8 million km^2) could be developed for biomass hydrogen, about 159 EJ per year could be produced. Biomass might also make a significant contribution in the industrialized countries. Excess cropland within the European Economic Community (some 15 million hectares) could produce about 3.0 EJ of hydrogen per year, and from 30 million hectares of idled cropland in the United States, about 5.9 EJ of hydrogen could be produced.

It is clear that land and water requirements will be important issues in the development of biomass energy supplies. However, pressure on biomass supplies could be reduced by using energy as efficiently as possible. Indeed, if biomass hydrogen is to play a large role in meeting transportation energy needs, development of highly efficient end-use technologies such as fuel cell vehicles is essential (DeLuchi 1992; Johansson et al. 1993).[4]

---

[4] Supply-and-demand scenarios for the United States illustrate the implications of end-use efficiency for land use.

DeLuchi, Larson & Williams (1991), using data from Idaho National Engineering Lab (1990) and Fulkerson et al. (1989), estimated that in the year 2030 as much as 45 EJ of primary biomass energy could be produced from better management of existing commercial forests, from energy crops and trees, and from urban and agricultural residues. They compared this estimate to the amount of primary biomass energy that would be required to fuel the highway vehicle fleet in the year 2030, considering different vehicle technologies and fuels. They found that if highway vehicles used internal-combustion engines fueled by methanol derived from biomass, virtually all of the 45-EJ maximum supply would be needed. If the vehicle fleet used fuel cells fueled by methanol derived from biomass, two-thirds of the total biomass primary energy supply would be required, and if the fleet used fuel cells fueled by hydrogen derived from biomass, almost half of the potential biomass supply would be required.

Considering that biomass would be demanded by other energy sectors, such as electricity generation, and perhaps by nonenergy sectors, as well as by transportation, it is clear that the use of biomass-derived fuels in transportation, even with fuel cell vehicles, would, *at the level of vehicle efficiency assumed by DeLuchi, Larson & Williams (1991)*, place great pressure on biomass supplies. This could lead to the development of huge biomass energy farms, with their attendant environmental risks. For example, in the DeLuchi, Larson & Williams (1991) scenario, if the entire 45 EJ of potential biomass supply were demanded by all sectors, then some 78 million hectares of additional land would be devoted to producing energy crops alone (not counting land already in commercial forests). This is an area equal to California, Oregon, and Washington states combined, about 10% of the land area of the lower forty-eight states.

Pressure to develop bioenergy supplies could be eased by greatly improving the efficiency of energy use. For example, the transportation-energy-demand scenarios in DeLuchi, Larson & Williams (1991), discussed in the preceding paragraphs, are based on rather conservative projections by the EIA (1990) of improvements in vehicular fuel effi-

Hydrogen from Wind Power

Wind power is a large and widely distributed resource that would require less land and much less water than biomass (see Tables 8-12 and 8-13). In practice, only a fraction of the global wind-electrolytic hydrogen potential of almost 1,200 EJ per year (see Table 8-13) could be developed because of rugged terrain and competing uses for land. Even with restrictions, however, wind resources would far exceed local electricity demands in many places, and the wind hydrogen potential would be large.

To supply an amount of hydrogen equivalent to current fossil fuel use (300 EJ) would require 6% of the world's land area. If all light-duty vehicles in the United States were replaced with hydrogen fuel cell vehicles, the projected hydrogen demand (based on projected driving levels in 2010) would be about 4.8 EJ/year. This amount of wind hydrogen could be produced on about 2% of the U.S. land area. Wind hydrogen plants would require only about two-thirds the land areas required for biomass hydrogen. Moreover, wind systems would not "use" land in the same way that biomass plantations would. Only a small portion of the total wind farm area would be taken up by the footprints of the turbine towers. The rest of the area would be available for other uses, such as farming or grazing. Unlike biomass plantations, wind (or PV) systems would require relatively little attention after they were built. There would be no large-scale inputs of chemicals or water on-site, and at any given time there would be no human activity throughout most of the site.

Hydrogen from Solar PV

Although PV hydrogen would be more expensive than hydrogen from biomass, it is by far the most widely available and least constrained resource. Moreover, PV land requirements would be much lower than for any other option, about one-thirtieth of those for biomass. Enough PV hydrogen to meet the world's foreseeable fuel needs could be produced on about 0.5% of the earth's land area (2% of the global desert area) (see Table 8-13). If all light-duty vehicles in the United States were converted to fuel cells, the PV hydrogen requirement could be met with only about 0.1% of the U.S. land area (or about 1% of the

---

ciency by the year 2030. If fleet average fuel consumption were half the level used by DeLuchi, Larson & Williams (1991) the total demand by a hydrogen-powered fuel cell highway fleet could be met by biomass residues and better management of existing forests—that is, without energy crops—with more than 5 EJ of potential supply left over for other sectors.

U.S. desert area). Of course, PV hydrogen production would not be limited to deserts; it could be produced in any reasonably sunny location. And because PV systems are modular, small systems might even be built on top of buildings, garages, or storage areas, with no "extra" land requirement.

Water Requirements for Renewable Hydrogen Production

The water requirements for electrolytic hydrogen production are modest, and electrolytic hydrogen could be produced even in deserts. Typically, a small percentage of the annual rainfall falling on the area covered by a solar hydrogen plant would be sufficient to supply feedwater for electrolysis. For example, the annual water consumption of a PV hydrogen plant corresponds to 2.7 cm of rain per year over an area equal to the plant size, which amounts to only 14% of the annual rainfall in El Paso, one of the most arid places in the United States (Ogden & Williams 1989).

In contrast, achieving a biomass productivity of 15 dry tonnes per hectare per year would require rainfall of 75 to 150 cm per year (Hall et al. 1993).

Hydrogen as a Transport Fuel

It is becoming increasingly likely that over the next ten to twenty years, significant opportunities could open to introduce hydrogen as a clean transportation fuel. In particular, the California Air Resources Board has mandated that starting in 1998, 2% of all passenger cars and light trucks sold in the state must be zero-emission vehicles (ZEVs). By 2001, 5% of light-duty vehicles must be ZEVs, and by 2003, 10% (CARB 1990). The only vehicles that could be developed in this time frame to rigorously meet the ZEV standards are fuel cell vehicles run on hydrogen and electric-battery vehicles. (Although methanol fuel cell vehicles would not be ZEVs, because the reformer would emit some CO and NO_x, emissions would be close to zero, only about 1% or less than those of a comparable gasoline-powered car.)

Hydrogen fuel cell cars could offer the following potential advantages as compared with other zero-emission or near-zero-emission vehicles:

- Because hydrogen storage is less heavy and bulky than advanced electric batteries, the range of a hydrogen fuel cell vehicle would probably be longer.

- High-pressure gas cylinders could be refueled in several minutes, as compared with several hours for recharging electric batteries. (With high-power charging equipment, it may be possible to charge batteries in 15–30 minutes, but this is not yet technically proven. Moreover, it would be difficult to use such equipment in residences because of the high power required.)

- Biomass is the only renewable energy source that could be used to produce methanol. Hydrogen could be produced from a wide variety of sources, such as PV and wind, which are less geographically constrained than biomass and potentially much larger.

There is already considerable experience with experimental hydrogen internal-combustion-engine vehicles (ICEVs) (DeLuchi 1989), which have been developed by Daimler-Benz, BMW, and Mazda, among others. Recently, a number of companies, including Ballard Power Systems (Canada), Daimler-Benz (Germany), Elenco (Netherlands), Energy Partners (United States), H-Power (United States), Roger Billings (United States), and Siemens (Germany), have begun developing experimental hydrogen fuel cell vehicles for the zero-emission-vehicle market.

Assessment of Hydrogen Fuel Cell Vehicles

In a fuel cell electric vehicle (FCEV), a hydrogen-air fuel cell provides electricity to an electric drivetrain similar to those used in battery-powered electric vehicles (Lemmons 1990; SAE 1991). Hydrogen fuel is stored directly (as a compressed gas or hydride) or in the form of methanol, which is reformed on-board to produce hydrogen. In some designs, peak-power demands are met by a small supplemental battery or perhaps an ultracapacitor.

Recent studies by DeLuchi (DeLuchi 1992; DeLuchi & Ogden 1993) have modeled fuel cell vehicles based on proton exchange membrane (PEM) fuel cells, which offer high power density, quick start-up time, modest operating temperature (100° C), and the potential to reach low costs in mass production. PEM fuel cells are now being developed and should be available within a few years (Prater 1990).[5]

---

[5] The critical technology in the hydrogen fuel cell vehicle is the fuel cell itself. The other major components—the battery, the hydrogen storage system, and the electric powertrain—have been successfully developed technically, and could go into commercial production soon. The development of the fuel cell has lagged behind the development of these other components, and consequently its cost and performance cannot be characterized as well. We have assumed that high specific power and high energy efficiency can be achieved at relatively low cost. For this assumption to be realized, low-cost, high-performance membranes must be found, and the fuel cell auxiliaries must be designed to be compact and require a minimum amount of energy. Demonstration projects underway now, or scheduled to begin soon, should provide a clearer picture of the ultimate technical and economic potential of the fuel cell.

The supplemental peak-power battery is assumed to be a bipolar lithium–iron disulfide battery, a promising technology now under development, which has the high power density needed for peak power. High-pressure compressed-hydrogen-gas cylinders are chosen for hydrogen storage because they are simple, commercially available, and able to be refilled quickly.

Based on post-2000 cost and performance projections for fuel cell, battery, and gasoline vehicle technologies, hydrogen fuel cell vehicles are compared with gasoline internal-combustion-engine vehicles (ICEVs), methanol fuel cell electric vehicles (MeOH FCEVs), and battery-powered electric vehicles (BPEVs) (see Table 8-14) (DeLuchi 1992; DeLuchi & Ogden 1993). To facilitate comparison, the weight, range, and performance of the vehicles have been chosen to be comparable. Figure 8-3 shows the life-cycle cost, and also the break-even gasoline price that would make the total life-cycle cost of the gasoline vehicle equal to that of the alternative vehicle (DeLuchi & Ogden 1993).[6]

Rather surprisingly, we see that fuel cell vehicles fueled with hydrogen from solar or wind would have a life-cycle cost comparable to that of a gasoline vehicle or an electric-battery car. With biomass hydrogen or methanol, the life-cycle cost would be even lower. Even though the initial cost for the hydrogen fuel cell vehicle would be $8,000 higher than that for the gasoline car, and renewable hydrogen would cost 1.5 to 2.5 times as much as gasoline, the life-cycle cost is about the same (or slightly lower for biomass hydrogen) because (1) hydrogen can be used two to three times as efficiently as gasoline, so that the fuel cost per kilometer is less; (2) the lifetime of the fuel cell vehicle is 33% longer, so that the contribution of the vehicle cost to the life-cycle cost is only slightly higher than for gasoline; and (3) maintenance costs are lower for FCEVs than for ICEVs.

Although discussions of alternative fuels often center around fuel cost, Figure 8-3 shows that the delivered cost of hydrogen is not a good indicator of hydrogen's economic competitiveness. Fuel costs are only a small fraction of the total life-cycle cost (typically about one-eighth for the vehicles listed in Table 8-14), and moreover, the high efficiency of fuel cell vehicles yields a lower fuel cost per kilometer than for a

---

[6] It is assumed that hydrogen is produced from solar or wind at a delivered cost of $23.4/GJ without taxes or from biomass at a delivered cost of $13.2/GJ. (Delivered hydrogen costs are based on midrange fuel production costs plus the costs of hydrogen compression, storage, and distribution, and filling station costs.) Methanol from biomass is estimated to cost $13.0/GJ delivered, electricity 7 cents/kWh, and gasoline $1.21/gallon (a price projected for the year 2000) (Ogden & Nitsch 1993).

Table 8-14. Cost and Characteristics of Alternative-Fueled Vehicles

| | **VEHICLE TYPE** | | | |
	Battery EV[a]	**H₂ FCEV**[b]	**MeOH FCEV**	**Gasoline ICEV**[c]
Fuel storage system	—	compressed gas @ 55 MPa	metal tank	metal tank
Fuel cell	proton exchange membrane (PEM)			
Battery	bipolar lithium alloy/iron sulfide			
Driving range (km)	400	400	560	560
Power to wheels (kW)	85	73	76	101
Delivered fuel price (excluding tax)				
(Biomass, PV/wind)				
($/gallon gasoline equivalent)	2.54	1.71, 2.97	1.69	1.21
($/GJ)	19.4	13.0, 22.5	13.0	9.3
Refueling time (min)	30–360	2–3	2–3	2–3
Gasoline-equivalent fuel economy				
(1/100 km)	2.0	3.2	3.8	9.1
(mpg)	120	74.0	62.4	25.9
Curb weight (1,000 kg)	1.44	1.24	1.27	1.37
Initial price (1,000 $)	28.2	25.4	24.8	17.3
Vehicle life (1,000 km)	257	257	257	193
Annual maintenance cost ($)	388	434	450	516

Source: Adapted from DeLuchi & Ogden (1993).
Notes:
[a] Electric vehicle (EV).
[b] Fuel cell electric vehicle (FCEV).
[c] Internal-combustion-engine vehicle (ICEV).

gasoline vehicle, even though the fuel is much more expensive. For high-quality fuels such as hydrogen and electricity, which can be used very efficiently and cleanly, the total life-cycle cost, the fuel cost per kilometer, and the break-even gasoline price are better economic indices than the delivered fuel cost.

Hydrogen fuel cell vehicles fueled with PV or wind hydrogen would start to compete with gasoline ICEVs on a life-cycle cost basis

Table 8-14. (continued)

LIFE-CYCLE COST OF TRANSPORTATION FOR ALTERNATIVE VEHICLES
(cents/km)

Cost Component	Battery EV	Solar/Wind H_2 FCEV	Biomass H_2 FCEV	Biomass MeOH FCEV	Gasoline ICEV
Purchased electricity	1.48	0.20	0.20	0.22	
Vehicle (excluding fuel cell, battery, storage)	7.59	7.18	7.18	7.22	11.17
Battery	7.08	2.15	2.15	2.03	
Fuel storage system		2.23	2.23	2.62	
Fuel for vehicle (excluding taxes)		1.96	1.13	1.33	2.82
Maintenance	1.69	1.89	1.89	1.96	2.89
Miscellaneous other costs	5.12	4.91	4.91	4.87	4.56
TOTAL COST (cents/km)	22.96	21.33	20.50	20.29	21.45
Break-even gasoline price including tax ($/gallon)	2.11	1.43	1.09	1.00	1.50

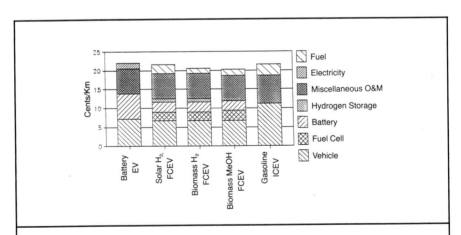

Figure 8-3. Life-Cycle Cost of Transport (400-Km Range— Compressed H_2 Gas @ 55 MPa) (1990$)

at a break-even gasoline price of about $1.50/gallon (about $1.10/gallon for biomass hydrogen). However, hydrogen fuel cell vehicles might be attractive from society's point of view, even at lower gasoline prices, because of their substantial local and global environmental benefits.

Emissions of Greenhouse Gases and Other Pollutants

The great attraction of hydrogen fuel cell vehicles is pollution-free operation. Whereas numerous undesirable compounds are emitted from gasoline and diesel fuel vehicles, or are formed from the emitted compounds, a hydrogen FCEV emits only water. Hydrogen FCEVs do not produce CO, NMOCs, NO_x, particulates, SO_x, oxidants (such as ozone), carcinogenic aromatic compounds (such as benzene), toxic metals (such as lead), aldehydes, or greenhouse gases. They are environmentally superior even to hydrogen ICEVs, which produce some NO_x as a result of the relatively high temperature of the internal-combustion engine, and small amounts of CO and HC from combustion of the lubricating oil. (PEM fuel cells operate far below the temperature required to produce NO_x, and do not consume oil.) Only battery-powered EVs can match the zero-emission performance of hydrogen-powered FCEVs (see Table 8-15).

Solar FCVs and BPEVs are the cleanest transportation options available. The extent to which they would improve urban air quality depends, of course, on the extent to which they would penetrate the vehicle fleet. Because FCEVs could be refueled much more quickly than could BPEVs, they probably would attain a greater market share, and hence ultimately could provide greater total air-quality benefits. The use of solar electricity to recharge BPEVs, or to make and compress hydrogen for FCEVs, would eliminate not only emissions of urban air pollutants, but all fuel-cycle emissions of greenhouse gases as well (see Table 8-15).[7]

The use in FCEVS of fuels derived from biomass also would provide a very large reduction in emissions of greenhouse gases, relative to gasoline. Biomass-fueled FCEVs would produce more greenhouse gas emissions than the all-solar/FCEV cycle (see Table 8-15), largely because of emissions from planting, fertilizing, harvesting, transporting, and gasifying biomass (DeLuchi 1991). Even in the very near

---

[7] If solar power were used to make but not compress the hydrogen, and instead the U.S. average power mix were used for compression (to 550 bar for vehicle storage tanks), the reduction in greenhouse gas emissions (relative to the gasoline fuel cycle) would be between 85% and 90%, versus 100% in the case where solar power is used for compression (see Table 8-15).

Table 8-15. Percentage Change in G/Km Emissions from Alternative-Fuel Light-Duty Vehicles Relative to Gasoline Vehicles, Year 2000

Feed/Fuel/Vehicle	CRITERIA POLLUTANTS[a] NMOC	CO	NO_x	SO_x	PM	Greenhouse Gases[b]
NG/methanol/ICEV	−50	0	0	−100	lower	−2
U.S. power mix/BPEV	−95	−99	−56	+321	+153	−11
NG/hydrogen/FCEV	−100	−100	−100	−100	−100	−43
Biomass/hydrogen/FCEV	−100	−100	−100	−100	−100	−67[c]
Biomass/methanol/FCEV	−90	−99	−99	−100	−100	−86[c]
Solar/hydrogen/FCEV	−100	−100	−100	−100	−100	−87[c]
Solar/hydride/ICEV	−95	−99	?[d]	−100	lower	−88[c]
Solar power/BPEV	−100	−100	−100	−100	−100	−100
All-solar/H_2/FCEV	−100	−100	−100	−100	−100	−100[e]
Baseline emissions on gasoline, g/km	0.48	3.81	0.28	0.03	0.01	305.3

Source: Adapted from DeLuchi (1993).

Note: The percentage changes shown are with respect to the baseline g/km emissions shown at the bottom of this table. ICEV = internal-combustion-engine vehicle; BPEV = battery-powered electric vehicle; FCEV = fuel cell vehicle.

[a] The estimates of relative emissions of criteria pollutants are based on data summarized in Sperling and DeLuchi (1991), and DeLuchi & Ogden (1993).

[b] The percentage changes refer to the sum of emissions of CO_2, CH_4, N_2O, CO, NO_x, and NMOCs from the entire fuel production and use cycle (excluding the manufacture of vehicles and equipment). Emissions of gases other than CO_2 have been converted to an equivalent amount of CO_2, where equivalence is defined in terms of the amount of global warming caused over a given time period. Results based on DeLuchi (1991).

[c] With renewable hydrogen or methanol, greenhouse gas emissions are reduced but are not necessarily eliminated. With biofuels, some emissions result from fossil fuel use while cultivating, fertilizing, and harvesting biomass. For these cases, it is assumed that the hydrogen is compressed for delivery to the vehicles at the service station using the projected mix of power sources in the United States in the year 2000 (EIA 1990).

[d] Hydrogen internal-combustion-engine vehicles built and tested to date have shown a wide range of NO_x emissions. A hydrogen engine can be designed to operate at a very high air-to-fuel ratio (that is, very lean), and will have very low NO_x emissions because of the reduced temperature. However, if such an engine is operated at full power, which requires an air-fuel mixture of 1:1, the NO_x emissions from the engine will increase substantially.

[e] If solar power is used for hydrogen compression, greenhouse gas emissions for solar hydrogen would be zero.

term, natural-gas-derived hydrogen in an FCEV would provide a large reduction in emissions of greenhouse gases, compared with the use of gasoline (see Table 8-15).

Strategy for Developing Solar Hydrogen as a Transportation Fuel in the United States

To compete economically with battery-powered electric vehicles (BPEVs) in the emerging zero-emissions-vehicle market, hydrogen fuel cell vehicles would have to be developed, tested, and commercialized on a large-enough scale to significantly reduce fuel cell costs.

Potential Markets

The first experimental hydrogen FCEVs could be developed within the next few years.[8] Testing in small experimental fleets will be an important step toward gaining experience with vehicle and refueling technology and evaluating consumer acceptance. Beyond this, the next step might be introduction of modest-sized test fleets of several hundred to a few thousand vehicles that would be centrally refueled. With a commitment from industry, it is possible that these modest-sized fleets of FCEVs could be ready starting around the year 2000, in response to the California market. Then, if hydrogen FCEVs were successful in fleet service, the hydrogen distribution network might be expanded to general consumers. During the early decades of the next century, FCEVs might come to capture a large share of the ZEV market—say, 100,000 vehicles per year or more—and FCEV costs would decrease as vehicle production levels increased.

Meeting the Demand for Hydrogen

How would hydrogen be produced to satisfy these potential markets? Over the next ten years, as hydrogen fuel cell vehicles are tested and readied for commercialization, only small quantities of hydrogen would be used, and the least-expensive option would probably be truck-delivered pressurized industrial hydrogen derived from natural gas.[9]

---

[8] Energy Partners project that their hydrogen fuel cell "Green Car" will be operational in 1994; Ballard is testing a hydrogen fuel cell bus in 1993; and the USDOE with GM will be investigating a range of possibilities for fuel cell automobiles, including those with hydrogen storage, testing a vehicle by 1996.

[9] The use of hydrogen from natural gas in FCEVs would result in a 40%–50% reduction in greenhouse gas emissions, compared with gasoline emissions (see Table 8-15). Although this reduction is not as large as that for renewable hydrogen, it is greater than the reduction

After the year 2000, hydrogen FCEVs might be used in midsized private and government fleets. At this point, the source of hydrogen would become more of an issue, both in terms of cost and in terms of greenhouse gas emissions. Fuel requirements for a fleet of 1,000 FCEVs would be about 75,000 GJ/year (or 0.5 million SCF of hydrogen per day). At this scale, instead of truck delivery, it would be less costly to produce hydrogen at the filling station, either from steam reforming of natural gas or via electrolysis.[10] (Biomass hydrogen systems, which have strong economies of scale, would probably be too expensive to compete at this small scale.) By the time 1,000-vehicle fleets of FCEVs are introduced, say between 2000 and 2010, wind and PV may well have reached low-enough costs to compete with steam reforming of natural gas on strictly economic terms (see Table 8-16).[11]

In the longer term, large numbers of FCEVs might be introduced as general-purpose ZEV passenger cars. In Table 8-11, a "city supply" system for 300,000 cars is described. Hydrogen fuel would be produced at a nearby centralized plant, and piped via a local citywide distribution system from the plant site to urban consumers at local filling stations. At this scale, biomass gasifier systems would benefit from economies of scale, and biomass hydrogen would be the least-expensive renewable option, costing only about half as much as PV or wind hydrogen.[12] However, land and water requirements would be sig-

---

offered by other near-term alternatives to gasoline, including methanol, compressed or liquefied natural gas, propane, and diesel fuel used in ICEVs (DeLuchi 1992). In addition, FCEV fleets operating on hydrogen made from natural gas would emit no criteria pollutants (see Table 8-15).

[10] A different strategy for meeting hydrogen demand soon after the year 2000 would be to build a larger centralized hydrogen plant and serve, say, ten cities, each with a fleet of 1,000 FCEVs. In a large plant, hydrogen could be produced at considerably lower cost from either steam reforming of natural gas or biomass gasification. However, because of the high capital costs of small-scale pipeline distribution, this option probably could not compete economically with small-scale decentralized production of electrolytic hydrogen. Moreover, it would be more complicated because of the pipeline infrastructure development.

[11] In Table 8-16 we describe several small-scale hydrogen production systems. The delivered cost of hydrogen for transportation would be about $17–$20/GJ for steam reforming and $17–$26/GJ for PV or wind hydrogen. Even if renewable electrolytic hydrogen is more expensive than fossil hydrogen, the government still may want to adopt policies to encourage its use, in recognition of its environmental benefits and to gain valuable experience in the design and operation of PV and wind electrolysis plants.

[12] Delivered costs for biomass hydrogen would be about $12–$15/GJ ($1.6–$1.9/gallon gasoline equivalent), as compared with about $20–$27/GJ ($2.6–$3.6/gallon gasoline equivalent) for PV or wind hydrogen. Moreover, the capital costs for biomass hydrogen plants would be much lower, about $140 million, as compared with $600–$1,000 million for PV or wind.

Table 8-16. Delivered Cost of Solar Hydrogen from Small Plants, ca. Year 2000

	ELECTROLYSIS (10 MWp)			Steam Reforming of Natural Gas
	PV	Wind	Hydro	
Capital costs (10⁶ $)				
Power system	5–11	8.5	—	2.1 Reformer plant
Electrolyzer	2.3	4.0	4.0	—
Compressor	0.5	0.5	0.5	0.1 Compressor
Storage	0.9	0.9	1.3	0.9 Storage
Filling station	0.5	0.5	0.5	0.5 Filling station
TOTAL	9–15	14.4	6.3	3.6
Contributions to hydrogen cost ($/GJ)				
Power system	7–14	13.6	—	5.0 Plant capital
Electrolyzer	4.4	5.9	5.2	2.3 O&M
Compression	2.3	2.3	1.1	0.8 Compression
Hydrogen storage	1.4	1.4	1.4	1.4 Storage
Filling station	2.5	2.5	2.5	2.5 Filling station
				5.4–8.1 Natural gas
Cost of hydrogen to consumer station				
($/GJ)	17.8–25.0	25.5	17–24	17–20
($/gallon gasoline)	2.5–3.6	3.7	2.4–3.5	2.4–2.7
Break-even gasoline price with tax ($/gallon)	1.28–1.54	1.56	1.25–1.50	1.25–1.36
Land used by power system (hectares)	12–19	47–160		
Energy delivered/year	70,000–90,000 GJ			
Vehicles fueledᵃ	1,200	1,200	1,600	1,000

Note: Costs and performance for PV and wind electrolysis systems are taken from Tables 8-7 and 8-8. Costs are given in 1989$. Hydrogen costs are computed based on the higher heating value. Estimates of the number of hydrogen fuel cell cars assume an efficiency equivalent to 60 mpg gasoline.
ᵃ Fuel cell fleet vehicles with an efficiency equivalent to 60 mpg gasoline, driven 48,000 km/yr.

nificant.[13] The production and use of biomass-derived hydrogen also would result in greater emissions of greenhouse gases than would the use of solar electrolytic hydrogen.

Even though much of the United States is close to good solar, wind, or biomass resources, it might become necessary in some cases to build pipelines to transport hydrogen long distances in the United States. The costs of such a scheme are given in the rightmost column of Table 8-11 for a 75-GWp "solar export system" involving a 1,000-mile pipeline from a PV hydrogen system in the southwestern United States to distant markets. The cost of hydrogen from this system would be comparable to those in the "city supply" case.[14]

At large production scales (and where suitable land and water are available), biomass would likely be the least-expensive renewable source of hydrogen. However, PV electrolytic hydrogen would require much less land and water and would result in lower emissions of greenhouse gases than biomass-derived hydrogen. Choosing among renewable hydrogen production technologies thus depends on the resource availability and on balancing the financial with the environmental costs and benefits. The long-run environmental benefits of solar- and wind-electrolytic hydrogen and the possibility of starting at very small scales without incurring large cost penalties argue for starting down this path soon. It also would be desirable to develop biomass gasifiers for hydrogen production (at both large and small scale), both because biomass is the least-expensive renewable feedstock for hydrogen, and because it is the only renewable feedstock for methanol, which might turn out to be the preferred hydrogen carrier for fuel cell vehicles (DeLuchi, Larson & Williams 1991).

Conclusion

With projected advances in the technology of fuel cells, solar-electric power generation, and biomass gasification, hydrogen from renewable resources could become attractive as a clean transport fuel in the early part of the next century. With renewable hydrogen used in fuel cell vehicles, greenhouse gas emissions could be greatly reduced and eventually eliminated, and emissions of regulated pollutants would be zero.

---

[13] Assuming production of 15 dry tonnes/hectare/year of wood chips from short-rotation intensive-cultivation trees and rainfall of 75–150 cm/year, a biomass gasifier hydrogen plant processing 1,650 dry tonnes/day would require 367 km^2 of plantation land (a circle 11 km in radius).

[14] The delivered cost of hydrogen to the consumer for PV and wind electrolysis systems does not depend much on the scale. Savings in compression and storage costs at large scale are balanced by increased transmission and distribution costs for large systems.

For the initial tests of FCEVs, hydrogen could come from the most convenient and lowest-cost source, which probably would be natural gas. The first renewable hydrogen energy systems might be introduced around the year 2000, with small PV hydrogen and wind electrolysis systems supplying hydrogen for small fleets of fuel cell vehicles. If these trials were successful, the use of hydrogen fuel might be expanded to the general public. At this scale, biomass hydrogen systems would become economically interesting, although the amount of hydrogen available might be limited by environmental constraints and by the availability of land. By contrast, wind and especially solar resources are huge and together could meet all the potential demand for hydrogen. In the long term, hydrogen would be produced from the best local resource, balancing environmental with traditional economic criteria. Hydrogen fuel cell vehicles could become an important part of a strategy for reducing greenhouse gas emissions and improving urban air quality.

References

Barnett, A. 1991. Astropower, Newark, Del. Personal communication.

Boes, E. 1991. Sandia National Laboratory, Albuquerque, N.M. Personal communication.

Buchner, H. 1984. "Hydrogen Use-Transportation Fuel." *International Journal of Hydrogen Energy* 9:501–15.

Buchner, H., and R. Povel. 1982. "The Daimler-Benz Hydride Vehicle Project." *International Journal of Hydrogen Energy* 7:259–66.

California Air Resources Board. 1990. "Proposed Regulations for Low-Emission Vehicles and Clean Fuels." California Air Resources Board Staff Report. Sacramento, Calif. August 13.

Candelario, T. R., S. L. Hester, et al. 1991. "PVUSA-Peformance, Experience and Cost." 22nd Institute of Electrical and Electronic Engineers Photovoltaics Specialists Conference. October.

Carlson, D. E. 1989. "Low-Cost Power from Thin-Film Photovoltaics." In *Electricity: Efficient End-Use and New Generation Technologies and Their Planning Implications.* T. B. Johansson, B. Bodlund, and R. H. Williams, eds. Lund, Sweden: Lund University Press.

———. 1990. Solarex, Thin Films Division. Personal communication.

Carpetis, C. 1984. "An Assessment of Electrolytic Hydrogen Production by Means of Photovoltaic Energy Conversion." *International Journal of Hydrogen Energy* 9:969–91.

Cohen, J. M., T. C. Schweitzer, S. M. Hock, and J. B. Cadogan. 1989. *A Methodology for Computing Wind Turbine Cost of Electricity Using Utility Economic Assumptions.* Presented at the Windpower '89 Conference.

Conover, K. 1989. "Photovoltaic Operation and Maintenance Evaluation." EPRI GS-6625. Palo Alto, Calif.: Electric Power Research Institute. December.

Craft, R. (Electrolyzer Corporation). 1985. Personal communication.

DeLaquil, P., M. Geyer, D. Kearney, and R. Diver. 1993. "Solar Thermal Electric Technology." In *Renewable Energy: Sources for Fuels and Electricity.* T. B. Johansson, H. Kelly, A. K. N. Reddy, and R. H. Williams, eds. Washington, D.C.: Island Press.

DeLuchi, M. A. 1989. "Hydrogen Vehicles: An Evaluation of Fuel Storage, Performance, Safety, and Cost." *International Journal of Hydrogen Energy* 14:81–130.

———. 1991. *Emissions of Greenhouse Gases from the Use of Transportation Fuels and Electricity.* Center for Transportation, Argonne National Laboratory, Research Report No. ANL/ESD/TM-22. Argonne, Ill. November.

———. 1992. *A Life Cycle Cost Analysis of Fuel Cell Vehicles.* Institute of Transportation Studies Research Report UCD-ITS-RR-98-14. University of California, Davis.

DeLuchi, M. A., E. D. Larson, and R. H. Williams. 1991. "Hydrogen and Methanol Production from Biomass and Use in Fuel Cell and Internal Combustion Engine Vehicles." Center for Energy and Environmental Studies Report No. 263. Princeton University, Princeton, N.J.

DeLuchi, M. A., and J. M. Ogden. 1993. "Solar Hydrogen Transportation Fuels and Their Use in Fuel Cell Vehicles." *Transportation Research* (in press).

Dutta, S., D. L. Block, and R. L. Port. 1990. "Economic Assessment of Advanced Electrolytic Hydrogen Production." *International Journal of Hydrogen Energy* 16:387–95.

Electric Power Research Institute (EPRI). 1986. *Technical Assessment Guide.* Vol. 1. *Electricity Supply.* EPRI P-4463-SR. Palo Alto, Calif.

Energy Information Administration (EIA). 1990. *Energy Consumption and Conservation Potential: Supporting Analysis for the National Energy Strategy.* SR/NES/90-92. Washington, D.C. December.

Fein, E., and K. Edwards. 1984. *Electrolytic Hydrogen in Three Northeast Utilities Service Areas.* Electric Power Research Institute ERRI EM-3561. Palo Alto, Calif.

Feucht, K., G. Holzel, and W. Hurwich. 1988. "Perspectives of Mobile Hydrogen Transportation." In *Hydrogen Energy Progress VII*. Vol. 3, pp. 1963–74. T. N. Veziroglu and A. N. Protosenko, eds. New York: Plenum Press.

Fulkerson, W., et al. 1989. *Energy Technology R&D: What Could Make a Difference?* Vol. 2. *Supply Technology*. Oak Ridge National Laboratory ORNL-6541/V2/P2. Oak Ridge, Tenn. December.

Furuhama, S. 1988. "Hydrogen Engine Systems for Land Vehicles." In *Hydrogen Energy Progress VII*. Vol. 3, pp. 1841–1954. T. N. Veziroglu and A. N. Protosenko, eds. New York: Plenum Press.

Gregory, D. P., C. L. Tsaros, J. L. Arora, and P. Nevrekar. 1980. "The Economics of Hydrogen Production." American Chemical Society Report 0-8412-0522-1/80/47-116-003.

Hall, D. O., J. Woods, A. K. Senelwa, and F. Rosillo-Calle. 1993. "Biomass for Energy: Future Supply Prospects." In *Renewable Sources for Fuels and Electricity*. T. B. Johansson, H. Kelly, A. K. N. Reddy, and R. H. Williams, eds. Washington, D.C.: Island Press.

Hammerli, M. 1984. "When Will Electrolytic Hydrogen Become Competitive?" *International Journal of Hydrogen Energy* 9:25–51.

———. 1990. Hammerli Associates, Ontario. Personal communication.

Hock, S. M., R. W. Thresher, and J. M. Cohen. 1990. Proceedings of the American Society of Mechanical Engineers, Winter Annual Meeting, Dallas, Tex., November 25.

Hubbard, H. M. 1989. "Photovoltaics Today and Tomorrow." *Science* 244:297–304.

Hug, W., J. Divisek, J. Mergel, W. Seeger, and H. Steeb. 1990. "High Efficiency Advanced Alkaline Electrolyzer for Solar Operation." In *Hydrogen Energy Progress VIII*. Vol. 2, pp. 681–96. T. N. Veziroglu and P. K. Takahashi, eds. New York: Plenum Press.

Idaho National Engineering Lab (INEL). 1990. *The Potential of Renewable Energy*. SERI/TP-260-3674. Prepared for the U.S. DOE Office of Policy, Planning and Analysis. Golden, Colo.: Solar Energy Research Institute. March.

Intergovernmental Panel on Climate Change (IPCC). 1990. *Climate Change: The IPCC Scientific Assessment*. J. F. Houghton, G. J. Jenkins, and J. J. Ephraums, eds. Cambridge, England: Cambridge University Press.

International Energy Agency (IEA). 1991. *Proceedings of the 2nd International Energy Agency Hydrogen Production Workshop, Julich, Germany, September 4–6.*

Johansson, T. B., H. Kelly, A. K. N. Reddy, and R. H. Williams. 1993. "Renewable Fuels and Electricity for a Growing World Economy: Defining and Achieving the Potential." In *Renewable Sources for Fuels and Electricity*. Washington, D.C.: Island Press.

Kevala, R. J. 1990. "Development of a Liquid-Cooled Phosphoric Acid Fuel Cell/Battery Power Plant for Transit Bus Applications." *Proceedings of the 25th Intersociety Energy Conversion Engineering Conference*. Vol. 3, pp. 297–300. P. A. Nelson, W. W. Schertz, and R. H. Till, eds. New York: American Institute of Chemical Engineers.

Larson, E. D., and R. Katofsky. 1992. "Production of Hydrogen and Methanol from Biomass." In *Advances in Thermochemical Biomass Conversion*. Interlaken, Switzerland. May 11–15.

Larson, E. D., and R. H. Williams. 1992. Princeton University, Center for Energy and Environmental Studies. Personal communication.

Lehmann, P. 1990. "Experimental PV Electrolysis System." Presentation at the 8th World Hydrogen Energy Conference, Honolulu, July 22–27.

Lemmons, R. A. 1990. "Fuel Cells for Transportation." *Journal of Power Sources* 29:251–64.

Leroy, R. L., and A. K. Stuart. 1978. "Unipolar Water Electrolysers: A Competitive Technology." In *Hydrogen Energy System*. T. N. Veziroglu and W. Seifritz, eds.

Lucas, E. J., E. A. DeMeo, G. M. McNerney, and W. J. Steeley. 1990. "The EPRI-Utility US Windpower Advanced Wind Turbine Program—Status and Plans." Windpower '90 Conference.

Matlin, R. 1990. Chronar Corporation, Princeton, N.J. Personal communication.

Metz, P. D., and M. Piraino. 1985. "Technoeconomic Analysis of PV Hydrogen Systems." *Final Report for PV Electrolysis Project*. Ch. 3.0, BNL-B199SPE(3). Upton, N.Y.: Brookhaven National Laboratory.

Miles, T. R., Sr., and T. R. Miles, Jr. 1992. "Environmental Implications of Increased Biomass Energy Use." NREL/TP-230-4633. Golden, Colo.: National Renewable Energy Laboratory. March.

Nesbitt, K. A., M. A. DeLuchi, and K. S. Kurani. 1991. *Household Electric Vehicles Market: A Near-Term Constraints Analysis*. University of California, Davis: Institute of Transportation Studies.

Nitsch, J., H. Klaiss, J. Meyer, et al. 1990. "Conditions and Consequences of a Development Strategy for a Solar Hydrogen Economy." Study for the Enquette Commission of the German Parliament on Technology Assessment and Evaluation. Bonn.

Noel, G. T., D. C. Carmichael, R. W. Smith, and J. H. Broehl. 1985. "Optimization and Modularity Studies for Large-Size, Flat-Panel Array Fields." Battelle-Columbus, Institute of Electrical and Electronics Engineers Photovoltaics Specialists' Conference, Las Vegas, Nev., October.

Ogden, J. M. 1991. "Hydrogen from Solar Electricity." Paper presented at the National Hydrogen Association 2nd Annual Meeting, Arlington, Va., March 13–15.

Ogden, J. M., and J. Nitsch. 1993. "Solar Hydrogen." In *Renewable Sources for Fuels and Electricity*. T. B. Johansson, H. Helly, A. K. N. Reddy, and R. Williams, eds. Washington, D.C.: Island Press.

Ogden, J. M., and R. H. Williams. 1989. *Solar Hydrogen: Moving Beyond Fossil Fuels*. Washington, D.C.: World Resources Institute. October.

Patil, P. G., R. A. Kost, and J. F. Miller. 1991. "U.S. Research & Development Program on Fuel Cells for Transportation Applications." In *EVS-10 Hong Kong, The 10th International Electric Vehicle Symposium: Symposium Proceedings*, 657–69, December 3–5.

Pirani, S. N., and A. T. B. Stuart. 1991. "Testing and Evaluation of Advanced Water Electrolysis Equipment and Components." In *Proceedings of the 2nd International Energy Agency Hydrogen Production Workshop, Julich, Germany, September 4–6*.

Prater, K. 1990. "The Renaissance of the Solid Polymer Fuel Cell." *Journal of Power Sources* 29:239–50.

———. 1991. Ballard Power Systems. Testimony on S.1269, the Renewable Hydrogen Energy Research and Development Act of 1991. Hearings before the United States Senate Committee on Energy and National Resources, Subcommittee on Energy Research and Development. June 25.

Protosenko, A. N. 1988. "Liquid Hydrogen in Air Transporation." Paper presented at the 8th World Hydrogen Energy Conference, Moscow, USSR, September 24–28.

Schucan, T. 1990. Paul Scherrer Institute, Switzerland. Personal communication.

Schwarz, J. A. 1990. "The Effect of Impurities on Hydrogen Storage Capacity on Activated Carbons at Refrigeration Temperatures." In *Hydrogen Energy Progress VIII*. Vol. 3, pp. 973–84. T. N. Veziroglu and P. K. Takahashi, eds. New York: Plenum Press.

Shusnar, G. J., J. H. Caldwell, R. F. Reinoehl, and J. H. Wilson. 1985. "ARCO Solar Field Data for Flat Plate PV Arrays." Paper presented at the 18th Institute of Electrical and Electronics Engineers Photovoltaic Specialists' Conference, Las Vegas, Nev., October.

Smith, D. 1991. Pacific Gas and Electric Company, San Francisco. Personal communication.

Society of Automotive Engineers (SAE). 1991. Fuel Cells for Transportation: Topical Technical Workshop, Washington, D.C., November 13–15.

Sperling, D. A. 1989. *New Transportation Fuels*. Berkeley and Los Angeles: University of California Press.

Sperling, D. A., and M. A. DeLuchi. 1991. *Alternative Transportation Fuels and Air Pollution*. Report to the OECD Environment Directorate, Organization for Economic Cooperation and Development, Paris. March.

Steeb, H., A. Brinner, H. Bubmann, and W. Seeger. 1990. "Operation Experience of 10kW PV Electrolysis System in Different Power Matching Modes." In *Hydrogen Energy Progress VIII*. Vol. 2, pp. 691–700. T. N. Veziroglu and P. K. Takahashi, eds. New York: Plenum Press.

Stuart, A. K. 1991. "A Perspective on Electrolysis." In *Proceedings: Transition Strategies to Hydrogen as an Energy Carrier—of the First Annual Meeting of the National Association*. EPRI GS-7248. Palo Alto, Calif.: Electric Power Research Institute. March. 13-1 to 13-9.

Stucki, S. 1991. "Operation of Membrel Electrolyzers Under Varying Load." In *Proceedings of the 2nd International Energy Agency Hydrogen Production Workshop, Julich, Germany, September 4–6*.

U.S. Department of Energy (USDOE). 1990. *Solar Thermal Electric Technology Rationale*. Solar Thermal and Biomass Power Division, Office of Solar Energy Conversion. August.

Wang, Q., M. A. DeLuchi, and D. Sperling. 1990. "Emissions Impacts of Electric Vehicles." *Journal of the Air and Waste Management Association* 40:1275–84.

Werbos, P. J. 1987. "Oil Dependency and the Potential for Fuel Cell Vehicles." SAE Technical Paper Series #871091. Warrendale, Pa.: Society of Automotive Engineers.

Winter, C. J., and J. Nitsch. 1988. *Hydrogen as an Energy Carrier*. New York: Springer-Verlag.

Zegers, P. 1990. "Fuel Cells in Europe." *Journal of Power Sources* 29:133–42.

Zweibel, K. 1990. *Harnessing Solar Power: The Photovoltaics Challenge*. New York: Plenum Press.

———. 1991. Solar Energy Research Institute, Golden, Colo. Personal communication.

Table A-1. Economic Parameters Used in Computing the Levelized Cost of Solar Electricity

Investment in Electricity and Hydrogen Production, Transmission, and Distribution	
Real rate of return on investment	0.061
Yearly insurance cost (fraction of initial capital cost)	0.005
Yearly property taxes (fraction of initial capital cost)	0.015

Source: These values are suggested by the Electric Power Research Institute for utility-owned electricity production systems (EPRI 1986).

Appendix: Methods for Calculating the Levelized Cost of Solar Electricity and Hydrogen

We have computed the levelized cost of electricity in constant 1989 U.S.$, using the economic assumptions in Table A-1, which are suggested by EPRI for utility-owned power plants (EPRI 1986).

Wind Electricity

For wind electricity, the electricity cost is given by:

$$Ce(\$/kWh) = (CRF + INS + TAX) \times Ct(\$/kW)/(a \times p \times 8{,}760 \text{ hr/yr}) + COM(\$/kWh)$$

where:

Ce = levelized production cost of wind electricity ($/kWhAC)
CRF = capital recovery factor = $i/[1 - (1 + i)^{-N}]$
i = real discount rate
N = system lifetime (years)
INS = annual insurance fraction of capital cost
TAX = annual property tax fraction of capital cost
Ct = installed capital cost of system ($/kWpeak)
a = availability
p = annual average capacity factor
COM = annual operation and maintenance costs ($/kWh)

The annual average capacity factor for the system *at a particular wind power energy density* can be calculated by:

$$p = Et/[Pw \times a \times 8{,}760 \text{ hr/yr}/1{,}000 \text{ (kW/W)}] \times L$$

where:

p = annual average capacity factor
Et = annual gross energy capture per unit of turbine area (kWh/m²/yr)
Pw = annual average power density of wind (W/m²)
a = availability
L = loss factor for wind turbine spacing, wiring losses

Et can be calculated from the measured or estimated gross energy capture per turbine:

$$Et = Ea/A$$

where:

Ea = gross energy capture per turbine (kWh/yr)
A = area swept by turbine blades (m²) = $pi \times (d/2)^2$
d = turbine diameter (m)

Solar Thermal-Electric Systems

For solar thermal-electric systems, the cost of electricity is given by:

$$Ce(\$/kWh) = (CRF + INS + TAX) \times Cst(\$/kW)/(8,760 \text{ hr/yr} \times p \times a)$$
$$+ COM(\$/kWh) + Pgas(\$/GJ)/nelec \times 0.0036 \text{ GJ/kWh}$$
$$\times fgas$$

where:

Ce = levelized production cost of solar electricity ($/kWhAC)
CRF = capital recovery factor = $i/[1 - (1 + i)^{-N}]$
i = real discount rate
N = system lifetime (years)
INS = annual insurance (as a fraction of capital cost)
TAX = annual property tax (as a fraction of capital cost)
Cst = installed capital cost of system ($/kWpeak)
p = total system capacity factor = solar capacity factor × $1/(1 - fgas)$
a = kWh generated annually/(8,760 × system capacity)
COM = annual operation and maintenance costs ($/kWh)
$Pgas$ = gas price ($/GJ) = gas price ($/MBtu)/1.055
$nelec$ = efficiency of steam-turbine electricity generation from gas = .29
$fgas$ = kWh generated annually from gas/total kWh generated annually

Photovoltaic Electricity

The cost of photovoltaic electricity in $/kWh is given by:

$$Ce = (CRF + INS + TAX) \times (1 + ID)$$
$$\times [(Cmod + Cbos)/(nmod \times nbos) + Cpc \times Ip]$$
$$\div (insol \times 8,760) + COM/(nmod \times nbos \times insol \times 8,760)$$

where:

Ce = levelized production cost of solar electricity (\$/kWh)
CRF = capital recovery factor = $i/[1 - (1 + i)^{-N}]$
i = real discount rate
N = PV system lifetime (years)
INS = insurance cost (as a fraction of capital cost)
TAX = property tax (as a fraction of capital cost)
ID = indirect-cost factor
$Cmod$ = capital cost of PV modules (\$/m²)
$Cbos$ = area-related balance-of-system capital cost (\$/m²)
$nmod$ = PV module efficiency at average operating temperature
$nbos$ = balance-of-system efficiency (= DC system efficiency/ module efficiency)
Cpc = power-related balance-of-system capital cost (\$/kW)
Ip = maximum insolation (kW/m²) = 1 kW/m²
$insol$ = annual average insolation on tilted, fixed, flat-plate array (kW/m²)
COM = annual operation and maintenance costs (\$/m²/year)

For a DC photovoltaic system, the cost of power-related balance-of-system equipment would be \$75/kW; for an AC system, \$150/kW. For a DC system, $nbos = 89\%$; for an AC system, $nbos = 85\%$.

Levelized Cost of Electrolytic Hydrogen

The levelized cost of electrolytic hydrogen, Ceh (in \$/GJ), for a large DC electrolysis plant can be expressed as (Hammerli 1984, 1990; Leroy & Stuart 1978):

$$Ceh = Cehc + Cehe$$

where:

$Cehc$ = capital component of electrolysis cost (\$/GJ)
= $[1/(nr \times 8,760 \text{ hr/yr} \times 0.0036 \text{ GJ/kWh})]$
$\times [(CRFel + INS + TAX + OM)/CF] \times Celec$
$Cehe$ = DC electricity cost component of electrolysis cost (\$/GJ)
= $Ce/(0.0036 \text{ GJ/kWh})/ne$

and:

nr = electrolyzer efficiency at rated voltage = $(Vr/1.481$ volts)

Vr = rated voltage of electrolyzer (in volts)

$CRFel$ = capital recovery factor = $d/[1-(1+d)^{-Nel}]$

d = real discount rate

Nel = electrolyzer lifetime (years)

INS = annual insurance cost (as a fraction of capital cost)

TAX = annual property plus income tax (as a fraction of capital cost)

OM = operation and maintenance cost (as a fraction of capital cost)

CF = electrolyzer capacity utilization factor = $no \times pelec$

no = coupling efficiency between power source and electrolyzer

$pelec$ = annual average capacity factor of power source

$Celec$ = installed capital cost of electrolysis plant ($/kWDCin)
    = $Cem \times \{(1-f1) \times (ir/i) + f1 + 0.5 \times f2 \times [1+(ir/i)]\}$

Cem = electrolyzer cells and accessories unit capital cost ($/kW of DC power input, at $V = Vr$)

V = operating voltage of electrolyzer (in volts)

$f1$ = fraction of electrolyzer cells and accessories capital cost that is independent of current

ir = rated electrolyzer current density (in milliamps/cm^2)

i = operating current density (in milliamps/cm^2)

$f2$ = installation-related costs, as a fraction of the cells and accessory cost—half of this cost is independent of the operating current density, and the other half increases linearly with operating current density

Ce = cost of DC electricity (in $/kWh)

ne = electrolyzer efficiency (DC input power to hydrogen energy figured on a higher heating value basis) = $1.481/V$

Typical values for $f1$, $f2$, ir, i, Vr, V, and Cem are shown in Table A-2.
    For an AC electrolysis plant, terms are added for the rectifier capital cost and O&M. The total hydrogen cost is:

$$Ceh = Cehc + Cehe$$

where:

$Cehc$ = capital component of electrolysis cost ($/GJ)
    = $[1/(nr \times nrect \times 8{,}760 \text{ hr/yr} \times 0.0036 \text{ GJ/kWh})]$
    $\times [(CRFel + INS + TAX + OM)/CF \times Celec \times nrect$
    $+ (CRFrect + INS + TAX + OM)/CF \times Crect]$

Table A-2. Cost and Performance of Large PV Electrolysis Plants

	Unipolar	Bipolar	SPE (projected)
Vr = rated voltage (V)	1.74	1.85	1.65
V = operating voltage range (V)	1.7–2.0	1.7–2.0	1.65
ir = rated current density (mA/cm²)	134	215	1,076
i = operating current density range (mA/cm²)	134–310	250–1,000	1,000–2,000
ne = efficiency at $V = Vr$ (= H$_2$ out [HHV]/DC in)	0.85	0.80	0.90
$f1$ = capital cost fraction independent of current	0.90	0.80	0.50
$f2$ = installation cost as a fraction of capital cost	0.45	0.45	0.75
Cem = capital cost of electrolyzer modules ($/kWDCin)	189	222 (1 atm.) 283 (30 atm.)	222
$Celec$ = installed capital cost DC electrolysis plant at rated current density ($/kWDCin)	274	322 (1 atm.) 410 (330 atm.)	388
OM = annual operation and maintenance cost as a fraction of capital cost per year	2%	2%	2%
Nel = electrolyzer lifetime (yr)	20	20	20
$Crect$ = capital cost of rectifier ($/kWACin)	130	130	130
$nrect$ = rectifier efficiency	96%	96%	96%
$Nrect$ = rectifier lifetime (yr)	10	10	10

Source: Parameters other than capital and O&M costs are from Leroy & Stuart (1978). The capital estimates for large unipolar electrolyzers and pressurized bipolar electrolyzers are from Craft (1985). Capital costs for atmospheric pressure bipolar and SPE (solid polymer electrolyte) electrolyzers are from Fein & Edwards (1984). Operation and maintenance costs are from Hammerli (1984).

$Cehe$ = AC electricity cost component of electrolysis cost ($/GJ)
= $Ce/(0.0036 \text{ GJ/kWh})/(ne \times nrect)$
$nrect$ = rectifier efficiency AC to DC conversion
$CRFrect$ = capital recovery factor for rectifier
= $d/[1 - (1 + d)^{-Nrect}]$
$Crect$ = capital cost of rectifier ($/kWACin)
Ce = cost of AC electricity (in $/kWh)
$Nrect$ = rectifier lifetime (years)

and the other variables are the same as for the DC plant. Typical values for these variables are given in Table A-2.

Table A-3. Cost and Performance Parameters for the Hydrogen Refueling Station

HYDROGEN REFUELING: INPUT DATA	
Compressor Station	
Fixed cost of compressor ($/hp, 1975$)	300[a]
Compressor cost per unit of output ($/hp/million standard ft^3 [SCF] of hydrogen/day, 1975$)	2.10[a]
Ratio of PPI for current year to PPI for 1975	2.07
Cost of electricity to the commercial sector ($/kWh)	0.070[b]
Annual cost of servicing, labor, and new parts (fraction of initial cost)	0.05[c]
Salvage value of compressor (fraction of initial cost)	0.20
Initial temperature of hydrogen (degrees K)	288.80
Initial pressure of hydrogen (psi)	50
Compressor output pressure divided by vehicular storage pressure	1.05
Number of stages of compression	6
Compressor efficiency	0.85
Storage and Refueling Equipment	
Cost of storage cascade, including manifolding, support, safety equipment, and transportation ($/SCF/1,000-psi storage)	0.27[d]
Storage capacity of station (SCF) divided by total SCF demanded during peak period	0.016
Gas deliverable from storage at maximum vehicular storage pressure (fraction of total SCF of storage)	0.10
Cost of refueling equipment, including meters and safety equipment ($/refueling line)	9,000[e]
Salvage value of storage and refueling (fraction of station initial cost)	0.15
Annual cost of servicing, labor, and new parts (fraction of initial station cost)	0.02

Source: See DeLuchi (1992) for documentation and sources not shown here.

Notes:

a We derived these coefficients from a cost-function graph presented in Darrow et al. (1977). Compressor manufacturers we have spoken with recently have confirmed our cost results (Barker 1991; Tothe 1991; Ward 1991).

b This is the commercial-sector price projected by the EIA (1990) for the year 2000.

c This is the maintenance-cost factor estimated by two major compressor manufacturers, Dresser-Rand (Tothe 1991) and Norwalk (Barker 1991).

d Based on an estimate done for us by CP Industries (Carrozza 1991) of the cost of a 44,400-SCF storage cascade designed specifically for hydrogen at 9,300 psi.

e According to one supplier, a custom-produced complete refueling system designed to deliver 400 to 500 SCFM of natural gas at 3,600 psi would cost about $11,000 (Patterson 1991). Mass production would bring this cost down considerably. However, the cost of an 8,000- or 9,000-psi system would be higher than the cost of a 3,600-psi system.

Table A-3. (continued)

HYDROGEN REFUELING: INPUT DATA (continued)

Land, Building, and Other Initial Costs

Other station capital and engineering cost (fraction of cost of compressor, storage, refueling)	0.03
Cost of buildings ($)	20,000
Cost of hook-up to gas line ($)	2,500
Price of land ($/acre)	200,000
Land required for buildings, exits, and entrances (sq ft)	4,500
Land required per refueling bay (sq ft/bay)	150
Land required for gas storage (sq ft land/1,000 SCF storage × 1,000 psi pressure)	50.0
Real rate of increase in value of land (fraction of original cost per year)	0.03

Hydrogen Throughput

Number of refueling lines (or bays)	8
Rate of delivery of gas to vehicle (SCF/min [SCFM])	400
Average length of time spent pulling in and out of refueling bay, removing and replacing pump, and paying (min)	2.5
Ratio of average nonpeak demand to peak demand (assume peak demand = station capacity)	0.33
Hours of peak (maximum) demand rate	2.00
Hours open per day	20
Days open per year	360
Fraction of tank filled per refueling	0.75

Operating Costs

Wage rate ($/hr)	7.50
Average number of shifts per hour	1.50
Overhead on salaries (multiplier)	1.60
Other station operating cost: supplies, water, sewage, garbage, etc. ($/yr)	5,000

Table A-3. (continued)

HYDROGEN REFUELING: CALCULATED RESULTS

Compressor

Compressor power needed (kW)	632
Required capacity of compressor (SCFM at 1 atm, 293.15 K)	1,400
Ratio of compressor capacity (SCFM) to nonpeak hydrogen demand (SCFM per nonpeak operating hour)	3.03
Ratio of compressor capacity (SCFM) to peak hydrogen demand (SCFM)	1.00
Average compressor operating hours per operating day	7.9

Hydrogen

Final pressure of hydrogen from compressor (psi)	8,400
Hydrogen compressibility factor	1.38[f]
Ratio of specific heats of hydrogen	1.47[f]

Demand for Fuel

Hydrogen throughput (million Btu/yr)	76,658
Hydrogen throughput (SCF/yr at 1 atm, 293.15 K)	$2.40\ 10^6$
SCF per vehicle (at 1 atm, 293.15 K)	778
Maximum hydrogen demand rate in an hour (SCFM at 1 atm, 293.15 K)	1,400
Vehicles per hour per refueling line, nonpeak hours	4.5
Maximum station capacity (vehicles per refueling line, one hour; assume this is peak)	13.5
Average number of vehicles per operating day	857
Total refueling time per car, including pulling into bay, delivering fuel, and paying (min)	4.45

Storage System and Land

Required hydrogen storage capacity at station (SCF)	26,319
Nonpeak demand provided by station storage (hrs)	0.1
Land required (acres)	0.134

Notes:
[f] Calculated as a nonlinear function of the temperature and pressure of hydrogen, using data from the National Bureau of Standards (Hilsenrath et al. 1955) and CP Industries (Dowling 1991).

Table A-3. (continued)

HYDROGEN REFUELING: CALCULATED RESULTS (continued)	
Cost	
Cost of compressor engine ($/hp, 1975$; based on regression of $/hp and hp)	57
Compressor cost ($/kW)	980
Capital cost of compressor ($)	619,471
Capital cost of storage cascade ($)	58,896
Other station capital and engineering costs ($)	22,511
Cost of land ($)	26,890
Total initial cost of station, including all equipment, installation, and engineering cost ($)	822,268
Total station operating cost ($/yr)	424,489
Levelized total initial cost, including resale of land and equipment ($/yr)	73,650
Hydrogen retail markup, before all taxes, $/million Btu	**6.50**

Chapter 9

Why Is Energy Use Rising in the Freight Sector?

Marianne M. Mintz and Anant D. Vyas

Over the past twenty years, both the demand for freight services and the consumption of fuel by those modes conventionally considered to be freight carrying—namely, truck, rail, marine, and air cargo—have grown steadily in the United States. Although freight modes now account for only 22% of the carbon dioxide emissions from the transportation sector (Vyas 1990), it is a growing share and much of the future growth in CO_2 emissions by the sector will come from these modes (USDOE 1991b). This chapter discusses trends in CO_2 emissions, energy use, and fuel efficiency. Historical data come from various published sources; forecasts were developed by the authors as part of a larger effort to project total transportation energy use for the Office of Transportation Technologies (OTT) within the U.S. Department of Energy (DOE). The forecasts use a series of disaggregate consumer choice models developed for OTT and other DOE offices and generate a wealth of detail, only a small portion of which is summarized here. In effect, the models simulate the processes whereby households select particular types of personal passenger vehicles and shippers select particular transportation modes to transport their goods or deliver their services. Key variables include exogenous forecasts of vehicle and modal attributes, retail fuel prices, economic output and distribution, commodity densities, and demographic trends. See Mintz & Vyas (1991) for a further discussion of these inputs, and descriptions of the models and their underlying theory.

The work on which this chapter is based was sponsored by the U.S. Department of Energy, Assistant Secretary for Conservation and Renewable Energy, under contract W-31-109-Eng-38.

243

Trends in Energy and CO_2 Emissions

Total transportation energy use, which nearly doubled between 1960 and 1985 (USDOE 1991a, 13), is expected to grow only a third as fast between 1985 and 2010 (Mintz & Vyas 1991, 5). Trends in demographics and vehicle fuel efficiency are expected to constrain near-term growth in fuel consumption by personal vehicles. For nonpersonal vehicles (freight modes and commercial aircraft), the outlook is somewhat different. The economic and demographic data on which recent forecasts are based show shifts in the U.S. economy and continued growth in disposable personal income (Mintz & Vyas 1991, 10). These trends should spur fuel consumption in nonpersonal transportation, with little relief from modest improvements in vehicle fuel efficiency. As a result, fuel consumption by freight modes is expected to increase by over 50% between 1985 and 2010, and total energy use by nonpersonal vehicles should surpass that for autos and other personal vehicles before 2005 (see Figure 9-1).

Figure 9-2 shows both the long-term historical trend and our baseline forecast of energy consumption by transportation mode. Viewed in this manner, the 1973–1974 and 1979 oil crises appear as clear breaks in the trendlines for automobiles. Figure 9-3 indexes the data, thereby showing growth (or decline) relative to each mode's energy use in 1970. Over this forty-year time frame, consumption by light-duty vehicles (autos and light trucks) grows 44% (only 11% from 1990 to 2010), whereas consumption by rail and marine modes (barges, coastal and Great Lakes shipping, and U.S. fuel purchases for international shipping) grows by nearly 70%.

Energy consumption by air modes (domestic air carriers and U.S. fuel purchases by international carriers) and heavy-duty highway vehicles (buses and trucks over 10,000-lb gross vehicle weight) provides an even sharper contrast, with aircraft more than doubling and heavy-duty vehicles more than tripling their fuel use over the forty-year time frame. Disaggregating modal consumption by fuel type, emissions of carbon dioxide may be estimated by applying standard carbon-release rates. Figure 9-4 displays the resulting trend. Again, diesel and jet fuel (used by trucks and aircraft) account for most of the growth in CO_2 emissions. (Note that the baseline forecast includes no alternative-fuels use, and that values shown include CO_2 emissions from fuel processing and transportation, as well as from combustion.)

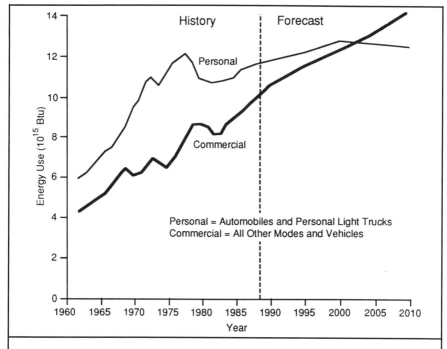

Figure 9-1. Transportation Energy Use by Personal Versus Commercial Modes, 1960–2010

Source: Mintz & Vyas (1991, 58).

Fuel Economy and Energy Intensity

Depending on mode, trends in energy efficiency are expressed in terms of energy intensity (Btu/ton-mile) or fuel economy (mpg). Before we present those trends, a brief discussion of data issues is in order.

Data Issues

Energy intensity may be computed from various time-series data sets of industry associations, government agencies, or private groups. The *Transportation Energy Data Book*, published by Oak Ridge National Laboratory (Davis & Hu 1991), is also a source. For rail and marine modes, ton-miles and fuel use are routinely reported, and energy intensity is a relatively straightforward calculation (see annual volumes of AAR; USACOE; USDOE, *Annual Energy Review*; USDOT, *Carload Waybill Statistics*). Because of inconsistencies in the data, how-

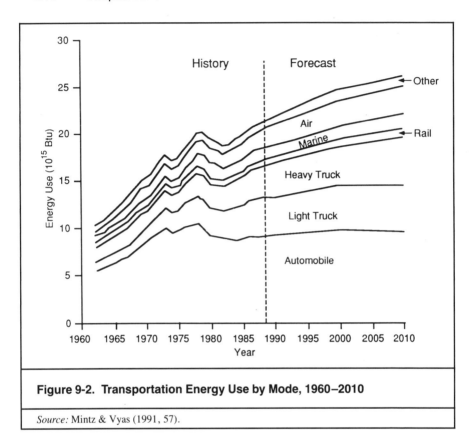

Figure 9-2. Transportation Energy Use by Mode, 1960–2010

Source: Mintz & Vyas (1991, 57).

ever, trends are not always what they seem. For example, in the 1980s, many class 1 railroads[1] spun off their regional and local operations into independent short lines. Operations on these typically lower-volume tracks had been included in the totals reported for class 1 railroads. Thus, some of the apparent improvement in rail energy intensity may be due to a reporting change. Likewise, because Alaskan oil development greatly increased the share of domestic maritime traffic represented by relatively efficient coastal tankers, maritime energy intensity should not be aggregated across area of operation.

For trucks, the data are even less reliable. The Eno Foundation has estimated domestic intercity ton-miles of travel (TMT) by truck (both ICC regulated and nonregulated) since 1950 (Smith 1991, 44). Data

---

[1] Railroads with annual operating revenues above a threshold set by the Interstate Commerce Commission (ICC). In 1988, that threshold was $92 million.

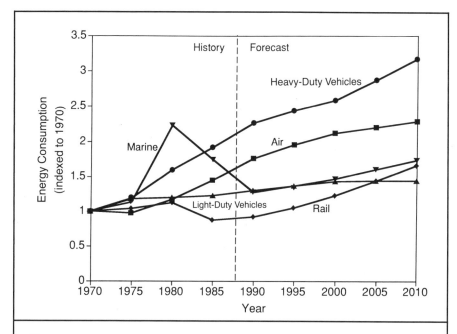

Figure 9-3. Energy Consumption by Mode (Indexed to 1970)

Source: Data from Mintz & Vyas (1991).

for ICC-regulated trucks are obtained from ICC reports; data for non-ICC trucks are estimated from trends in vehicle-miles of travel and average loads (tons/vehicle-mile) of contract/specialized ICC trucks as reported to the ICC (Smith 1991, 44). In effect, Eno assumes non-ICC trucks share the same characteristics as contract/specialized ICC trucks, an assumption that may or may not be correct.

Air freight data are also problematic. Because much cargo is carried in the lower hold, or "belly," of passenger aircraft, ton-miles must be disaggregated by aircraft type—passenger or all-cargo. To our knowledge, no such consistent, disaggregated time-series data exist. Thus the following discussion excludes air freight.

Rail Modes

Since 1970, railroads appear to have improved their energy intensity by over 30% (Davis & Hu 1991, 2-28). Although some of this improvement may be attributed to technological factors, the operational efficiencies wrought by mergers and consolidations, changes in

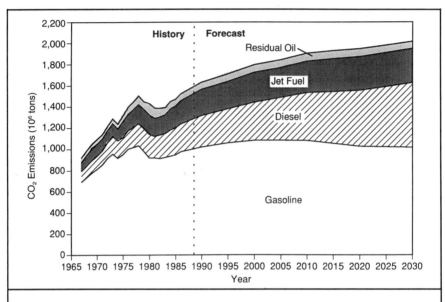

Figure 9-4. Carbon Dioxide Emissions by Type of Transportation Fuel, 1965–2030

Source: Vyas (1990).

work rules and in the mix of traffic, and the increased prevalence of unit trains were at least as important. Some of these factors—for example, shifts from boxcars to piggyback cars—tend to reduce fuel efficiency since the ratio of load to gross weight may decline. Other factors—like dedicated piggyback services, double stacking, and unit trains—tend to increase fuel efficiency. Deregulation of the rail freight industry also enhanced carriers' ability to abandon marginally profitable routes, to restructure operations, and in many cases, to upgrade equipment. As mentioned above, many low-volume routes were reorganized into regional or local railroads, which are not included in national statistics. Hence reporting differences could also have been a factor.

Rail power units that are in use now employ relatively old technologies. The technology picture is not expected to change much over the forecast period since the majority of rail power units are relatively new. A manufacturer exchange program, in place from the mid-1970s through the mid-1980s at General Motors' Electromotive Division, caused a turnover of power units. Under that program, attractive pricing encouraged railroads to replace rather than rebuild existing power units. Many locomotives with older two-stroke engines were replaced with current-technology two-stroke units. However, the program reduced the potential for further improvement in energy intensity as replacement demand is likely to be depressed for some time. Even though locomotives with energy-efficient four-stroke engines are now possible (Baumgartner & Mikulicic 1989), long locomotive life spans (approximately twenty years) and a relatively young fleet are likely to slow their penetration; technological improvements would require upwards of twenty years to produce a discernible impact. Although there is plenty of historical precedent for rapid, dramatic technological changes in rail equipment (for example, shifts from steam to diesel engines, from hand brakes to air brakes, and from smaller to larger engines to power longer, heavier consists), the base case contains no precipitating policy or event to induce such change. Thus operational improvements are assumed to be the principal source of future efficiency gains. Although research is assumed to continue on methods to use coal, residual oil, and relaxed-specification diesel oil in medium-speed diesel engines, alternative fuels are not considered in the baseline scenario.

Marine Modes

As it was for railroads, the energy intensity of inland marine modes (towboats and Great Lakes vessels) has improved substantially since 1970. In the future, little change is anticipated in either the fuel consumption or energy efficiency of waterborne modes, since long vehicle life cycles and low fuel costs (as a portion of total operating costs) provide little incentive for fuel efficiency improvement.

The past improvements in energy intensity are attributable to transport of large volumes of Alaskan oil and increase in domestic coastal traffic because oil tankers and coastal vessels have relatively more efficient power units and duty cycles than push/tow boats operating in inland waterways. The forecast scenario assumes steady declines in Alaskan oil output, so this beneficial effect is assumed to slowly erode over time.

Marine engines are two-stroke diesels with long operating lives. Current-technology four-stroke engines with higher stroke-to-bore ratios may be able to reduce fuel use; however, short of wholesale engine replacement (which could take up to thirty years), little improvement is foreseen. Some other technological and operational

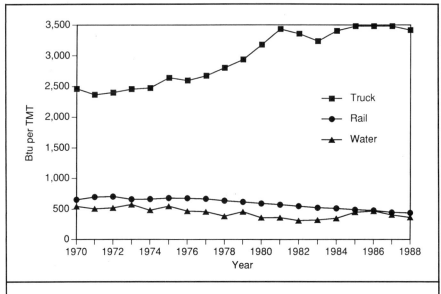

Figure 9-5. Recent Trends in Freight Mode Energy Intensity, 1970–1988

Source: Data from Davis & Hu (1991, 2-28).

improvements (see Mintz & Vyas 1991) could lower the energy intensity but are deemed not to be cost-effective under the forecast-scenario fuel prices.

Heavy Trucks

According to the Federal Highway Administration, the fuel economy of the entire fleet of heavy-duty combination (tractor-trailer) trucks rose from 4.78 mpg in 1970 to 5.34 mpg in 1989, an improvement of only 12% (see annual volumes of USDOT, *Highway Statistics*). Whereas fuel economy increased steadily in the 1970s, it declined somewhat in the 1980s. Many factors contributed to this lack of progress, including inefficient fleet management; low load factors (including an excess of empty backhauls); poor driver training; increased urban congestion; higher speed limits on rural interstate highways; shifts within the stock of heavy trucks toward larger, less fuel-efficient vehicles; disproportionate growth in travel by these larger vehicles; and slow turnover of older, less fuel-efficient rolling stock.

Expressed in terms of energy intensity, the truck picture is even more discouraging. As shown in Figure 9-5, whereas the average energy intensity of railroad and inland waterway operations declined by approximately 33% between 1970 and 1988, the energy intensity of intercity or line-haul trucks rose by nearly 40% over this time frame.

In passenger cars, the passenger and freight load is a small percentage of gross operating weight. In contrast, the load of heavy trucks is large relative to the gross weight of the vehicle, and reductions in tare weight are as likely to permit additional loading as to improve fuel economy. Thus, although weight reduction still offers substantial opportunity for improving the fuel economy of light-duty vehicles, it is not as promising for heavy trucks. Rather, the fuel efficiency of heavy trucks is expected to improve from continued advancements in engine technology (primarily higher-torque/lower-rpm engines) better engine/drivetrain matching, and more highly integrated aerodynamic designs. Although increased penetration of off-the-shelf conservation measures, such as low-profile tires and electronic engine and transmission controls, should provide some benefit, recent data suggest the impact may be quite modest.

Penetration of the less costly of these measures was first spurred by sudden increases in the price of fuel during the 1970s and has continued because of diesel fuel and road use tax increases in the 1980s. According to the *1987 Truck Inventory and Use Survey* (TIUS), 20% of all class 8 trucks (that is, those operating at gross combination weights above 33,000 lb) were equipped with aerodynamic devices, 14% had wide axle/drive ratios, 13% had fuel economy engines, and 6% had radial tires (USDOC 1990). However, the resulting improvements in on-the-road fuel economy were quite modest. In 1987, the average class 8 truck with no energy conservation devices got 5.2 mpg, whereas the average truck equipped with a host of devices and other modifications to conserve fuel (for example, aerodynamic devices, axle ratio changes, high-torque-rise/low-rpm engine, radial tires, road speed governor, variable fan, engine retarder, electronic vehicle monitoring system) got 6 mpg, an improvement of only 15.3%. Moreover, when data were controlled for vehicle age, it appears that the presence or absence of conservation devices had little effect on fuel economy. Vehicle age—a variable that includes improvements in engine and drivetrain technology, in aerodynamic design, and presumably in maintenance and proportion of duty cycle in line-haul operation—was far more significant. The data show not only that many energy conservation devices provide little or no fuel economy improvement, but that some combinations of devices actually reduce fuel economy. There are several explanations for the apparently poor performance. Perhaps truck buyers are not specifying the most fuel-efficient combination of devices for their vehicle's mission. Perhaps individual devices are not performing as claimed. Alternatively, an increasing share of "base" vehicles are entering service with factory-equipped devices that are so transparent to truck buyers that they are unaware of them.

Because of this relatively disappointing impact, our projections of efficiency improvements through implementation of conventional technologies are less optimistic for heavy-duty trucks than for passenger cars. Over the next twenty years, another 12% improvement in fleetwide fuel economy—from continued advances in aerodynamics, increased penetration of electronic engine and transmission controls, and improved tires and lubricants—is expected (Mintz & Vyas 1991). Although individual new vehicles may achieve far greater improvements, the combination of a "less than ideal" operating environment and continued tight profit margins is likely to depress the average fuel economy of the truck fleet.

Factors Affecting Truck Energy Intensity

Virtually all of the above-noted increase in truck energy intensity occurred between 1960 and 1980. These two decades coincide with major structural changes in the economy and dramatic oil price shocks, as well as continued increases in urban traffic congestion. Deregulation of the transportation industry occurred somewhat later and thus was probably not a factor (although it may be argued that increased modal competition prevented truck energy intensity from deteriorating further).

Economic Factors

Between 1960 and 1980, the economy underwent major structural changes. The service sector became an even larger component of output, imports of manufacturer and consumer goods grew phenomenally, the composition of industrial output shifted toward lower-density commodities, and the cost of capital grew to historically high rates.

Services. Continuing a much longer trend, the service sector rose from 26% of GNP in 1960 to 31% by 1980 (see Figure 9-6). As a result, physical output—ton-miles (assuming no change in average length of haul) and vehicle-miles (assuming no change in average load)—should have grown less than the total economy. However, vehicle-miles (VMT) grew considerably faster (3.7% per year) (see annual volumes of USDOT, *Highway Statistics*). Much of this growth can be attributed to fast-growing service industries—such as pizza and small-package delivery services; lawn care, home and office cleaning, and other maintenance services; and communications—all of which

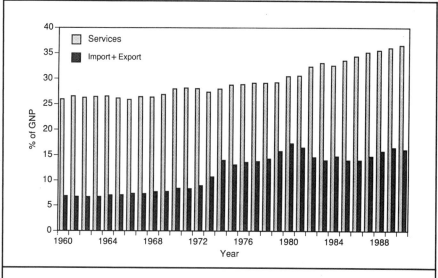

Figure 9-6. Service Sector Output and Merchandise Trade as a Percentage of GNP, 1960–1990

Source: Data from DRI (1987, 1990).

rely on trucks, mainly light trucks. Given the increasing service orientation of the economy, this suggests that ton-miles may be an increasingly inaccurate indicator of truck activity, and Btu/TMT may be an equally inaccurate measure of efficiency. However, because ton-miles are commonly used to describe activity for other freight-carrying modes, the metric permits analyses of modal competition. Miles per gallon is certainly a potential substitute, but since it takes no account of load factors, one can argue that it is too coarse a metric.

Imported Goods. Over this time frame, the value of imported goods tripled as a share of GNP, rising from 2.95% in 1960 to 9.06% in 1980, while exports doubled, rising from 3.96% to 8.24% (see Figure 9-6). As imports displaced domestic production, fewer of the inputs to the production process came from traditional domestic sources, and finished goods began to compose a larger share of ton-miles. Because of their higher value and susceptibility to damage in shipment, finished goods generally require more elaborate packaging. This reduces not only density (weight per unit volume) but also average load, as trucks quite often as not "cube out" before they "weigh out." This is consistent with trends shown in Eno's data, which provide

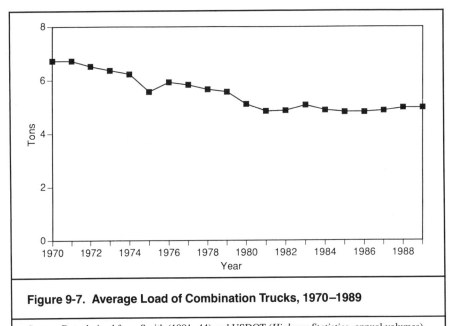

Figure 9-7. Average Load of Combination Trucks, 1970–1989

Source: Data derived from Smith (1991, 44) and USDOT (*Highway Statistics*, annual volumes).

the basis for Figure 9-7. Despite increased weight limits, the data show that the average load of combination trucks dropped by 25% between 1970 and 1980. Less-than-truckload (LTL) trucks[2] accounted for all of this drop, possibly due to cubing out. Since the average load of truckload (TL) trucks rose slightly through 1980, the data suggest two disparate trends—namely, cubing out in LTL trucks and weighing out in TL trucks.

All else equal, increasing the share of total goods movement represented by imported goods should also increase average length of haul, and because a relatively longer portion of this increased length of haul is line haul, the net effect should be improved energy intensity. As shown in Figure 9-8, between 1970 and 1980, average length of haul rose for all freight modes. Although the average for LTL trucks rose the most (34%), the average for inland waterways and railroads also

---

[2] LTL trucks typically carry multiple loads, each generally under 10,000 lb, under separate waybills.

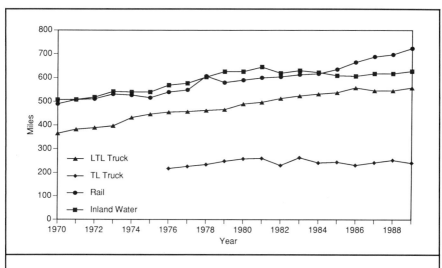

Figure 9-8. Average Length of Haul by Freight Mode, 1970–1987

Source: Data from Smith (1991, 71).

rose (by 23% and 20%, respectively).[3] However, as noted above, longer lengths of haul did not improve truck energy intensity, at least not on an overall modal basis.

Commodity Density. Relatively stronger growth in low-density commodity sectors like plastics and electronics (as compared with steel and agricultural products, for example) is another key factor behind cubing out. So, too, is the continued trend toward materials substitution—not just in vehicles, but in virtually all consumer goods.[4] (See the following discussion on load composition.)

Cost of Capital. High inflation and historically high real interest rates also affect truck energy intensity. In 1960, the prime rate was 4.82%, with inflation roughly 1.6% according to the implicit price deflator; by 1980, the prime rate stood at 15.27%, with inflation

---

[3] It is unclear why average loads on inland waterways have risen. Presumably, individual barges are more heavily loaded. Part of the increase in rail loads may be due to the exclusion of local and regional movements.

[4] For example, according to the Aluminum Association's Automotive and Truck Committee, the average use of aluminum in cars increased about 65% between 1974 and 1984 (Rowand 1986).

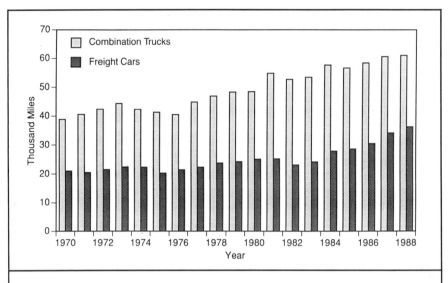

Figure 9-9. Annual Utilization of Combination Trucks and Class 1 Railroad Freight Cars, 1970–1988

Source: Data derived from AAR and USDOT (*Highway Statistics*, annual volumes).

roughly 9.1% (DRI 1987, A.2–3). Since the high cost of capital encourages firms to minimize capital expenditures, the immediate effect is a tendency toward longer vehicle replacement cycles, increased leasing, and/or more intense equipment utilization. Between 1970 and 1980, the average utilization of combination trucks rose 25% (from 38,819 to 48,472 miles as shown in Figure 9-9). Between 1980 and 1990, this average rose another 24%, to over 60,000 miles. Freed from regulatory constraints, the utilization of rail freight cars rose an even more dramatic 45% between 1980 and 1988 (see Figure 9-9).

Although increasing equipment utilization improves productivity, it does not necessarily improve energy intensity. This is not surprising, since equipment rental, depreciation, and purchased transportation typically exceed fuel as a percentage of operating expenses (see annual volumes of AAR; ATA 1991; Sweirenga 1991) (see Figure 9-10). Thus truckers generally have more incentive to improve the productivity of their equipment dollar than they do their fuel dollar. Figure 9-10 also displays expense distributions for rail and air modes. Surprisingly, for both truck and rail modes, the fuel share of operating costs is below 10%. For air, the fuel share is considerably higher, presumably a key

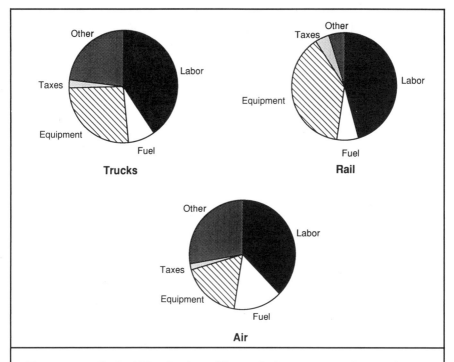

Figure 9-10. Typical Distribution of Truck, Rail, and Airline Operating Expenses

Source: Data derived from AAR (1988, 11); Sweirenga (1991); USDOC (1987, 586).

factor behind airlines' greater tendency to adopt energy conservation measures.

Traffic Congestion

Traffic congestion may be a major factor behind increased truck energy intensity. As shown in Figure 9-11, nearly 45% of urban interstate mileage and roughly 70% of peak-traffic volume are congested in the peak hour. For autos, much of the discrepancy between EPA-test and on-the-road fuel economy may be due to congestion (Mintz, Vyas & Conley 1991; Westbrook & Patterson 1989). The same may be true for trucks, especially those engaged in the distribution portion of inter-modal services. In 1990 approximately 29% of rail car loadings were trailers or containers (AAR 1991, 24–26). Assuming that the majority of these intermodal trips entail some urban pickup and delivery, traffic

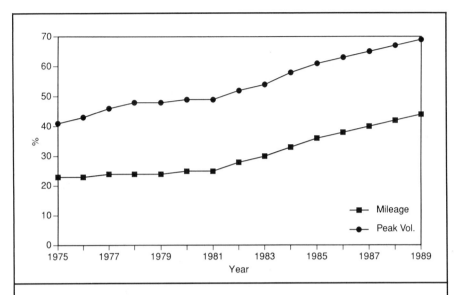

Figure 9-11. Percentage of Urban Interstate Highway Mileage and Peak-Hour Traffic Under Congested Conditions, 1975–1989

Source: Data from USDOT (*Highway Statistics*, 1990, 164).

congestion should increase the energy intensity of intermodal trips. Because it is not clear whether the truck portions of such trips are being correctly accounted for in the data, increased intermodalism may be another factor behind the apparent increase in truck energy intensity.

Load Composition

As mentioned above, loads of lower-density commodities often cube out, whereas loads of higher density commodities weigh out. Thus, even though *average* loads may be declining, an increasing number of trucks are operating with very heavy loads. This may be seen in Figure 9-12, which plots trends in the percentage of traffic volume and axle loadings on rural interstates by two categories of heavy trucks (those with four or fewer axles, and those with five or more axles). Between 1970 and 1980, the heavier of the two classes rose from 8% to 14% of traffic volume and from 74% to 91% of axle loadings. Meanwhile, the lighter of the two truck classes stayed at roughly 5% of traffic volume but dropped from 24% to 7% of axle loadings. This corresponds with TIUS results showing a bimodal distribution in truck loads and utili-

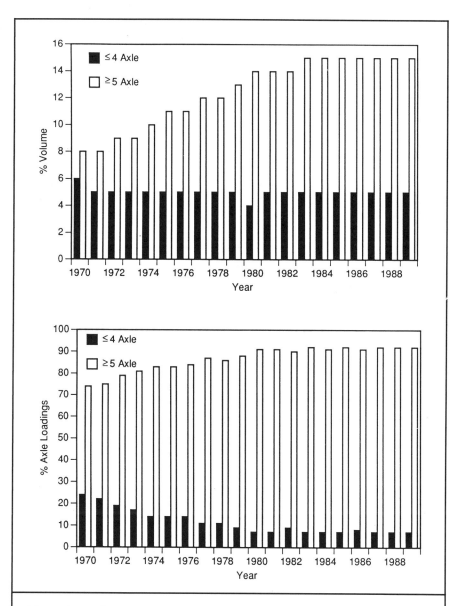

Figure 9-12. Shares of Traffic Volumes and Axle Loadings on Rural Interstate Highways by Trucks with Five or More Versus Fewer Axles, 1970–1989

Source: Data from USDOT (*Highway Statistics*, 1990, 189).

zation—that is, some heavy trucks are extremely productive, carrying very heavy loads and operating far more than 100,000 miles per year, whereas the majority are lightly loaded and utilized (USDOC 1990).

Fuel and Other Costs

The increase in truck energy intensity came at a time when the price of diesel fuel was rising relative to that of gasoline (see annual volumes of USDOE, *Annual Energy Review*). Thus, fuel price was probably not a factor on an overall modal basis, although it no doubt affected the purchase decisions of individual firms. As stated earlier, labor and equipment costs account for a higher portion of average truck operating expenses than does fuel. Since labor alone represents 51% of truck operating expenses (USDOC 1987, 586), popular cost-cutting strategies include switching from union to nonunion personnel; reducing crew sizes, turnover, and absenteeism; and relying on independent contractors in place of employees. Partly because of this cost cutting and partly because of a general driver shortage, firms are placing an increasingly high priority on attracting and retaining good drivers. Thus, new trucks are being equipped with more driver amenities, such as air conditioning in both cab and sleeper compartments, sound systems, improved suspensions, microwave ovens, and automatic transmissions. Although the resulting loss in fuel efficiency has not been quantified, 1,000 lb of driver amenities could easily exact a penalty of 0.1–0.2 mpg.

Conclusions

Most of the increase in transportation energy use that has occurred over the past thirty years has come from growth in commercial aviation and heavy trucks. Of all transportation modes (freight or passenger), heavy trucks experienced the fastest growth, tripling their energy use between 1960 and 1990. Because this trend is expected to continue, nonpersonal transportation modes are expected to consume more energy than autos and light trucks by the year 2005.

Over the past two decades, the energy efficiency (or mpg) of the heavy truck fleet has improved relatively little, whereas the energy intensity (Btu/TMT) has increased. A variety of factors are to blame, including traffic congestion, tight profit margins, driver behavior and other operating constraints, shifts in the composition of economic output and truck loads, and relatively high-cost labor and equipment and low-cost fuel. Fuel-conserving devices appear to have made little impact on improving the efficiency of heavy trucks, although newer vehicles presumably incorporating advancements in engines, transmissions, and aerodynamic design are approximately 15% more fuel-efficient than older models. Because of these modest gains in fuel efficiency, increases in miles traveled have produced and will continue to produce near-comparable increases in fuel use.

Despite inconsistent data, freight railroads appear to have made considerable progress in streamlining their operations and improving energy intensity. This trend is essentially complete for the near term.

Aside from increased coastal traffic due to North Slope oil development, the energy consumption characteristics of domestic waterborne commerce have been relatively stable despite increase in average length of haul. This trend is expected to continue.

References

AAR. Annual. *Railroad Facts*. Washington, D.C.: Association of American Railroads.

ATA. 1991. *American Trucking Trends*. 1990–91 ed. Alexandria, Va.: American Trucking Associations.

Baumgartner, P., and N. Mikulicic. 1989. "The New Four-Stroke Diesel Engine Sulzer S20." *Motortechnische Zeitschrift* 50 (11): 502–508.

Davis, S., and P. Hu. 1991. *Transportation Energy Data Book*. 11th ed. Oak Ridge National Laboratory Report ORNL-6649. Oak Ridge, Tenn. January.

DRI. 1987. *History Tables*. Lexington, Mass.: Data Resources, Inc./McGraw-Hill.

———. 1990. *History Tables for the U.S. Economy: 1965–89*. Lexington, Mass.: Data Resources, Inc./McGraw-Hill.

Mintz, M., and A. Vyas. 1991. *Forecast of Transportation Energy Demand Through the Year 2010*. Argonne National Laboratory Report ANL/ESD-9. Argonne, Ill. April.

Mintz, M., A. Vyas, and L. Conley. 1991. *Minorities and Fuel Economy Standards: Differences in EPA-Test vs. In-Use Fuel Economy*. Paper presented at the Socioeconomic Energy Research and Analysis Conference, Baltimore, Md., June 27–28.

Rowand, R. 1986. "Continued Gains Seen for Aluminum in Autos." *Automotive News* (Detroit).

Smith, F. 1991. *Transportation in America*. 9th ed. Waldorf, Md.: Eno Transportation Foundation.

Sweirenga, J., Air Transport Association. 1991. Personal communication to M. Mintz. August 12.

USACOE. Annual. *Domestic Waterborne Commerce of the United States*. Fort Belvoir, Va.: U.S. Army Corps of Engineers.

USDOC. Annual. *Transport Economics*. Washington, D.C.: U.S. Department of Commerce, Interstate Commerce Commission.

————. 1987. *Statistical Abstract of the United States, 1988*. 108th ed. Washington, D.C.: U.S. Department of Commerce, Bureau of the Census. December.

————. 1990. *1987 Truck Inventory and Use Survey*. Public use data tape. Washington, D.C.: U.S. Department of Commerce, Bureau of the Census.

USDOE. Annual. *Annual Energy Review*. U.S. Department of Energy, Energy Information Administration. Washington, D.C.

————. 1991a. *Annual Energy Review 1990*. U.S. Department of Energy, Energy Information Administration Report DOE/EIA-0384(90). Washington, D.C. May.

————. 1991b. *Limiting Net Greenhouse Gas Emissions in the United States*. Vol. 1. *Energy Technologies*. U.S. Department of Energy Report DOE/PE-0101. R. A. Bradley, E. C. Watts, and E. R. Williams, eds. Washington, D.C. September.

USDOT. Annual. *Carload Waybill Statistics: Territorial Distribution, Traffic and Revenue by Commodity Class*. Washington, D.C.: U.S. Department of Transportation, Federal Railroad Administration.

————. Annual. *Highway Statistics*. Washington, D.C.: U.S. Department of Transportation, Federal Highway Administration.

Vyas, A. 1990. "Supporting Analysis for the U.S. Department of Energy Study on Limiting Greenhouse Gas Emissions in the United States." Argonne, Ill.: Argonne National Laboratory.

Westbrook, F., and P. Patterson. 1989. "Changing Driving Patterns and Their Effect on Fuel Economy." Paper presented at the 1989 SAE Government/Industry Meeting in Washington, D.C. Warrendale, Pa.: Society of Automotive Engineers. May 2.

Chapter 10

Characteristics of Future Aviation Fuels

Oren J. Hadaller and Albert M. Momenthy

W
hich fuel? This is a question that surfaces every time there is a supply and price scare associated with crude oil. Up to now, each flurry of activity has subsided after the panic ended and legislators realized that no alternative fuel proved to be more affordable or more available than those from petroleum. Now there are an increasing number of environmental concerns, such as global warming, driving the search for the replacement of petroleum-based fuels. However, studies indicate that the currently used aviation fuel is as likely to satisfy these concerns as the few alternative fuels that are suitable for use in aircraft. Hydrogen, publicized as the most environmentally benign alternative to petroleum, will become economically acceptable only after the world has exhausted its fossil fuel resources or a low-cost, abundantly available source of electric power, such as nuclear fusion, is developed.

Improving efficiency will be the principal way to lessen the impact of aircraft on the environment until a technically and economically practical nonfossil-based fuel is discovered. Improving efficiency has always been and will continue to be a primary objective of aircraft operators and manufacturers (see Figure 10-1).

Supply

Until recently the number of years crude oil reserves were expected to support the current consumption rate varied very little from year to year. Each year, the oil consumed was shown to be replaced by the addition of new reserves, primarily in the Middle East. Because these estimates indicate no margin for growth and because reserve additions are primarily in an unstable area of the world, these numbers are often

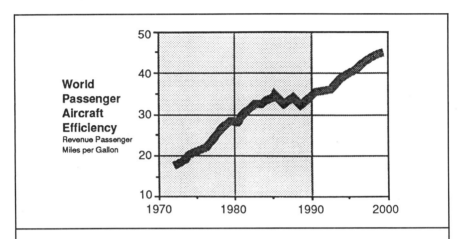

Figure 10-1. Improving efficiency will continue to be a primary objective of aircraft operators and manufacturers.

used to substantiate outlooks showing near-term problems with crude oil availability along with greatly inflated crude oil prices, and hence a need to develop alternative fuels. However, the use of such data for this purpose is deceptive because

- "proved reserves" reflect crude oil availability restrictively defined by technical and economic conditions—they are not an absolute, or even commercial-development, limit

- "proved reserves" assume no new technology beyond that in an advanced stage of development at the time of estimate

- incentives for reporting new discoveries have been greatly reduced by unyielding and often unreasonable attacks on their development by a variety of special interest groups

During the early 1980s, oil exploration activity stimulated by expectations of ever-increasing prices boosted estimates of crude oil reserves, even within the restrictive definition of "proved reserves."[1] If the definition is revised to include oil likely to be recovered at a cost of less than $20 per barrel, there is sufficient crude oil to last well into the

---

[1] *Proved reserves* are generally taken to be those quantities that geological and engineering information indicate with reasonable certainty can be recovered in the future from known reservoirs under existing economic and operating conditions (BP 1991a).

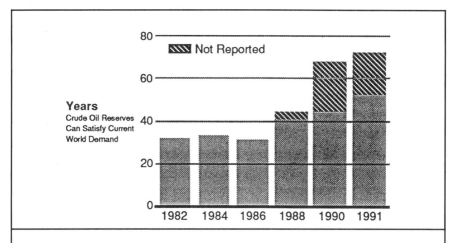

Figure 10-2. Reserves of petroleum at ≤$20 per barrel are sufficient to last well into the next century.

next century (see Figure 10-2). This more optimistic, and realistic, view of oil has pushed availability arguments for developing alternative fuels into the background; thus the current rallying point is the environment.

There is a growing realization among environmentalists that an energy source that could replace a significant amount of coal or petroleum must have abundant reserves. Therefore, natural gas has become increasingly popular as the clean fuel of the future. There is little agreement, however, as to the magnitude of natural gas reserves. Reserves reported for conventional gas[2] in the United States (approximately 4% of the world total) appear to be about the same as for crude oil in terms of availability at the current price and rate of production (BP 1991b). Estimates of recoverable gas from unconventional sources, such as coal seams, tight sands, and Devonian shale, vary from almost none to several times more than that available in the form of conventional gas (see Figure 10-3). Estimates for methane hydrates are in the category of thousands of years—but many scientists dispute the geological hypothesis for its formation, and hence there is still some question as to the existence of such massive quantities of gas (AGA 1980, 1989).

---

[2] *Conventional gas* is defined as that which is contained as a gas phase or in solution with crude oil in natural underground reservoirs.

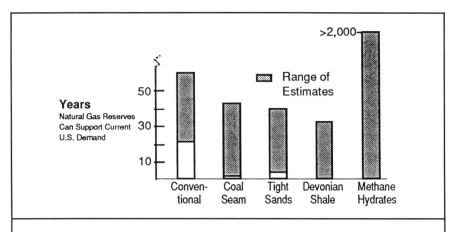

Figure 10-3. There is plenty of natural gas, but how much is low-cost conventional?

Conventional Fuels

During the past two decades, environmental considerations have had an increasing impact on both personal and business activities. Until recently, environmental problems have been treated as local issues, principally identified with large urban areas. Now a concern has developed that is of a more global nature. This concern is the "greenhouse" effect—a global warming caused by the introduction of infrared-radiation-absorbing gases into the earth's atmosphere. These gases include carbon dioxide (CO_2), the chlorofluorocarbons (CFCs), methane (CH_4), nitrous oxide (N_2O), and ozone (O_3). Of these, the most prevalent and publicly recognizable is CO_2. There is little question that a higher demand for fossil fuels will increase the production of CO_2. Therefore, the obvious solution to global warming is to limit or reverse this growth through conservation or substitution of nonfossil sources of energy. Unfortunately, the social, economic, political, and technical problems associated with accomplishing this reversal are enormous. For example:

• Many nations are planning to use more coal to boost their standard of living, particularly the countries of South and East Asia. These plans are not likely to be reversed.

• Nuclear power is the only nonfossil energy source with a real potential for replacing significant quantities of fossil fuels. The current

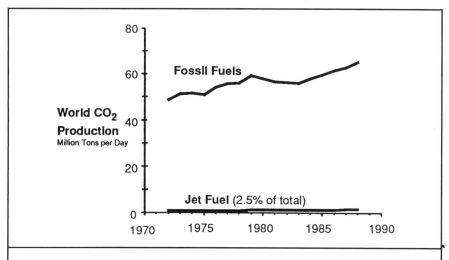

Figure 10-4. Aircraft account for a very small fraction of the world's production of CO_2.

worldwide trend is to back away from nuclear power, and this industry is not likely to recover in the near future.

- The world's population is increasing at such a rate that steps to improve energy efficiency are counteracted by increases in the number of energy users. Past attempts to limit population growth have had limited success.

Therefore, those worried about global warming are having a difficult time identifying projects that can produce reportable results in a reasonable time. This situation can lead to actions that are not necessarily justified on the basis of technical or economic merit.

Aviation is not a major producer of carbon dioxide. Aircraft consume about 2.5% of the fossil fuel used (see Figure 10-4). However, aviation is one of the few petroleum users projected to have a continuing growth in fuel consumption (see Figure 10-5). During the past twenty years, the CO_2 produced by the growth in aviation has been somewhat offset by improvements in aircraft efficiency. Aggressive programs to improve the efficiency of aircraft will continue in the future. Improving efficiency will be the most cost-effective and technically feasible method for reducing aircraft-generated CO_2 until an affordable nonfossil-based alternative fuel is developed.

A major shortcoming in regulations designed to solve environ-

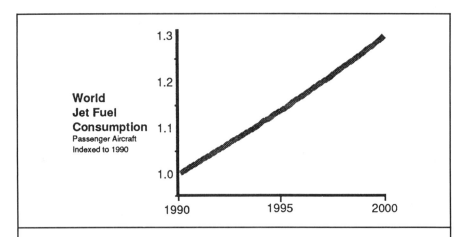

Figure 10-5. Jet fuel consumption is forecast to grow at a moderate rate during the next decade.

mental problems is that analyses required to identify negative aspects of the proposed action are often neglected. Each processing step used to upgrade or modify a raw material uses energy. If this energy is from a fossil fuel, the CO_2 produced in the transformation will increase as the thermal (conversion) efficiency decreases. Therefore, regulations that increase the fuel-processing requirement also increase the CO_2 produced per unit of usable end-product energy (see Figure 10-6).

The most notable environmental action related to transportation that will drop fuel production efficiency, and hence increase overall CO_2, is the substitution of methanol manufactured from natural gas for gasoline from petroleum (efficiency <70% versus efficiency >90%) (LeBlanc & Rovner 1990). However, it is the less advertised actions requiring changes to the composition of fuel that are likely to cause the biggest overall drop in fuel production efficiency. These include

- lower diesel and gas oil sulphur (≤0.05 wt.%) and aromatic content (≤20 vol.%)

- lower gasoline aromatics (≤1.0 vol.% benzene; ≤25 vol.% total)

- increased U.S. gasoline oxygen content (11 vol.% as methyl tertiary butyl ether [MTBE])—now being recognized as a source of increased CO_2 (Morton 1991)

- a worldwide product demand shift—less residual (heavy fuel oil), more product upgrading

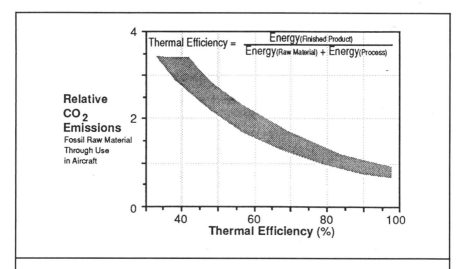

Figure 10-6. Regulations that result in more fuel processing will increase the amount of CO₂ produced per unit of usable energy.

It is becoming more evident that there are likely to be sources of regulation-caused CO_2 that have not been identified, much less quantified. However, regulations that have already been passed will add more CO_2 to the atmosphere than that from projected increases in the consumption of jet fuel (see Figure 10-7). The largest drop in efficiency outside the United States will be from the increased use of hydrogen to reduce the sulphur content of diesel and gas oil (O'Brien 1991; White 1991) (see Figure 10-8). A drop in the efficiency of U.S. refineries also involves an increased use of hydrogen to saturate aromatics, plus the requirement for an oxygenate additive, such as MTBE, in gasoline (the energy used to produce hydrogen and additives is a charge against refinery efficiency) (Scherr, Smaalley & Norman 1991).

Although current regulations governing the composition of fuels apply only to diesel and gas oil, they are likely to indirectly cause a lowering of the sulphur and aromatic content of jet fuel (see Figure 10-9). This is partly because product marketing requirements will not allow a total segregation of diesel, jet fuel, and gas oil. Boeing data show that the average sulphur content of 90% of currently delivered jet fuel is below 0.1 wt.% (Hadaller & Momenthy 1989). This has resulted in an average jet fuel sulphur content (0.04 wt.%) that is about an order of magnitude lower than the 0.3 wt.% specification maximum

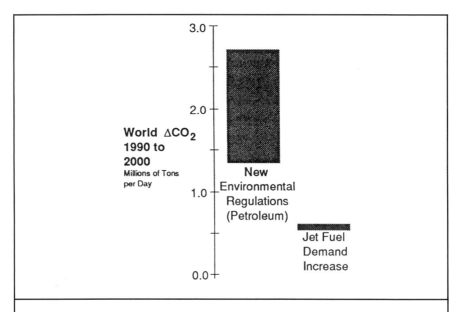

Figure 10-7. The CO_2 added to the atmosphere by the growth in aviation will be small relative to that resulting from new regulations.

(see Figure 10-9). Analyses of jet fuel samples from refineries that would be able to satisfy projected year 2015 product demand and composition requirements indicate that the average jet fuel sulphur content is likely to drop to 0.02 wt.%.

Aromatics are believed to be a primary cause of particulate emissions in diesels. Therefore both federal and state regulations controlling the aromatic content of diesel fuel have been passed. The most stringent of these is a California regulation that limits its aromatic content to 10 vol.% by 1993 (Stodolsky 1990). Even though California tends to lead the world in fuel-related regulations, few countries could afford the costs associated with such a severe diesel fuel restriction. Unless a clear benefit is demonstrated for an aromatics reduction to 10 vol.%, a more likely restriction for worldwide diesel fuel is 20 vol.%.

There are no plans to require a reduction in the aromatic content of jet fuel. However, any reduction in the aromatic content of diesel is likely to result in a reduction in the aromatic content of the total distillate pool. If the worldwide aromatics limit for diesel is forced to be 20 vol.%, a refiner's need to maintain flexibility in the marketing of distillate fuels is likely to force the average aromatic content of jet fuel to

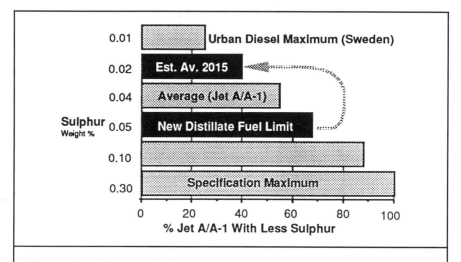

Figure 10-8. New restrictions on the sulphur content of fuels, particularly diesel, will indirectly cause a reduction in the sulphur content of jet fuel.

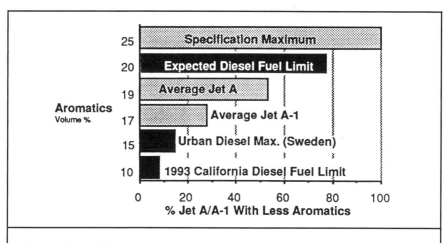

Figure 10-9. A forced reduction in the aromatic content of diesel is likely to result in a reduction in the aromatic content of jet fuel.

less than 15%. A reduction in the aromatic content of jet fuel would result in a fuel that is cleaner burning (lower radiation) and has a higher energy per unit weight. Unfortunately, it also means a lower density and lower energy per unit volume.

The search for an abundant clean fuel has revived various concepts for replacing transportation fuels derived from crude oil. Until recently, liquid methane was the only natural-gas-derived fuel considered satisfactory for aircraft. Recently, processes have been developed that allow the manufacture of conventional jet fuel from natural gas (Quinlan 1991). Of particular interest to aviation is that several of these processes that have reached the demonstration plant stage of development produce distillate fuels (including jet fuel) (van der Burgt et al. 1989; Velocci 1991). The jet fuel from such processes has low to no sulphur or aromatics.

Alternatives

A fundamental requirement for a commercial aircraft jet fuel is that it have

• a heat of combustion per unit mass sufficiently high to allow the transport of revenue producing payload—not just mission fuel

• a heat of combustion per unit volume sufficiently high to allow the storage of fuel without compromising aircraft design or performance

It is very difficult to quantify "sufficient" in terms of either mass or volumetric heat of combustion. However, these properties for conventional jet fuel (kerosene) rarely cause an aircraft design compromise or prevent the consideration of a mission. On the other hand, the volumetric heat of combustion for liquid hydrogen is so poor that it would force design compromises even if it were not a cryogen. Design compromises associated with liquid methane (for example, fuel in the fuselage) are primarily related to the fact that it is a cryogen (see Table 10-1).

The liquefied petroleum gases, propane and butane, have been proposed as alternative fuels for aircraft ("USSR" 1991). These fuels are not cryogens, but they have many of the storage and transfer problems associated with a cryogen. In-depth studies of these fuels have not been conducted because the natural supply is not sufficient to support a world aviation fleet. Manufacturing propane and butane offer no availability, cost, or environmental advantages as replacements for conventional jet fuels.

The alcohols, methanol and ethanol, have such poor mass and vol-

Table 10-1. Fuel Properties Comparison

Fuel	Net Heat of Combustion (Btu/lb)	Net Heat of Combustion (Btu/gal)	Boiling Point (° F @ 1 atm)
Conventional	18,400–19,000	116,000–127,000	>100
Hydrogen	51,500	29,675	−423.2
Methane	21,500	76,193	−258.7
Propane	19,774	96,121	−43.7
n-Butane	19,506	97,973	31.1
Ethanol	11,550	76,000	172.9
Methanol	8,640	57,370	148.5

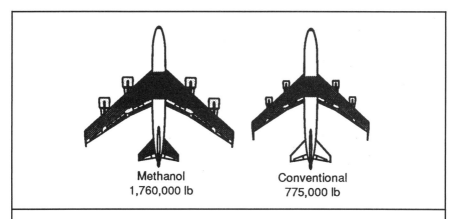

Methanol
1,760,000 lb

Conventional
775,000 lb

Figure 10-10. Alcohol-fueled aircraft would be very large, heavy, and inefficient.

umetric heats of combustion that they would not be satisfactory commercial aircraft fuels (see Table 10-1 and Figure 10-10). They are important to the aircraft industry only because their widespread production and use would influence the properties, supply, and cost of conventional jet fuels.

Therefore, only the cryogens, methane and hydrogen, have sufficient positive attributes to justify serious attention as possible replacements for kerosene-type aircraft fuel (*Seattle Times* 1990). In addition,

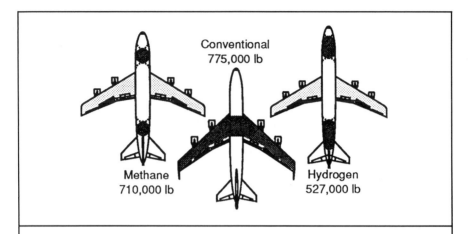

Conventional
775,000 lb

Methane
710,000 lb

Hydrogen
527,000 lb

Figure 10-11. Methane and hydrogen must be stored in the body of aircraft.

they are perceived by environmentalists to be clean fuels, particularly hydrogen.

Cryogenic fuels cannot be handled by a conventional aircraft fuel system. The use of cryogens will require the development of new technology, or significant improvements in existing technology, before an aircraft that satisfies realistic commercial requirements can be designed (Momenthy 1977). The normal boiling points of hydrogen and methane are considerably below the lowest ambient temperature (see Table 10-1). This means that the aircraft fuel system must be

• thermally insulated from the environment and primary aircraft structure

• cooled to the liquid saturation temperature prior to or during the initial stages of tank loading or fuel transfer

The fuel tanks of aircraft using cryogens must be insulated pressure vessels. In comparison to other fuel tanks they would be very large in terms of energy stored. These tanks would have to be located in the fuselage instead of the wings to minimize boiloff losses as well as because of their large size (see Figure 10-11).

The greater volume of cryogen necessary for payload and range performance equivalent to that for conventional fuels would require a larger fuselage. However, the gross weight, and hence energy consumption, of large long-range aircraft using cryogenic fuels, particu-

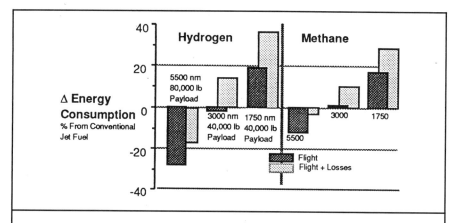

Figure 10-12. Aircraft fueled with cryogens are not necessarily more efficient than those using conventional jet fuel.

larly hydrogen, may be less than those of aircraft using conventional fuels because of their greater energy content per unit weight. The weight and vaporization losses associated with cryogens lower and even reverse this energy advantage for small short-range aircraft (see Figure 10-12).

The complex nature of the thermodynamic processes associated with the storage and use of cryogens in commercial aircraft offers many challenges for the design of a fuel delivery system (see Figure 10-13). For the fuel system to behave in a stable manner, the fuel storage and pumping system must be designed as a unit. Insulation must be sized to minimize vaporized fuel losses and at the same time ensure the satisfaction of inlet pressure requirements of a pump that must deliver fuel over a wide range of flow rates.

The pumping of cryogens in space vehicles is state of the art. However, space vehicle flow rates vary over a relatively narrow range, and pump life requirements are counted in seconds; cost is a secondary consideration. In addition, the acceleration vector of a space vehicle is directed toward the pump inlet and increases as the fuel is used; thus the pump has at least some effective liquid head for subcooling. The acceleration vector of an aircraft is somewhat random and cannot be used to satisfy pump inlet pressure requirements (see Figure 10-14). Helium is the only pressurant available for hydrogen tanks, and it is too expensive for commercial aircraft operations. Nitrogen can be used with methane, but the solubility of nitrogen in liquid methane is a problem. Without inert gas pressurization, no existing pump can sat-

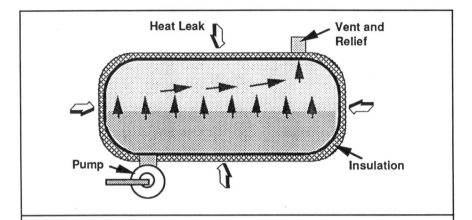

Figure 10-13. The storage and transfer of cryogens in aircraft involve the interaction of complex thermodynamic and fluid dynamic processes.

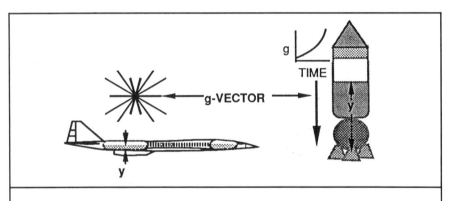

Figure 10-14. Commercial aircraft and space program mission, life, cost, and performance requirements are not compatible.

isfy commercial aircraft weight, life, and delivery requirements. The development of such pumps will require a significant extension of existing technology or, preferably, some imaginative approaches to the transfer of hydrogen from tanks to engines.

In contrast to the operation of conventionally fueled aircraft, in a cryogen-fueled aircraft the duty cycle—the demand for fuel during taxi, takeoff, cruise, and descent—will play an important part in establishing fuel system concept feasibility. Analyses of system perfor-

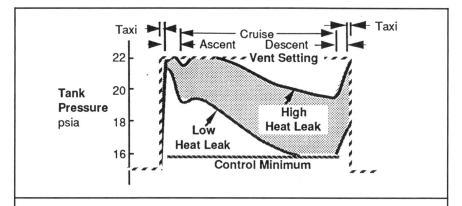

Figure 10-15. Cryogen tanks must be insulated so that the heat leak is low enough to minimize vaporized fuel losses and high enough to prevent the pressure from dropping to where unstable liquid boiling occurs.

mance must account for realistic aircraft mission duty cycles before fuel system thermal protection requirements or the practical use of the cryogen as a coolant can be established.

Currently there is no workable insulation concept for commercial aircraft fuel systems. Vacuum jackets are too heavy or delicate, and currently available foam insulation cannot withstand the imposed temperature variations without unacceptable repair and inspection operations. At this point, it is not even clear how much insulation is required. Having too little insulation results in venting, and hence loss, of fuel, particularly during the taxi phases of operation. Too much insulation can cause the tank pressure to drop to the saturation point of the liquid, which can cause unstable system operation or pump cavitation. In any case, the sizing of insulation must satisfy all mission phases—taxi, ascent, cruise, and descent (see Figure 10-15).

A selling point for cryogens has been their potential for use as the coolant for high-speed aircraft engines and structure. The ability to take advantage of a significant percentage of this cooling capacity in a practical commercial aircraft may prove to be quite difficult. The use of fuel cooling requires a matching of the fuel flow demanded by the engines to airframe and engine cooling requirements (a function of Mach number) (see Figure 10-16). Such a match has not been demonstrated for commercial aircraft.

Entirely new and more complex ground distribution and storage systems must be developed for servicing, safing, and maintaining the

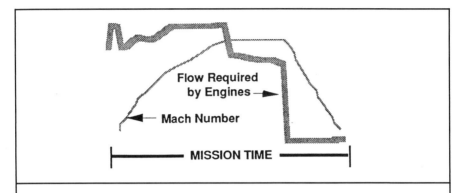

Figure 10-16. The use of cryogens to cool the structure of high-speed aircraft may not be practical.

aircraft (Alder 1986; NASA 1976). A gas liquefaction facility and fuel storage area must be located at or near the airport for safety and to limit boiloff (losses). In addition, practical commercial aircraft requirements, such as a one-hour turnaround time, will make the currently simple fueling of aircraft a relatively complex task. At the very least, the saturation pressure of the cryogen in the ground loading system must be matched to the saturation pressure of the cryogen in the aircraft tanks.

Cost and Global Warming

The cost would be enormous to develop the new airplanes and fuel-handling systems required to use radically new types of aircraft fuels, such as liquid hydrogen and liquid methane (Hadaller & Momenthy 1988). Even if only the cost of fuel is considered, the most optimistic cost, including all alternatives, is at a parity with the price of aviation fuel derived from petroleum (see Figure 10-17). However, cost does not equal price. The cost of 90% of the jet fuel currently produced is under 30 cents per gallon (see Figure 10-18). This is the petroleum-based jet fuel cost that should be used in alternative-fuel comparisons, not the current price. If the ground rules used in fuel comparisons are not consistent, the conclusions are meaningless.

More CO_2 is produced by the manufacture and use of most alternative fuels than by the refining and use of fuels from crude oil (see Figure 10-19). The use of coal to produce hydrogen is the most environmentally unclean of the energy systems; hydrogen from water using

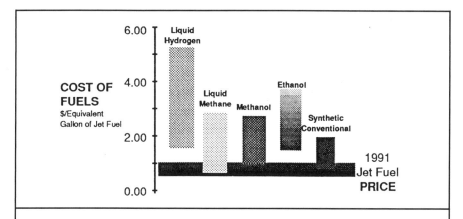

Figure 10-17. The cost of some alternatives is close to a parity with the price of jet fuel. However, cost does not equal price.

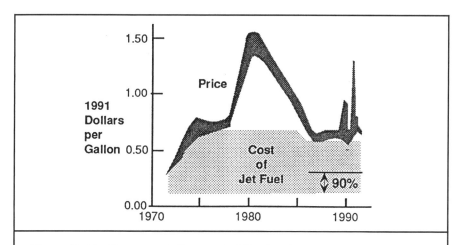

Figure 10-18. The cost of all nonsubsidized fuels, including jet fuel, is considerably lower than price.

nuclear power is the cleanest of those processes that could produce the large amounts of fuel required by aircraft. Hydrogen will become economically acceptable only after the world has exhausted its fossil fuel resources, or after a low-cost, abundantly available source of electric power, such as nuclear fusion, is developed. Without this low-cost

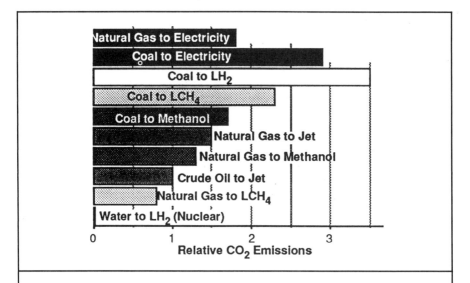

Figure 10-19. The manufacture and use of most alternative fuels produce more CO_2 than the refining and use of fuels from crude oil.

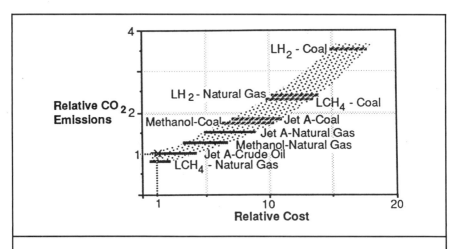

Figure 10-20. Unless the energy required for upgrading is supplied by a nonfossil source, the manufacture and use of most fuels will produce more CO_2 than those derived from petroleum.

electric power, the environmentally benign production of hydrogen from water is not possible.

Of the alternative fossil fuel options, those derived from natural gas appear to be the most environmentally benign. However, methane is also a greenhouse gas, and losses from natural gas systems would reduce their environmental advantage over other fuels.

The CO_2 produced in the upgrading of fossil fuels increases with decreasing conversion efficiency. Process energy and capital equipment costs also increase with decreasing conversion efficiency. Unless the energy required for upgrading is supplied by a nonfossil source, the production and use of most alternative fuels will increase the production of CO_2. Unless there is a real petroleum shortage or there are politically imposed costs, alternative fuels will cost more than petroleum-based fuels (see Figure 10-20).

References

Alder, H. P. 1986. "Hydrogen in Air Transportation: Feasibility Study for Zürich-Airport, Switzerland." Eidgenössisches Institut für Reaktorforschung. EIR-Report No. 600. Wurenlingen, Schweiz. September.

American Gas Association, Gas Supply Committee. 1980. "The Gas Energy Supply Outlook: 1980–2000." A.G.A. #F00728. October.

————. 1989. "The Gas Energy Supply Outlook: 1989–2010." A.G.A. #F00889. September.

Boeing Company. 1976. "An Exploratory Study to Determine the Integrated Technological Air Transportation System Ground Requirements of Liquid-Hydrogen-Fueled Subsonic Long-Haul Civil Air Transports." NASA Contractor Report. NASA CR-2699. September.

BP. 1991a. "BP Statistical Review of World Energy." British Petroleum Co. June.

————. 1991b. "BP Review of World Gas." British Petroleum Co. August.

Hadaller, O. J., and A. M. Momenthy. 1988. "Development of Fuels for Supersonic and Hypersonic Commercial Transports." Outlook for Supersonic & Hypersonic Aircraft. Transportation Research Board. Circular #333. June.

————. 1989. "The Characteristics of Future Fuels—Part I." Boeing Document D6-54940. August.

LeBlanc, J. R., and J. M. Rovner. 1990. "Remote Gas Conversion in Worldscale Methanol Plant." *Hydrocarbon Processing*. March.

Momenthy, A. M. 1977. "Fuel Subsystems for LH2 Aircraft: R & D Requirements." *International Journal of Hydrogen Energy* 2: 155–62.

Morton, P. 1991. "An Industry Going Nowhere." *Oilweek*. July 15.

O'Brien, D. J. 1991. "Global and Regional Trends in Investment Implications for the Oil Industry." In *Proceedings of the 2nd Jakarta International Energy Conference '91*. Jakarta. October.

Quinlan, M. 1991. "Competition from Gas." *Petroleum Economist*. January.

Scherr, R. C., G. A. Smaalley, Jr., and M. E. Norman. 1991. "Clean Air Act Complicates Refinery Planning." *Oil & Gas Journal*. May 27.

Seattle Times. 1990. "Cleaner Jet Burns Hydrogen in Engine." May 21.

Stodolsky, F. 1990. "Energy and the Clean Air Act." *Energy Matters* (TRB Committee on Energy and Travel Demand) 1, No. 2 (December).

"U.S.S.R. Pushes CNG, LNG as Motor Fuel." 1991. *Oil & Gas Journal*. May 6.

van der Burgt, M., et al. 1989. "The Shell Middle Distillate Synthesis Process." London: Shell International Petroleum Co. November.

Velocci, A. L., Jr. 1991. "Creating Liquid Fuels from Natural Gas." *The Lamp* (Exxon Corp.) 73, No. 3 (Fall).

White, L. 1991. "Sulphur Dioxide Emissions from Oil Refineries and Combustion of Oil Products in Western Europe (1989)." Brussels: CONCAWE Air Quality Management Group. April.

Chapter 11

Transportation on a Greenhouse Planet: A Least-Cost Transition Scenario for the United States

John M. DeCicco, Steven S. Bernow, Deborah Gordon, David B.
Goldstein, John W. Holtzclaw, Marc R. Ledbetter, Peter M.
Miller, and Harvey M. Sachs

T he results presented here are drawn from a collaborative study undertaken by energy conservation organizations to develop an end-use-based energy strategy for the United States (UCS et al. 1991). The project analyzed the potential for policy-driven pursuit of efficiency and renewable resources to significantly reduce the economic costs, environmental impacts, and petroleum dependency of energy use in the United States. Separate analyses were performed for transportation, residential, commercial, industrial, and electric-utility sectors; the transportation sector analyses were conducted by the authors of this chapter.[1] Sectoral results were integrated using the

[1] Other members of the America's Energy Choices project contributed to the development and refinement of the transportation analysis, particularly Howard Geller, Jeff Hall, Dan Lashof, Alden Meyer, and Mary Beth Zimmermann. We are also most grateful to a number of individuals who provided information for the project and reviewed drafts of the report on which this chapter is based. The extensive comments and constructive criticisms provided were invaluable to us in developing this work. We also thank David Greene and Dan Santini, editors of these proceedings, and the reviewers, who provided many helpful comments on the conference draft.

LEAP energy and environmental accounting model.[2] The overall analysis and results of the study, including extensive supporting policy recommendations, are documented in the *America's Energy Choices* report (UCS et al. 1991). This chapter focuses on a selected scenario from that analysis and discusses the resulting projections of energy use and CO_2 emissions for the year 2030.

Four scenarios, termed the reference, market, environmental, and climate stabilization scenarios, were developed for the America's Energy Choices study. Projections were made for forty years out, to year 2030, with intermediate results for years 2000 and 2010. These scenarios are fully discussed in UCS et al. (1991).

The *reference scenario* reflects a continuation of current policies, practices, and trends. It is not a frozen efficiency projection and roughly corresponds to the EIA/SR (1990) reference projection; the key differences will be noted shortly.

The *market scenario* incorporates technologies for efficiency and renewable supplies that are estimated to be cost-effective to energy consumers without consideration of externalities. Public-policy changes would be needed to overcome some of the market failures and institutional barriers to the adoption of the technologies. Particularly in the near term, we hold the efficiency levels to what we judge might be achievable even though they may fall short of the estimated cost-effective levels. For example, technology penetration limitations restrict the year 2000 target for automobile fuel economy to 40 mpg even though our analysis indicates a cost-effective level of 43 mpg.

In the *environmental scenario*, some externalities are monetized by assuming fuel tax levels based on estimated costs of air pollution emissions and other societal costs (such as petroleum security costs). Greenhouse gas emissions costs—for example, as might be reflected with a carbon tax—are not included. The incorporation of externalities allows us to select even greater levels of efficiency and makes certain renewable supplies more competitive with conventional energy supplies. We consider our environmental scenario to approach a least-societal-cost reconfiguration of energy utilization in the United States in that major external costs are incorporated into decision making and in that cost-effectiveness is evaluated from a societal (rather than private) perspective. The environmental scenario is the particular focus of this chapter.

Finally, a *climate stabilization scenario* was developed. This scenario incorporates a carbon tax of $25/ton in addition to the externality

---

[2] LEAP stands for "Long-range Energy Alternatives Planning," a computerized energy-planning system (Tellus 1990).

costs included in the environmental scenario. Additional efficiency improvements and fuel shifts are also assumed as needed to achieve absolute reductions of CO_2 emissions of 20% by 2000 and 50% by 2030, relative to the 1988 level. Not surprisingly, the shifts needed for the 2000 target appear nearly impossible to realize. Nevertheless, the climate stabilization scenario usefully indicates the changes needed to meet such specific near-term greenhouse gas emissions reduction goals.

Greenhouse gas emissions reduction targets would pertain to the U.S. economy as a whole, not to each individual sector. Nevertheless, it is instructive to examine the results for the transportation sector alone. Compared with 1990 CO_2 emissions of 1.9 Gt/yr (10^9 tons per year), 2030 CO_2 emissions are 50% lower in the environmental scenario. In the reference scenario, by comparison, CO_2 emissions grow by 32% over the forty-year horizon. The environmental scenario thus represents a cut of 62% of the 2.5 Gt/yr otherwise projected for 2030. As discussed below, these reductions are achieved largely through efficiency improvement, with help from mode shifting and fuel substitution. We believe that this case represents a projected outcome that would be societally cost-effective and achievable through aggressive policy measures and a significant shift of investments into efficiency and renewable resources. Although the environmental scenario reflects a net societal benefit, it is not necessarily a "no losers" scenario, since the requisite investment shifts would entail major changes in the allocation of economic resources.

Assumptions and Analyses

We took as our starting point the EIA (Energy Information Administration, U.S. Department of Energy) transportation sector model (EIA/TED 1990) and the National Energy Strategy service report (EIA/SR 1990). We then developed a reference case using the efficiency levels and fuel mix projections from the EIA work. Our reference case differs from EIA's in terms of the underlying activity levels that drive transportation demand. Our reference case technical efficiency and fuel mix assumptions are essentially the same as EIA's. The energy savings and CO_2 emissions reduction estimates made here are for our environmental scenario relative to the reference scenario.

For personal travel, we made our own projection of vehicle-miles of travel (VMT). Figure 11-1 shows historical and projected VMT for various scenarios (the policy scenario projections are discussed below). Our VMT projection is driven higher than EIA's in the midterm by demographic data, but then drops lower as population stabi-

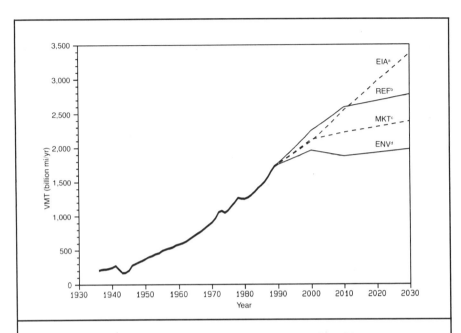

Figure 11-1. Past and Projected Light-Duty Vehicle Travel in the United States

Source: UCS et al. (1991), Figure C1.
Notes:
a EIA = EIA/SR (1990) reference scenario.
b REF = Reference scenario used in this analysis.
c MKT = Market scenario.
d ENV = Environmental scenario.

lizes and some assumed saturations in vehicle ownership and women's driving come into play.[3] Alone, this difference accounts for an 18% drop, or 2.9 quads in year 2030 light-duty vehicle energy demand in our reference case as compared with EIA's.

The demand for freight services is driven by the amount and types of industrial output. Our industrial sector is modeled differently from EIA's, generally reflecting trends toward lowered materials intensity and a shift toward services (UCS et al. 1991, 60–61; Williams, Larson & Ross 1987). To maintain the same level of overall economic activity

---

[3] We use the projections of Spencer (1989) for population over age sixteen, adjusting for projected immigration and deducting the portion over age eighty-five, which cuts another 1% by 2030; see Appendix C of UCS et al. (1991) for further details.

(GNP) as projected by EIA, we assumed increased growth in the commercial-services sector, which does drive part of freight transportation demand. However, these shifts result in our reference case freight demand being 2.2 quads (23%) lower than EIA's in 2030.[4] Some truck-to-rail mode shifting is assumed in the environmental scenario, but the overall level of freight service demand (ton-miles) is the same as in the reference scenario.

For the environmental scenario, we based our projections of potential efficiency improvement on a combination of identified technologies plus extrapolations on rates of technical improvement. For the near term, which we identify as projection year 2000, our technology improvements are based on conservation supply curves developed for automobiles (Ross, Ledbetter & An 1991) and heavy trucks (Sachs et al. 1991). These two modes currently account for about two-thirds of transportation energy use, and their respective assessments list only measures for which estimated efficiency benefits and technology costs are known. Aircraft efficiency is based on the assessment of Greene (1990). Although cost-effectiveness was not identified for all of the measures, we assigned progressively higher identified efficiency levels to our more aggressive scenarios. The technology efficiency levels used for the environmental scenario highlighted in this chapter are intermediate levels, between those used for the market and climate stabilization scenarios presented in UCS et al. (1991).

Light-Duty Vehicles

In the reference case, the average rated fuel economy of new light-duty vehicles is assumed to improve 47% (new cars at 41 mpg) over the forty-year period through 2030 (Table 11-1). In contrast, a full implementation of presently existing measures cost-effective up to a fuel price of $1.47/gallon (1990$) could yield a 53% improvement (new cars at 43 mpg) over the next decade (Ross, Ledbetter & An 1991). A conservation supply curve showing the fuel economy improvement as a function of cost of conserved energy is shown in Figure 11-2, which also lists the cost/benefit assumptions for the technologies used. Average vehicle size and performance are based on the 1987 new-car fleet, and the technologies considered include only those that have been demonstrated to date. Table 11-1 shows the assumed fuel economies of new vehicles by scenario and year. For the environmental scenario, the

---

[4] The comparison is for the comparably modeled domestic freight modes (truck, rail, domestic shipping), which EIA projects at 9.7 quads in 2030 (EIA/SR 1990, 202), versus our reference projection of 7.5 quads.

Table 11-1. Projected Fuel Economies of New Automobiles

	1988	2000	2010	2030
EPA test (55/45) mpg				
Reference[a]	28.6	33	37	41
Least private cost[b]		40	50	56
Least societal cost[c]		43	54	75
Climate stabilization[c]		46	59	75
On-road vs. test shortfall				
Reference[d]	20%	20%	25%	30%
Least private cost[e]		25%	200%	0%
Least societal cost[e]		20%	10%	0%
Climate stabilization[e]		20%	10%	0%
Annual rates of on-road improvement[f]				
Reference	4.1%[g]	1.1%	0.7%	0.5%
Least private cost		3.0%	2.9%	1.7%
Least societal cost		4.3%	3.7%	2.1%
Climate stabilization		5.3%	3.7%	1.8%

Notes:
a EIA/SR (1990), Table G-3.
b For 2000, authors' target, based on Ross, Ledbetter & An (1991); for 2010 and 2030, the medium-risk and high-risk estimates, respectively, given by EEA (1991) for 2010, adjusted downard to reflect elimination of shortfall.
c As in note *b*, with more ambitious schedule and assuming further technical improvements, optimization for on-road driving, and improvement of driving conditions (e.g., speed limit enforcement), so that shortfall is eliminated and the 75 mpg (EEA high-risk estimate for 2010) is achieved by 2030.
d EIA/SR (1990), Table 3-4, p. 85.
e Authors' targets, as discussed in notes *b* and *c*.
f For new vehicles, from previous year to projection year, as calculated from the test mpg and shortfall assumptions.
g New automobiles, 1977–1988, from Heavenrich, Murrell & Hellman (1991), Table 1, and assuming a 15% shortfall in 1977.

corresponding evolution of the fuel economy of the entire vehicle stock is given in Table 11-2.

Most of the technologies assumed for the environmental scenario are already in use, although many of the engine and load reduction technologies have been applied to enhance power performance rather than to improve fuel economy in recent years. Idle-off, or engine start-stop, has been used in some European cars, but its market has been limited. A significant fraction of driving time is spent in idle. Idle-off

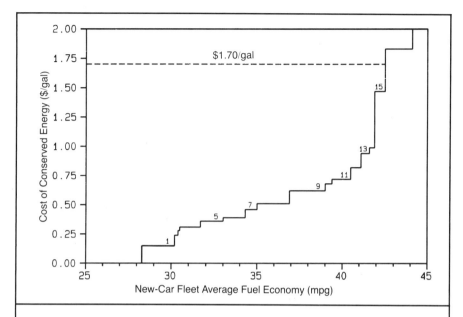

Figure 11-2. Cost of Fuel Economy Improvement for Automobiles

Technology	Indiv. New-Car Mpg Increase (%)	Retail Price Increase ($)	Market Share Increase (%)	COST/BENEFIT ASSUMPTIONS Avg. Cum. Consumer Cost ($)	Cum. Fleet EPA Mpg	Cost of Conserved Energy ($/gal)	Cum. Avg. CCE ($/gal)
Baseline: 1987 new fleet					28.3		
Transmission management	9.0	60	75	45	30.2	0.15	0.15
Roller cam followers	1.5	15	37	51	30.4	0.24	0.15
Torque converter lockup	3.0	35	16	56	30.5	0.28	0.16
Overhead cam	6.0	74	69	107	31.7	0.31	0.21
Advanced friction reduction	6.0	80	80	171	33.0	0.36	0.25
Intake valve control	6.0	80	75	231	34.3	0.39	0.27
Front-wheel drive	10.0	150	23	266	35.0	0.46	0.29
4 valves/cylinder	6.8	105	100	371	36.9	0.51	0.33
Idle-off	15.0	250	50	496	39.0	0.62	0.37
Accessory improvements	1.7	29	80	519	39.4	0.68	0.38
Aerodynamic improvement	4.6	80	85	587	40.5	0.72	0.40
Multipoint fuel injection	3.5	67	56	624	41.1	0.82	0.42
Continuous variable transmission	4.7	100	45	669	41.6	0.94	0.43
Lube & tire improvements	1.0	22	100	691	41.9	0.99	0.44
5-speed auto overdrive transmission	4.7	150	40	751	42.5	1.47	0.47
Weight reduction	6.6	250	85	964	44.1	1.83	0.56
Advanced tires	0.5	20	100	984	44.2	2.01	0.57

Source: UCS et al. (1991), Table C8, based on Ross, Ledbetter & An (1991), assuming a 3% discount rate and 10-year term.

Table 11-2. Summary of Light-Vehicles Analysis, Environmental Scenario

	1990	2000	2010	2030
VMT, base (billion mi)	1,762	2,250	2,610	2,820
Land use/TDM effect	0.0%	−13.0%	−30.0%	−34.0%
Cost of driving effect	0.0%	0.5%	2.2%	4.4%
Net light vehicle VMT	1,762	1,969	1,884	1,986
Light truck fraction	0.29	0.31	0.32	0.32
Gasoline price (1990$/gal)	1.09	1.32	1.59	1.94
Avg. driving cost (cents/mi)	5.8	5.4	4.3	3.1
New-vehicle fuel economy (EPA mpg)				
Automobiles	28	43	54	75
Light trucks	21	32	41	56
Average new light vehicle	25	39	49	68
On-road fuel economy (mpg)				
Shortfall, on-road vs. EPA	20%	20%	10%	0%
New light-vehicle average	20.2	30.8	44.3	67.8
Stock fuel economy (on-road mpg)				
Automobiles	21	27	41	69
Light trucks	15	20	31	52
Stock average on-road	19	25	37	62
Average energy use (kBtu/mi)	6.65	5.10	3.34	2.01
Average annual improvement rate				
New light-duty vehicles		4.3%	3.7%	2.1%
Light-duty vehicle stock		2.7%	4.3%	2.6%
Relative efficiency by fuel type				
Petroleum	1	1	1	1
Natural gas	1.0	1.0	1.0	1.0
Biofuels	1.0	1.0	1.0	1.0
Hydrogen	1.0	0.9	0.9	2.5
Electric (end-use from grid)	2.5	2.3	2.3	2.5

Table 11-2. (continued)				
	1990	**2000**	**2010**	**2030**
Shares of VMT by fuel type				
Petroleum	100.00%	97.67%	68.22%	5.83%
Natural gas	0.00%	0.40%	0.96%	0.08%
Biofuels	0.00%	1.92%	24.43%	66.38%
Hydrogen	0.00%	0.00%	0.00%	0.00%
Electric (end-use from grid)	0.00%	0.01%	6.39%	27.71%
End-use consumption (quads)				
Petroleum	11.715	9.812	4.296	0.233
Natural gas	0.000	0.040	0.060	0.003
Biofuels	0.000	0.193	1.539	2.650
Hydrogen	0.000	0.000	0.000	0.000
Electric (end-use from grid)	0.000	0.001	0.175	0.442
LIGHT-VEHICLE TOTAL (QUADS)	11.7	10.0	6.1	3.3
Source: UCS et al. (1991), Table C16.				

is not particularly costly to implement, and its fuel savings are among the largest of any available technology (see Figure 11-2). Current market conditions offer no incentive to introduce such a technology (similar concerns have been raised for transmission management, also noted in Figure 11-2). However, idle-off is an example of a measure that would become viable with stronger efficiency standards, feebates, and other policies to encourage the direction of technological advances toward improving fuel economy. We assume that reaching these levels of vehicle efficiency will require such policy changes, including, at minimum, strengthened Corporate Average Fuel Economy (CAFE) standards. The environmental scenario also assumes a gasoline tax of $0.50/gallon, which begins to cover some of the societal costs of automobile use.[5] The resulting gasoline price in 2000 would be $1.70/gallon, which implies the cost-effectiveness of all but the last two measures in Figure 11-2.

By 2030, we assume new cars would reach a fuel economy of 75

---

[5] Overall societal costs of automobile use were recently estimated to be $0.15–$0.30 per vehicle-mile of travel, or $3.00–$6.00 per gallon of gasoline for the current fleet average of 20 mpg (Moffet 1991).

mpg. This value matches the "risk level 3" estimate of EEA (1991) for the year 2010, which we are applying as a target for twenty years later than the EEA assessment. New cars rated at 75 mpg are also well within the range of existing prototype vehicles (see, for example, Bleviss 1988, Table 3-2). Achieving this level of improvement includes further refinement of existing technologies, identified in Figure 11-2, as well as new technologies now in active development, such as two-stroke engines, regenerative braking, electric and electric-hybrid drive trains, advanced batteries, fuel cells, and advanced materials substitution. Not all technologies would be used in all vehicles, of course, since some of these technologies address the same sources of inefficiency, particularly losses at part load. Advanced emissions control technologies, such as heated catalysts, heat batteries, and NO_x reduction catalysts may also come into play—the latter, for example, through its facilitation of lean-combustion-engine designs (which include lean-burn four-stroke and two-stroke spark-ignition engines and direct-injection diesel engines). Cost information is not available for technologies beyond those already fully demonstrated. For 2010 and later, therefore, we are assuming that applications of the identified technologies will be cost-effective compared with the assumed gasoline price of $2.10/gallon (1990$, including externalities taxes).

Table 11-1 lists the vehicle fuel economy assumptions for our various scenarios, and Figure 11-3 shows the resulting new-vehicle energy intensities, with past history shown for comparison. In the environmental scenario discussed here, there is a two-thirds reduction in light-vehicle energy intensity by 2030, corresponding to an average improvement rate of 3.1%/yr for new vehicles and 3.0%/yr for the entire stock. Assertive public policies will be required to effect such a transformation of the U.S. personal transportation fleet. The likely efficacy of ongoing increases in CAFE standards is analyzed by DeCicco (1992). Besides stronger standards, other helpful policies include market incentives (feebates), an increased gasoline tax, advanced vehicle competition and demonstration programs, strategic procurement of efficient vehicles by governmental and other fleets, and steady research and development support for advanced vehicle technologies. A degree of vehicle mix shifting may also be appropriate, which could ease the burden on technology improvement. From a CO_2 reduction perspective, obvious improvements in the mix would be a reversal of the popularity of inefficient light trucks (which are now one-third of new-vehicle sales) and an increase in specialized smaller vehicles, such as "sporty" but efficient two-passenger cars and commuter cars.

We acknowledge that automotive fuel economy improvements as

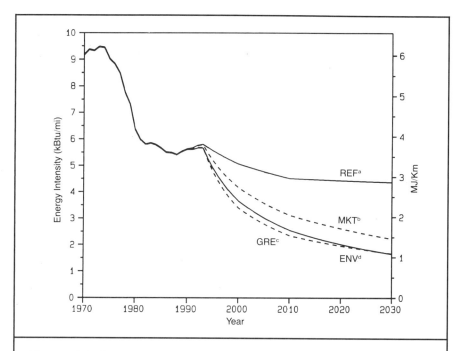

Figure 11-3. Past and Projected Energy Intensity of New Automobiles

Source: From UCS et al. (1991), Figure C2. Historical data from Heavenrich, Murrell & Hellman (1991) and USEPA (1980); projections based on new-vehicle rated fuel economy and shortfall assumptions shown here in Table 11-1.
Notes:
[a] REF = Reference scenario (same as EIA/SR 1990).
[b] MKT = Market scenario.
[c] GRE = Climate stabilization scenario.
[d] ENV = Environmental scenario.

significant as those in our environmental scenario are controversial. We do not acknowledge that there are significant technical or economic barriers to such improvement; rather, the barriers are mainly political and informational. This is an area in which a transition to vehicles having lower environmental impact may not be a "no losers" policy shift. Certainly, the resulting curtailment of gasoline demand would affect the petroleum industry. Ongoing significant fuel economy improvement would place burdens on the automotive industry that could constrain profitability but which are unlikely, of themselves, to affect employment. Historically, there is no evidence that cost-effective improvements in fuel economy have adversely impacted employment in the automotive industry, and future increases in fuel economy will not involve in any fundamental way a shift of production overseas. Rather, comprehensive studies, such as Womack, Jones & Roos (1990), indicate that the poor competitive position of some U.S. domestic automakers is the result of not keeping up with advances in production efficiency and management practice. On the other hand, measures taken to significantly decrease VMT (as discussed below) may dampen demand for motor vehicles.

A summary of the light-vehicle analysis is given in Table 11-2. We did not do an independent analysis of vehicle fuel types, but rather based our projected allocations and relative vehicle efficiencies by fuel type on the very high-conservation case of EIA/SR (1990). Since our scenario pushes efficiency farther, there should be no constraints on fuel availability. We lump alcohol-fueled vehicles (both combustion and fuel cell) together under the category "biofuels," which is projected to contribute two-thirds of the light-duty-vehicle supply by 2030. The next-largest category is electric vehicles. A hydrogen category is listed as a placeholder, since hydrogen utilized in a fuel cell is a promising possibility that could displace some of the other fuels over the forty-year horizon; biomass-derived methanol could also be used in fuel cell vehicles (DeLuchi, Larson & Williams 1991).

Personal Travel Demand

The reference scenario represents a continuation of the now-dominant patterns of urban and suburban growth. These involve heavy automobile dependence, as reflected in low densities, segregated uses, and subsidized road building. In contrast, the environmental scenario assumes a combination of policy changes to achieve denser urban development patterns, to institute transportation demand management, and to directly impose on users the full costs of their automobile use.

We assume a phase-in of mixed-use infill development strategies, so that after 2000, 75% of new population growth settles as urban infill and the remaining 25% is suburban infill, essentially halting sprawl onto vacant land. The resulting densification serves to greatly decrease VMT per person in the affected regions. Auto trips are shorter and at higher average occupancy, and there are shifts to walking, transit, and bicycling, as we presume development policies will also better facilitate these modes. We estimate that phase-in of densification can shave 5% from VMT growth by 2000 and 21% by 2030. This projection of VMT reduction is based on a number of studies that document a relationship between higher residential density, reduced automobile VMT, and increased transit usage (Newman & Kenworthy 1989; Pushkarev,

Table 11-3. Projected Impacts of Transportation Demand Management (TDM) in the Environmental Scenario

Measure	VMT Reduction
Commercial area parking charge of $0.01/min	4.6%
Subsidized transit and ride sharing	2.1%
Subsidized off-peak transit	1.5%
Employee parking charge of $3/day	1.2%
Regional congestion pricing to achieve only slightly congested roads (level of service C)	1.1%
Mileage- and smog-based registration fee (average $125/vehicle)	0.2%
$1.50/gal gasoline price adder, incorporating $0.50/gal tax (externalities other than greenhouse emissions) plus $1.00/gal for pay-at-the-pump insurance	6.1%
TOTAL[a]	16.5%

Source: From UCS et al. (1991), Table C3, derived from Harvey (1990).
Note:
[a] The total is less than the sum of the separate VMT reduction effects of the individual measures because of overlapping impacts on travel decisions, as indicated by the regional transportation modeling analysis on which the results were based.

Zupan & Cumella 1982).[6] For example, studies in the San Francisco, New York, and Chicago areas show that VMT declines 30% each time density doubles, if neighborhood commercial business is allowed (Holtzclaw 1990). Further documenting and quantifying these relationships and delineating the differences between and across metropolitan areas is a priority for further research.[7]

Transportation demand management (TDM) measures complement the densification to achieve further reductions in VMT. The measures listed in Table 11-3, based on the analyses of Harvey (1990), would themselves yield a 16.5% reduction of VMT. In combination with densification, the TDM measures add a net 13% reduction by 2030. Overall, the result is a 34% reduction of VMT compared with our reference case in 2030. This holds net growth in VMT to just 6% above the 1990 level, as shown by the lower curve in Figure 11-1. The

---

[6] See also other studies reviewed in Newman & Kenworthy (1989) and in Holtzclaw (1990).

[7] Some of the uncertainties and issues involved as well as research needs are discussed by Deakin (1990) and Burwell, Bartholomew & Gordon (1990).

VMT reductions account for about one-third of the reduction in light-vehicle energy use; the rest comes from improved fuel economy.

The densification and TDM effects induce increases in urban transit usage. In the reference case, transit passenger-miles of travel (PMT) is flat over the forty-year horizon. The environmental scenario projects a fivefold increase in PMT by 2030 (average PMT growth rate of 4.3%/yr) based on a relation indicating that transit PMT grows by one-sixth the shrinkage in VMT (Holtzclaw 1990), relative to the reference case.

Regarding the investment needed for transit, on the basis of statistics reported in Gordon (1991) we estimate that there is no added cost (capital and operating) beyond what would have been needed for roads (construction and maintenance) displaced by shifting demand from personal vehicles to transit. For example, with the funding allocation flexibilities established in the Intermodal Surface Transportation Efficiency Act of 1991 (ISTEA), nearly one-half of highway program capital authorizations can be more broadly spent, including use for transit capitalization (see, for example, STPP 1992). This broadened funding ability will help to ensure that there are ample resources available to implement the infrastructure developments needed in our environmental scenario. It will also be essential to develop the planning capabilities and political will, at all levels of government, needed to successfully redirect the resources into a more efficient multimodal transportation system. Efforts to improve air quality, such as those required by the Clean Air Act Amendments of 1990, will be helpful in this regard. It should be noted that personal vehicle travel is not shifted exclusively to transit, since much of it goes to higher vehicle occupancy, walking and biking, or reduced travel distance.

This level of VMT reduction assumes the adoption of regulations and financial incentives that would achieve densification with compact, mixed-use infill development, particularly in transit corridors. These policies would be designed to discourage sprawl and encourage infill development in cities, towns, and surrounding suburbs. Relevant policies include zoning regulations, urban growth boundaries, greenbelt preservation, environmental regulations, incentives for dense and mixed-use development, and an enhanced integration of transportation and land use planning. Transportation demand management will also play a crucial role. Some TDM measures reduce direct transportation costs by providing better transit alternatives. Other measures increase the direct costs of driving (for example, via parking pricing and other user fees) to induce mode substitution, thereby reducing the externalities (air pollution, resource depletion, congestion costs) associated with driving. As noted above, a shift in public expenditures is also needed to expand transit capacity, moving revenues away from highways. In the environmental scenario, few or no new highways would be needed after 1995, since new development is shifted into areas where roadway infrastructure is already in place. A proportionately greater share of highway funding would be directed toward maintenance as well as toward making roadway infrastructure more conducive to use of efficient modes through enhancements such as high-occupancy-vehicle (HOV) lanes, good access to transit nodes, and making improvements to facilitate pedestrians and bicyclists.

A shift away from nearly exclusive automobile reliance and toward the alternative transportation and densification strategies contemplated in our environmental scenario will be controversial and will face considerable political hurdles. However, the other option of continuing down the current path of largely uncontrolled sprawl faces its own significant obstacles. Moreover, there are ancillary benefits, such as the potential for a revitalization of decaying urban centers, which can help to generate support for pursuing the environmentally motivated scenario outlined here. Public education on the economic, societal, and environmental benefits of such a shift in development will be essential to facilitate the transition and to build the political support needed to implement these policies.

Freight

Our freight transportation analysis starts with a set of freight service demand levels, in ton-miles per year by industrial subsector, from the 1985 recalibration of the Argonne National Laboratory (ANL) FRATE model (Vyas 1990). These statistics are used instead of the EIA activity-by-mode values (for example, truck VMT, rail ton-miles) to permit estimates of mode-shifting potential. The service demand levels for the eleven industrial subsectors were projected using the growth rates of our industrial sector model (UCS et al. 1991). We do not incorporate macroeconomic effects (for example, energy price changes) of different scenarios into the freight analysis; neither do we feed back the results of our industrial-sector analysis. Therefore, the results reflect only the effects of efficiency and mode changes within the freight transportation sector alone. The 1990–2030 freight mode efficiency improvements developed for the environmental scenario are shown in Table 11-4. A summary of the freight demand, energy intensity, and fuel mix assumptions along with the resulting end-use energy requirements is given in Table 11-5.

Regarding the technical potential for improving freight energy efficiency, a cost-benefit analysis was available only for near-term

Table 11-4. Freight Energy Efficiency Improvements in the Environmental Scenario, 1990–2030

ASSUMPTIONS REGARDING TRUCK-TO-RAIL MODE SHIFT POTENTIAL[a]

Commodity Group	Shipping in 1985 (10^9 ton-mi)	Current Truck Share	Portion That Cannot Shift to Rail
Chemicals, rubber, plastics	286	41%	80%
Primary metals	113	68%	80%
Food	358	73%	80%
Paper	98	50%	100%
Refinery	488	18%	100%
Stone, clay, glass	158	79%	100%
Metal durable	189	80%	80%
Other manufacturing	216	75%	80%
Agricultural	453	67%	100%
Mining, including oil wells	1,296	3%	100%
Construction	151	100%	80%
Retail trade	140	100%	90%

TECHNICAL EFFICIENCY IMPROVEMENTS BY MODE[b]

Mode	1990–2030 Improvement of Ton-Mi/Btu
Truck	101%
Rail	63%
Waterborne (domestic)	25%
Pipeline	25%
Air cargo	168%

AVERAGE FREIGHT SECTOR EFFICIENCY IMPROVEMENT

Weighted by ton-miles and including mode shift effect	75%

Notes:
a Based on UCS et al. (1991), Table D3. Activity and mode share data are from the ANL FRATE model (Vyas 1990). Mode shift limitation assumptions are our own.
b Based on UCS et al. (1991), Table D10, with truck efficiency equivalent to heavy trucks reaching 10.5 mpg (see Figure 11-4) and air cargo efficiency equivalent to passenger aircraft at 100 SM/gal (see Table 11-7).

Table 11-5. Freight Transportation Analysis Summary, Environmental Scenario

	1990	2000	2010	2030
Activity (10^9 ton-miles)				
Truck	1,755	1,952	2,192	2,613
Rail	830	939	1,069	1,350
Water	851	863	888	898
Air	7.8	9.5	11.7	16.5
Pipeline	846	862	888	901
TOTAL	4,288	4,626	5,049	5,778
Truck loading (tons/vehicle)	5.59	5.59	5.59	5.59
Truck VMT (10^9)	314	349	392	467
Truck mpg	8.6	10.6	13.0	17.3
Energy intensity index				
Truck	1	0.815	0.664	0.498
Rail	1	0.895	0.796	0.612
Water	1	0.950	0.900	0.800
Air	1	0.793	0.512	0.373
Pipeline	1	0.950	0.900	0.800
Energy intensity (Btu/ton-mile)				
Truck	2,808	2,288	1,864	1,397
Rail	443	396	353	271
Water	402	382	362	322
Air	18,809	14,916	9,630	7,016
Pipeline	271	257	244	217
Energy by mode (quads)				
Truck	4.927	4.465	4.086	3.650
Rail	0.368	0.372	0.377	0.366
Water	0.342	0.330	0.321	0.289
Air	0.146	0.142	0.113	0.116
Pipeline	0.229	0.222	0.217	0.195
Other (not modeled) (quads)				
Natural gas pipelines	0.535	0.537	0.544	0.527
International shipping	0.717	0.851	0.984	1.047

Table 11-5. (continued)

	1990	2000	2010	2030
Energy by fuel (quads)				
Petroleum	6.490	5.931	5.204	3.572
Natural gas	0.535	0.729	1.006	1.913
Electricity (end-use)	0.239	0.232	0.226	0.205
Renewables	0.000	0.027	0.204	0.500
TOTAL ENERGY USE (QUADS)	7.263	6.918	6.642	66.190

Source: UCS et al. (1991), Table D10.

heavy-truck technologies. Trucking is, of course, the most important freight mode from an energy perspective. Air freight is more energy intensive, but it includes a smaller and more specialized fraction of all shipping, much of which is carried as belly cargo on passenger aircraft. Air freight is assumed to have the same efficiency improvement as passenger air (discussed below). For other modes, the efficiency improvement projections from the EIA/SR (1990) very high-conservation case are used.

Our estimates of the potential improvements in freight truck fuel economy are based on Sachs et al. (1991). The estimated conservation potential for heavy-truck efficiency technologies is shown in Figure 11-4, which plots the estimated cost of improvement against achievable fleet fuel economy relative to a baseline fleet at 5.2 mpg. Including engine technologies now in development, the estimated cost-effective heavy-truck fuel economy is 8.7 mpg. We also assume that lower road speed, corresponding to an enforced 55-mph speed limit, is desirable in the environmental case. Highway speed is not limited because it is cost-effective for an individual driver; particularly for freight trucking, the private cost might be high, as shown in Figure 11-4. Rather, speed limits are imposed for broader societal reasons (safety, environmental protection, decreased dependence on oil imports). Speed reduction brings the heavy-truck fuel economy potential up to 9.1 mpg, a 75% improvement over the baseline. Finally, since this assessment is based on near-term technologies, for the environmental scenario we extrapolate to a year 2030 potential of 10.5 mpg, or roughly a doubling (100% improvement) of the baseline.

Since the Sachs et al. (1991) analysis covered only "heavy-heavy" (within class 8) trucks, we assumed that a similar level of improvement could be achieved by freight trucks on average. The heaviest trucks

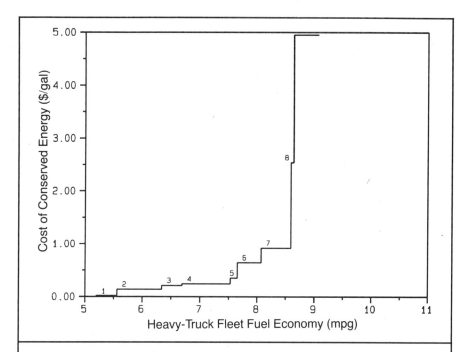

Figure 11-4. Cost of Fuel Economy Improvement for Heavy Trucks, 1990–2030

Technology	Cost ($)	Lifetime (mi)	MPG Benefit	Penetration	Fleet Mpg	CCE ($/gal)
Drive train	1	750,000	7%	100%	5.6	0.00
Other available engine technology	1,500	500,000	15%	100%	6.3	0.14
Aerodynamics—tractor	3,000	750,000	14%	48%	6.7	0.21
Engine control technologies	4,000	750,000	16%	100%	7.5	0.24
Aerodynamics—trailer	2,000	750,000	5%	48%	7.7	0.35
Tires	700	80,000	8%	100%	8.1	0.64
Engines in development[a]	10,000	750,000	10%	100%	8.6	0.92
Weight reduction	3,000	750,000	1%	100%	8.7	2.54
Speed reduction[b]	15,000	200,000	15%	55%	9.1	4.95

Source: Sachs et al. (1991), Figure 1, which can be referenced for further details.
Note: Assumes a baseline fuel economy of 5.2 mpg and a 3% discount rate.
[a] Includes turbocompounding, bottoming cycles, low-heat-rejection diesels.
[b] Not a technology, but rather the cost of longer driving times.

dominate the freight activity in terms of VMT. The light and medium classes of freight trucks are bracketed by passenger vehicles and heavy trucks, and as noted earlier, even higher levels of improvement are projected for light-duty vehicles. Therefore, we are comfortable with this assumption even though a specific assessment for all classes for freight trucks was not performed. We scaled the average freight truck fuel economy by the improvement in heavy-truck fuel economy using the ratio of the 8.6 mpg EIA/SR (1990) baseline for all freight trucks to the 5.2 mpg Sachs et al. (1991) baseline for heavy trucks. The resulting fuel economy and energy intensity projections are given in Table 11-5.

The present modal breakdown of intercity freight (ton-miles) is rail, 37%; trucks, 26%; oil pipelines, 21%; domestic water shipping, 16%; and air, 0.35% (Smith 1990). At present, a small fraction of purely domestic freight moves in intermodal service (containers or trailers on flatcars or dedicated vehicles, and "carless" trailers). There are many barriers to increasing intermodal shipping, of which the most important is that intermodal service takes longer for hauls less than about 500–600 miles, whereas, based on statistics in Smith (1990), average shipment distances are 252 miles (truckload) and 548 miles (less than truckload). Intermodal shipping has, however, doubled in the past decade and has good continued-growth potential in selected markets (Roberts & Fauth 1988). This may seem to run counter to the trend toward greater time-value of shipments; however, it is not conventional bulk-commodity rail service that we see growing. Rather, it is expanded competitiveness of intermodal services, which take advantage of inherent efficiencies of rail and the congestion avoidance possible with the use of an exclusive, fully scheduled right-of-way. Rail shipping uses about one-fourth as much energy per ton-mile as trucks do. Increasing the intermodal share will save energy if the rail system is near enough to origins and destinations. If not, the postulated savings are lost in drayage—that is, extra truck shipping to and from the rail terminals.[8]

Using an analysis of intermodal potential by commodity subsector, summarized in Table 11-4(a), we estimated that a maximum of 12% of intercity truck ton-miles could move to rail by 2030. In the environmental scenario, this shift is phased in starting with a 3.3% shift by the year 2000 and is reflected in the activity (ton-mile) projec-

---

[8] Because rail routes are more circuitous than truck routes, one should add approximately 10% to the ton-miles shifted. Such an adjustment would increase rail ton-miles by about 3%, which, using our projected activity levels, would imply an additional 0.01 quad; this was neglected in our analysis.

Table 11-6. Freight Transportation Results, Reference Versus Environmental Scenarios

ENERGY END-USE		
	Quads	Change Relative to 1990
1990	7.3	—
Reference scenario 2030	9.8	+35%
Environmental scenario 2030	6.2	−15%
FUELS MIX, ENVIRONMENTAL SCENARIO FOR 2030		
Fuel	**Quads**	**Share**
Petroleum	3.6	58%
Natural gas	1.9	31%
Biofuels (renewable)	0.5	8%
Electricity (52% renewable)	0.2	3%
Source: UCS et al. (1991), 93, and Appendix E, 16–17.		

tions given in Table 11-5. No shifts occur in the other modes. In particular, we did not consider the potential impact of new services that may become important over a forty-year horizon, such as shipment via highly automated and integrated transportation networks, high-speed rail, and displacement by electronic media.

Freight energy demands by mode were partitioned into renewable and nonrenewable fuels; we did not analyze splits within these categories (for example, alcohol versus biodiesel). Although we assumed moderate increases in natural gas as a land freight fuel, its contribution could be significantly higher, particularly for meeting near-term CO_2 emissions constraints. Natural gas is widely available, relatively low-cost, and burns rather cleanly. Compressed or liquefied natural gas may be suitable for fleet vehicles, heavy trucks, and rail (where liquefied natural gas might be carried in tenders behind the locomotive). For the freight sector environmental scenario, we did not attempt to specify the form of renewable fuel use, which could be alcohol or hydrogen in combustion engines or fuel cells.

As summarized in Table 11-6, the year 2030 environmental scenario projection for freight transportation energy end-use is 37% lower than the reference case projection. The reduction is achieved mainly through efficiency improvements, with a 1.2%/yr average rate of technology efficiency improvement between 1990 and 2030. Accounting for the truck-to-rail mode shift, there is 1.4%/yr average improvement rate in ton-miles moved per Btu. In the reference case, by comparison, there is essentially no average improvement, since the relatively small technology efficiency gains in all modes are offset by the projected higher activity growth rates of the more intensive modes, truck and air.

Although energy requirements and CO_2 emissions by the freight subsector can fall in absolute terms, the potential drop is not nearly so dramatic as that for light vehicles. Presently, light vehicles are the dominant transportation energy use, and they are projected to remain so in the reference case. In the environmental scenario, however, freight becomes the dominant user of transportation energy by 2030. The absolute fall in energy consumption from present levels is 15%, so there is a greater burden on fuel switching in the freight subsector if we seek a 50% cut in CO_2 emissions by 2030.

Although technology cost projections have large uncertainties, we estimate that these energy use reductions would be cost-effective in every scenario. With changes in land use patterns and urban transportation policies there could be additional savings, but we did not analyze the impact of these factors for freight transportation as we did so for personal travel. Changes that could impact freight energy needs include the following: Production could be located closer on average to consumption (although this would run counter to recent trends toward a more global economy). Land use and traffic policies could be implemented to facilitate freight movement; such policies could include HOV rush-hour lanes that convert to freight-only at night, and other congestion-limiting measures as discussed under personal transportation policies.

Intercity Passenger Travel

Reference case projections of personal air travel through 2010 were obtained from EIA/TED (1990). Activity levels and fuel efficiency were extrapolated to 2030 in a way consistent with pre-2010 trends and the EIA/SR (1990) results. Table 11-7 summarizes our intercity travel analysis. Overall intercity travel demand, as measured by passenger-miles of travel (PMT), is expected to more than triple by 2030, growing at average rates of 3.5%/yr between 1988 and 2010 and 2.5%/yr between 2010 and 2030. With reference case efficiency assumptions and no mode shifting, the resulting energy use would grow from the present level of about 2.9 quads to 5.4 quads by 2030.

Significant improvements in aircraft efficiency are possible, especially over the long run as the stock is replaced (Greene 1990). Presently, passenger-aircraft fuel economy averages 39 seat-miles per

Table 11-7. Intercity Air and High-Speed Rail, Summary of Analysis (All Scenarios)

Scenario and Year	1988	2000	2010	2030
Reference				
Air PMT (10^9)	513	762	1,082	1,772
Air SM/gal	39	52	62	73
Air energy intensity index	1.000	0.765	0.629	0.534
Air energy use (quads)	2.91	3.31	3.86	5.37
Market				
Air PMT (10^9)	513	762	1,017	1,577
HSR PMT (10^9)	0	0	65	195
Air SM/gal	39	51	62	73
Air energy intensity index	1.000	0.765	0.629	0.534
HSR energy intensity index	1.000	1.000	0.904	0.740
Air energy use (quads)	2.91	3.31	3.63	4.78
HSR energy use (quads)	0.00	0.00	0.09	0.21
TOTAL: AIR + HSR (QUADS)	2.91	3.31	3.72	4.99
Environmental				
Air PMT (10^9)	513	762	984	1,479
HSR PMT (10^9)	0	0	98	293
Air SM/gal	39	51	73	100
Air energy intensity index	1.000	0.765	0.534	0.390
HSR energy intensity index	1.000	1.000	0.904	0.740
Air energy use (quads)	2.91	3.31	2.98	3.27
HSR energy use (quads)	0.00	0.00	0.13	0.32
TOTAL: AIR + HSR (QUADS)	2.91	3.31	3.11	3.59

Source: UCS et al. (1991), Table C11.
Note: High-speed rail (HSR) efficiency improvements are assumed to be 1%/yr for all scenarios, starting from the year 2000 base of 0.9 kBtu/seat-mile (SM).

Table 11-7. (continued)				
Scenario and Year	1988	2000	2010	2030
Climate stabilization				
Air PMT (10^9)	513	762	952	1,382
HSR PMT (10^9)	0	0	130	390
Air SM/gal	39	51	79	150
Air energy intensity index	1.000	0.765	0.9494	0.260
HSR energy intensity index	1.000	1.000	0.904	0.740
Air energy use (quads)	2.91	3.31	2.67	2.04
HSR energy use (quads)	0.00	0.00	0.17	0.43
TOTAL: AIR + HSR (QUADS)	2.91	3.31	2.84	2.46
Parameters				
Jet fuel energy content: 135 kBtu/gal				
Base air energy intensity: 3.462 kBtu/SM (fully loaded)				
Base HSR energy intensity: 0.900 kBtu/SM (fully loaded)				
Load factor (both air and HSR): 0.61				

gallon (SM/gallon). The reference scenario projects improvement to stock average performance of 73 SM/gallon by 2030. In the environmental scenario, we assume this level of improvement by 2010 and a further improvement to 100 SM/gallon by 2030. This is within the levels estimated by Greene (1990), who identified aircraft technologies that could eventually push fleet efficiencies into the 110–150 SM/gallon range. The result is a 27% reduction in air energy use by 2030. We did not specifically analyze fuel substitution possibilities and thus assume continued use of petroleum fuels and their CO_2 emissions rates for aircraft.

Because of the large growth in air travel, the resulting airport congestion, and anticipated limits in new airport construction, several regions of the country are considering high-speed trains for intercity passenger service. The options include various forms of fast steel-wheel trains, such as the French *train de grande vitesse* (TGV), as well as magnetic levitation (Maglev) vehicles. We do not attempt to distinguish these in our analysis but classify them together as high-speed rail (HSR). HSR options are considered to be competitive (on both energy cost and travel time) at distances of generally 600 miles or less, which are estimated to account for about one-third of current domestic air PMT. By air, these shorter trips are more energy-intensive than longer flights. In the environmental scenario, we assume a phase-in of HSR, so that one-half of the shorter trips are shifted from air to HSR by 2030. We assume that HSR options will use 900 Btu/SM[9] in 2000 and improve at 1%/yr thereafter. HSR energy use then grows to 0.32 quads by 2030, contributing a net 8% reduction of intercity travel energy use compared with the reference case. Counting the aircraft efficiency improvements, the environmental scenario projection of energy use for intercity travel in 2030 is 3.6 quads, which is 33% lower than the reference projection.

Findings and Inferences

Table 11-8 summarizes the energy end-use results for our transportation sector analyses. All scenarios are shown, with a breakdown into light vehicles, freight, intercity passenger travel, and urban transit. For the environmental scenario on which this presentation focuses, we project a reduction in transportation energy use to 39% below the present level, in contrast to a 30% increase in the reference case. The largest reduction in the environmental scenario is by personal light vehicles, for which end-use drops from 11.7 quads in 1990 to 3.3 quads in 2030, versus rising to 13.3 in the reference case. Driving-age population is projected to grow at 0.6%/yr over the forty-year horizon; energy end-use shrinks at an average rate of 3%/yr in the environmental scenario, versus growth of 0.3%/yr in the reference case.

It is instructive to break down the reductions in energy use into components of technology improvement and mode shift. This is shown for the environmental scenario in Table 11-9. Consistently for all subsectors, it turns out that improved technology efficiency is responsible for three-fourths of the reduction, with shifts to more efficient mode accounting for the remainder. This is significant because the majority of the technology improvements have already been identified at present even though the projection is for forty years out. Widespread commercialization of the efficient transportation technologies involves some uncertainty, and costs are not fully identified. Nevertheless, there is still room for technological innovation, the further potential gains from which are not reflected in the scenarios. The mode shift portion rests on assumptions about policy changes to profoundly affect land use patterns and transportation infrastructure. As noted earlier, the personal travel mode shift projections are largely grounded in comparative data for areas that have developed according to different patterns; however, there is a lack of data on areas that have made a transition through time

---

[9] A midrange value of rail and Maglev estimates obtained from D. Rote (1991).

Table 11-8. Transportation Energy End-Use Summary (All Scenarios)

Scenario (By End-Use Activity)	PROJECTED ENERGY END-USE (quads)			
	1990	2000	2010	2030
Reference				
Light vehicles	11.70	13.30	13.80	13.30
Freight	7.26	7.90	8.66	9.81
Intercity passenger	2.91	3.31	3.86	5.37
Urban transit[a]	0.15	0.15	0.15	0.15
TOTAL	22.0	24.7	26.5	28.6
Market				
Light vehicles	11.70	11.40	8.50	5.40
Freight	7.26	7.20	7.30	7.05
Intercity passenger	2.91	3.31	3.72	4.99
Urban transit[a]	0.15	0.19	0.26	0.23
TOTAL	22.0	22.1	19.8	17.7
Environmental				
Light vehicles[b]	11.70	10.00	6.10	3.30
Freight[b]	7.26	6.92	6.64	6.19
Intercity passenger[b]	2.91	3.31	3.11	3.59
Urban transit[a]	0.15	0.25	0.40	0.33
TOTAL	22.0	20.5	16.3	13.4
Climate stabilization				
Light vehicles	11.70	9.60	5.50	3.30
Freight	7.26	6.72	6.61	5.88
Intercity passenger	2.91	3.31	2.84	2.46
Urban transit[a]	0.15	0.34	0.40	0.33
TOTAL	22.0	20.0	15.4	12.0

Source: UCS et al. (1991), Table C13.

Notes:

a Urban transit results are from UCS et al. (1991), Table C5, assuming an average transit efficiency improvement rate of 1.3%/yr. This is based on a 50%–50% share split between bus and rail transit, and energy intensity (Btu/VMT) decreasing by 43% for buses and by 39% for rail (EIA/SR 1990, 218). We did not do a specific conservation assessment for bus efficiency. Rather, we assumed that buses have an efficiency improvement potential similar to that of freight trucks. Some heavy-truck measures (such as engine, tire, and lubrication improvements) are directly applicable; others (such as aerodynamics) are less so; however, other significant options (such as regenerative braking) not assumed for heavy trucks are applicable to buses.

b For the environmental scenario, light-vehicle results are from Table 11-2, freight results are from Table 11-5, and intercity passenger results are from Table 11-7.

Table 11-9. Breakdown of Transportation Sector Energy Use Reductions in 2030, Environmental Scenario Versus Reference Scenario

	ENERGY USE (quads) Reference Scenario	QUADS OF REDUCTION (% reduction)		ENERGY USE (quads) Environmental Scenario
		Efficiency	Mode Shift	
Personal travel (nonintercity)	13.45	7.50 (77%)	2.29 (23%)	3.66
Freight	9.81	2.73 (76%)	0.87 (24%)	6.19
Intercity travel	5.37	1.35 (76%)	0.43 (24%)	3.59
TOTAL	28.63	11.59 (76%)	3.60 (24%)	13.44

Source: UCS et al. (1991), Table C12.
Note: The breakdown for each subsector was obtained by factoring the ratio of environmental (ENV) to reference (REF) scenario energy use (E), into an efficiency portion (p), and a mode shift portion (q), according to $E_{ENV}/E_{REF} = (1-p)(1-q)$. The absolute energy reduction, $E_{ENV} - E_{REF}$, was then broken into two components proportional to p and q. The percent contributions of technology improvement and mode shift to the reduction are thus taken to be $p/(p+q)$ and $q/(p+q)$, respectively.

from highway-mode intensive transportation to denser development and a multimodal transportation system.

These results show that although there is a larger burden on technology improvement in achieving energy use reductions consistent with a greenhouse-constrained economy, technology cannot be expected to achieve the needed energy use reductions alone. Significant policy changes are needed to push both technology improvement and shifts to more efficient modes. The three-to-one ratio suggested here is not fully certain, of course, and technological advances could reduce the burden on mode shifting. This breakdown was not, however, foreordained, since the analyses were done independently under similar guidelines about likely cost-effectiveness, externality costs, and policy change.

Besides reducing energy consumption through efficient technologies and shifts to less intensive modes, the other important way to cut CO_2 emissions is to switch to renewable fuels. With the steep energy use reductions indicated here, there is a smaller burden on fuel switching, which increases the possibility that the CO_2-renewable fuel supply system can be sustainable in the broader sense of having minimal disruptions to natural ecosystems. Petroleum use now accounts for essen-

Table 11-10. Transportation Sector Energy Use and CO_2 Emissions in 2030, Environmental Scenario Versus Reference Scenario

	Energy End-Use (quads)	CO_2 Emissions (10^9 tons/yr)	CO_2 Factor (10^6 tons/quad)
Base year estimates for 1990	22.0	1.90	86
Reference scenario in 2030 (change from 1990)	28.6 (+30%)	2.50 (+32%)	87 (+1%)
Environmental scenario in 2030 (change from 1990)	13.4 (−39%)	0.95 (−50%)	71 (−17%)

tially 100% of the 22 quads, or 11 Mbd (million barrels per day), used by the transportation sector. By 2030, it drops to 7 quads (54% of end-use) in the environmental scenario versus 27 quads (94% of end-use) in the reference case. Further reductions in petroleum use and its attendant CO_2 emissions could be obtained from greater use of biofuels or renewably generated hydrogen. For example, DeLuchi, Larson & Williams (1991) suggest that hydrogen- or methanol-powered fuel cell vehicles may offer significant environmental benefits and be economically competitive with petroleum-powered vehicles on a life-cycle-cost basis. Presently, however, it is premature to pick winners or losers among the various renewable fuel options. Our results are therefore based on use of a generic biofuel, which is assumed to supply 3.2 quads (23%) of transportation energy end-use by 2030 in the environmental scenario.

Table 11-10 shows the environmental scenario results for transportation sector CO_2 emissions in 2030, assuming no net CO_2 emissions from biofuels. The 50% absolute reduction in CO_2 emissions is obtained in part by fuels substitution, mainly in the light-vehicles subsector, so that CO_2 emissions per unit of energy consumption are reduced by 17%. As noted regarding the energy use reduction breakdown in Table 11-9, the 15-quad cut in transportation energy end-use is achieved largely through efficiency improvement, which is responsible for 76% of the reduction. Mode shifting accounts for the remainder. In addition to a halving of CO_2 emissions, other air pollution from the transportation sector is also significantly reduced. We assume that the more stringent of the emissions levels specified in the 1990 Clean Air Act Amendments (for example, Tier II tailpipe standards) are completely phased in by 2030 in all scenarios (see UCS et al. 1991, Appendix I). Since we did not differentiate scenarios by emissions standards for criteria pollutants, differences in emissions projections between scenarios depend only on reduced levels of VMT and overall transportation sector fuel use. The environmental scenario projects emissions reductions relative to the reference scenario of 50% for nitrogen oxides and reactive hydrocarbons (NO_x and RHC) and 30% for sulfur oxides and particulates (SO_x and TSP) by 2030.

Issues for Further Analysis

The large reductions in transportation sector energy use and CO_2 emissions projected for the environmental scenario will clearly require significant changes in transportation and energy policy. The technical and economic feasibility of the technology improvements invoked in the analysis has the firmest underpinning among the assumptions used. Published information on efficient technologies was used for the major energy-intensive transportation modes—light-duty vehicles, heavy trucks, and passenger aircraft. Indeed, the assumptions are technologically conservative since neither new innovations nor technology breakthroughs are assumed over the forty-year horizon of the study. Extrapolations regarding similarity in improvement rates were assumed for some of the other modes, and these estimates should be refined with further analysis.

The potential for significant mode-shifting adopted in our environmental scenario is based on cross-sectional analyses of Holtzclaw (1990) and extrapolations of the regional TDM assessments of Harvey (1990). These results are more controversial because they go beyond the possibilities suggested by conventional transportation planning models used in the United States. Nevertheless, comparisons with areas having much lower levels of highway mode activity than are presently typical in the United States provide evidence that automobile dependency is not necessary for healthy economic development. Although such results are provocative, what is less clear is the process by which such a transition can be made. Needed are better time series data on land use characteristics for areas that have undergone different development patterns, resulting in significantly different per capita VMT.

The alternative-fuels aspects of the analysis also need further development. In particular, there is scope for greater use of natural gas, particularly as a transitional fuel in earlier years. As noted earlier, we did not include any hydrogen use in the environmental scenario, although by 2030 this may be a promising fuel in electric vehicles powered by fuel cells.

There are a number of economic issues raised by the analysis as well. The meaning of least societal cost in the context of transportation planning needs to be better refined. Our definition is based on the few energy-related environmental externalities for which societal costs estimates are available, primarily regulated air pollutants, plus petroleum security costs. Other societal costs are also involved, which could affect the outcome of the analysis in either a positive or negative way. Our technology cost information is also limited, with the most complete information being available for near-term technologies. Further analysis is needed to refine the estimates of longer-run cost-effectiveness; this will be an ongoing effort in the transportation and energy policy.

The environmental least-cost paradigm behind our analysis implies that the environmental scenario is in some sense a "no regrets" scenario, since the changes are estimated to be cost-effective to society, if not always to private individuals. It is not necessarily a "no losers" scenario, since there are dislocations involved that would place different burdens on and yield different benefits to various groups of consumers and industries. In particular, the petroleum and other fossil fuel industries would be under pressure to either diversify into the provision of less environmentally damaging energy services or face significant losses of income. Such potential economic changes certainly bear further examination, since political feasibility may hinge on a sharing of benefits with parties who would otherwise have a vested interest in business-as-usual. Further economic issues yet to be addressed include macroeconomic effects, energy price feedbacks, equity, and fiscal changes involved in the imposition of environmental taxes, such as those considered in the environmental scenario.

Conclusion

Under the assumptions of our environmental scenario, significant reductions in petroleum use, overall energy use, and carbon dioxide emissions are projected by the year 2030. The technology changes, mode shifts, and fuel substitutions utilized in making the projections are estimated to be cost-effective when considering environmental externality costs along with the direct investment and operating costs of transportation technologies.

Relative to a reference projection that assumes no changes from present policies and trends, the environmental scenario achieves energy end-use reductions of 73% for personal travel in light-duty vehicles, 37% for freight modes, and 33% for domestic air travel by the year 2030. Overall, transportation sector energy use is cut 53%, from the reference projection of 28.6 quads down to 13.4 quads in 2030. Consistently across the subsectors, about three-fourths of the reduction is due to technology efficiency improvement, and the remainder is from shifting to more efficient modes. Petroleum use, which is now nearly 100% of the 22 quads (11 Mbd) used by the transportation sector, falls to 7 quads (3.6 Mbd) in the 2030 environmental projection, versus 27 quads (14 Mbd) in the reference case. These significant energy use reductions, coupled with a moderate use of renewable fuels (3.2 quads), yield a 50% absolute reduction in CO_2 emissions from the U.S. transportation sector, which are presently 1.9 billion tons per year. Further emissions reductions would be possible with a greater shift to renewable fuels, such as hydrogen, which were not fully analyzed in the present study.

Major changes in transportation and energy policy would be required to achieve the benefits identified in the environmental scenario. The requisite policy assumptions were briefly mentioned here and are fully discussed in the longer report on which this paper is based (UCS et al. 1991). Our projection of the significant reductions of CO_2 emissions that could be achieved following our environmental scenario does involve considerable uncertainties. However, our examination of the options for improving efficiency and using renewable resources suggests that the greater source of uncertainty has to do with political and institutional barriers rather than technology or cost hurdles. Clearly, significant new investments will be required to follow a strategy such as that outlined in our environmental scenario. However, our results indicate that following such a path will be less costly to the United States than a continuation down the present transportation path of increasing reliance on inefficiently used fossil fuels. The CO_2 emissions reductions projected for the environmental scenario are all achieved at net economic benefit according to the factors considered here. This is what we mean in characterizing our environmental scenario as a "least-cost transition scenario." The results provided here offer a positive vision of the environmental and economic benefits of a transportation system more compatible with a greenhouse-constrained world. Presenting such a vision is an important step toward building the public support needed to change transportation policies in a way that will move the United States toward an environmentally sustainable economic system.

References

Bleviss, D. 1988. *The New Oil Crisis and Fuel Economy Technologies: Preparing the Light Transportation Industry for the 1990s.* New York: Quorum Press.

Burwell, D. G., K. Bartholomew, and D. Gordon. 1990. "Energy and Environmental Research Needs." In *Transportation, Urban Form, and the Environment*. Special Report 231. Washington, D.C.: Transportation Research Board.

Deakin, E. A. 1990. "Jobs, Housing, and Transportation: Theory and Evidence on Interactions Between Land Use and Transportation." In *Transportation, Urban Form, and the Environment*. Special Report 231. Washington, D.C.: Transportation Research Board.

DeCicco, J. M. 1992. *Savings from CAFE: Projections of the Future Oil Savings from Light Vehicle Fuel Economy Standards*. Washington, D.C.: American Council for an Energy-Efficient Economy. May.

DeLuchi, M. A., E. D. Larson, and R. H. Williams. 1991. *Hydrogen and Methanol: Production from Biomass and Use in Fuel Cell and Internal Combustion Engine Vehicles: A Preliminary Assessment*. Report No. 263. Princeton, N.J.: Center for Energy and Environmental Studies, Princeton University. August.

EEA. 1991. *An Assessment of Potential Passenger Car Fuel Economy Objectives for 2010*. Report prepared for the U.S. Environmental Protection Agency by Energy and Environmental Analysis, Inc. Arlington, Va. July.

EIA/SR. 1990. *Energy Consumption and Conservation Potential: Supporting Analysis for the National Energy Strategy*. Service Report SR/NES/90-02. Washington, D.C.: Energy Information Administration. December.

EIA/TED. 1990. *Transportation Energy Demand Module for the PC-AEO Spreadsheet Model*. Washington, D.C.: Energy Information Administration.

Gordon, D. 1991. *Steering a New Course: Transportation, Energy, and the Environment*. Cambridge, Mass.: Union of Concerned Scientists.

Greene, D. L. 1990. *Energy Efficiency Improvement Potential of Commercial Aircraft to 2010*. Report ORNL-6622. Oak Ridge, Tenn.: Center for Transportation Analysis, Oak Ridge National Laboratory. June.

Harvey, G. 1990. *Draft Transportation Control for State Clean Air Plan* (June) and *Final Transportation Control Measure Plan* (November), prepared for the Metropolitan Transportation Commission, Oakland, Calif.

Heavenrich, R. M., J. D. Murrell, and K. Hellman. 1991. *Light-Duty Automotive Technology and Fuel Economy Trends Through 1991*. Ann Arbor, Mich.: U.S. Environmental Protection Agency. June.

Holtzclaw, J. 1990. *Explaining Urban Density and Transit Impacts on Auto Use*. San Francisco: Sierra Club. April.

Moffet, J. 1991. "The Price of Mobility." Draft Report. San Francisco: Natural Resources Defense Council. November.

Newman, P. W. G., and J. R. Kenworthy. 1989. *Cities and Automobile Dependence: A Sourcebook*. Aldershot, England: Gower Technical.

Pushkarev, B. S., J. M. Zupan, and R. S. Cumella. 1982. *Urban Rail in America: An Exploration of Criteria for Fixed Guideway Transit*. Bloomington: Indiana University Press.

Roberts, P. O., and G. R. Fauth. 1988. "The Outlook for Commercial Freight." In *A Look Ahead: Year 2020*. Special Report 220. Washington, D.C.: Transportation Research Board, National Research Council.

Ross, M., M. Ledbetter, and F. An. 1991. *Options for Reducing Oil Use by Light Vehicles: An Analysis of Technologies and Policy*. Washington, D.C.: American Council for an Energy-Efficient Economy. June.

Rote, D., Argonne National Laboratory, Argonne, Ill. 1991. Personal communication. April.

Sachs, H. M., J. M. DeCicco, M. Ledbetter, and U. Mengelberg. 1991. *Fuel Economy Improvement for Heavy Trucks: A View of Existing Technology, Future Possibilities, and the Potential Improvement*. Washington, D.C.: American Council for an Energy-Efficient Economy. August.

Smith, F. 1990. *Transportation in America*. 8th ed. Waldorf, Md.: Eno Foundation for Transportation.

Spencer, G. 1989. *Projections of the Population of the United States, by Age, Sex, and Race: 1988 to 2080*. Current Population Reports, Series P-25, No. 1018. Washington, D.C.: Bureau of the Census. January.

STPP. 1992. *Special issue: Transit and the New Legislation*. Bulletin #12. Washington, D.C.: Surface Transportation Policy Project. January 14.

Tellus (Tellus Institute and Stockholm Environment Institute). 1990. *LEAP (Long-range Energy Alternatives Planning): A Computerized Energy Planning System*. Vol. 1. *Overview*. Boston: Tellus Institute. January.

UCS et al. (Alliance to Save Energy, American Council for an Energy-Efficient Economy, Natural Resources Defense Council, and Union of Concerned Scientists). 1991. *America's Energy Choices: Investing in a Strong Economy and a Clean Environment*. Cambridge, Mass.: Union of Concerned Scientists. December.

USEPA. 1980. *Passenger Car Fuel Economy: EPA and Road.* Report EPA 460/3-80-010. Ann Arbor, Mich.: U.S. Environmental Protection Agency. September.

Vyas, A., Argonne National Laboratory, Argonne, Ill. 1990. Personal communication. December.

Williams, R. H., E. D. Larson, and M. H. Ross. 1987. "Materials, Affluence, and Industrial Energy Use." *Annual Reviews of Energy* 12:99–144.

Womack, J. P., D. T. Jones, and D. Roos. 1990. *The Machine That Changed the World.* New York: Rawson Associates.

About the Editors

David L. Greene is senior research staff member in Oak Ridge National Laboratory's Center for Transportation Analysis. He earned a B.A. degree from Columbia University in 1971, an M.A. degree from the University of Oregon in 1973, and a Ph.D. in Geography and Environmental Engineering from The Johns Hopkins University in 1978. Dr. Greene joined the staff of Oak Ridge National Laboratory in 1977. In 1980, he founded the Transportation Energy Group at ORNL, which under his direction became the Transportation Research Section and has since become the ORNL Center for Transportation Analysis. Dr. Greene spent 1988–1989 in Washington, D.C. as a Senior Research Analyst conducting research on automotive fuel economy and alternative transportation fuels policy in the Office of Domestic and International Energy Policy, U.S. Department of Energy. He has written fifty articles for professional journals in addition to an equal number of technical reports. His research has been recognized by awards from the Martin Marietta Energy Systems, Inc. Active in the Transportation Research Board and the National Research Council, he recently served on the NRC's Committee on Automobile and Light Truck Fuel Economy and is current Chairman of the TRB's Section on Environmental and Energy Concerns.

Danilo J. Santini is manager of the Environmental and Economic Analysis Section within the Center for Transportation Research at Argonne National Laboratory. He earned a Bachelor of Architecture degree from the Massachusetts Institute of Technology in 1968, a Master's degree in Business and Economics from the Illinois Institute of Technology in 1972, and a Ph.D. in Urban Systems Engineering and Public Policy at the Technological Institute of Northwestern University in 1976. He joined Argonne National Laboratory in 1974, as Assistant Staff Scientist and in 1979 he was promoted to Staff Scientist. In 1982 he joined Argonne's Center for Transportation Research and in 1992 was named Section Manager. He has authored or coauthored numerous journal articles and book chapters, as well as technical reports and conference papers on transportation and energy issues, including research examining the interactions of energy and the macroeconomy. In 1985 he authored conference papers that anticipated the worst oil price collapse in 50 years. He is a member of several professional associations and is most active in the Transportation Research Board. He served as president of the Chicago Energy Economists for 1985–1986.

About the Authors

Steven S. Bernow received a Ph.D. in Physics from Columbia University in 1970 and is a founder of Tellus Institute, a nonprofit organization that since 1976 has done research and policy analysis on resource and environmental issues. He focuses on integrated energy and environmental planning in regional, national, and international contexts and is a contributing author of *America's Energy Choices*, a comprehensive analysis of the potential for energy efficiency and renewable resources across all fuels and sectors.

Mia Layne Birk is Program Associate-Transport Specialist at the International Institute for Energy Conservation (IIEC), where she has been directing IIEC's transportation activities. Ms. Birk has a Master's degree in International Relations from Johns Hopkins University and a Bachelor's degree in Government and French from the University of Texas at Austin.

John J. Brogan is Director of the Office of Propulsion Systems for Transportation Technologies in the U.S. Department of Energy. The Office of Propulsion Systems conducts research and development and testing and evaluation of advanced ground transportation propulsion systems, including gas turbine, advanced diesel, Maglev, and fuel cell electric- and hybrid-powered systems.

John M. DeCicco received his Ph.D. in Mechanical Engineering from Princeton University in 1988 and is a Research Associate with the American Council for an Energy-Efficient Economy (ACEEE). The current focus of his work is energy efficiency in the transportation sector, particularly the assessment of technologies for advancing vehicle efficiency and options for reducing energy use and environmental impacts through transportation planning.

Mark A. DeLuchi does research on the energy economic and environmental aspects of transportation fuels and systems.

David B. Goldstein has been Co-Director of the Natural Resources Defense Council's Energy Program since 1980. He has led research and implementation efforts in a variety of areas, including energy planning, efficiency standards, and economic incentives.

319

Deborah Gordon is Transportation Program Director for the Union of Concerned Scientists and is the author of *Steering a New Course: Transportation, Energy, and the Environment*. Before joining UCS in 1989, she worked at the Lawrence Berkeley Laboratory (1988–1989) and as a chemical engineer with Chevron U.S.A. (1982–1987).

Oren J. Hadaller is a Principal Engineer in the Boeing Commercial Airplane Group's Technology and Product Development organization. Since 1978, he has been involved in research on fuel supplies, characteristics, and alternatives.

Susan M. Haltmaier is a Senior Associate in the Energy and Environmental Research Group of DRI/McGraw-Hill where she is responsible for analyzing the impact of emerging environmental policies on domestic and international markets. Following graduation from Wellesley College and the London School of Economics, she has spent over ten years analyzing the energy industry with Kidder, Peabody & Co., Charles River Associates, Sun Co., and the Chase Manhattan Bank.

John W. Holtzclaw has a B.S. degree in Engineering Physics, an M.S. degree in Nuclear Engineering, and a Ph.D. in Urban Sociology. He is presently a consultant for the Natural Resources Defense Council (NRDC) and the Sierra Club in urban land use, transportation, and socio-economic interactions.

Marc Ledbetter is a Program Manager at Battelle Pacific Northwest Laboratory, Portland, Oregon, specializing in energy efficiency technology and policy analysis. Mr. Ledbetter was Deputy Director of ACEEE when he contributed to this book.

Paul MacCready, Ph.D., founder and Chairman of AeroVironment Inc., is best known as the "father of human-powered flight" for his development of the Gossamer Condor and Albatros that won aviation's largest cash prizes. His company work covers products and services in the connected fields of environment, alternative energy, and efficient vehicles (including key roles in creating the solar-powered GM Sunraycer and the battery-powered GM Impact car), all fitting the theme of "doing more with less" and helping move civilization toward a desirable sustainability that includes nature.

John Mason is Vice President, Engineering and Technology, Allied Signal Aerospace Company, retired, and was SAE's 1990 president. Currently he consults for Garrett Automotive Group of Allied Signal, teaches for Cal State Long Beach, and chairs the Energy and Environment task force of Fisita, an international automotive organization.

Stephen Meyers has been a Staff Scientist in International Energy Studies at the Energy and Environment Division at Lawrence Berkeley Laboratory since 1982.

Robin Miles-McLean is Chief of the Transportation Section in the Office of Mobile Sources, U.S. Environmental Protection Agency.

Peter M. Miller is a Senior Scientist with the Natural Resources Defense Council.

Marianne Millar Mintz specializes in transportation energy forecasting and policy analysis for Argonne National Laboratory's Center for Transportation Research. She has over 20 years' experience in transportation and energy analysis and has authored more than 50 publications in the field. Her Master's degree is in Public Service Systems from UCLA's School of Architecture and Urban Planning.

Albert M. (Al) Momenthy is Manager of Transportation Energy for the Boeing Commercial Airplane Group. He is responsible for analyses and forecasts covering the production, properties, application, and economics of fuel for transportation.

Joan Ogden is a physicist at Princeton University's Center for Energy and Environmental Studies, where her main research interest is assessment of renewable energy systems.

Peter Reilly-Roe is responsible for policy development and alternative transportation fuels and energy efficiency in transportation for Energy, Mines and Resources Canada.

Harvey Sachs is Director, Policy Research, at the Center for Global Change of the University of Maryland. His work focuses on barriers that inhibit adoption of efficient and renewable technologies, and on specific strategies to remove the barriers.

Lee Schipper, Ph.D., is Staff Senior Scientist at Lawrence Berkeley Laboratory, and coleader, International Energy Studies at Lawrence Berkeley Laboratory, and visiting Researcher at the Stockholm Environment Institute.

Michael Shelby, Ph.D., is Chief of the Energy Policy Branch in the Office of Policy Analysis at the U.S. Environmental Protection Agency. The Energy Policy Branch develops policy options to mitigate greenhouse gas emissions that contribute to climate change.

Ruth Steiner is a graduate student in City and Regional Planning at the University of California at Berkeley.

Sek R. Venkateswaran is a Project Manager with the Transportation Technologies Group at Energetics, Inc. He manages several analytical projects for government and industry clients to assess advanced vehicle propulsion and alternative fuel technologies and their potential energy and environmental impacts. He has an M.S. degree in Mechanical Engineering from the University of Maryland.

Anant Vyas conducts research on new transportation engine technologies, alternative fuels, advanced materials, and modal energy demand. He also works on projects relating to mobile source emissions and consumer response to new technologies.

Michael P. Walsh is a mechanical engineer who has spent his entire career working on issues related to motor vehicle pollution control and energy consumption. His history includes service with the U.S. Environmental Protection Agency and private consulting for the U.S. Congress, United Nations, and World Bank.

Index

acid rain
  causes of, 1
  and nitric acid, 6
Advanced Gas Turbine (AGT) program, 164
Advanced Turbine Technology Applications Program (ATTAP), gas turbine engines, 164
aerodynamic drag. *See* air drag
Africa, potential resources for renewable hydrogen production (table), 211
agriculture
  contribution to global warming, 2
  effects of ozone on, 6
AGT Program. *See* Advanced Gas Turbine (AGT) program
air conditioning (motor vehicle), as source of CFCs, 8, 43
air drag
  improvements in, 65
  and motor vehicle energy use, 153–55
air freight
  freight transportation analysis summary (table), 299–300
  problematic data concerning, 247
  technical efficiency improvements (table), 298
  See also aircraft; freight transport
air pollution
  in Bangkok (Thailand), 96
  health effects, 96
  in Islamabad (Pakistan), 98
  and motor vehicle fuel efficiency, 43–44
  sources of, 1–2
  in Surabaya (Indonesia), 97–98
  in urban areas of developing countries, 92, 104
  See also pollutants; smog

air travel
  compared with other modes in OECD countries (graphs), 59–60
  in developing countries, 72
  domestic air travel energy intensities in OECD countries (graph), 67
  energy intensities of, 58, 58n
  and load factor, 66–67
  in passenger travel in OECD countries, 66–67
  in Europe, 55
  in the former East Bloc, 74–75
  growth in OECD countries, 58–60
  international, 75–76
    graph, 76
  See also air freight; aircraft; aviation fuels
aircraft
  alcohol-fueled (illustrated), 273
  aviation fuels
    alternative, 272–81
    conventional, 266–72
  CO_2 emissions from, xviii, 2–3, 267
    graph, 267
  economics of, versus cars, 150
  emissions (North America) (tables), 41
  energy intensities in OECD countries (graph), 52
  fuel efficiency, 66–67, 304, 306
    improving, 44, 66–67, 263, 267
  fuel share of operating costs, 256–57
  hydrogen-fueled (illustrated), 274
  intercity passenger travel, 304–6
  methane-fueled (illustrated), 274
  technology improvements, 311

323

as source of electricity for electric
vehicles, 47
commercial buildings, as sources of
CO_2, 3
commercial transportation. *See*
freight transport
compressed natural gas (CNG)
efficiency of, 178–79
energy use and CO_2 emissions
(table), 181
and four-stroke engine efficiencies
(table), 177
as a motor fuel, 98, 99, 156, 303
and vehicle weight, 176
See also natural gas
compression ratio
and ethanol, 73
for gasoline and alternative fuels
(table), 137
and IC engine efficiency, 129–
37
versus idealized cycle efficiency
of IC engines (graph), 132
versus peak efficiency (graph),
134
"concept" vehicles, 44. *See also*
fuel efficiency
constant-pressure cycle (of diesel
engines)
ideal and actual, 129–36
pressure-volume diagram, 131
constant-volume cycle (of SI
engines)
ideal and actual, 129–30, 133
pressure-volume diagram, 130
conventional gas. *See* natural gas
cryogens
as aviation fuels, 272–78
compared with conventional jet
fuels (graph), 275
cooling the structure of high-
speed aircraft with (graph),
278
insulating cryogen tanks, 277
in space vehicles, 275
storage and transfer of (illustrated), 276

tank pressure of cryogen tanks
(illustrated), 277
See also hydrogen; methane
crystalline solar cells, 196. *See also*
photovoltaic (PV) systems

DeCicco, John M., 319
on a least-cost transportation transition scenario for the U.S.,
xix–xx, 283–316
deforestation
contribution to global warming, 2
as source of CO_2, 2–3
DeLuchi, Mark A., 319
on solar hydrogen transportation
fuels, xvii–xviii, 189–241
Department of Energy. *See* DOE
(Department of Energy)
developing countries
energy use in freight transport,
83–85
meeting transportation needs of,
91–92
oil importing requirements of, 91–
92
per capita travel, 72, 86
travel energy use in, 71–74, 86–
87
graph, 54
See also rapidly developing
countries
diesel engines
constant-pressure cycle, 129–33
exhaust aftertreatment, 144
exhaust emissions, 136–37, 144
as a fuel-efficient alternative,
136–37, 171
ideal and actual engine cycles,
129–36
improving part-load fuel economy,
141–42, 144
limited-pressure cycle, 129–33
low-heat-rejection, 142
turbocharging, 139–41, 144
See also diesel fuel
diesel fuel
as an alternative to gasoline, 156